'A Bloody Difficult Subject'

'A Bloody Difficult Subject'

Ruth Ross, te Tiriti o Waitangi and the Making of History

Bain Attwood

AUCKLAND UNIVERSITY PRESS

First published 2023

Auckland University Press
University of Auckland
Private Bag 92019
Auckland 1142
New Zealand

www.aucklanduniversitypress.co.nz

© Bain Attwood, 2023

ISBN 978 1 86940 982 1

A catalogue record for this book is available
from the National Library of New Zealand

This book is copyright. Apart from fair dealing for the purpose of private study, research, criticism or review, as permitted under the Copyright Act, no part may be reproduced by any process without prior permission of the publisher. The moral rights of the author have been asserted.

Every effort has been made to trace copyright holders and obtain permission to reproduce copyright material. The publisher apologises for any errors or omissions in this book and would be grateful if notified of any corrections that should be incorporated in future reprints or editions.

Book and jacket design by Duncan Munro

Map design by Tim Nolan/Blackant Mapping Solutions

Cover image: Ruth Burnard and her typewriter, *c.* 1944, Peter Boyd Collection

This book was printed on FSC® certified paper

Printed in China by Everbest Printing Investment Ltd

*For Ruth Ross's descendants
and in memory of my mother, Margaret Finlayson Attwood
(30 July 1926 – 27 August 2016)*

Contents

Map ix
Preface xi

PART 1: *Ruth Ross*

Chapter 1: The Government Printer 3
Chapter 2: School Publications 33
Chapter 3: The New Zealand Journal of History 63

PART 2: *Te Tiriti*

Chapter 4: Reading 'Te Tiriti o Waitangi' 93
Chapter 5: The Waitangi Tribunal, the Legal Scholars and the Historians 119

PART 3: *History*

Chapter 6: Politics, Public History and Juridical History 143
Chapter 7: Revisionist Histories 171
Chapter 8: The Advantages and Disadvantages of History 197

Appendix: Te Tiriti o Waitangi/The Treaty of Waitangi 215
Illustrations 219
Abbreviations 221
Notes 223
Bibliography 251
Acknowledgements 277
Index 279

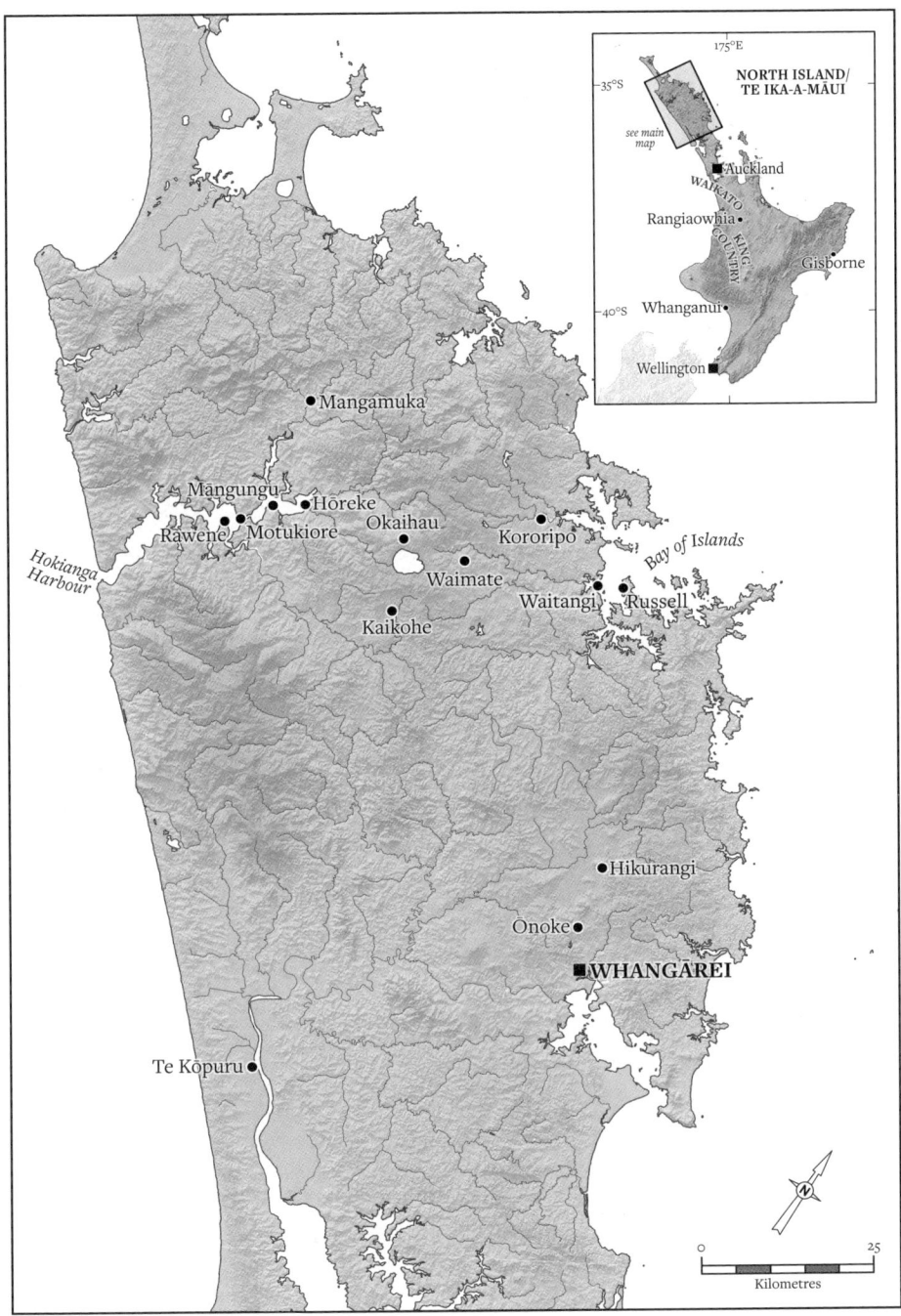

Preface

In May 1955 a thirty-five-year-old woman and her family left their suburban home in Auckland at short notice, moving to Motukiore, a small, remote community in the Hokianga, on the north-west coast of the North Island of New Zealand. Her husband took up a position as the principal teacher at the local Māori school. She took care of the house, raised their two young boys, created a vegetable garden, taught at the school for a while, established a country library service and befriended the local Ngāpuhi people. Shortly after they arrived, she began to write a story for school children about the historic 1840 Treaty of Waitangi,[1] or what she called te Tiriti o Waitangi — the Treaty's name, as most New Zealanders now know, in the Māori language.

It would be many years — not until 1972 — before this woman, Ruth Ross, published a learned article in the *New Zealand Journal of History* about te Tiriti; as she remarked to the journal's editor, she found the Treaty 'a bloody difficult subject'. Yet, within a decade, her article in this specialised academic journal had become famous, and shortly afterwards it was taken up in a way that helped to transform both Pākehā and Māori understanding of the Treaty, and make te Tiriti central to the country's law, politics and culture. The Treaty/te Tiriti came to be regarded as the nation's founding document, always speaking as the measure for a just distribution of resources in New Zealand society, and fundamental to the understanding of the country's history.[2]

Ross was on first-name terms with well-known figures in post-Second World War New Zealand, most notably her fellow historians J. C. Beaglehole and Keith Sinclair, the writer Frank Sargeson, the poet James K. Baxter, the artist Ralph Hotere and the literary editor Charles Brasch. But whereas they are still remembered by many New Zealanders, she has been forgotten beyond a small circle of historians and lawyers. I have written this book with the conviction that, by grappling with three difficult subjects — Ross herself, te Tiriti, and history — and the relationships between them, we can learn a great deal about Aotearoa New Zealand society, culture and politics of the last seventy years.

I seek to address several questions. When, why and how did this remarkable woman come to write about te Tiriti? How and why was her 1972 article received in ways that were at cross purposes to her intentions? Why has historical knowledge about the Treaty changed so dramatically in New Zealand since she started to write about it in the 1950s? How might histories about te Tiriti best be told, for what purposes and to what ends? And how might the different forms of knowledge that Māori and Pākehā have about 'history' be negotiated?

For some time now — and largely due to Ross's work — it has been taken for granted that te Tiriti/the Treaty comprises two language texts (the English and the

Māori), that there are significant differences between them, and that the Māori one is the most important. Consequently, it is difficult to comprehend that that is not how the Treaty was once seen and that this was not the main point Ross was trying to make about it. She could never have imagined that her article would be received in this way, that so much would be read into it, and that this would be fundamental to the enormous impact it had. These developments would have dumbfounded her, for she had other, quite different things to say: that the Treaty was hastily and inexpertly drafted; that the English text was badly translated into te reo Māori; that the Treaty was so ambiguous and contradictory that it was taken to mean whatever anyone wanted it to mean; and that it could never provide the basis for any legal change that would give the help Māori desperately needed. As this suggests, the story I am about to tell is full of unexpected turns, unforeseen circumstances and unanticipated outcomes.

In seeking to answer the questions I am addressing in this book I have found three concepts useful. The first is the public life of history. A renowned historian, Dipesh Chakrabarty, formulated this concept several years ago to make sense of the public controversies about history that have been taking place lately in countries like New Zealand. He used it to distinguish what he called history's public life from what he regarded as its cloistered life. By the cloistered life of history — the second concept I have used — Chakrabarty meant the life that the discipline of history enjoys in universities as it is taught, studied and researched, and discussed and debated in journals, monographs, seminars, conferences and the like. History is like any other discipline in this respect, but it differs from most other disciplines in the humanities and the social sciences in that it does not present as many strong barriers to those who wish to participate in the conversations it prompts and the controversies it stirs up. Anyone, whether they are academically trained or not, can presume to do history, discuss and debate it.

By the public life of history Chakrabarty meant the discussions and debates that occur about history in the public domain. As he pointed out, these interact with those that take place inside the universities, moulding one another even to the extent that they can affect the discipline's basic terms, such as 'research', 'sources', 'facts' and 'truth'. Sometimes this means that the relationship between the two lives of history is awkward and tense. This is particularly so when historical claims are made that trained historians find difficult to defend in the light of their professional knowledge and the protocols of the discipline. In short, being the kind of discipline it is, history is not only prone to having a public life but is perennially open to the pressures that emanate from that life. These pressures tend to vary between countries and across time, but they have been marked in democracies in recent times. In the New Zealand case, nowhere has this been more evident than in the conversations and controversies that have arisen about the Treaty of Waitangi/te Tiriti o Waitangi.[3]

The third concept I have used, which I have called the private life of history, refers to the ways that history works as an emotional force in the lives of the discipline and its practitioners. In contemplating the work of their peers, historians tend to overlook that it is influenced by both rational and irrational forces. In recent times, historians have been more willing to acknowledge the role that subjective factors play in historical research and writing. Nonetheless, they are inclined to countenance only those factors that are generated by social, cultural and political circumstances. Most are inclined to shy away from the role that the human psyche plays in their own work and that of their fellow historians. This neglect of the private life of history can be attributed partly to historians lacking the historical sources and the analytical tools that are required if one is to recover, and make sense of, its influence, but it mostly springs from a reluctance to engage with and reflect upon this factor. Yet the accounts that historians have provided about the highly charged matter of the Treaty are as likely to be the result of the powerful emotional forces that are at work in the relationship between the past and present as they are of their reasoned response to the historical traces they have unearthed and the stories that others have told about it over time. To be able to understand the stories they have told about the Treaty satisfactorily, we need to be willing and able to chart the relationship between the public, cloistered and private lives of history.

In this book I approach Ruth Ross, te Tiriti o Waitangi, and the lives of history as someone whose position might be described as that of an inside outsider. While I was born and bred in New Zealand, I migrated to Australia in 1981 to undertake a doctorate in history and have worked there ever since (except for short stints in universities in the United Kingdom and the United States). My research has often referenced New Zealand's history and one of my recent books, *Empire and the Making of Native Title*, is devoted to a consideration of matters that touch on the Treaty. But I have not been party to the public discussions and debates that have taken place about te Tiriti in recent decades. More to the point, unlike many of the other Pākehā historians who have written about the Treaty in the last thirty years, I have not been involved in the work of the Waitangi Tribunal. For better or worse, then, I come to the subject matter of this book with a degree of distance.

This said, I have met nearly all the scholars I write about in this book. Some, such as John Miller, Keith Sorrenson, Judith Binney and Keith Sinclair, were my teachers in a formal sense. Others, like Andrew Sharp, Paul McHugh and Mark Hickford, have taught me much in other ways. Still others, including Claudia Orange and Rachael Bell, have given me help in researching this book. Sadly, I never met Ruth Ross, though as a postgraduate student in the late 1970s I might have walked past her in the corridors of the Victorian terrace house that housed many of the staff of the department of history at the University of Auckland, or in the hallway of the modern prefabricated building next door where she had an office at the time. I have had the good fortune to spend time with her surviving son Duncan and his family, which has helped me to get to know her, but it is the wonderful collection of papers that she bequeathed to the Auckland War Memorial Museum Library (probably at the urging of her younger son, Malcolm) that has been the main source of my knowledge about her and her work.[4]

I am not suggesting that my position makes the perspectives I bring to Ross, te Tiriti and the making of history superior to those of other historians, but I do think it means that my interpretation differs from that of most of the scholars who have written about the Treaty in recent times. The distance that any historian constructs in their work about the past invariably carries both advantages and disadvantages. At best, all a historian can do is to reflect on their own relationship to the stories that have been told, the historians who have created many of them, and the narrative that he or she chooses to tell in turn, and then act accordingly.

The plot of this book can be quickly summarised. Part 1, dealing mostly with the period between the early 1950s and the early 1970s, is concerned with describing what Ross wrote about the Treaty and explaining how and why she did so. Part 2, treating the period between the early 1970s and early 1990s, is devoted to a consideration of the reception of her work and how this and other factors influenced the telling of a story about te Tiriti in the context of the operations of the Waitangi Tribunal, which was established in 1975 to address the past neglect of its principles. Part 3, covering the period from the early 1990s to the present, is a story that, like the history of the Treaty itself, does not have an ending as it examines ever-widening questions about the lives of history and democracy in New Zealand.

I do not seek to provide a comprehensive account of Ross's life and work, te Tiriti, or the historical writing about it. But I do endeavour to provide enough of an account of each of these difficult subjects for readers to make sense of them and their interaction with one another. Some readers might feel that the ground I am about to cover has been well and truly trodden in recent years and that consequently there is little if anything new to say. I hope to show that this is far from being the case, and to stimulate deeper understanding about te Tiriti o Waitangi and the role that the lives of history have played and continue to play in New Zealand.

PART 1
Ruth Ross

Chapter 1
The Government Printer

For some time now, historians familiar with Ruth Ross's famous article about te Tiriti o Waitangi have assumed that it originated in the early 1970s.[1] This made sense. It seemed to be the product of a moment when the Treaty and the rights of Māori as the tangata whenua were beginning to become prominent in public discourse in New Zealand. But her article was actually the fruit of research and thinking she had done twenty years earlier.[2]

To make sense of what Ross wrote about te Tiriti over two or more decades, we need to identify the various contexts in which she did this work. These include the relationship between her writings and New Zealand society, culture and politics; the intersections between her life and her research; the connections between each of her writings on the Treaty; and the relationship between her intentions and what she ultimately wrote.

The reasons why Ross became attracted — and in time attached — to the Treaty as a historical subject are neither simple nor straightforward. She once claimed she had strayed into it. This exaggerates what happened. But whereas the involvement of many historians in research on the Treaty in recent decades can be attributed readily to the dominant social, cultural and political forces of the day, hers cannot. Instead, it was the outcome of a complex set of factors, which include her upbringing and family circumstances, her training at university, her early historical research, and her relations with several people, most of whom were men.[3]

Ruth Guscott and J. C. Beaglehole

Ruth Guscott, later Ross (1920–1982), was born and educated in Wanganui (now better known as Whanganui), about 200 kilometres north of Wellington. It was New Zealand's largest urban area after its four main centres, but still only a small city of approximately 25,000 people. She and her brother spent a lot of their free time as children in the country, their father being a livestock agent dealing with cattle and sheep. This gave her a lifelong affinity with the land and its people. She excelled at school but found life at home intellectually barren. Her father was a rather stolid, sober and dull man (though he had what she once called an 'incongruously romantic weakness' for some expressions of popular Māori culture). Guscott came to find both her parents puritanical, authoritarian, conservative and repressive, and rebelled against what she felt they stood for. In particular, she seems to have withdrawn emotionally from her father as she grew up, though this probably meant that she sought out other men as father figures. While her upbringing does not seem to have been especially religious in nature, she was repelled by her paternal grandparents' rabid Irish Protestantism and bigoted anti-Catholicism. In 1938 she left home to go to Wellington to begin a Bachelor of Arts degree at Victoria University College (later known as Victoria University of Wellington), determined to follow in the footsteps of an aunt who was her namesake (but known as Lill).[4]

Guscott started her studies at Victoria University College with the intention of majoring in English literature and history. However, after hearing the historians J. C. Beaglehole (1901–1971) and F. L. W. (Fred) Wood (1903–1989) lecture, she decided to concentrate on history. Both these men were part of an injection of new blood that had taken place recently at the university, and Guscott and her contemporaries were among the first generation of New Zealand students to be taught by historians who had received professional training in the discipline. On taking up their posts in the mid-1930s Wood and Beaglehole sought to transform the practice of history in New Zealand. This involved the introduction of certain methods of research. Students were required to focus on what were called 'primary sources' — that is, traces of the past that had been created at or near the time of the events they were studying — rather than distil the work of other historians. They were expected to treat any account of the past critically, even sceptically, to be rigorously accurate and even pedantic as far as historical facts were concerned, and to interpret the past in a dispassionate manner. They were encouraged to write in a certain way, arguing a case rather than just telling a story, and marshalling the primary sources in support of their contentions, rather than quoting them for their own sake.[5]

The kind of questions Guscott's teachers asked of the past differed from those of earlier practitioners of history in New Zealand. As far as Wood and Beaglehole were concerned, what made the country's past a proper subject for academic research was its connection to Britain and its place in the wider Anglophone empire. New Zealand history had yet to be conceived as a field of study and no New Zealand university offered it as a subject. The questions Beaglehole and Wood asked about the past influenced the kind of sources they and their students used. They largely relied on ones that had been created at the imperial centre rather than on the colonial periphery. All this meant that they tended to marginalise local historical information and knowledge that had long been the realm of journalist-historians; and to distinguish their work from that earlier amateur tradition of historical writing about New Zealand's past, which they tended to denigrate as antiquarian.[6]

At Victoria University College Guscott quickly proved herself to be a keen, brilliant and diligent student. She had enormous integrity and a fierce commitment to truth as she perceived it. As such she could be stubborn, even intractable. She suffered fools less gladly than most, but was just as demanding of herself. She was also very kind and fiercely loyal to her friends. She struck her teachers and fellow students as outgoing, confident and independent-minded, and seemed to thrive on argument. She was unusual, too, in that she rebelled against the gender conventions of the day that expected women to be self-effacing and subordinate. (We have already noted her swearing, which was exceptional in an age when such behaviour was considered to be 'unladylike'.) But she was actually an introvert and quite unsure of herself, which no doubt owed something to being a young woman in a world dominated by men. At this time no woman held a permanent position in a department of history in New Zealand even though there were many female students. Guscott came to depend on the high regard in which she was held by her male teachers.[7]

Victoria, like the other university colleges in New Zealand, was small. The students attending classes during most of Guscott's time numbered fewer than a thousand, and the Department of History had only two staff. This meant teachers and students got to know one another well. Both Beaglehole and his wife Elsie, and Wood and his wife Joan, befriended their young students, inviting them into their homes and introducing them to their circle of friends. Ross would later claim that she felt closer to the Woods and more at home with them, but she enjoyed Beaglehole's gossip, wit and jokes, and found him the more stimulating intellectually. He had what his son and biographer Tim Beaglehole has described as an affectionate manner with young women. Guscott liked to spar with him.[8]

Relations between staff and students could be close. Many years later, after Beaglehole died, Ross told an acquaintance, 'I wept on his shoulder once in my student days, for love of someone else', before going on to recall: 'I've always loved him, but I don't honestly believe I was ever in love with him.' In the early 1940s Beaglehole had a sexual relationship with another of his former students, Janet Wilkinson (later Paul), who was one of Guscott's colleagues at the time. But to her Beaglehole was

5

more of a father figure, just as he was for several of his other female students. One of them — Ruth Fletcher (later Allan) — once called him her 'fairy godfather'.⁹

Guscott continued to enjoy Beaglehole's patronage and friendship after leaving Victoria University College. She owed her first job as a historian to him. Near the end of 1941 she was appointed as a research assistant in the Historical Branch of the Department of Internal Affairs in Wellington, previously known as the Centennial Branch, which had been formed in 1937 by an enterprising senior public servant, Joe Heenan, to undertake a wide-ranging set of activities to mark the centenary in 1940 of the British annexation of New Zealand. A part-time adviser from the Branch's beginnings, Beaglehole had recently taken charge. Determined to ensure that one of the Centennial's projects that had faltered — a historical atlas — would not be put on hold until the Second World War came to an end, he insisted that he be allowed to hand-pick two new research assistants, both of them pretty, clever young women: Guscott and Wilkinson.¹⁰

Guscott jumped at the chance, though she thought New Zealand's history was boring. It was a decision that was to change her life. By this time she had completed her major in history but not her degree.¹¹ It is not altogether clear why she decided to set aside her studies, but we know that she intended to resume them at a later date and to do postgraduate work in history. Many years later, one of her best friends claimed that Guscott found full-time study something of a treadmill and the prospect of doing practical or public work as a historian more congenial. There is probably something in this, but part of her would have liked to have become an academic (and there is evidence to suggest that she would have been a brilliant teacher).¹²

In the next couple of years, three more of Beaglehole's talented female students — Nan Wheeler (later Taylor), Mary Boyd (née Mackersey) and Frances Fyfe (later Porter) — were to join Guscott at the Historical Branch. As research assistants, their position in the Branch — and, later, its companion, the War History Branch — was subsidiary to that of men, which was in keeping with traditional attitudes about the place of women in New Zealand society. They were known by the men in the Historical Branch and elsewhere as 'Beaglehole's babies', and the Branch was called 'Beaglehole's kindergarten'. Beaglehole never seems to have encouraged any of these women to go to Oxford, Cambridge or London to do a doctorate, as bright young men were at this time.¹³

Yet this was only one side of the coin. The war provided many women with unusual opportunities for work as men were conscripted to serve in the armed forces. They had a chance to prove that they were capable of any task or position of responsibility that was put their way. In this case the Historical Branch gave these young women an opportunity to enter the historical profession at a time when few if any junior lectureships were open to them. For her part, Boyd reckoned that they felt lucky to have interesting work and be part of a lively community of scholars, writers and artists; that they were grateful to the men who recommended their appointments; that they felt they were equals to their male colleagues; and that they were happy in the work they had because they did not intend to spend the rest of their lives working as research assistants. But Boyd was one of the fortunate ones: in 1947 she was appointed as a temporary junior lecturer at Victoria University College when Beaglehole was granted leave to work on James Cook's journals, and shortly afterwards she got a tenured position when the permanent junior lecturer, John Owens, went off to Oxford to do graduate work. By contrast, Guscott's career as a full-time historian was short-lived. Later she would feel ambivalent about her time at the Branch: on the one hand she relished learning how to do historical research on her own; on the other she resented Beaglehole's lack of guidance and oversight. Most importantly, she came to feel that she had never been capable of being anything more than a research assistant.[14]

But this conviction lay in the future. For the time being she enjoyed the opportunity to do an enormous amount of research on European trade and settlement in northern New Zealand in the two to three decades prior to 1840. She took to this work readily, acquiring skills and habits that were to serve her well for the rest of her life. Several months after she started, Beaglehole sang her praises, telling Heenan that she demonstrated 'a capacity for rapid work in a sphere of very complex and sometimes contradictory evidence, and a skill for formulating argument and conclusions'.[15]

Six weeks after she had begun work at the Branch, Guscott came across a rich body of historical sources in the bowels of the Department of Lands and Survey. This archive of files concerning early Pākehā claims to Māori land captured her imagination and sparked her curiosity about the history of New Zealand in the decades preceding British annexation in 1840. She dashed off a bold memorandum to Heenan, seeking to impress on him the value of this hidden trove of material. She argued that it was significant because it concerned a matter that had been a source of conflict between Māori and Pākehā since the beginning of New Zealand's history. 'In fact', she told him, 'the whole question of land claims was so very important in our history that I do not think a true perspective can be gleaned of the land problem until much of the material on these files can be made available to the research student.'[16]

As well as becoming interested in these land matters, Guscott was intrigued by another issue central to the Treaty of Waitangi: the reasons why the British government had chosen in 1839 to instruct New Zealand's first governor, William Hobson, to make a treaty with the Māori chiefs, the role this had or had not played in the British Crown assuming sovereignty, and the legal status that the Treaty had had since. Her growing fascination with this subject almost certainly owed something to her meeting and falling in love with a brilliant young lawyer, R. W. (George) Burnard, who had been a couple of years ahead of her at Victoria University College. He had a strong interest in constitutional law and it seems the young couple had numerous conversations about sovereignty and the Treaty, not least because this matter had recently been discussed in a book by a legal scholar who also worked for the Department of Internal Affairs, N. A. Foden. 'The early constitutional history of New Zealand is one of my hobby horses which I am inclined to ride whether the occasion merits it or not', Guscott confessed to another historian, Marie King, in August 1943. Several months later, in Auckland, she would spend an evening with a former secretary of the Auckland Law Society discussing these questions — 'Tore Foden to pieces and put his arguments back together again rather the worse for wear yet altogether singularly untouched' — and another evening with a fellow historian doing the same thing — 'there were quite a few constitutional-legal points we pulled to small pieces. Thoroughly enjoyed myself.'[17]

Part of the attraction of the Treaty for Guscott lay in the fact that the legal questions surrounding this matter of sovereignty were controversial. '[The] controversial points are unending', she told King; 'historian disagrees with historian and lawyer with lawyer'. As we will see, Ross enjoyed a good fight between scholars. But this was not all. She saw herself as a rebel and relished challenging points of view that she believed were dominant, especially historical ones that had become the subject of myth. The role that missionaries had played among Māori in early colonial New Zealand is one example; the Treaty another. In her mind at least, these were entangled. It is hard to exaggerate the degree to which the work she would do on the Treaty was fuelled by her hatred of the missionaries, or at least the Anglican missionaries, and one of them in particular, Henry Williams, who was principally responsible for translating the Treaty into te reo Māori. She was angered by the way they were portrayed by some historians (such as the High Anglican librarian-historian Harold Miller), in large part because she believed that the missionaries' evangelising had had a destructive impact on the fabric of Māori life.[18]

Besides, she had been taught that it was the role, even the duty, of the historian, to be sceptical about myths. Several years earlier, in a short history of New Zealand, Beaglehole had referred to the Treaty as a myth, declaring that it was 'curious . . . in view of the troubled career of the Treaty, its uncertain observance, the ambiguities of its interpretation, to observe the veneration in which it has been surrounded — not so much for its content or its intention . . . but for its actual place in the history of New Zealand as a canon of inter-racial relations . . . [which] have not been conspicuously successful'. Yet he allowed that every nation must have its myths, and thought it might not be in the best of taste to attack this one. Guscott would have no such compunction. In a historical outline of Russell as the first seat of government in New Zealand, which she was instructed by Heenan to prepare and which was eventually published (on Beaglehole's suggestion) as a small book, *New Zealand's First Capital*, she criticised Hobson's treatment of the matter of sovereignty on his arrival in 1840, expressed scepticism about the Treaty's status, and was scathing about the way in which the site for the country's first capital had been chosen. In the process she savaged two well-known historians, tearing strips off one for overlooking important historical sources and mistranscribing others, and taking issue with the other over his interpretation of a key historical figure.[19]

In undertaking much of her research at the Historical Branch, Guscott relied on the historical methods she had been taught at university. But she soon discovered that it required careful reconstruction of the past on the basis not only of official historical documents that were held in metropolitan centres like Wellington but of fragments of information that were held elsewhere. Moreover, she found it necessary to call on the knowledge of local amateur historians and other such people. In these circumstances, she realised, apropos academic and antiquarian history, that it was 'sometimes difficult to tell where one branch of the species ends and the other begins', thereby bringing into question the sharp distinction between the two that the discipline of history insisted upon.[20]

Most of her research focused on Pākehā but required her to pay attention to the history of Māori. The Branch had decided that the atlas should begin not with the European discovery of the islands of New Zealand but the Polynesian discovery, and provide a series of maps about Māori before 1840 (after which there would be a succession of maps on the progress of British settlement). As a result, Māori people were very much a presence in the research that Guscott undertook into the early history of Europeans, or Pākehā as she soon started to call them. The archive that she had encountered within weeks of starting at the Branch, which was known as the Old Land Claim files, included a large amount of written Māori testimony. The same was true of the records of the Native Land Court (established in 1865) that she became familiar with.[21]

The nature of Guscott's research meant she engaged with Māori people in person. In making field trips to places such as Gisborne to consult written records, she ended up conducting with Māori what a later generation of New Zealand historians, most notably Tony Simpson, Michael King and Judith Binney, would call 'oral history'. On one memorable occasion Guscott met an elderly man, or kaumātua, Henare Ruru, and his sister, and listened to them reminiscing at great length. As Ruru's sister understood only a little English and spoke it less, this meant, Guscott observed, that 'the conversation [had to] be bilingual and three cornered'. Perhaps this gave her a taste for the work of translation that she came to believe was essential for the task of understanding the Treaty. At the very least it is apparent that she enjoyed these field trips immensely and especially her conversations with elderly Māori men.[22]

One of these field trips proved especially consequential in the medium term. In March 1944, after doing several weeks of documentary research in Auckland, Burnard (as she now was) set out for the far north, which was one of the most important areas of Pākehā settlement prior to 1840 and where, that year, the Treaty had first been proffered to local Māori at Waitangi in the Bay of Islands. Her principal destination was the old house of a Pākehā trader, F. E. Maning, at Ōnoke in the Hokianga, where she hoped to find the minute books he kept during his time as a judge of the Native Land Court (1865–76). As she admitted to one of her correspondents, she had become 'a bit Maning mad'. Burnard was undoubtedly attracted to him for the same reason she found many of the European traders of this period intriguing: they were often known as 'Pakeha-Maori' because they settled in Māori communities, adopted their modes of living, and were treated by them as though they were Māori. She enjoyed a certain frisson in challenging the conventional historical accounts of these men, arguing that they had a less harmful impact on Māori than the missionaries had. Burnard was all the more sympathetic to Maning because in his early days in New Zealand this Irishman was ambivalent about British colonisation and government, urged the northern chiefs not to sign the Treaty, and was consequently attacked (wrongly) by Hobson and the Protestant missionaries as an agent of the French Catholic bishop, Pompallier. In other words, Maning was one of the reasons Burnard was attracted to the Treaty as a subject.[23]

She thoroughly enjoyed her time in the far north even though the Bay of Islands was a difficult place to get around without your own car, and the Hokianga was even harder. She cadged a lift with a local Native Land Court man and hitched a ride on the back of a lorry amid several Māori and numerous cream cans. But she was particularly taken by the Hokianga. 'I thought the place gloomy, overpowering, dingy, a backwater', she soon told a local Pākehā historian, John Lee. 'But the hasbeenness, its squalor, its depressing mists and rain, its ignorance and complete lack of interest in its past . . . got me. Perhaps it was just my reaction, but I was fascinated as I have been fascinated by no other place in New Zealand. I want to go back. To live there would be hell. But to go back for a few weeks to potter about with equipment for all weathers and with a launch — that is one of the things I simply must do.'[24]

She would eventually return to the Hokianga, not for several weeks but for several years, and there she would write her finest piece of work about the Treaty. However, she had little time for Waitangi. She had planned to visit it briefly, but a change in the weather ruled this out and she reckoned she was not sorry, claiming she could not stand either it or Russell because so much had been done in recent years to reconstruct them as historic places.[25]

Several months after Burnard returned to Wellington from this eight-week field trip, she suffered a devastating loss. Her husband died, having fallen seriously ill just two months earlier. George was only twenty-six years old and they had been married less than a year. To make matters worse, doctors at Wellington Hospital had been unsure what was ailing him and were stonily silent. Finally, they realised he was suffering from Hodgkin's disease, a rare form of cancer of the lymphatic system akin to leukaemia that can often go undiagnosed for many years. They ordered him to move to a warmer place to convalesce, but before he and Ruth could set off for Gisborne he was struck down by tuberculous meningitis. Its onset was rapid: he did not even have time to make a will, and he and Ruth were probably unable to say a last farewell to one another.[26]

If the personal papers Ross left to the Auckland Institute Library (now known as the Auckland War Memorial Museum Library) are any guide, she seldom talked about this trauma in later years. But on one occasion she admitted that his death had brought a very happy period in her life to 'a bloody and brutal end', and on another that it had turned her world 'inside out'. Wishing to escape the pain and anger she felt, she threw herself into a new project that was connected in her mind to the Treaty, namely Maning, and resumed work on another project that was similarly connected to it: shortly after her return from the far north she had sought permission to work on a project that she described as 'Old Russell with its outcropping of constitutional history of the Hobson period' and which she confessed was 'more of a personal fetish than a public utility'. After George died she worked on this over several months, which resulted in the publication of *New Zealand's First Capital*.[27]

By the time Burnard had completed this fine essay, she could see little future for herself as a historian. She was sceptical that anyone was going to see the atlas project through, singling Beaglehole out for criticism, and began to seek work elsewhere. She was also finding it difficult to have much confidence in her abilities as a historian.[28] But no offers of work were forthcoming and she had to stay put. Finally, sometime between VE Day and VJ Day, she was transferred to the War History Branch, after a plan for a comprehensive programme to prepare an official history on New Zealand's involvement in the Second World War had come to fruition. But the Branch made little use of her skills. As she recalled, she catalogued its small library of books, looked after the maps, made morning and afternoon tea, collected the money for the tea and badgered five unwilling men into washing the dishes.[29]

There was an upside though: she met Ian Ross, a man ten years older than herself,[30] who had recently returned from the war after enlisting shortly after its outbreak and serving for its duration. A few weeks later, just before Christmas, they married. She would later remark that they wed on the spur of the moment — which was not uncommon at the end of the war — and had a couple of children in quick succession — also not uncommon at this time, in what became known as the post-war baby boom.[31]

After becoming pregnant with her first child, Ross resigned from the War History Branch and, not long after she gave birth, the young family moved north to Auckland. There, they had no place of their own to live because of a severe housing shortage and so lived in discomfort and disorder for a few years. Ruth had little time to call her own, let alone do any work other than caring for her husband and children, and she felt horribly confined. In these post-war decades, marriage, home and family were more than ever considered to be a woman's domain. Women, or at least those of the middle class, were discouraged from doing paid work after they married, even if they did that work at home, and it was generally held that the needs of children should be regarded as paramount and that the best childcare was provided in the home. Only after Ruth, Ian and their two sons, Duncan and Malcolm, moved into their own home on Auckland's North Shore in 1950 and the two boys started kindergarten and school, was she able to resume paid work outside the home. But when she did so, it was as a historian, partly thanks to her friends, who ensured that her skills would not be overlooked.[32]

The *Facsimiles* commission

In 1952 Ross was offered freelance work by the School Publications Branch of the Department of Education, and in May the following year she received a commission to work on the Treaty. Beaglehole was responsible for the latter. He had persuaded the Government Printer, R. E. Owen, to reprint *Facsimiles of the Declaration of Independence and the Treaty of Waitangi* — a small volume that had been compiled and introduced by H. Hanson Turton (1818–1887) in 1877 and reprinted in 1892 — merely so he could offer Ross work. Turton's book comprised facsimiles — that is, exact copies — of a series of documents: the Māori text of the 1835 Declaration of Independence (in which northern chiefs proclaimed they were sovereign at the same time as they asked for the protection of the British king) and the signatures or marks of the signatories and witnesses to it; one of the English-language drafts of the Treaty; seven sheets of the Treaty in the Māori language, and the signatures or marks of the signatories and the witnesses that were made on them at several places including Waitangi; the sheet of the Treaty in English that was signed at Waikato Heads and the signatures or marks of the signatories and witnesses there; and the printed version of the Treaty in te reo Māori that was produced in February 1840, which included some signatures made in the Waikato.[33] Ross was to present these facsimiles to a new audience by writing a new introduction.[34]

She was thrilled to be offered the job, telling Beaglehole she would love to do it. As well as being attracted and attached to the Treaty for the reasons I have already discussed, she wanted an intellectual challenge and knew that this task would provide it. Shortly after beginning work on it, she remarked to Beaglehole: 'what a hell of a subject . . . The ground to be covered is appalling . . . [full of] snags and pitfalls'.[35]

From the outset, though, she was anxious about taking on the job. She was concerned about the subject matter. 'I know from past experience, that once one gets launched on Waitangi stuff, the work involved is never ending', she told Beaglehole. She was worried about what the commission might require of her and whether she had the time and resources she would need to do it. How long was the introductory essay to be? When would it be due? Were the historical sources readily available? She found research time-consuming because she was wedded to a particular historical method. 'The tough Beaglehole school of research was first-rate; but it can make things difficult', she explained to one of her correspondents. 'I won't include a damn thing that I haven't got a clear-cut authority for. However water-tight my theory [by which she meant her argument] seems to me, laboriously built up by weighing this fact against that, one set of circumstances against another, I still can only state it as a supposition. The damned pettifogging detail that holds one up.' In fact, no matter what the scope of the historical task she undertook, Ross always felt she had to research it thoroughly, irrespective of how much work this entailed. At the same time, research was the most enjoyable part of being a historian as far as she was concerned.[36]

Beaglehole tried to reassure her. A straightforward introduction of 10,000 words was all that was required; no laborious historical research was needed; no original argument was called for. But Ross knew how hard she found it to juggle research and writing with her responsibilities as wife and mother, and that gathering the historical material took her, as she put it, 'a hell of a lot of time'. 'Public Library opens at 9.30 of a morning, and the Museum [Library] at 10, and I have to be back here at 2 p.m. to escort my beginner [Malcolm] over the main road [from kindergarten], so it doesn't leave much time', she explained to Beaglehole. 'And I find that one day's [research] a week knocks me for a loop and puts the entire household out of plumb for that week.' A little later, she would describe her working habits to her friends Dora and Graham Bagnall in these terms: 'I go like mad for about six weeks, then I find the weeds are shoulder high, no one has any whole garments to wear, and I've had it in more ways than one, and I just have to call a halt for a while.'[37]

Ross's family responsibilities soon threatened to sabotage the job even before she had a chance to start on it. Her brother fell ill and so her aging father was going to come and live with her (her mother having died the previous year after being seriously ill with diabetes for twenty years). She herself fell ill with flu and badly poisoned fingers, and the boys were sick and home from school. For a moment it seemed she would have to give up the commission. She was bitterly disappointed but could not see any way out of this situation. She feared that in her present circumstances she would 'crack up' if she tried to do it. To make matters worse, she was concerned that she was letting Beaglehole down. But he was sympathetic to her predicament, telling her there was no need for her to start on the job until she was ready. The crisis was averted when other arrangements were made for her father's care, though another bout of illness for Ross and her children, the summer school holidays, and other commitments meant she was unable to begin work on the commission until March 1954.[38]

Just two weeks after she started, Ross was able to rough out a tentative plan of how she was going to approach the task. She sent this in a letter to Beaglehole for comment, as he had suggested she do. This kind of document is as rare as it is invaluable. Seldom do historians leave such a rich contemporary record of what or how they are thinking about their research and writing. Ross's letters are especially revealing because she often wrote them as though she was thinking out loud. Furthermore, she felt more able to be forthright and say what she thought than she did in much of her public writings, or at least her academic ones. Talking about her letter-writing, she once referred to 'my customary unbuttoned fashion'.[39]

The plan Ross sent to Beaglehole reveals that she had already begun to formulate a bold contention about the Treaty. 'One thing that will be said', she informed Beaglehole, 'is this: whatever the treaty may or may not be (my own private opinion is that it is, was and ever will be, a complete balls-up . . .), it was the expression of the Colonial Office's intentions. An incomplete, hasty, ill-conceived and incompetently carried out expression if you like, but at least the intentions were clear'. In 1972 she would conclude her *New Zealand Journal of History* article in very much the same terms, even using some of the same words.[40]

Ross had arrived at this contention through two discrete lines of inquiry. The first concerned how the British Crown had assumed sovereignty in 1840 and the precise moment at which it had done so. As far as she was concerned, the Treaty's legal significance — or rather the lack of it — was made clear several months after it had first been signed by a small number of chiefs at Waitangi on 6 February 1840 but was still to be taken around the country to secure the consent of the other chiefs. In May Governor Hobson simply proclaimed that New Zealand had fallen under Queen Victoria's rule, thereby rendering the process of obtaining signatures irrelevant. 'Once Hobson had proclaimed the Queen's sovereignty in May, and the British govt. had approved those proclamations, then that was that', Ross insisted. 'By various legal forms the Queen assumed sovereignty, and nothing could alter the situation — no matter how many chiefs had not signed the treaty.'[41]

Her other line of inquiry concerned the drafting of the Treaty. Re-reading a relatively recent newspaper editorial about Waitangi and the Treaty had provoked her to consider this matter. 'Waitangi is the very cradle of New Zealand's civilisation', the editor of the *Auckland Star* had asserted. 'In the truest sense, the treaty known by its name is our equivalent of Britain's Magna Carta. The word [Waitangi] itself, the single word, even when spoken without mention of the celebrated treaty, is evocative of so much that is of paramount importance in our brief story.' Ross considered this to be hogwash, but it was another passage in the editorial that had really caught her attention and raised her ire: 'Queen Victoria is credited with having herself written the treaty.' This led to a humorous exchange between her and her husband: 'What Ian and I would like to know', she wrote to Beaglehole, 'is did [the Queen] first write it in English and translate it into Maori, or vice versa?' Yet the newspaper's absurd claim about the authorship of the Treaty had suggested a line of thought to her that she sensed might be worth investigating.[42]

Ross began to set this out in her letter to Beaglehole. 'The Treaty of Waitangi as signed by the chiefs is in the Maori language, with the exception of the one [sheet] signed by the Waikato chiefs. Why this one sheet is in English, heaven alone knows.' At that stage she had yet to compare this English-language version with the facsimile of the draft in the Turton volume, or the English versions that Hobson sent to the British Colonial Office. But as she wrote to Beaglehole she got a little closer to formulating what was to become a crucial part of her interpretation of the Treaty: 'The point I am working up to, is there an official English version of the Treaty? The Treaty as the chiefs signed it, with the exception of the Waikatos, was a Maori Treaty only. No English version was attached to what they signed, therefore there can be no official version of what they signed, only a translation.' This point led her to ask Beaglehole whether any authoritative translation had recently been made either of the main sheets of the Treaty (into English) or the Waikato sheet (into Māori). 'Now could it be', she asked, 'that a Maori scholar (and I mean a Maori scholar and not a scholar of Maori) translating the Treaty into English would produce something which does not entirely coincide with the Treaty the Waikatos signed, or (if they differ) with the English versions as they may appear in P.P. [the British Parliamentary Papers] or elsewhere?'[43]

In other words, Ross was starting to have an inkling that the Māori-language version of the Treaty might differ in certain respects from the versions produced in English, and that this mattered because it was the Māori version, not the English version, that most of the chiefs had put their names to. For the moment, though, she had little sense of the implications of this line of thinking, partly because she lacked confidence. 'This is all very tortuous, and I don't know whether I have outlined it intelligibly or not', she commented to Beaglehole. She had not been able to think it through sufficiently, but she did have a sense that she was on to something important and was excited. She did not know whether anyone else had investigated this matter but hoped they had not.[44]

Several days later, Ross wrote to Beaglehole again, her mind bubbling over. 'Second thoughts on this vexatious matter', she announced, almost as if there had been no break in a conversation she had been having in her mind with him. 'I think I must concede that there is an *official* English *version* — but it is not the Treaty of Waitangi, except the Waikato sheet. That is, the treaty as we understand it, as Hobson and the Colonial Office understood it, was signed by the Waikatos only. This opens up all sorts of interesting possibilities.' She did not explain what she thought they were, however, merely noting in regard to the first part of the Treaty's second article that the official English version read that the Queen guaranteed the signatories 'full, exclusive and undisturbed possession of their lands and estates, forests, fisheries and other properties which they may collectively or individually possess', whereas a translation of the Māori version into English stated that she guaranteed them 'the entire chieftainship of their lands, their villages, and all their property'. But Ross did sense that the Māori version 'could be rather a different kettle of fish' from the English one.[45]

At this point, though, she faltered, fearful that there was a danger that she was becoming unduly preoccupied with the differences between the English and Māori texts. She tried to persuade Beaglehole that this was not the case: 'Do not suppose that I am concentrating on this point to the exclusion of all else.' But, most of all, she wanted his guidance about her focus on the Treaty texts and the Māori one in particular. 'I would like a directive', she told him, 'whether to abandon it, or whether to pursue it.'[46]

Beaglehole never responded to this plea for help, much to Ross's annoyance. Ten weeks later, she gave up waiting and sought the help of another historian, Keith Sinclair (1922–1993), a senior lecturer at Auckland University College and well on his way towards becoming one of the best-known New Zealand historians of his generation. By this time she seems to have abandoned the approach she had described to Beaglehole and adopted a different line of inquiry. 'I am looking at the ruddy thing more or less from the angle — why it is, or thought to be, important — how it has been interpreted — how it has affected native policy from 1840 onwards', she wrote. As she recognised, this was a ridiculously large task for a 10,000-word essay: '[It will] take me from Maori land tenure to Wiremu Kingi, from the Kororareka flagstaff to Potatau, from the Kohimarama conference to the Kotahitanga movement, from the Ratana grand tour to the Tirikatene petition, from Mrs Whina Cooper to the Hon. [E. B.] Corbett [the current Minister for Maori Affairs], and so on ad infinitum.'[47]

In the next few months, however, Ross resumed working along the lines she had initially proposed, though she found it difficult. In November 1954 she told the Bagnalls: 'I'm supposed to be doing an introduction for the re-issue of the facsimiles for the Govt. Printer. I think I'm treating it mainly from a purely textual viewpoint, which, as I neither speak nor read Maori, is rather barmy . . . [This angle] has been largely ignored — or so it would seem from my inadequate reading . . . I'm anything but the obvious person to do it. Consequently my progress is a series of flounderings and near-drownings, and I don't seem to be getting very far very fast.'[48]

To understand why Ross chose to adopt a textual viewpoint or approach — by which she meant one that sought to determine the meanings and implications of the Treaty by concentrating on its texts rather than the contexts in which it was made (though in fact she considered the latter to a large degree) — we need to understand how this came about. According to her own account,[49] she began by reading, or rather re-reading, *The Treaty of Waitangi, or How New Zealand Became a British Colony*, by the journalist-historian Thomas Lindsay Buick, who had been one of the most influential historical writers in New Zealand in the early decades of the twentieth century. It is not surprising she started there: first published in 1914, with a second edition appearing in 1933 and a third in 1936, his was the only book-length account of the Treaty. Her re-reading of it proved to be important to her research in several ways.[50]

On being offered her commission, Ross had originally intended to tell the story of the Treaty meetings, as Beaglehole had suggested she do. But she realised that Buick had already done this and saw no point in merely producing what he had done. Driven to look for a different angle, Buick was helpful again. He not only referred to most of the relevant historical sources and quoted large chunks of them; he also alerted Ross to the possibility that the Māori text of the Treaty differed in at least one regard to the English texts, and discussed the matter of translation, as had another historian, James Rutherford (1906–1963).[51]

But Buick's book was primarily important because it was a powerful expression of the nationalistic myth about the Treaty. This had become ascendent in recent decades, largely due to Buick's numerous writings and talks about the Treaty; to the former Governor-General of New Zealand, Lord Bledisloe, buying and bequeathing land at Waitangi to the nation in 1932; and to the celebrations of the Treaty that took place there in 1934 and 1940. Buick told a story about the Treaty as if it were a compact between Māori and Pākehā, claiming that it provided the foundation for New Zealand's nationhood because it was the means by which Britain had acquired sovereignty, and amounted to a 'Maori Magna Carta' because of the rights it bestowed on them. A desire to overthrow this myth drove most of the work Ross was to do on the Treaty throughout her life.[52]

After reading Buick, Ross turned to what she called the most obvious historical sources: Hobson's despatches to the Colonial Office, and various eyewitness accounts of the Treaty signings. Her attention then shifted to a pamphlet war that broke out in the 1860s about the legal implications of the Treaty. The way she read the pamphlets written by the former Chief Justice William Martin both reflected and reinforced the course her research increasingly took. He discussed the texts of the Treaty and the translation of particular English words into the Māori language, and the differences in meaning between the two language texts. 'So far as I know', she told Beaglehole, 'that was [the] first occasion when the actual treaty, i.e. the text and its meaning, was taken out and aired. And how!'[53] Martin, she contended, had 'made most effective play of the fact that while [in the Māori text] the Crown granted to Maori "te tino rangatira"'(which he translated as 'full chieftainship'), Māori 'gave to the Crown only "te kawanatanga"', which he 'translat[ed] as "governorship" (which he or someone else pointed out is not "sovereignty")'. She was struck by the fact that Martin had argued that 'while "te tino rangatira" was something which the chiefs knew well, "te kawanatanga" was an unknown meaningless thing [to them]'.[54]

However, she believed that the treatment Martin and the other pamphleteers had given the differences between the two language texts was inadequate because they had not gone 'into the translation problem enough'. Consequently, she felt she had no choice but to delve into this herself, which served to increase the attention she gave to the Treaty texts.[55]

On the grounds that the Church Missionary Society missionary Henry Williams and his son Edward had been responsible for translating the Treaty from English into Māori at Waitangi, Ross decided that she needed to understand what they thought the Treaty meant. She formed the view that the Māori text they created must have had a closer resemblance to the Māori language as the missionaries had previously rendered it in their translation of the Bible into Māori, than to spoken Māori. As a result, she decided that to comprehend what she called '"treaty" Maori', she had 'to take a close look at "bible" Maori'. She spent several months doing this, painstakingly reading the King James version of the New Testament and pre-1840 translations of it. To make more sense of the concepts of property and sovereignty in the Treaty that the Williamses had to translate, she read the work of the anthropologist Raymond Firth and drew on what she had recently learned by taking a short Adult Education course in anthropology at Auckland University College.[56]

The attention Ross gave to the Treaty texts — and her claim that the Treaty's meaning was to be found in those texts — was peculiar in both senses of that word: strange and unique. Historians who have discussed Ross's work on the Treaty have overlooked this point.[57] While it was commonplace among academic historians at that time to make a fetish of historical documents or texts, they nevertheless concentrated on historical contexts. Ross herself saw her so-called textual approach as singular and odd and so felt the need to legitimise it. She found warrant for this in the commission she had received from the Government Printer. 'As it is an introduction to the facsimiles I'm to write, the textual viewpoint seems the obvious method of approach', she told the Bagnalls.[58]

Just as Ross's focus on the Treaty texts was peculiar, so too was the attention she gave to the Māori one and her claim that *it* was the Treaty. The foremost Māori leader of his generation, Apirana Ngata (1874–1950), and the historian James Rutherford, had previously discussed the Māori text, but they had given most of their attention over to the English one and accepted it as the official version. Hence, not only does Ross's emphasis on the texts need to be explained, but that on the Māori one does as well. One might argue that the explanation lies in the historical fact that this was the text that most of the chiefs signed. But, as the historian E. H. Carr pointed out a long time ago now in his famous book *What is History?*, historical facts do not speak for themselves. They only speak when the historian calls on them to do so, the historian decides which facts have the floor, and this depends on the historian's interpretation and judgement, which are influenced by the present and are subjective to some degree.[59]

The Māori text was important for Ross for several reasons. She was sympathetic to the plight of Māori as the underdogs in New Zealand society. As she had long had a rebellious spirit, she was critical of the fact that the Treaty had come to be interpreted primarily through a Pākehā lens — and an official one at that. She was deeply committed to the importance of being truthful and so was troubled by the possibility that the terms of the Treaty had not been represented to Māori in such a way that they had been able to understand what they had been asked to cede. It also seems that the issue of consent was very important to Ross. Finally, her deep prejudice against Christian missionaries or, to be precise, the Anglican evangelical missionaries, which was almost certainly a result of her upbringing, meant that she was unusually concerned with the role that two of their number had played in translating the English text into Māori.[60]

Ross's commitment to understanding the Māori text deepened as she sought the help of several Māori. At this time it was unusual for an academically trained historian to consult Māori, but during her time at the Historical Branch she had met and talked with Māori, enjoyed doing so, and learned how helpful it could be. As she worked on her commission she received assistance from Matt (Matiu) Te Hau (1912–1978), who had recently taken up a position as the Māori Adult Education tutor at Auckland University College, and Pei Te Hurinui Jones (1898–1976), a Ngāti Maniapoto leader who was an interpreter, scholar, translator, genealogist and writer and who had spent many years researching Tainui traditions. As she acknowledged at the time, she could not have done her work on the Māori text without their help. By the same token, her singular preoccupation with the texts owed much to the fact that she was working in isolation from Pākehā academic historians. 'I did discuss the matter once or twice, but only briefly, with Keith Sinclair', she told Beaglehole at one point. 'Otherwise Waitangi was a topic of unacademic conversation at home and with various Maori friends.'[61]

As time went by, Ross found it harder and harder to continue working on her commission. She had trouble getting hold of the manuscript and archival sources she wanted to consult, knew her approach was unconventional, and realised her critical take probably meant that the Government Printer would blanch at publishing her findings. She had been aware of most of these hurdles from early in the piece but they weighed on her mind increasingly. In part this was so because she lacked confidence in her capacity as a historian and was torn between the pleasurable feeling she derived from her belief that the textual approach was the hardest road possible to the Treaty route, and the painful feeling that she lacked the wherewithal to bring her project to fruition. This made it difficult for her to pursue the path she had chosen. A few months after she started, she reported that her work on the Treaty was becalmed; by March 1955 she had decided to set it aside for a while in the hope that a way forward would become clear to her; and by May that year she decided she had better abandon it.[62]

But her deep personal investment in the Treaty and her dogged determination saw her return to the job in February 1956, several months after moving to the Hokianga. She started to plan a trip to Wellington so she could finish off the research. More than ten years had passed since she last had some acquaintance with the records she needed to examine. She wanted to see the originals of the documents that had been reproduced in the facsimiles, the instructions that Hobson had given to the agents who took the Treaty sheets around the country to get the consent of other chiefs, and their reports of the Treaty meetings they had held. She hoped that the Dominion Archives (the forerunner of the National Archives of New Zealand) had been able to wrest the relevant records from the various government departments where she had last seen them. The condition of these records had troubled her for some time, prompting her to ask Beaglehole where they were now being held: 'they used to be in the Police Cellar providing a diet for fleas and rats — or rather the rats ate the documents, the fleas ate the rats, and the cats that ate the rats delivered themselves of their kittens on whatever pile of papers was around'. Her anxiety about making this trip grew after she agreed to speak about her research to a gathering of the Victoria Historical Association, which comprised teachers and senior students in the Department of History at Victoria University College as well as a few professional historians who had connections to the Department.[63]

Ross's Treaty paper

The seminar paper that Ross prepared for this occasion has a clarity that is lacking in most, if not all her later writings about the Treaty,[64] probably because she was more confident about her interpretation than she would ever be again. She began it boldly by declaring that a great deal had been written about the Treaty but that most of it was confused. She then suggested that those responsible for that work had made a mistake in assuming that the English version was the Treaty. She conceded that it stated what the British Crown understood the Treaty to be, but pointed out that this version (the Waikato sheet aside) was not the Treaty that either the representatives of the Crown or the chiefs had signed. At this stage she did not spell out the implications of this fact, remarking instead: 'That the Crown was only one signatory of the treaty seems to have been lost sight of by many historians and successive governments.' However, later on, when she discussed contemporary debate about the Treaty, she stated: 'I take it that because the greatest number of Maori signatories signed the Maori text, and the British Crown signed six Maori texts to one English version, that the Maori text is the treaty.' This is one of the few occasions in her work on the Treaty that Ross spelt out what underpinned her insistence that the Māori text was *the* Treaty.[65]

She moved on to argue that the job of translating the English text into Māori in 1840 had presented enormous problems as it was 'studded with concepts' that were 'foreign to Maori thought at the time', and that this had been aggravated by Hobson's lack of understanding of what was involved and his undue haste. 'Had [he] waited a while and called in William Williams and [Robert] Maunsell, instead of making do with Henry Williams and son', she asserted, '*probably* the Maori text *would* have been closer in meaning to the English version'. Before she presented her paper Ross must have decided that she had overstated this point, as she changed 'probably' to 'possibly' and 'would' to 'might'.[66]

Ross suggested that the Māori text of the Treaty raised three questions for the historian: what, respectively, did Hobson and the British government, Henry Williams and his son, and the Māori chiefs think it meant? She did not spell out her reasoning but it seems clear that she believed that this was the case once a historian accepted that the Treaty (the Waikato sheet aside) was an agreement written in the Māori language. She suggested that the first question was relatively easy to answer: Hobson and the British government thought the Māori text meant the same as the English text and they regarded it as merely one of several devices to attach New Zealand to the British Crown — and not a legally binding one at that. In keeping with this point, she argued that the Treaty meetings were probably staged for the sake of appearances. She observed that Hobson did not even wait for all of them to take place before he issued his proclamation in May 1840 declaring British sovereignty over the whole of New Zealand, and she pointed out that while he had claimed the North Island by virtue of cession, he had simply claimed the southern islands on the grounds of the legal doctrine of discovery. As far as she was concerned, both these actions drew into question the belief that British sovereignty rested on the Treaty. At this point in her presentation she departed from her text to draw attention to a document she had just come across in the Dominion Archives: a little-known proclamation that Hobson had issued in May 1840 that left no doubt that he *had* claimed the southern islands on the basis of discovery.

Ross told her audience that she had found it difficult to answer the question of what Williams and his son thought their translation would convey to Māori. While she had undertaken research on pre-1840 missionary translations of English into Māori in the hope that this would shed light on the matter, it had only made the matter murkier than ever as far as she was concerned.[67]

She reckoned the question regarding Māori understanding was the most difficult to answer, largely because the historical sources that reported the discussions that took place at the Treaty meetings had what she called 'a pakeha bias', or more specifically what she regarded as an official and a missionary bias. She implied that this problem was aggravated by the fact that the Pākehā officials and missionaries who had created the historical record were reluctant to attribute the opposition among

Māori to 'its most natural cause' — an 'acute perception of what signing the treaty could entail', that is the loss of their independence — and had blamed the likes of Maning instead.[68]

In turning her attention to the Māori text in an attempt to answer this question, Ross began by suggesting that the preamble conveyed the spirit if not the precise meaning of the English version, but she quickly pointed out that 'the real guts' of the Treaty lay in its articles. She reminded her audience of the English version: 'In the 1st [article] the Maori chiefs ceded to [Queen] Victoria "all their rights and powers of sovereignty". In the 2nd the Maori were guaranteed "full exclusive and undisturbed possession of the lands, estates, forests, fisheries which they may collectively or individually possess so long as it is their wish and desire to retain the same in their possession", and the Maori granted to the Crown the pre-emptive right of purchase. By the 3rd the Maori were given all "the rights and privileges of British subjects".'[69]

How were the key concepts in these articles conveyed in the Māori text? she asked. The first article in the English text, which had stated that the chiefs ceded to the British Crown 'absolutely and without reservation all the rights and powers of Sovereignty', had been translated as that the chiefs 'ka tuku rawa atu ki te Kuini o Ingarani ake tonu atu te Kawanatanga katoa o o ratou wenua'. Ross remarked: 'This I am told means "give up all rights to te Kuini o Ingarani [the Queen of England] for ever to the kawanatanga of their land".' But she doubted 'kawana' and 'kawanatanga' would have meant anything to the chiefs in 1840, as she believed that the missionaries had coined these words (in the course of seeking to translate 'governor' and 'governorship' in the scriptures). Moreover, she insisted: 'governance is not sovereignty, governorship is not sovereignty, and government — which I understand is the present meaning of kawanatanga — is not sovereignty'. By contrast, she argued, the concept of 'mana' approximated more closely to the concept of sovereignty than 'kawanatanga', insofar as there was anything in Māori thought at the time that did, and was the closest possible one-word translation of 'sovereignty'. If the translators had rendered this article so that chiefs gave to the Queen forever 'te kaha katoa me te mana katoa o rangatiratanga' instead of 'te kaha katoa me te kawanatanga katoa', the Treaty would have got a very different reception than the one it did, she stated, implying that many chiefs would simply not have agreed to sign. At this stage she pointed out that whoever was responsible for translating into Māori the 1835 Declaration of Independence — she thought it was Henry Williams — had used the words 'te Kingitanga [ko] te mana', and she went on to argue that if a word had to be coined to denote sovereignty, 'kingitanga' would have served better than 'kawanatanga', presumably because she thought the former implied supreme power, like that of a king, rather than merely that of a governor.[70]

Turning to the first clause of the second article, Ross suggested that its guarantee to Māori of 'ki nga rangatira ki nga hapu, ki nga tangata katoa o Nu Tirani, te tino rangatiratanga o o ratou wenua o ratou kainga me o ratou taonga katoa' offered a good deal more than the English text's guarantee of 'full, exclusive and undisturbed possession &c', because it invoked the attributes of a rangatira, most significantly that of mana. If this clause did mean that Māori had retained 'te tino rangatiratanga', she suggested, there must have been 'precious little left [for them] to cede to the Queen'. She asked her audience: 'Isn't this a possible explanation of Nopera [Panakareao]'s much quoted saying — the shadow of the land goes to the Queen, the substance stays with us?' She pointed out that this remark had been invoked repeatedly to evidence a claim that Māori knew they were signing away their sovereignty while retaining possession of their land. But she believed a different interpretation could be given to it. 'The shadow — kawanatanga — was freely given, its full implications not being comprehended, while the substance — te tino rangatiratanga — was retained, so well understood and valued, and so all-embracing, that if the Queen wanted what was left over, then she was welcome to it.'[71]

Ross summed up what she saw as the key difference between the Māori and English versions of this clause by stating: 'the English version accents that "sovereignty" was ceded, and the possession of land retained [by Māori], while the Maori text accents the retention of "te tino rangatiratanga o ratou taonga katoa", which must have included mana. For how could the land be retained, and the mana go? So that those who did sign may have done so thinking that all the attributes of mana would be retained, and would regard the Queen's mana, the kawanatanga, as some jumped-up thing, a pakeha whimsy, a shadow, something of no importance at all.' She also suggested that 'taonga' had a broader meaning than 'possessions', stating: 'We think of "possessions" as material possessions . . . I am told that "taonga" can include not only these things but language, custom, way of life, manner of thought, in short, what the anthropologists term "Maoritanga".'[72]

Ross had comparatively little to say about the second clause of the second article, as she thought that the meaning of the Crown's right of pre-emption — that is, its exclusive right to buy land from Māori — had been made relatively clear to the chiefs in the missionaries' translation. In respect of the Treaty's third article, she noted that whereas in the Treaty's preamble the term 'just rights and privileges' had been translated as 'rangatiratanga', here 'the rights and privileges of British subjects' was translated as 'nga tikanga katoa rite tahi ki ana mea ki nga tangata o Ingarani'. She seemed to suggest that Māori would have understood 'nga tikanga' rather differently than 'rights and privileges', but did not pursue the point.[73]

Having completed her account of what she saw as the differences between the Treaty's Māori and English texts, Ross provided what amounted to a conclusion to the main part of her paper, or at least she tried to make clear what her main take on the Treaty was. (As she admitted more than once, she found it difficult to keep the big picture in mind and struggled to see the wood for the trees, and even found it difficult to remember how that saying went, inverting 'the wood' and 'the trees'.) She declared: 'In moments of cynicism, despair and overwork, I am very tempted to say that the treaty of Waitangi was ... a fraud and a hoax, a snare and a delusion — to both contracting parties.'[74]

Ross then launched into a discussion of the legal matters that a historical consideration of the Treaty tended to throw up, though this saw her stray into a mire she had hoped to avoid but to which she was drawn repeatedly. Her discussion here was by no means coherent, comprising instead a series of disconnected points as she shifted back and forth between the present and the past. But it is important to try to make sense of what she was trying to say as this can enable us to understand the essence of her principal argument about the Treaty.

Ross began this part of her talk by speaking of what she called 'this so-called treaty'. She had formed her sceptical take on it after reading lawyers' opinions and conducting her own historical research. She wrote: 'This collection of signed sheets is not a treaty according to either international or municipal law — which I gather all revolves round the argument that New Zealand was not in 1840 a sovereign and independent state. (And according to European conventions — which appear to be all that counted — it certainly was not.)' At this point in her typewritten paper, she scribbled a couple of observations that had evidently occurred to her. She remarked: 'The interesting point here is that the British Crown ... "acknowledged New Zealand was a sovereign and independent state so far at least as is possible to make that acknowledgement in favour of a people composed of numerous and petty tribes, who possess few political relations to each other, and are incompetent to act, or even to deliberate, in concert" — those were [Colonial Secretary] Normanby's instructions to Hobson.' In other words, she was pointing out that the British government did not regard Māori as truly sovereign. Consequently, in keeping with the logic of contemporary legal opinion about the Treaty, she asked her audience: 'if the Maori rangatira were not sovereign and independent rulers, how could they cede to the Queen something they did not possess?' In other words, Ross was asking how had the British government been able to envisage that the Māori chiefs were able to engage in a process in which they were expected to cede their sovereignty when it did not regard them as truly sovereign.[75]

At this point in her presentation Ross reverted to her typewritten text. As she did so, her main argument became clearer: 'If a signed document is not treated as a treaty, either in conception, drawing up, signing nor subsequent action, then ergo, it is not a treaty.' Her argument becomes clearer still when we consider the next remarks she made. If the British government had not truly regarded the Treaty of Waitangi as a treaty, she commented, this was even truer of Hobson. Earlier in her paper she had asserted that Hobson was unconcerned about who signed the Treaty or how they did so. Here, she argued that he regarded the agreement made at Waitangi as *the* Treaty and so considered all subsequent meetings or signings as merely ratifying it. Indeed, she claimed that the way in which Hobson went about establishing British sovereignty in New Zealand — by issuing proclamations declaring invalid all titles to land not confirmed by the Crown and declaring himself Governor over such parts of it as had been or might be acquired in sovereignty — *before* he made the Treaty at Waitangi, revealed that he was ignorant of what both British law and Māori custom required. Finally, she added that even if it was conceded that his intentions were good — and she thought they were — 'they only served to pave the road to chaos and ruin'. In short, she argued that the Treaty was a contradictory mess and that this had led to an even greater mess over time.[76]

In the last part of her paper Ross discussed another dimension of the Treaty that interested her: the way in which it was now regarded by both Māori and Pākehā. The observations she made in this context shed further light on the main thrust of her interpretation of the Treaty, largely because in making them she pointed out the implications of her argument about the differences between Māori and English texts of the Treaty for contemporary policy-making. She noted that the Treaty was often referred to by Māori and Pākehā alike as 'the Maori Magna Carta'. This, she jested, might be appropriate given that 'very few people know just what the Magna Carta was about' and 'it was not what people generally believe it to have been!'. But she was mostly concerned with how the Treaty was seen by Māori, asserting that they seemed to regard it as the basis of their civil rights and so accorded it a great deal of respect. Ross noted that there had been, and perhaps would continue to be, 'periodic agitations' by Māori 'to have the treaty given full authority at law, incorporated into the statute books, recognised by the courts &c &c'. But she went on to state emphatically that it was not the basis of many of the rights Māori currently enjoyed, and to suggest that any agitation to lend legal authority to it could only be mounted by those who had never looked closely at it, whether in the Māori version or the English one.[77]

There were several reasons why Ross doubted any good could come from incorporating the Treaty — by which she meant the Māori text — into New Zealand law. One stumbling block was its actual meaning. Ross suggested that if a dozen leading Māori scholars were each to independently translate the Māori text into English, 'the result might be a dozen different translations'. More importantly, perhaps, she held that whether it was interpreted to mean that the chiefs had ceded sovereignty or merely 'te Kawanatanga katoa o o ratou wenua', no attempt to give it legal standing would make any difference to the historical fact that New Zealand was now a British settler dominion. Even though she recognised that Māori were justified in claiming that the undertaking the Crown had given to respect their rights in land in the second article had been repeatedly breached in the last 115 years, she could not envisage a situation in which this promise could be upheld. Likewise, she realised that if the Treaty was incorporated into New Zealand law on the basis of her argument that

Māori had not ceded sovereignty according to the Māori text, all the legislation passed since 1840 would become invalid because 'its very enactment [would be] contrary to te tino rangatiratanga o o ratou taonga katoa', and she did not think this would meet the interests of either Pākehā or Māori. She admitted that on this score she had 'a certain sympathy with [the permanent under-secretary of the British Colonial Office] Mr James Stephen's view [of 1843 and 1844] — "it [the assumption of sovereignty by the British Crown] may be unjust or impolitic or inconsistent but it is *done*"', adding: 'you can't put the clock back'. Finally, Ross told her audience that she could see no value in the third article of the Treaty becoming part of New Zealand law. While this would mean that the rights and privileges they enjoyed on the same basis as other New Zealand citizens would be upheld, the *special* rights and privileges that Māori alone enjoyed — she gave the Maori Land Court, separate Māori representation in Parliament, Māori trust boards and Māori land development schemes as examples — could be withdrawn.[78]

These remarks of Ross's disclose a vitally important point. Her account of the Treaty, like that of any historian, was shaped to a large degree by her present and how she imagined the future. She could not conceive of the possibility that any of the points she had made in her argument about the Māori text of the Treaty could have beneficial outcomes because of the nature of the dominant political, legal and cultural discourse of the day. She was unable to imagine a situation in which Māori understandings of the Treaty based on the Māori text could be accorded a similar weight, let alone a greater one, to Pākehā understandings based on the English text; or one in which the Treaty was regarded in international and domestic law as a valid agreement between two sovereign powers; or one in which Māori were considered to be anything other than as individual subjects who at best had a rightful claim to the same rights and privileges as other New Zealanders, rather than a collective who had rights on the basis of being the country's indigenous people.

The trip to Wellington

Hardly any academic historians in New Zealand were undertaking research at this time in the field that would only come to be known as Māori history in the closing decades of the twentieth century. The historian Alan Ward (1935–2014), who was writing a postgraduate thesis about Māori land in 1956, later recalled that '[f]ew Victoria University people then knew or cared much about the field'. This response can be seen in the reaction to the paper that Ross presented to the Victoria Historical Association. Apparently, its members regarded her approach to the Treaty as idiosyncratic and dismissed it (and had Beaglehole been there, rather than overseas on sabbatical leave, he would have done the same). This provoked a crisis that resulted in her giving up the Government Printer commission.[79]

We only have Ross's account of what happened when she gave her paper, but for our purposes this is sufficient as what matters is how she perceived the reception she got. She found the criticism she received very painful, so much so that she spoke about it repeatedly in the years that followed. The opportunity to speak to the Victoria Historical Association meant a great deal to her. It was the first time she had had a chance to air her views to a historically informed audience, and she was anxious that her textual approach might be, as she put it, 'off beam'. For that reason alone, she was apprehensive about giving the paper, but this was all the more the case because as an introvert she hated speaking publicly. 'In fear and trembling I'd agreed [to talk]', she remarked a month after she had given her paper, 'but that was nothing to how I felt when all the learned bods were assembled.'[80]

The text of her paper was punctuated with questions such as 'Would you agree?', and several uses of 'possibly' and 'probably', and in presenting it she betrayed more of the anxiety she felt about her approach and argument. 'I struggled along in a most unlecturish way,' she told one of her correspondents the following month, 'timidly put my little theories forward ... marshalling my little army of piddling details, voicing my innumerable doubts'. Much later, she told another correspondent that she had undoubtedly spoken incoherently.[81]

In most of her accounts of the adverse reaction she felt she got to her paper, she singled out her erstwhile friend Mary Boyd. 'She told me my approach was a waste of time' and 'dismiss[ed] my preoccupation with the text as "historically worthless"', she reported. There is little reason to doubt that Boyd made comments of this kind, even though Ross could be quite a raconteur when she felt she had the right audience — a few well-known friends — and so was inclined to embellish. As two of Boyd's former graduate students, Malcolm McKinnon and Doug Munro, have recalled, Boyd could be very forthright and frank as well as opinionated and intolerant,[82] apparently oblivious to the effect that this could have on friends, colleagues and students. This is to say that she was much like Ross in her personal demeanour (as Ross recognised), no doubt because it was difficult being a woman in the historical profession, or any profession, at this time, so much so that many women found it necessary to shore up their position by being stern, fierce and intractable. Moreover, as Ross herself was an exacting critic, she always feared that the tables could be turned, as they had been on this occasion, and this only made things worse. We do not know whether anyone else at Ross's talk shared Boyd's opinion, but she believed they did. This hurt. She tried to fend this feeling off later by using derisive terms for Victoria's History Department such as 'the academic gang'.[83]

It was Boyd's attack that stung Ross the most, however. Boyd had not only been a junior colleague at the Historical Branch, but Ross had taken her under her wing, they had become good friends, and even shared a house for a while. Ross might well have felt betrayed. Boyd's criticisms might also have troubled Ross because her opinion about the Treaty probably carried some weight as she had some expertise in the history of relations between Māori and Pākehā, having done an MA thesis on this subject for the period 1815–45.[84]

As well as feeling wounded by the dismissal of her approach to the Treaty, Ross was maddened by something that occurred at her presentation. According to her account, almost all her audience refused to accept that the document she had just found in the Dominion Archives — one of Hobson's proclamations of 21 May 1840 — existed. '[T]he whole gang were up in arms', Ross once recalled. 'Such a proclamation did not exist — that was final . . . I didn't know what I was talking about, such a proclamation did not, repeat not, exist.' She reckoned they would never have believed her had not Ian Wards, who had done a fair amount of research on the Treaty, remarked that he, too, had seen the document in question.[85]

To make matters worse, Ross was unable to go away, lick her wounds or let off steam afterwards, as the seminar had taken place in Boyd's home where she was staying during her visit to Wellington. But Ross was flabbergasted by what happened next. After everyone else had gone home, Boyd, referring to the Hobson document, remarked to her in an accusing tone of voice: 'you do keep your secrets'. Yet a night or so earlier, having asked Ross how she had got on at the Archives that day, she was told that Ross had made 'an exciting discovery', namely that document. 'Oh, she [Boyd] said in a completely disinterested tone and went on to talk about something else.' Sometime after Ross had given her paper, Boyd realised that a collection of historical documents she and some of her colleagues had been compiling was not as thorough as they thought, having overlooked this document. 'But that chastening thought was soon forgotten,' Ross claimed; 'after all the proclamation in question was of minor significance.' Boyd eventually recognised she had treated her old friend badly and tried to patch things up, albeit without apologising. 'We did enjoy seeing you again and hope you'll repeat the visit after not so long a gap next time', she wrote to her several months later, 'but I still feel guilty about the Treaty.' Their friendship was to survive, which was a credit to them both.[86]

Ross partly found her trip to Wellington difficult because it deepened a rift in her relationship with academic history and its practitioners that had begun to develop a couple of years earlier, after she began to feel they were disparaging of one of her historical interests: New Zealand's participation in the Second World War. She responded in kind, writing in May 1956 to the elderly journalist, writer, broadcaster and historian Alan Mulgan (1881–1962): 'An academic study of history is very narrowing I feel.' A month later she explained to him what she meant: 'the new scientific spirit of historical inquiry, in its stronger demand for proof, frequently misses out on some of the virtues of the older and less scientific historians'. She cited the writings of

James Cowan (who had written extensively about Māori and the New Zealand Wars) as an example, observing that they had 'life, and character and atmosphere to burn', before going on to complain: 'It is the fashion in historical circles today to decry the work of the earlier New Zealand historians . . . But poking borax at Cowan and co. can go, does go, too far.'[87]

Work on the Treaty was a case in point. 'Recently', she told Mulgan, 'I read a very learned article in a very learned journal on the treaty of Waitangi by Trevor Williams.' She conceded that the article by this Oxford don was a good one but observed that he had been very critical of Buick's *Treaty of Waitangi*: 'It was a book, said Mr Williams, which had no value — or words to that effect — for any serious historian.' 'Now that is sheer bunkum', she exclaimed. 'Heaven knows the book in question has many faults . . . But it is a book which no serious historian, interested in the treaty of Waitangi, can afford *not* to read . . . above all else the book is readable. And how I wish that some of these scientific historians of today could *write* as clearly and well and as interestingly as their much scorned predecessors.'[88]

Ross felt estranged from the academic circle to which she had once belonged. 'I didn't enjoy the trip to Wellington last year and have no desire to repeat it', she told Beaglehole a year or so later. 'Whether it is I or others who have changed I don't know, but the mixture certainly isn't as before.' A few years later she told her former colleague, Janet Paul, that she had felt like 'a fish out of water — sort of Rip van Winkle in reverse'. But there was more to it than this. 'Nearly all my academic friends', she told an American friend, 'took the line of — what on earth did you want to go and shut yourselves off from the world in Hokianga [for], depriving your children of their intellectual equals, cutting yourself off from a "cultural" life, &c. &c. ad nauseam.' She confided to another correspondent: 'I didn't bother to enquire why the supposition that the kids here were Duncan's and Malcolm's intellectual inferiors. They are Maoris so they must be. And yet the woman [who made this remark] is a most "enlightened" member of the Wellington "intelligentsia", who would be horrified if I pointed out to her that her argument rested on that premise.' (I assume the woman in question was Joan Wood.) Ross tried to make light of what had happened in a letter to yet another one of her associates, claiming her trip was 'great fun' and had 'a certain comic opera flavour', but it is clear that she felt hurt. Unable to deal with this, she became increasingly critical of academic historians at the same time as she would continue to crave their recognition, and research and write in the ways the discipline of history demanded.[89]

For the time being, though, Ross was so distressed by the reaction to her presentation that shortly afterwards — possibly the next day — she took herself off to R. E. Owen, the Government Printer, and, as she put it, 'chucked' the Waitangi job (which was a course of action made easier by the fact that she had not received any payment for the work she had done). In subsequent years she would repeatedly tell a story about this moment, often with a flourish that disguises how painful she found the episode. It went more or less like this: I worked on the project, time permitting, for the best part of two years and then went down to Wellington to tie up the last few threads. Or so I thought. In fact it all seemed so hopeless that I went along to the Government Printer and told him I'd have to quit the job. The information I required doesn't exist. I couldn't do this research by hit-and-raid research runs. Money wasn't the stumbling block. I'm a part-timer. My job is at home looking after my husband and children and I won't leave them to struggle along on their own. In any case, the Treaty is the subject of entrenched New Zealand myth and no government department will publish a volume that argues that the Treaty was a hopeless mess, a half-conceived, ill-executed, unfinished job. Oh well, I came home a wiser woman and wrote a primary school bulletin about the treaty instead, which is more to my liking than a scholarly editorial introduction. So, the work for the facsimiles volume wasn't a wasted effort![90]

There was a grain of truth in this story, but it does not provide a satisfactory explanation of why Ross gave up the job. She did so primarily because she was pained and angered by the reception of her paper. Giving up the commission was an attempt to get rid of these troubling feelings. Another psychological force might have played a role in her hasty decision to quit. Partly it was a feeling that she was not up to the task, partly it was a fear that she had become unduly preoccupied with the Māori text. 'That damned text has become something of an obsession with me', she confessed to the archivist and historian Michael Standish. Indeed, she seems to have felt that her textual approach was mad. She acknowledged that a worthwhile introduction could be written for the facsimiles without searching the archives thoroughly, but admitted that *she* could not do that. Those who knew Ross well might have attributed this to her 'over-developed conscience' or her 'stern perfectionism'. There is no doubt some truth in these observations but they do not explain her passionate attachment to the Treaty.[91]

Ross regretted throwing the job in that day in Wellington, and so this was not the end of the matter. Shortly afterwards, she told Wood and Standish that the problem she had encountered lay in her being too far away from the sources she needed to consult, thereby leaving the door open to the possibility of her picking up the job again. This is what happened: Wood was willing to see whether he could get a grant from the university to meet the costs of her doing the research, and Standish approached Beaglehole to ask whether the Archives and the university could join forces to provide the necessary funding. Ross's response to these developments makes it clear that she found it difficult to relinquish a job she had dearly wanted to do and to tell Beaglehole she had given it up. But she vacillated over whether she wanted to take it up again. It seems that she needed Beaglehole to want her to do so. But several months passed without her hearing a word from him, prompting her to send him a short letter telling him she had given up the job and suggesting he get an archivist to do it.[92]

A few weeks later, Beaglehole scribbled off a letter to Ross that might have been typical of those he wrote to his former women students, given that he often adopted a bantering tone with them (as he did in his correspondence with family members). 'About all I can say to you, in answer of yours . . . is that you're a bad girl, & I should really say B-G and I'm sorry I haven't said it earlier', he wrote. This was so, he claimed, because he had told her at the outset that 'a straightforward historical introduction' was all that was required and that this meant that she did not need to conduct much research or provide any historical revision. 'But of course I knew you'd hare off to rewrite the history of the Maori race & pakeha-Maori relations before you finished.' After some more banter of this kind, he told her it was 'damn silly' for her to 'turn the job in at this stage'. He then suggested a way forward that he and Standish had discussed, and told her to get in touch with Standish to discuss the matter. In concluding, he told Ross: 'Don't give me any cheek in return, & say I didn't tell you this, that, or the other thing. Besides, if you come to Wellington, you can give Mary [Boyd] more advice on the rearing & education of children.'[93]

If Ross still had it half in mind to resume this Treaty commission, which she almost certainly did, this letter put paid to any immediate prospect of her doing so. Beaglehole had tried to help but the way he did so was ill-judged. In any case, the assistance he offered was merely of a material kind and Ross needed and wanted much more than that, namely his guidance, encouragement and approval. In signing off, he told her he was leaving for Tonga in a week's time and suggested there was no time for her to reply. This meant that she just bided her time before composing a six-page letter in response. She began this by angrily dismissing his claim that neither historical research nor historical revision was needed, and proceeded to explain how she had gone about the work in order to persuade him that a great deal of research and revision *was* needed. Yet, having done so, she faltered, expressing doubts about her textual approach, reporting the critical reaction to her presentation in Wellington, and apologising for the length of her letter. She also found it necessary to insist that she was giving up the job even though her letter revealed that she still harboured the hope of reviving it.[94]

Beaglehole, however, must have decided to wash his hands of the whole business. At any rate, he never replied to her letter. This upset her. She feared he was no longer interested in the Treaty and the facsimiles volume and had given up on her. For several months she hoped she would get some sign from him that this was not the case, so much so that she seems to have conflated herself with her namesake, Ruth Allan, who had recently died, commenting on a tribute to her that Beaglehole had written: 'my first reaction was — I hope he showed *her* he thought very highly of her. His opinion meant a lot to her.'[95]

Ross's confidence in herself as a scholar, tenuous at the best of times, had been shaken by the response of academic historians — and particularly that of her beloved teacher and patron — to her highly original scholarship on the Treaty. She more or less resigned herself to a belief that it was historically worthless and that no good could ever come of it. This made it difficult, if not impossible for her to continue to work in this vein. Fifteen years would pass before she felt able to pick up the threads of her novel approach in an academic forum. In the meantime she had to seek other outlets for her research on the Treaty, even though she realised that few, if any, of them were really suitable, and she was only willing to make some of the adjustments that were necessary to meet their requirements.[96]

Chapter 2
School Publications

By the time Ross abandoned her Government Printer job she already had another avenue for pursuing her passionate interest in the Treaty.[1] It was another public commission. The School Publications Branch of the Department of Education had agreed to her writing a piece for its series of school bulletins, which were small books really, of about 12,000 words. Her Waitangi bulletin, as she called it, was initially aimed at primary school children in Standards 3 and 4 who were between nine and eleven years old, but later this was changed to Forms 1 and 2 and eleven- to thirteen-year-olds.[2]

School Publications had been founded as the publishing wing of the New Zealand Department of Education in 1939. Its task was a humble one: to replace the dull and unimaginative textbooks that were currently available. But with national consciousness beginning to stir, the dynamic Director of Education Dr C. E. Beeby (1902–1998) was keen to have material that would reflect and mould the experience of New Zealand school children. School Publications was not only authorised to seek contributions from educationalists and subject specialists but also to commission work from the best available local writers and artists.[3]

For the social studies curriculum, which encompassed history, School Publications required its authors to present historical work in the form of a narrative, allowed them to use fictional techniques, urged them to represent the past from the point of view of historical actors, and encouraged debate and even a degree of controversy. This meant Ross could break free from the shackles of her training in the discipline of history. But this was not the only factor that enabled her to produce her best piece of work about the Treaty. Her family's move to Motukiore in the Hokianga also proved decisive.

School Pubs

Ross had been lobbying School Publications — or School Pubs as it was affectionately known — for a commission to do a bulletin about the Treaty before Beaglehole approached her to offer the Government Printer job. 'By the way, who is doing the Waitangi and whaling and sealing bulletins?' she asked Pat Earle (1917–2014), one of the School Publications editors, in March 1953. 'If they aren't farmed out yet — any chance of me getting the Waitangi one? I work on the principle that there is no harm in asking.' She sketched out the kinds of stories she could tell about the making of the Treaty.[4]

But Earle refused to be rushed and Ross received the Government Printer job soon after. Nevertheless, in June 1954 she again 'touted for the Waitangi job' (her words), writing to Pat Hattaway (1912–1970), the chief editor at School Publications, to press her case. Ross had clashed with School Pubs recently after the Department of Education had prohibited a bulletin she had written about an early Pākehā trader from making any reference to the consumption of alcohol or passing any critical remarks about the work of Christian missionaries among Māori. Consequently, she felt she had to provide some kind of a guarantee that she would not make any remarks about those touchy subjects in a bulletin on the Treaty. 'I *think* I can promise to be neither offensive nor controversial', she wrote. 'And I would love the job.' There can be no doubting her interest. As she remarked to Hattaway, 'Ian says I am suffering from Waitangi-itis.'[5]

She had to wait several more months before there was any movement at School Pubs. It was the responsibility of their editors to commission authors; Earle had resigned and a replacement had to be found; and his successor had to learn the ropes before commissioning any new work. It appears that Ross raised the matter of the Waitangi bulletin with Earle's successor, the historian Michael Turnbull (1922–1998), shortly after he took up his position in October 1954.[6] The two of them were soon on first-name terms. It turned out they had met during their school days — and had even danced together once. The boyish Turnbull remembered the occasion; Ross did not. By the end of November he had agreed she could do the bulletin.[7]

Ross had already done a lot of work for School Pubs. She had begun a few years earlier by 'boiling down' (Earle's words) Herman Melville's famous 1851 novel *Moby Dick* to a single story of Captain Ahab's quest for the notoriously hard-to-catch whale, but afterwards nearly all the writing she had done focused on the far north of New Zealand in the two decades before British annexation. She had compiled a collection of historical documents entitled *European Trade and Settlement in New Zealand before 1840* for a series to be used by senior students, but had then gone on to produce material for primary school pupils, completing several short stories for the *School Journal* and two bulletins, all of which concerned relations between Māori and Pākehā.[8]

Ross relished the work she did for School Pubs. In part this was because she embraced its fundamental purpose, which her mentor Beaglehole had described as one of 'making [children] feel that life in New Zealand [could] be a worth-while and interesting experience; that New Zealand has a tradition and contemporary ways of living of its own; that New Zealanders are doing fascinating and important things here and now, that can be best written about and drawn by New Zealanders'.[9] But she was also aware that School Pubs had acquired a reputation for excellent writing, fine artwork and high production standards. Given her perfectionism, they were a good fit, or so it seemed. She appreciated the fact that this extraordinary organisation provided a stimulating environment in which to work and sustained many local writers and artists. It was part of a lively literary and artistic scene and many of those who worked for it on commission were men and women who were playing a major role in the development of New Zealand writing and painting. Several of its in-house editors were gifted writers. They included two poets, Alistair Campbell and James K. Baxter. The latter would succeed Turnbull and thereby become Ross's editor for her Waitangi bulletin. The painter Rita Angus illustrated one of her stories for the *School Journal*.[10]

School Pubs suited Ross, too, because it encouraged its authors to take an independent line and challenge conventional opinion. Moreover, it gave its writers an opportunity to develop a theme in some depth. This was especially true of its social studies bulletins, which gave Ross a chance to sink her teeth into something substantial. She also welcomed the challenge of writing history for school children, regarding it as 'a fascinating and a teasing problem', though, despite her protestations to the contrary, she hoped this would not comprise the sum of her work as a historian.[11]

What is more, Ross found School Pubs congenial because it was committed to publishing material about Māori culture and history. At this time it was publishing a series of bulletins about post-1840 Māori history by the novelist and short story writer Roderick Finlayson. Ross read them in draft and welcomed what he had written. 'It seems to me that Finlayson has got his history from Maori sources — and what a harvest he has reaped', she told Turnbull. 'I am absolutely thrilled that he has worked this way, and more delighted than I can say with the results.'[12] She relished the fact that he conveyed a Māori perspective of the New Zealand Wars of the 1860s and 1870s, something she believed that a recently published book that dealt with this subject — H. C. M. Norris's *Armed Settlers: The Story of the Founding of Hamilton, New Zealand, 1864–1874* — had failed to provide, thereby obscuring what she called 'the other side of the picture, the dispossessed Maori'. In seeking to impress upon the Department of Education the importance of Finlayson's bulletins, she asserted: 'it is high time that pakeha New Zealanders, young and old, took a look at New Zealand history from the Maori angle'. School Pubs, then, offered her an environment in which she could pursue her growing interest in Māori history and do what she could to prompt Pākehā to stop 'ignoring the unpalatable past' and acknowledge 'that injustice has been done to the Maori', as she put it. She began to speak of her approach to the Treaty in terms of 'the Maori angle' and 'the Maori point of view', telling more than one of her correspondents that this was what interested her most about it.[13]

Most of all, perhaps, School Pubs enabled Ross to free herself from the straitjacket imposed by the historical training that had come to shackle her work on the Treaty for the Government Printer because of the emphasis it placed on grounding historical knowledge in written historical sources. This requirement had constrained her, given the approach she had chosen to adopt: the sources she needed to understand the Māori text of the Treaty, or to recover Māori perspectives of it, were not readily available or simply did not exist.

School Pubs encouraged its historical writers to make up things, including historical sources, within reason. This went against the grain for any author trained in the discipline of history. As Ross wrote to an American academic, R. W. (Pat) Kenny: 'Your instinctive choice would probably be, like mine, to stick to facts'. However, in writing for school children she had learned that this was a mistake. 'There are times of course where one must stick to the facts, every detail correct so far as one can make it, down to the most minute details', she declared, '[but] you can do a better job by letting your imagination run riot'.[14]

School Pubs not only required its historical writers to produce accounts in the form of narrative and to adopt a variety of literary devices to give life to what might otherwise be the bare bones of history. It urged them to present a picture of the past from the perspective of the historical actors. By the time Ross tackled her Waitangi bulletin her experimentation with literary techniques included making up historical characters and inventing dialogue for them.[15] She had abandoned the mode of writing she had previously learned, which emphasised analysis and argument at the expense of stories full of pace and colour that were difficult to derive from historical sources. She came to find this quite liberating and to prefer writing historical fiction, up to a point. At one stage she agreed to contribute more stories to the *School Journal* on the condition that they could be fictional. 'If they are to be written on specific blokes who actually existed in solid flesh and bone, then so far as I am concerned, they must be correct in every detail', she told Turnbull. 'I have enough acquaintance with the background material to ensure the stories would be accurate in the round, and would not be hampered by gaps in the material on a specific bloke as I would if I used actual historical characters.' For time-strapped women writers — Elsie Locke is another example — writing historical fiction had another advantage. Ross put it like this: 'I wouldn't have the time to do the research for factual stories, whereas I have an over-flowing supply to hand for fictional ones.' In short, School Pubs encouraged and enabled her to work in ways that were discouraged by the cloistered life of history.[16]

Soon after Turnbull agreed that she could write a bulletin about the Treaty for School Pubs, Ross began to envisage how she might do it. By January 1955 she had decided it would probably be set in the Hokianga, that it would deal with the Treaty meeting at Māngungu, and that it would be done in the form of a play or a series of plays.[17]

The path to Motukiore

Before Ross started to work on her Waitangi bulletin in earnest, though, a momentous change took place that was to influence her work on the Treaty profoundly: she, Ian and their boys moved from Auckland to Motukiore. Several factors brought about this change, but the most important was her reaction to a public lecture J. C. Beaglehole gave in April 1954 and published shortly afterwards.

In *The New Zealand Scholar* Beaglehole discussed what he saw as the predicament of any colony, riffing on a lecture that the American essayist and novelist Ralph Waldo Emerson had delivered at Harvard University in 1837 in which he had pondered the fact that New England derived its culture and thus its sense of belonging from another country, and called on Americans to speak their own minds so they could make themselves feel at home in their new land. Beaglehole followed suit, arguing that New Zealand could be regarded as a province, culturally speaking, and insisting that while there was undoubtedly an unconscious New Zealand tradition there was a need to make this present in the lives and thought of New Zealanders.[18]

The heart of this lecture was autobiographical. Beaglehole had taken himself as a case study of the predicament he believed New Zealanders suffered from. He confessed that he had been uninterested in New Zealand on his return after doing a doctorate in London and had undergone a slow and awkward process of becoming a New Zealander. He recalled that in the early 1940s he and one of his younger colleagues at the Historical Branch had discussed the subject of a New Zealand tradition. 'We played a good deal with words like "indigenous" and "authentic" — even, I fear, with "autochthonous"', he wrote. Beaglehole went on to argue that it was the job of the New Zealand scholar, which he defined loosely as a thinker, to help make New Zealanders conscious of their country's tradition and thus of themselves. They could only do this, he contended, by being critical, in the broad sense of that word. He envisaged a special role for scholars who were academically trained historians — like Ross.[19]

After he had drafted this lecture, Beaglehole sent it to his former colleague at the Historical Branch, Eric McCormick (who had recently completed the manuscript of a book about the New Zealand expatriate artist Frances Hodgkins) for what he called 'some really savage criticism'. Nothing of the kind was forthcoming. But savage, if oblique, criticism was provided by Ross in a letter she composed after he sent her a copy of his lecture. Implicitly, she accused Beaglehole, who would soon win international renown as a scholar of the Pacific, of being obtuse in his understanding of New Zealand identity. Her letter warrants being quoted at length as it sheds light on the key factor that propelled the Rosses to move to Motukiore, where she would adopt a particular approach to telling the story of the Treaty.[20]

Ross's response to Beaglehole's lecture was deeply personal. What interested her most was its autobiographical aspect. She was surprised by what he had said because she had known him for a long time and thought she knew him well. 'Do you know it never occurred to me that you had been a victim of that intellectual schizophrenia which tears at some of my friends and which I have so long deplored', she began her letter to him. Most of all, she was puzzled. 'Nor can I understand how I always sensed in you the consciousness of belonging, if you yourself did not feel it. Of anyone I have ever known, or have ever known of, you have always been for me "the New Zealand scholar" and it is as unthinkable to me that your "New Zealandness" should not be felt by you'. Ross was surprised by her reaction to his lecture, remarking to her friends the Bagnalls: 'I have fewer illusions than some about the bloke, and have always been freer of awe than most of my kindergarten associates . . . but even so this was rather a shock.' She was so shaken by reading his personal testimony that she immediately sat down to work out her own attitude to being a New Zealander, producing in the course of three days a twelve-page single-spaced typewritten letter to him that she called 'a sort of counter-testimony'.[21]

Ross's reaction to Beaglehole's lecture owed much to the fact that she felt the business of being a New Zealander had been over-intellectualised in certain literary circles in the country. 'Of course we are New Zealanders, so why bellyache about it?' she told Beaglehole. 'I was born a New Zealander, I am a New Zealander, I behave, and speak and think as a New Zealander, I like being a New Zealander, I shall die a New Zealander — so what? That seems to me to be a completely normal state of affairs. I have never wanted to be anything else but a New Zealander, and I certainly have never felt that to be a New Zealander is to be torn between two worlds.'[22]

Ross thought this was the case because she had no hankering to go overseas. 'I see people set off on the Great Trek, and I see them return, and I stay put. I'm quite content to stay put', she wrote. 'To be a New Zealander is good. I am content to be just that. Life is enriching and rewarding still, and will continue to be. Minor riches and small rewards perhaps, but I find them worthwhile and satisfying.' Instead of seeing the rest of the world, she wanted to see more of New Zealand. 'If a few thousand [pounds] dropped into my lap tomorrow, I would not buy a ticket for London, for concerts and plays and galleries and lectures. I'm damned sure I never want to set foot in the U.S.A.', she wrote. 'I'd go North again, and look at the bare brown hills of the Bay [of Islands], and watch from Opononi the sand hills turn golden . . . I'd go to Kaeo and Mangonui and right up to Reinga. They say there is nothing to see up there, but I'd like to see what nothing is like . . . I'd like to leave Opotiki for all points east. I shall always wonder what the Urewera is like. I feel incomplete because I have never seen Cape Foulwind, nor Granity, nor Karamea.' She yearned to see the places such as Westport where her grandparents and Ian's grandparents had lived and worked. 'I'd like to see Southland where rabbits starved out my grandfather's sheep. And Pareora, near Timaru, where my father [as] a child of nine sat in [a] buggy.'[23]

Ross was unpersuaded by Beaglehole's contention that there was a need for a New Zealand tradition to be made plain. 'What is all this about making explicit the unconscious New Zealand tradition?' she asked. 'We are New Zealanders, and we've always been fully aware of it.' But at this point she paused, pondering whether this was true in her case or whether it owed something to the trip her family had made to Britain in 1931 when she was an eleven-year-old. '[A]re we only consciously New Zealanders because [my brother Colin and I] found ourselves at an early age on exhibit . . . Was it because we were then eyed curiously and unbelievingly by barbarous kinsmen that we knew ourselves for what we were? . . . One and all they regarded us with uncomprehending eyes, then said . . . "Why, we expected you to be different, but you're just like us". And Colin and I thought — like hell we are!'[24]

Ross recalled their encounter with British culture and heritage. 'I have a good memory, I see it all. Cathedrals and castles, palaces and parks, plays and galleries, pomp and circumstance . . . And what impression did it all make?' Likewise, she recalled their encounter with the landscape. 'I remember all of us, primed by friends and relatives of the beauties of the Scottish lochs . . . And on we drove ever waiting for the miracles of beauty to unfold themselves. And then at last, disappointed, we said — Yes that was nice, quite pretty, but we'd rather have Long Acre when the kowhai was flowering.' And she added: 'We said, the Whangaehu valley can lick this. Is this a forest, we asked? It's too tame, give us the bush at the back of Paparangi any day. What has this got, we said, that the Purapura hasn't. The bluebells make a fine show we granted, but those lakes in the sandhills in behind Kaitoke are more to our taste.'[25]

Ross acknowledged that her response might have been insular and short-sighted but rejected any suggestion that this was evidence for New Zealand being a province of the so-called old country. Instead, she insisted, it testified to the fact that she and her family in Britain were 'strangers in a foreign land'. She recalled that her family had recoiled from much of what they had seen at this time of the Great Depression. 'The silent men hanging round the streets, nothing to do, nowhere to go. The dole queues. The squalor and misery and poverty . . . We did not think possible that West Coast miners might be as badly off.' She also remembered their pulling up alongside a policeman somewhere on their travels to ask for directions: 'He said ... You're New Zealanders aren't you? We nearly fell on his neck for joy. Here at last was someone who knew us for what we were — of course we were New Zealanders.'[26]

Yet Ross insisted that this 'Grand Tour' was not responsible for her sense of being a New Zealander. 'I was born one, as my father and mother were before me, and we all knew it.' She wondered: 'Was the knowledge that we were the land's as the land was ours born in us too? Did we know that, because we were close to the soil itself, and knew it well[?]' She went on to tell Beaglehole of her forebears' struggles on the land as farmers, bushmen, shearers, fencers and stackers. 'They were New Zealanders and they thought as New Zealanders.' Ross told of her own relationship to the land. 'My home was in a town, but most of our free time was spent in the country. Hanging round the yards while my father drafted sheep, sometimes on the race-gate, but more often just sitting on the fence with the sun blazing, the dust rising, dogs yapping, the smell of sheep, and men sweating, shouting, swearing, working.' Later she declared that she would hear the sounds and recall the smell of those yards for the rest of her days.[27]

Ross admitted that she had been brought up on British history at school and university but held that she was nonetheless conscious of the New Zealand tradition. Besides, as far as she was concerned, the country's history, art and letters were only part of that tradition. 'For what can history, art and letters mean if you are not born knowing that the land you walk is your land, the sun that shines on you is your sun, the sea you swim in your sea. That is the real belongingness, only in that soil can these things take root ... The only New Zealander who need be in a predicament is he who knows not his own country'.[28]

In summing up, Ross faltered: '[A]m *I* saying these things too easily? Am *I* merely whistling to keep my courage up?' But this was only momentary. She concluded by telling Beaglehole a little story: 'As I sat on the steps in the sun opening the mail, the seven-year-old [Duncan] peered over my shoulder. "What" he asked "is a scholar?" I told him. "Oh" he said. "The New Zealand scholar? That's me. I'm a New Zealand scholar!" and sauntered off to dig in his garden.' In signing off, Ross expressed some of the feelings she had for Beaglehole: 'Yours, in affection, respect, gratitude, and dissent.' Once she completed the letter, she pondered whether she should hold on to it, recognising it was an 'outburst' and 'a bit below the belt'. But Ian doubted Beaglehole would be offended and so she sent it.[29]

In the next few months the sentiments Ross had expressed about being a New Zealander acquired more significance for her. The clash of opinions between her and Beaglehole became public knowledge, even stirring up some debate, after she shared her letter to Beaglehole with several friends who in turn discussed her views with some of their acquaintances. As this occurred, Ross began to consider in more depth an aspect of being a New Zealander that Beaglehole had overlooked and she had barely touched on, namely how Māori figured in the matter.[30]

She started to ruminate about this shortly after responding to Beaglehole's lecture and her thoughts evolved in the first few months of 1955, following a holiday she, Ian and the boys spent travelling around the Waikato. During the previous year she had become more and more interested in the history of this area and of the neighbouring King Country. She had remarked to the publisher Blackwood Paul, who was based in the Waikato: 'I honestly think no one knows much about the Waikato war.' She believed the same was true of the King Country. 'It shames me bitterly to admit it, but it is only within the last five years that it occurred to me why the King Country is called the King Country.' She had never heard of the Māori king Tāwhiao and the independent Māori state that continued to exist throughout much of the nineteenth century in that area, though it was, as she observed, 'fair slap bang in the middle of the North Island'. She came to believe that there was a good deal of material about the Waikato and the King Country that was untouched and that only a scholar of Māori could make use of it, telling Paul: 'Not necessarily a scholar who is also a Maori — though that would be very interesting, and probably very salutary for the pakeha — but a scholar of the Maori language, Maori life, and Maori history.'[31]

Ross had become fascinated with this time and place after hearing Matt Te Hau tell an Adult Education class at Auckland University College a story, based on oral tradition, about an incident that had taken place at Rangiaowhia during the New Zealand Wars. According to the historian Vincent O'Malley, after British troops had taken possession of Ngāruawāhia on the Waikato River in December 1863, they pushed up the Waipā Valley towards the rich agricultural land of Rangiaowhia, and there, at dawn on Sunday 21 February 1864, they charged into an unfortified village, killing many Māori by firing on them and torching at least one whare (house) with several people inside. As soon as the men of the Kīngitanga heard of this, they abandoned a position they had taken up at Pāterangi and dashed back to defend their families or to seek revenge for the deaths that had occurred the day before. But they came under attack from the British forces and suffered heavy losses at nearby Hairini. The assault on Rangiaowhia was regarded by the Kīngitanga as an act of treachery: Rangiaowhia was not a pā (fort) but a place of refuge for women and children; they had been given to understand it would not be attacked; and they had passed a message to the British troops, via Bishop George Augustus Selwyn, telling them that women and children were at Rangiaowhia and requesting that they not be harmed. This meant in their eyes that the British attack constituted a raid rather than a battle and that the deaths amounted to murder. In the years that followed there was seldom any acknowledgement among Pākehā that their forebears had killed civilians at Rangiaowhia, but what had occurred was bitterly remembered by the Kīngitanga.[32]

On hearing the story that Te Hau related, Ross concluded that what had happened there was 'an exceedingly horrible business' and 'a particularly nasty affair'. In the version of the story Te Hau had told, it was a church that had been set alight by the British troops during a religious service and the congregation had been burnt to death. Ross came to believe that this event marked a turning point in relations between Māori and Pākehā and that Māori never forgave and would never forget. She recognised that the oral tradition she had heard had probably exaggerated and distorted what happened and so in her view it amounted to a dubious source of historical information, but she nonetheless formed the opinion that what many Māori believed had happened was almost as important as whatever had taken place there. There can be little doubt about the impact this story had on her. Nearly twenty-five years later she was still troubled by it.[33]

Her fascination with the Rangiaowhia incident grew during 1954 after she read a draft of one of Finlayson's bulletins that provided an account of what had happened. She started to look out for anything that could add to her sketchy knowledge. The opportunity to learn more arose during her trip with her family around the Waikato as they visited one of Ian's wartime acquaintances who owned land at Rangiaowhia. One could look out from this property to the next ridge and see the spire of the Anglican church and then look across to a farmhouse where the Kīngitanga had fought at Hairini the following day. 'I can tell you it got me', she told Turnbull. 'You wonder whether you are standing on the very spot where Bishop Selwyn stood that Monday evening in 1864 and called out "E hoa ma ko au tenei ko Pihopa. Haere no mai. Ko au tenei ko Pihopa Herewini — Friends it is I, the Bishop. Come to me. It is I, Bishop Selwyn." And his listeners, lying in ambush on the edge of the wheatfield, fingered their triggers and argued whether to shoot or whether not to shoot.'[34]

As Ross recognised, Rangiaowhia and Hairini in the past, and Rangiaowhia and Hairini in the present, had become intertwined in her mind. This had profound implications for how she saw the matter of being a New Zealander, and a New Zealand tradition. She told Turnbull: 'Past and present at Rangiaowhia and Hairini are all mixed up with my ire with the Beaglehole and Brasch brigade and their beef about the inarticulate, or was it unconscious, New Zealand tradition . . . The people who bleat we are just a young country, not like the England where every stone and every track is steeped in history. Ughghgh — they make me mad. They have neither the eyes to see with, nor ears to hear with, and there is no damn sense or sensitivity in them.'[35]

These thoughts and feelings led Ross to contemplate making a move from suburban Auckland so that she and her family could have more of the connection to the land that she had recently insisted was fundamental to being a New Zealander. It seemed increasingly likely that she would favour a place that was connected to the tangata whenua (the first people of the land).[36] In April 1955 she and Ian agreed that they would sell up in Auckland and move to a rural area where Ian would teach in a Māori primary school (which was part of a system of schools that had first been established under the control of the Native Department in 1867 but later transferred to the Department of Education, and whose student numbers had reached a peak at this time). They decided they would like to make a home for themselves in the Waikato or the northern King Country. According to Ross, the reasons for making such a move were complicated, but in reality one was uppermost: she wanted an opportunity to live in a place in which the Māori past was present.[37]

Where they might go depended on what teaching positions in the Māori school service came up for Ian. As it turned out, the first offer was for the school at Motukiore on the Hokianga Harbour and so they went there. This suited Ross just as well as the Waikato or the King Country. As she explained to one of her correspondents: 'I made some slight acquaintance of the area . . . some ten years back . . . The north fascinated me and the prospect of living there for a couple of years pleases me. Also I've been commissioned to do two historical bulletins for School Pubs, one . . . has a Hokianga setting [the Waitangi bulletin], the other . . . has a Bay of Islands setting', which was a Hobson bulletin that was also to focus on the Treaty. Soon after she moved to Motukiore, Beaglehole sent her a letter in which he quipped: 'Your move & all that sounds very exciting. You could hardly be closer to the original, autochthonous soil. You ought to be thoroughly happy.'[38]

Motukiore and a Māori world

Motukiore was on the margins of mainstream New Zealand society. On a tidal creek on the south side of the Hokianga Harbour, even today it is an out-of-the-way place. Despite Motukiore's name, which meant an island of rats, it was not actually an island. Strictly speaking, that name belonged to a tiny bush-clad island that lay hidden in the middle of mangroves at the mouth of the creek on which the Rosses lived. Nonetheless, Motukiore was small, so small that Ross was surprised it could be found on a map. It comprised a string of widely scattered houses, shacks and nīkau whare, four miles from Hōreke, a small town (if it could be called that) which boasted a pub, a garage, a post office, a mill and a store. The Rosses went there each Friday to collect their mail and newspapers, while their groceries were delivered once a week by the store.[39]

The Hokianga was known as 'the roadless north'. What roads there were, were often impassable. Public transport was rudimentary, and the telephone at Motukiore was frequently out of order. There was no doctor in the area and a nurse visited only every other month. The weather, though subtropical, was unpleasant much of the time. But Ross and her family soon fell in love with the place. This was largely because of the people around them, nearly all of whom were Māori. Of the approximately thirty children in the school, the only Pākehā were the Rosses' two boys and three other children who all belonged to the same family. Ross remarked that local Māori had no marae, or meeting house, or church, but were nevertheless very much a community: 'a community of common background and means of livelihood; a community of closely inter-woven relationships and interests; a community of spirit'. The Rosses liked the community though it took a while to establish anything like a free and easy relationship with its members. Ross told one of her correspondents after they had been there two years: 'For the first year we felt we were treading on egg-shells in our relations with them. The second year we were still pretty wary. Now at last we feel at ease with them and they appear at ease with us.' This was unusual, the anthropologist Pat Hohepa would have said. Rural Māori communities, at least those in the Hokianga, were mistrustful of Pākehā and especially those in official positions.[40]

The Hokianga was still very much a Māori world, partly because it had avoided the devastating effects of war and confiscation and the influx of large numbers of Pākehā that had occurred in many other parts of New Zealand. Most of the people were Māori and the place had many historical associations. It was believed by Ngāpuhi to be the place at which the great Polynesian ancestral figure Kupe had arrived in Aotearoa on his voyage of discovery, as well as the place from which he returned to Hawaiki, and they held that the latter event was the origin of the name 'Hokianga' as 'hoki' means 'to return'. It was also one of the first areas in New Zealand to become an outpost of the British Empire. Just down the creek from the Rosses' house was the Hairini cemetery, one of the oldest burial grounds in northern New Zealand still in use. Along the road from the Rosses was Māngungu, the site of the first Wesleyan mission station in the north and the place where the Treaty meeting that was to feature in Ross's bulletin took place. They passed it every week going to and from the store at Hōreke.[41]

The local community, or at least those she called the rangatira, soon realised that Ross was interested in Māori history and were willing to talk and share some of their knowledge with her. The most senior of these men, Tutere Koroi, who was nearer eighty than seventy and had the greatest mana, was the Rosses' closest neighbour. In the first year they were there she began to have long conversations with him as well as two younger men, Eru Te Whata and Jack Taylor. Although Koroi's English was limited and Ross did not speak Māori, she found these conversations helpful. She learned the tribal affiliations of the community and that there were genealogical connections between its members and those who had signed the Treaty, either at Waitangi or at Māngungu. She also learned that the current lessee of land nearby was a descendant of the senior Ngāti Hao rangatira Eruera Maihi Patuone, and his younger brother Tāmati Wāka Nene, who had played a crucial role at the Treaty hui (meeting) at Waitangi on 5 February 1840. She was eager to discover a more local connection. At one stage she had some reason to believe that there were descendants of two men — Mohi Tāwhai and Matiu — who had signed at the Māngungu meeting.

The rangatira were keen for Ross to visit the cemetery at Hairini as they believed at least one of those signatories might be buried there, and they persuaded the local tribal committee to invite her and her family to visit so that she could check the names on the tombstones. This invitation was exceptional: those in the occupational role of a school teacher tended to be barred from places where local Māori ceremonies took place.[42]

Every second Sunday at Motukiore was 'Church Sunday'. It was common for some of the local community to go to the Rosses' house for a cup of tea and a bun after the service. One Sunday afternoon in October 1955, after most of the people had left, Ross got out the facsimile of the Treaty sheet that included the signatures of those who signed at Māngungu and showed it to Koroi and Te Whata. Later, she gave a vivid account of what happened in a letter she wrote to a couple of her acquaintances in Auckland. 'Eru and I get down on the floor and Tutere sits down . . . we get into the Hokianga signatures. Eru can't decipher them, but I've done a lot of poring over them, so I have a go, trying to get my tongue round the names of the chiefs and hapu [clans or descent groups], feeling rather self-conscious about my pronunciation. But sometimes it's right, and they nod, and sometimes it's wrong and they courteously correct, and we get going great guns.' But then the two men became engaged in argument: 'Whether that bloke came from Rahiri or Whirinaki, whether he was a Hikitu or a Ngatipiu and so on. And they place some chaps, and go into great details of who is that family and that hapu now.' Much to Ross's disappointment, they did not seem to know anything about the Treaty meeting at Māngungu. She was hoping for some local stories she could draw on for her Waitangi bulletin.[43]

They moved on to the other Treaty sheets. There was a lot of discussion between the two men as to who signed for what tribe and who did not sign. '[T]he tribes who didn't sign were the Waikato and the Ngatihaus and the Maniapoto and the Tuwharetoa, and they . . . all fought the [British] troops in the Waikato war. But up here there was only one war, the War in the North [of the mid-1840s], what happened in the Waikato they know nothing about it, and aren't interested. They fought their war up here long before the Waikato ever thought about it.' However, Ross, Koroi and Te Whata soon began to discuss the Māori text of the Treaty. The response she received from the two rangatira was in stark contrast to Beaglehole's and Boyd's. 'I trot out some of my pet theories on the wording and they get a great reception', she told her correspondents. 'So then I tell Eru that I'm supposed to be doing a new introduction for the Govt. Printer. And he looks at me. I think you'd better shut up Mrs Ross. They won't print that . . . They won't like that at all. But I think you are right. Yes I think you are right.'[44]

At this point Koroi and Te Whata resumed speaking in Māori, leaving Ross desperately wishing she knew enough te reo to understand what they were saying. But they soon resumed speaking in English. Te Whata focused on the articles of the

Treaty and began to tell Ross: 'If I go out and shoot a pigeon, the government will fine me, make me pay money. If I go and catch too many fish in the river, they will put me in prison. They say I am not to take the oysters off the rocks.' This prompted Koroi to interject apropos of another shellfish: 'and the toheroas, the toheroas'. 'Yes', responds Te Whata, 'all to get money out of the Maori, that's what the government do'. He pointed out that this was not proscribed by the Treaty: 'the Queen didn't say anything about pigeons, or fish, or oysters, or toheroas. She didn't say we mustn't take them . . . The Queen said we could keep our things — see what she says — o ratou taonga katoa — all our possessions. But the government takes no notice. Why don't they say no horse-racing and no beer, and leave us our pigeons and toheroas . . . But the Queen said nothing about toheroa. Tutere's head is down on his chest — the pakeha take everything, everything, everything.'[45]

Ross guided the two men's attention to the third article of the Treaty. 'But look, Mr Tutere, the Queen said the Maori should have the rights and the same laws as the pakeha. But you don't have the same laws as we do — not always. Sometimes the law is the same for Maori and pakeha, and sometimes there is one law for the pakeha and another for the Maori. What about your Land Courts? And what about the Maori Members of Parliament? If the government did what the Queen said, then we would all vote together for the same people.' Ross was surprised by the two men's reaction. She had not struck many Māori before who were of the same mind as her regarding the last of these matters: 'Ah yes, says Te Whata . . . We should all be on the same roll, we should all vote together and then it would be as the queen said it was to be — ka tukua ki a ratou nga tikanga katoa rite tahi ki ana mea ki nga tangata o Ingarani. Yes, yes, we should all vote together . . . And Tutere nods in agreement.' As Ross observed: 'So there are three of us busy agreeing that separate Maori representation should be abolished and the result could be more Maori representatives, and certainly greater actual Maori representation of Maori interest.'[46]

At this moment Ian returned from some tasks he had been doing and this reminded the two rangatira that there were some things that they should be doing too. 'Te Whata's conscience smites him and he grabs his hat and is out to the front door, protesting loudly that he must go home.' But he is unable to open the door and no one helps him. Ross offers the two men another cup of tea. 'I'm thirsty with so much talking. Yes, says Te Whata, we talk, talk, talk. And Tutere's head nods . . . yes, we talk, but it is good talk, very good talk. So Te Whata forgets about his conscience and sits down again, and once more there is another round of tea and buns.'[47]

Just as Ross found the response of these rangatira to her work on the Treaty encouraging, so too must she have found the response of her editor at School Pubs. 'I'm glad . . . you have chosen Hokianga', Turnbull told her after he learned the Rosses were shifting there, having already expressed the view that her writing would improve once she was unable to get to libraries to do ever more research. 'Do get

[Eric Lee-] Johnson [to do the drawings for your Waitangi bulletin] and then together you can create a genius loci, a feeling for place we must aim for in our bulletins more than we have so far.' A month or so later, Turnbull enthusiastically replied to the first letter Ross sent him from Motukiore. 'From the Bulletin angle', he wrote, 'I am so glad that you are getting into the place you want for the Waitangi bulletin.' And he gave this advice: 'I am wondering whether you can in some way bring in the Hokianga today. Could you, as historian, explore the place, find out where the events happened, question Jack Taylor and other Maoris, and then re-create the scene in dramatic form?'[48]

Soon after Ross moved to Motukiore she started to give more thought to how she would tackle her Waitangi bulletin. But it would be some time before she was able to commence work on it properly. She did not have the five hundred pounds a year that the English novelist Virginia Woolf famously reckoned was a prerequisite for a woman being able to write, though she did at least have Woolf's other requirement — a room of her own — one of the bedrooms in the house, where she had a couple of desks. Even once she began on her bulletin there were, as always, many demands on her time. Most involved caring for Ian, Duncan and Malcolm, but she was responsible for older family members also. During this period she had to oversee the care of her beloved Aunt Lill, which saw her hurtling back and forth between Motukiore and Auckland, a bus journey that took the best part of a day. (Ross did not drive. Her father had tried to teach her but this had gone so badly she never felt able to try again.) And after her aunt and father died Ross had to spend a good deal of time settling their estates. As the wife of the school teacher, she had the responsibility of nurturing relations with the local community, which was a role she enjoyed (and which led to her establishing a branch of the Country Library Service). Finally, the family was largely dependent on what she could grow. Ross loved getting out into the garden — and some of the local Māori women encouraged her by giving her rare kinds of kūmara (sweet potato) — but carving out a garden in a subtropical climate meant she was forever battling with weeds or bugs of some kind or another as there were no frosts to kill them off.[49]

As if these tasks were not enough, the ever restless Ross agreed to take on more work for School Pubs. She accepted a commission to write four stories for the *School Journal* and acted as an (unpaid) consultant to Turnbull, giving advice on school bulletins generally and Finlayson's in particular. Likewise, she spent a great deal of time assisting other historians with their work, providing an enormous amount of information, giving plentiful advice about historical sources, and commenting in detail on their manuscripts.[50] She was tremendously generous in this regard. But she was her own worst enemy: this work ate up her time. However, she found it difficult to decline requests for help. She also spent hours and hours writing to friends and acquaintances. The harder pressed she was, the more she seems to have sat down at her typewriter and hammered out long letters.[51]

In the light of all this work, Ross's life was hectic and this took its toll. To make matters worse, she slept poorly and found it difficult to read and write at times, as she had only one good eye. Sometimes Motukiore's isolation proved a problem. The local store did not run to ribbons and paper for her beloved typewriter and there were no large libraries in the area though the chief librarian at the Auckland Institute Library, Enid Evans, repeatedly came to the rescue by sending her books and copies of manuscript material that she had requested.[52]

Time-consuming as most of the tasks were, some of them proved helpful for Ross's Waitangi bulletin. For example, while she had to put her work on it on hold when Ian's assistant teacher left suddenly and she had to stand in at short notice, teaching half a dozen Māori infants to speak English forced her to think more about the issues of language and translation that would become central to the story she would tell. Likewise, some of the other writing she agreed to do for School Pubs was useful. One of the stories she wrote for the *School Journal* gave her what she described as 'the whole idea of relating the present face of the land, and the people now living on it, with those who preceded them'.[53]

Ross had decided before she and her family moved to the Hokianga that she would probably focus this bulletin on the Treaty meeting at Māngungu, but this did not necessarily mean that the angle she would take would be a Māori one. Only as she became immersed in the Māori world of Motukiore did this become the case. Had she not done so, it would have been difficult if not impossible for her to adopt this perspective. 'I could never [have] written this bulletin [in the way I did] without knowing the area and the people', she later said. 'Not only is the scene Motukiore but the people of the hapu are Motukiore people.' It helped enormously that she could, as she put it, 'prowl round' Māngungu and see what could be seen from the site of the old mission house. Certain landmarks — such as the peak of nearby Maungataniwha — became fundamental to her telling of the story. In a sense she was doing fieldwork in the way an anthropologist would.[54] This only became a common practice among a handful of Pākehā historians in the mid to late 1970s. More generally, it was unusual for a Pākehā to know as much about the Māori world as Ross came to do at this time. Most knew nothing of it.[55]

Ross started to understand how much Māori and Pākehā differed. She later observed: 'As a Pakeha living in a Maori community I couldn't help being aware of differences in Maori and Pakeha thought.' After hearing Māori being spoken around her, she became more and more of the opinion that her bulletin should comprise talk by the principal Māori figures at the Māngungu mission station. In the stories she wrote for the *School Journal* she used Māori words. She sought to impress upon the editors at School Publications the need for Pākehā children to learn how to pronounce them, and decided she would like to learn how to speak the language herself.[56]

Just as importantly, Ross realised how little most Pākehā at hui were able to understand what Māori were saying, just as she formed the view that the role of Pākehā on these occasions was primarily one of listening and trying to understand, rather than talking. A few years later she remarked to the editor of a magazine to whom she had submitted a short story: 'It often seemed to me that when a Maori tells a story, he tells a story. Never mind about the other fella. If he wants to listen — let him listen. If he understands — good. If he doesn't — too bad.' She explained: '[W]hat I've written — or tried to — is a story about a Pakeha in a Maori setting. If it has a main theme . . . [it] is the Pakeha's feeling of knowing or not knowing, of being inside yet shut out, of being carried along in a haze of half-understanding.'[57]

In this context Ross increasingly believed it was time that Pākehā New Zealanders of all ages started to look at New Zealand history from the Māori perspective. She reproved Alan Mulgan for his Eurocentrism in this regard: 'You appear to have fall[en] into the trap of using the phrase "the very early days" as synonymous with "the early days of European settlement". The very early days in the history of Hokianga surely were about a thousand years ago.' By the same token, she became concerned that local Māori were not passing on their knowledge to their young and so she advocated that Māori history, tradition and custom be taught at the school in Motukiore, which happened to coincide with the view of some progressive Education Department officials at this time.[58]

Drafting the bulletin

Soon after Ross received the commission from School Pubs for her Waitangi bulletin, she agreed to do one on Hobson that would focus on the Treaty but from the perspective of the British or the Pākehā. To her way of thinking, doing this bulletin licensed her to concentrate on a Māori perspective in her other bulletin. This said, she believed that she had to do both bulletins as she thought her account of the Treaty would otherwise lack balance.[59]

She wrote the first draft of her Waitangi bulletin during a burst of work in the middle of 1956. In keeping with what she had proposed initially, she set out to re-create the Treaty meeting at Māngungu largely by using the dramatic form. Much of the writing came easily to her. She reckoned that two of the scenes, which she was calling 'The Hapu' and 'The Meeting', more or less wrote themselves. She found 'The Meeting' easy to write as she had rich historical sources for it that she could précis, but it probably helped that she had got to know the place. This was certainly true for 'The Hapu'. 'The scene is actually a mile or so down our creek, the Perunui', she told

Baxter, her editor. 'Tamati's land on the point is still owned by his Maori descendants. Te Whaiti and Huirama are buried in the little cemetery between the point and the puriri [tree.] Pero is there too probably, for bones outnumber headstones.' The tree under which she set the kōrero (discussion) among the hapū was still there. 'I[n] its shade the hapu gathers for the feast on annual cemetery clean-up day', she observed. Similarly, the mountain range she described was still a looming presence. 'And up behind is Maramarua, the old Ngahengahe stronghold.'[60]

As these remarks suggest, the contemporary landscape informed her portrayal of the past, so much so that past and present became almost indistinguishable from each other, as they had for her at Rangiaowhia. Ross talked about this aspect of her bulletin the following year: 'I was writing about a place I was living in and, though I didn't realise it at the time, about people I knew. Pero, Huirama, Te Whaiti Matiu and young Hone have a lot in common with Jack Taylor, Eru Te Whata, Tutere, old man Wara and young Pakau. Whether that makes the thoughts, words, attitudes of my characters right historically I don't know, but it does help to give them some air of conviction.'[61]

She found it more difficult to hit on a way of conveying that most of what took place in nearly all the scenes was transacted in Māori. In her first draft she provided all the Māori text of the Treaty, and after she omitted this from the second draft she changed the title of the bulletin to 'Te Tirite [sic] o Waitangi' to help make her point about the Treaty being an agreement written in Māori. Moreover, she found it hard to represent the wide gulf that she believed existed between the ways Māori and Pākehā understood the Treaty, though once again language was crucial. 'One way of showing this', she told Te Hau, 'is by mood, another by differing phraseology and by such devices as never letting a Maori speaker refer to Hobson or the Queen except as the Kawana [or] the Kuini.'[62]

Baxter was very pleased with Ross's first draft. 'On a single reading I would say that you have succeeded admirably in building up the essential impression of events occurring in a real world of the senses', he told her. He suggested some changes but hoped they would be kept to a minimum. Ross was greatly relieved. She had looked forward to doing both her Waitangi and Hobson bulletins with Turnbull and had been apprehensive about Baxter's appointment as his successor. She felt she could not understand the current generation of New Zealand poets and Baxter was an unknown quantity for her. But she now realised he made 'awfully good sense' as an editor.[63]

Ross was concerned that she might not have succeeded in getting across one of her main contentions. 'One point I want to absolutely ram home is that the treaty of Waitangi is *not* the English draft', she told Baxter. She claimed that her 'whole interpretation of the treaty . . . [in her bulletin was] based on that one vital fact, that it is a Maori text'. (Strictly speaking, this was not so. It was that the Māori text differed from the English text.) Yet, having insisted that this was the case, she added a note to her typewritten letter to Baxter: 'Or am I just being perverse?' She was probably remembering the reaction of Boyd and her colleagues to the paper she had given just six months earlier.[64]

Given her self-doubt, Baxter's response was crucial. Fortunately, he was sympathetic to what she was trying to say, grasped the essence of her argument, and reassured her that she had mostly succeeded in getting it across to her readers. He recommended another way to get her main point across: 'Say, if you like — "Hobbs [the Wesleyan missionary] was speaking in Maori, reading the Maori text of the Treaty. This was the true Treaty of Waitangi, not the English draft of it. Whatever the chiefs understood from the Treaty was very different from what the men who framed the Treaty had meant, translating English ideas of law, government and the possession of land into a foreign language which had no words to express these ideas accurately".' Baxter added: 'I don't suggest you should put it just like that; you will have your own way of saying it; but to say it explicitly seems the only sure way out.'[65]

Baxter recognised what nearly everyone who knew Ross failed to register: that while she was outspoken, she was by no means confident about her ability; that this often caused her to be dogmatic; and that she needed a lot of reassurance. This is what he provided — and it worked. 'I was quite cock-a-hoop over what you said about it, even though you gave me credit for doing something I didn't know I'd done', she informed him. 'But I must say that to be told that the most recent thing I've done is the best is singularly pleasing.'[66]

She was delighted that her draft had been well received by Jack Taylor: 'By the way I got the secretary of the local tribal committee to read the draft', she told Baxter. 'He and his wife, according to the daughter, got quite animated over it at home, but his comments to me were few. Even allowing for his innate courtesy, I think he approved it. We know him well enough now, I think, to provoke candid comment had he disapproved.' She must have been chuffed by one of his remarks: 'He also said it was the first thing he's read which attempted to see the Treaty from the Maori angle'.[67]

At this point in the process Ross was keen to have School Pubs type up a decent version of her draft and send it off to Matt Te Hau, Pei Te Hurinui Jones, Keith Sinclair and Michael Turnbull. Apart from anything else, she had run out of puff, as she often did after an intense period of work. Nevertheless, by January 1957, typed copies were ready to be sent out. She was in favour of several readers outside School Pubs having 'a lash' at it. (She told Te Hau that she had made 'some dirty cracks' about the draft chapters of Sinclair's *Pelican History of New Zealand* and so felt she had to give him 'an opportunity for utu', which is often understood as a chance for revenge.) But she was apprehensive about how her bulletin might be received in-house, warning Baxter that if School Pubs sought to censor her on any issue that she considered fundamental to her treatment of the Treaty, such as the role the Protestant missionaries had played, she would feel obliged to withdraw it. Having said this though, she wondered whether she was 'preparing for war unnecessarily, like an old hen with one misbegotten chick?'. This was undoubtedly the case.[68]

Both Māori readers welcomed what Ross had written. Te Hau thought she had done excellent work. Jones's response was even more commendatory. 'It is evident that she had gone to a lot of trouble to capture the Maori atmosphere of the tribal gatherings', he told Baxter. 'The descriptive writing . . . are all true to the old-time orator[y] of the Maori. I cannot recall any other work in which such occasions have been so well described.' The response of these two readers meant a good deal to Ross. She was gratified by Te Hau's praise and elated by Jones's. Sinclair also rated it a first-class piece of work.[69]

But Ross remained anxious. She fretted about the reception her bulletin might get from the Department of Education. As it turned out, her concerns were misplaced as far as it went, though they were not in respect of Pākehā opinion more generally. In June 1957 the *New Zealand Herald* rejected a letter to the editor she had been prompted to write after the newspaper published what she regarded as '[a] more than usually stupid and ignorant sub-leader'. The point of her letter, though this was implicit rather than explicit, as was so often the case with her writings about the Treaty, was to question the significance of 6 February as a national day. She reiterated her argument that the signing of the Treaty that took place that day was not the grounds on which the British Crown had established sovereignty because, apart from anything else, the authority of the chiefs who signed reached no wider than their own limited tribal territories. She suggested that if New Zealand wanted to have a day of national celebration to mark the establishment of British sovereignty, 21 May 1840 was the most appropriate date, it being when Hobson had formally proclaimed that the sovereignty of New Zealand vested in the British Crown forever. Nevertheless, she insisted that 6 February should be commemorated on the grounds that Hobson had given certain moral guarantees to Māori on behalf of Queen Victoria that day.[70]

The 'guns of Te Horeke'

By July 1957 Ross's Waitangi bulletin seemed to be moving smoothly towards publication, only for School Pubs to throw a spanner in the works, or so it seemed to Ross. She had been given to understand that it could be 14,000 words long, but Baxter had been directed to tell her it could only be 12,000. To add insult to injury, he had taken it upon himself to make the required cuts and told her to 'clear [her] decks for action', though he did acknowledge that she might 'feel like an unjust Solomon' that he had 'butchered [her] child'. She was incensed by what she saw as his high-handed treatment. She had worked hard to find the time and summon the mental energy required to research and write the bulletin, and for this reason, as well as others, she was very prickly about any perceptible threat to her work. In a blistering nine-page letter she told Baxter *he* had better clear *his* decks for action. Not for nothing did Turnbull once joke about 'the guns of Te Horeke'.[71]

By this time there had already been some friction between Ross and Baxter. He had paid a visit to Motukiore several months earlier and all the Ross family had enjoyed his company immensely, but a couple of months later he had sent Ross a poem prompted by his time in the Hokianga, part of which he had quoted in a letter to her:

> ... Tell
> Historian, how the broken tribes were healed
> In a land of exhausted wells, north
> From that great ragged capital
> Flung like a coat to rot on garden earth.

Ross seems to have interpreted this as a barbed suggestion that she was so preoccupied with providing a Māori perspective of the past that she was neglecting the problems they faced in the present. Yet she had been troubled for some time about the economic poverty local Māori were suffering (as a result of a lack of capital to put their land into full production) and the concomitant depopulation that was occurring. She had also been critical of the role the Department of Maori Affairs was playing in encouraging the drift of young Māori to towns, exclaiming to the Bagnalls: 'Apparently the departmental view is that this district is over-populated!! My bloody oath, it makes you spit. The land could support twice and three times its present population, and support it well.' Given this, it is probably unsurprising that Baxter's poem had made her 'hopping mad'. She had retorted by writing some verse of her own:

> Look, poet, with more seeing eye
> At backblocks Hokianga.
> Are you so blind to obsequies
> Of dying Maoritanga?
>
> Reinga calls the old men north
> In hopeless tired pity
> While young and fit go south to rot
> In sweaty stinking city.
>
> Fine phrases jar discordantly
> When atrophied tongue is lying —
> No healing here of broken tribes
> Just one small hapu, dying.[72]

Now, she told Baxter in no uncertain terms, if her bulletin needed any cutting, *she* would do it. She went on to admonish him: 'You can't reduce a final draft by one seventh simply by lopping out ten large chunks . . . The whole thing must be re-assessed, re-aligned, in part re-written . . . Remember if Waitangi is ever published it appears over my name. I'm not screaming because you've "butchered my child" (though that you have indeed done), but because you've butchered history and, bless my soul, my historical argument! . . . Remember, this is a bulletin about *Maori* reaction to the treaty.' She was irate, too, about his recommendation that there be a glossary and his provision of one that had definitions that she believed bore little if any relation to the way she had used the words in her text. But after she had finished typing this letter she hesitated, scribbling a postscript in which she half-joked: 'How stands my rangatiratanga with School Pubs now?'[73]

Baxter, realising there was a very good chance Ross would withdraw the bulletin, was both conciliatory and firm. He conceded she should have been told earlier that she might have to reduce its length, and agreed to remove the glossary on the condition that she provide English equivalents in the text. He also told her she was right not to accept all the cuts he had made. Nevertheless, he pointed out that she had exaggerated the damage he had done to her historical argument. Ross was mollified and once she regained her composure and began working on the cuts that were required she was able to see that many of the changes Baxter had recommended made good sense.[74]

Baxter was full of admiration of her next draft and made few changes to it before sending it off to the printers for galley proofs to be prepared. 'You know,' he told Ross, 'you seem to put your very best into a rush job'. But, once again, she was enraged by what he had done. '[F]rankly, developments over Waitangi suggest that R. M. Ross and the School Publications Branch have come to the final parting of the ways', she told him. '[Y]ou had absolutely no right at all to send the Waitangi script to the printer . . . with any alterations at all about which I had not been consulted and to which I had not consented.' As far as she was concerned, what she had submitted was not the final draft: the length still needed to be adjusted; the introduction polished; the translation of Māori phrases arranged. She felt she had made this point clear to Baxter, that he had not taken any notice of her threat to withdraw the bulletin if what she wanted to say was overridden by School Pubs, and that he had given her an undertaking that nothing would be rushed. She felt that she was being pushed around. Likewise, she resented Baxter's remark that she did her best work when she had to rush. 'You are mistaken', she told him. 'I have always put the best of which I am capable into any job for School Publications. So far as Waitangi is concerned I've put three and a half years work into it — two on research and the rest on the script.' 'You say the alterations are "astonishingly few"', she continued. 'It is immaterial whether they are few or many, large or small. If I don't like them, they will be altered. You will send me the galleys and I will alter them as I see fit. Pat Hattaway once said

I had an over-developed conscience. Well I do have a conscience, and there will be no more altering of galleys than *I* consider absolutely necessary.' She was not done yet. 'The Waitangi script remains my property until I am paid for it. And I shall not choose to accept payment for it until I have seen the page proofs. Should anyone be so foolish as to publish a script which *I* have not passed for publication I would take the matter straight to the Director.'[75]

Ross brought her tirade to a close in this abrupt fashion: 'I think it probable that Waitangi will be my last job for School Publications. *If* I do Hobson, it will be on my terms . . . If, however, School Publications care to decide here and now that they would prefer some other author for Hobson — that is OK by me. For that matter, they can return the Waitangi script right now if they like — I'm easy.' Just as she had given up her other Treaty commission in a moment of anger, she was on the verge of doing the same with this one.[76]

Baxter proved to be more adroit in dealing with this crisis than Beaglehole had been with the one over the facsimiles volume. Had he not, this Waitangi job might have suffered the same fate as the other one. He pointed out to Ross that there had been a misunderstanding: he had assumed that the pruning and polishing she wanted to do could be handled at the galley proof stage (though he had not made this clear to her). He was also tactful, telling her that he thought the version at the printer was superior to the previous draft and that the bulletin was the best job she had done for School Pubs. But he told her that her demand to have the final say over any publication was untenable.[77]

On receiving Baxter's letter, Ross realised she had made a mistake in assuming that she would not have an opportunity to make any more substantive changes. Consequently, she felt obliged to explain her outburst. 'I was determined that past misfortunes [in the publication process] . . . would not be repeated with Waitangi', she told him. 'Apart from being wild with you over what appeared to me editorial high-handedness, my general fed-upness is with the School Publications set-up, not with you personally.' She also pulled back from some of the demands she had made. 'In the matter of historical presentation, I realise of course that I must satisfy you. It is your job to decide what is and what is not suitable for the classroom.' Nonetheless, she insisted that she had to satisfy herself that what she was saying was historically accurate. Ross also felt ashamed that she had blown her top at Baxter and found it necessary to apologise to him and retract some of what she said: 'I am indeed sorry that I so rudely and violently disrupted what has been a pleasant, harmonious and to me anyway fruitful association. I would very much like to do another job for you.' Nevertheless, she remained, as she put it, 'browned off' with School Pubs, though she realised this cut both ways, scribbling a note at the end of this letter: 'And surely School Pubs will be more than fed up with me!' As this suggests, Ross had some sense that she was her own worst enemy.[78]

Three weeks later, Baxter sent Ross the galley proofs. In returning them with her corrections she once again felt the need to tread carefully. 'Herewith the galleys. They seem to have become entangled with the cats' meat or the ducks' breakfast. Damned if I know how or when and I apologise profusely.' She was embarrassed by the fact that she had made a mistake in the way she had rendered the title of the bulletin and had to ask for the 'O' to be changed to lower case. Nevertheless, she insisted that some changes be made. She was dismayed by the new introduction she had written, recognising that she had failed to capture the essence of her argument; she called for the part entitled 'The Meeting' to be reset; and she asked for some minor corrections to be made. She found all these tasks difficult; she told Baxter, as she had told others on several occasions, that by the time her work reached this final stage she had lost all interest in it.[79]

One final matter remained to be dealt with: the illustrations. This was something close to her heart. On learning she had been formally commissioned to do this bulletin, she had set about trying to forge a collaboration between herself and an illustrator. She believed illustrations were an integral part of any bulletin and that better bulletins would be produced if authors and illustrators worked together closely. She had been bitterly disappointed by the quality of the illustrations that were done for some of her earlier work for School Pubs. At the very least she wanted the opportunity to talk things over with an illustrator and she expected them to read the story she had written and to illustrate *it*. On the suggestion of her friend Janet Paul, she had approached Eric Lee-Johnson, who was well known for his paintings of the Hokianga and lived nearby at Waimamaku. He was keen; School Pubs did a lot of spadework in commissioning him to do six to eight illustrations; and Ross felt she had pulled off a real coup. However, several months later ill-health forced Lee-Johnson to withdraw. This was a blow for Ross, but she decided she would make one last attempt to secure an illustrator — and a Māori one at that.[80]

Eventually she approached Hone Papita Raukura (Ralph) Hotere (1931–2013). Born and raised in the Hokianga, he was one of several young, developing Māori artists at the time and was currently working as an art adviser for Northland primary schools. He was keen to get the work and agreed to do some quick sketches. Ross was delighted with them and felt they could work together. However, Cliff O'Malley, the art editor at School Pubs, was of the opinion that Hotere's figure work was not up to scratch for the purposes of publication, though he realised that his feeling for the local scene was quite impressive; and Baxter reckoned that Hotere lacked the sophistication needed to handle the job. O'Malley's judgement did not altogether surprise Hotere and Ross. Hotere believed the sketches required more work before they were ready to be shown to School Pubs, while Ross had an inkling that she had made a mistake in sending them to Baxter and O'Malley prematurely and recognised that she had been overly ambitious in thinking she could persuade School Pubs to commission an artist unknown to them. Nonetheless, both she and Hotere were disappointed by this outcome.[81]

Ross now felt she had to resign herself to accepting E. Mervyn Taylor, who was a well-established artist and a well-known quantity as far as School Pubs were concerned. She was anxious, though, about what he would produce. She acknowledged he was a good artist but asked whether he knew the Hokianga. Baxter sought to reassure her, but she remained sceptical. There was a particular scene that she badly wanted to be depicted: 'Something which must, I feel, be illustrated is "away to the north the sharp peak of Maungataniwha standing sentinel against the sky". Not merely because from this side of the river, from the mouth of our creek east to Mangungu you can't get away from the sight of Maungataniwha, but because of Papahia's speech: "What is the Kawana come for? I will tell you. That he may be high, very high, like Maungataniwha, and us low on the ground, nothing but little hills"', she told Baxter. 'That is one of the most significant Mangungu speeches. It shows so clearly how jealous of their authority, how wary lest Hobson's purpose be to usurp that authority, the chiefs were. And more important still perhaps, how close was the communion between the Maori and his land.' She asked Baxter: 'Does [Taylor] know Maungataniwha? We *must* have Maungataniwha.' She was also worried about the artwork for the cover as Baxter had told her it was unlikely that School Pubs would put the Hokianga signatures or the Treaty on it as she had suggested.[82]

In the next few months Ross wrote to Baxter several times inquiring about what was happening with the illustrations and the cover and pleading with him to send up the drawings before the blocks were made. In February and March 1958 she finally got to see all the drawings Taylor had submitted. She was disappointed, telling Baxter that while they were nice drawings, they were patchy illustrations. In her view Taylor's knowledge of the material in her text — the scene, the characters and so forth — was either limited or uneven. She was concerned most of all about that one particular drawing. 'By my interpretation Papahia's "high, high, like Maungataniwha and us low like little hills" demands an audience . . . Either Taylor doesn't see it my way, or he hasn't seen Maungataniwha.'[83]

In sending these drawings, Baxter admitted he was lukewarm about them but felt that they should let them stand. Ross disagreed and called for changes to be made. Baxter was willing to compromise. Three illustrations would be redone, and another was to be redone or scrubbed. One of them was of Maungataniwha. This was more than Ross had expected: 'After all, Taylor has considerable standing which I haven't, except perhaps as a prize bloody nuisance.' The cover had been redesigned and this more or less met with her approval. 'The lettering of "Te Tiriti o Waitangi" is damn nice', she told Baxter. '"R. M. Ross A Primary School Bulletin" tend to spoil the effect, but I suppose you have to have it on the cover', she added. She did ask for some changes, though. The impression Taylor had given of the Treaty document was misleading. 'As for the 99.9 [per cent] of New Zealanders the treaty of Waitangi is myth and misconception', she wrote, 'I take a slightly dim view of my bulletin being illustrated by a completely non-existent document.'[84]

After all that had happened, Ross decided that this would be the last piece of work she did for School Pubs, though, as with the Government Printer, this was not without her feeling some regret, wondering whether she was doing the right thing, and knowing she had irritated those she had worked with. In telling Hattaway she was quitting, she wrote: 'I don't know your problems, Pat. Perhaps I have been one of the noisiest ones. For how many years have I been giving off with much ebullience (your description) at one or other of you for one thing or another? Well this is the last boiling over, I'm retiring, you can all rest in perfect peace.' Her decision meant she never wrote the Hobson bulletin that she had conceived as the companion to her Waitangi one, and this left her feeling that she was 'leaving the job half done'.[85]

Te Tiriti o Waitangi

Ross's bulletin about the meeting that was held at the Wesleyan Mission at Māngungu on the Hokianga Harbour on 12 February 1840, several days after the Treaty had first been signed at Waitangi, began with a brief introduction. She set out some of the key parts of her interpretation of the Treaty, which she had first advanced in her paper to the Victoria Historical Association. She also explained to her young readers the historical sources she had drawn on for the story she was about to tell, alerting them that these were penned by Pākehā and that there was no written Māori account of the events she was about to describe, and suggesting why this mattered by quoting a remark that a rangatira, Mohi Tāwhai, had made during the meeting at Māngungu: '"Our sayings will sink to the bottom like a stone, but the words of the Pakeha will float, like the wood of the whau tree, and always remain to be seen."'[86]

In the bulletin's four parts Ross cleverly told a story in which several lines of her argument about the Treaty were embedded. In the opening part she imagined a hui among the local hapū as a way of setting the scene from a Māori perspective for the meeting that would take place at Māngungu. In doing so she made clear that the treaty-making occurred in an ancestral stronghold in which traditional beliefs such as those about Kupe were as strong as ever and Māori were the more powerful party. But she revealed (in both this part and the next) that the Māori world had already undergone change and that this was making many rangatira apprehensive. They knew they had already lost a great deal of their land and were troubled by the prospect of losing more; their fears had been aggravated by some Pākehā in their midst warning that thousands of British were about to descend on them; and they knew first-hand the fate that had befallen the native people across the Tasman, following British colonisation there.[87]

Much of the hui Ross described was preoccupied with the Treaty that was to be presented to them shortly and about which they had heard many rumours since the meeting at Waitangi. She emphasised that te Tiriti was strange to them and that they were unable to grasp the reasons why the British emissary was seeking to make it, and the implications of their agreeing to putting their names or marks on this pukapuka (piece of paper). She stressed that there was much debate among the hapū and pointed out that some of it was on generational lines. There were those who feared that the Kāwana (Governor) or the Kuini (Queen) wanted to be able to assume authority over them and their lands and thus take their mana from them; others held that the Kāwana merely wanted authority so that he could keep miscreant Pākehā in order and thereby protect them; still others reckoned that Māori were not so weak that they needed protection from Pākehā, whom they scorned as tūtūā (nobodies). Some felt it was best to drive the Pākehā into the sea; others held that they were useful. One rangatira reported that at the meeting at Waitangi, Tāmati Wāka Nene had expressed the opinion that it was too late to drive these people from their shores and had asked the Kāwana to remain and be their protector so that their lands and customs were preserved. Ross made clear that there were differences between the tribes and suggested that their responses to the news about the Treaty were as much a consequence of the nature of intra- or inter-tribal relations as they were of the matters at stake.[88]

In the next part, 'Highway to Hokianga', Ross shifted the focus to the British. She described the official party as a way of drawing attention to its puny size as well as Hobson's delicate state of health. She invented a conversation between him and the missionary Richard Taylor, which began as they departed Waimate Mission (where the second Treaty meeting had taken place on 9 and 10 February), as a means of presenting her argument that the outcome of the meeting at Waitangi had been influenced by the intervention of Nene and Patuone but also owed much to the missionaries. Finally, she described the journey the official party made to the Hokianga in such a way as to make clear that these British newcomers were out of place and anxious whereas the missionaries felt at home, not least with the Māori guides.[89]

The third and by far the longest part of the bulletin, 'The Meeting', was the part told as a play, which Ross suggested children could act out in the classroom and for which she provided stage directions. This, as she remarked to Baxter, was really the guts of the bulletin. Here, as elsewhere, her aim was to create confusion and doubt in her readers' minds about what the Treaty meant. To do this, she sought to make several points that were in keeping with the interpretation she had arrived at several years earlier. First, there was the contradictory nature of the texts. The chiefs were to 'give up all rights to the Queen of England for ever in the kawanatanga —

the governorship of their lands', but '[t]he Queen of England agrees and consents [*i.e.* confirms] to the chiefs, to the tribes, to all the people of New Zealand te tino rangatiratanga — the absolute greatness, the full chieftainship — of their lands, their villages, and all their possessions'. This argument was conveyed by her account of the part of the meeting in which Hobson read the English text and the missionary, Hobbs, translated it into Māori.[90]

Second, there was the gulf between the British and Māori understanding because the concepts that lay at the heart of the Treaty could not be translated. Ross demonstrated this point in the following passage: 'When Mr Hobbs has finished he pauses a while, as though arranging his thoughts. Then he begins to explain matters, speaking sometimes fluently but more often hesitantly, and sometimes at a loss for words altogether. When this happens he glances down at the parchment in his hands, reads out a phrase or so, and continues to address the meeting until he is again stuck for the right words. His is a difficult task, the explanation of English ideas to this large gathering.' She remarked further: 'The agreement is written in the Maori language, but its ideas are as foreign to the Maori chiefs as its language is to Captain Hobson.'[91]

In her account of the prolonged debate that followed, Ross drew heavily on the available historical sources to make clear that while some rangatira were willing to allow the Kāwana to come and rule over the Pākehā, they wanted no such figure for themselves and were troubled that his coming would mean that they would lose both their authority and their land. She used the historical record to suggest that rangatiratanga and land were inseparable as far as the chiefs were concerned. The rangatira included Pāpāhia, who, she noted, had already signed the Treaty at Waitangi but who now spoke vehemently against it. '"What is the Kawana come for?" he asked. "'I will tell you ... That he may be high, very high, like Maungataniwha. [*Squats down*]. And us down low on the ground, nothing but little hills. [*Jumps up*]. No! No! No! Let us be equal. [*Wheels round to face Hobson*]. Why should one be high and the other low? That is bad."'[92]

Both in this and in the last part of the bulletin (called 'After-Thoughts') Ross suggested that Hobson and several of the missionaries were in error in attributing opposition to the Treaty to either Pākehā settlers, most notably F. E. Maning, or the French Catholics, most obviously Bishop Jean Baptiste Pompallier, rather than recognising that the chiefs had enough intelligence and independence to form their own views about it. 'Someone has put him up to this ... Speak your own thoughts', Hobson exclaimed at one point in response to the first rangatira who had spoken in the debate, the Ngāpuhi rangatira Makoare Te Taonui, to which he retorted: 'I *am* speaking my own thoughts.'[93]

Ross noted that in the end many chiefs signed, but she implied that it was difficult to know what this signified: 'Among those who make their crosses or write their names are some who have spoken in favour of Hobson staying, and some who wish to send him away, and others who . . . have not spoken at all.' She suggested in the last part of her bulletin that some had signed only because they were following the lead of others or wished to acquire the material goods (such as blankets) that were on offer. Likewise, she revealed that some had agreed to the Treaty even though they had no intention of conceding to the Crown the exclusive right to purchase their land, making clear instead that they would sell to whomever they pleased.[94]

'After-Thoughts' was a means of driving home her principal argument. Ross imagined conversations between Hobbs and his fellow missionary William Woon, and between the local hapū and Maning, two days after the meeting. She had Hobbs expressing scepticism about whether the chiefs had understood what they had agreed to cede: '"I did my best, Mr Woon, but how *can* one explain, in Maori, the meaning of sovereignty?" Hobbs asked impatiently. "Why, I'm not sure I know myself all that sovereignty implies. Do you?" "Well," hesitated the other, "the power and authority of a sovereign, a ruler, I suppose." "Yes," broke in Hobbs, "that is just the point. The power and authority of the Queen of England is rather different from the power and authority of a Maori chief, isn't it?" "It is, I agree" [remarked Woon].' She made her argument that a key concept had not been used in the Māori text of the Treaty by providing this exchange: '"Then do you imagine that the chiefs consider they have handed over their authority, their mana, to the Queen?" [Hobbs asked]. Woon sat up with a jerk. "No," he said abruptly. "I do not. Nor do I recollect, Mr Hobbs, that the term 'mana' was used in the wording of the treaty." "It was not," Hobbs said crisply. "Yet surely the real meaning of the chiefs' cession of sovereignty to the Queen is that their mana will be dwarfed by the mana of the Queen?" Woon nodded in agreement.' Ross suggested that the treaty-making had been hasty: 'Woon said rather heatedly: "The whole business has been too hurried."' Finally, she raised the question of whether the Treaty had been necessary, and suggested, through words she gave to Hobbs, that it *had* been — so that the British Crown could restrain the growing number of Europeans.[95]

In the second conversation, featuring Maning and the hapū, Ross represented the local group as unsure about what signing the Treaty had meant. This was where she told of how some had signed only to withdraw their consent later; of others who had signed for very mundane reasons, or despite there being aspects that displeased them (especially the clause that meant they could only sell their land to the Crown); and of another who doubted black marks on a piece of paper could signify anything much at all. In an aside she drew into question the degree to which Hobson was concerned to gain the consent of the chiefs by having Maning ask two rangatira whether the Governor had agreed to their request to remove their names from the Treaty. In closing, Ross suggested that Māori were facing a troubling future: 'Thunder at sea, a long way off.'[96]

Te Tiriti o Waitangi was published in November 1958. Ross's anxieties about its publication continued up to and beyond its release, largely but not only because she realised that her account of the Treaty was radically different to the popular myth of the Treaty. As it turned out, the bulletin was universally praised. Among academic historians, both Sinclair and Boyd gave it their seal of approval. But it was the reception it got from other quarters that meant as much if not more to Ross, or so she reckoned. She received many commendatory remarks from school teachers but was especially pleased with the reaction of Māori readers, young and old. Ross never felt altogether comfortable being praised. She seems to have been just as pleased by the fact that her bulletin generated some controversy. '[It] took place in the Horeke store and I'm sorry I wasn't a fly on the wall', she told Hattaway. 'The proprietor [a Pākehā] gave off much steam I believe, because I had suggested in the bulletin (did I?) that over the treaty the British gave the Maori a raw deal. "And so they did", retorted the senior assistant in the store [Jack Taylor], who naturally defends me through thick and thin as he was asked to read and check the draft. I believe it all got extremely heated.' Nonetheless, Ross was pleased with her work, which is noteworthy given that she was usually so critical of what she produced. She was right to feel proud.[97]

In some respects Ross had adhered to the rules of the discipline of history in writing *Te Tiriti o Waitangi*, but a good deal of what she accomplished was only made possible by her breaking those rules: that there be a sharp separation between the author and their subject matter; that there is a fundamental difference between fact and fiction; that there be an enormous amount of distance, if not a disjuncture, between past and present; that truth was universal rather than a matter of perspective; and that the historian must be disinterested or dispassionate.[98]

Ross realised she had effectively torn up the historian's rulebook, describing her bulletin in these terms: 'It's a curious sort of thing — fact and fancy . . . past and present all inextricably mixed. I don't know that you would call it history . . . Though I didn't realise it at the time, in the writing of it I drew as much on my own experience as I did on historical records.' Clearly, this Waitangi job had been enormously important to her. 'This bulletin meant a great deal more to me than just another piece of historical writing for kids', she confessed to one of her correspondents. This was the case, as she recognised, because of her emotional investment in its subject matter. 'There is no getting away from the fact that I was very much wrapped up in it', she admitted. 'The setting was local, the characters in it based on local people, the situation one which I have either experienced myself or had a personal almost emotional feeling about.'[99]

Chapter 3
The New Zealand Journal of History

It is time to start turning our minds towards the piece of work for which Ruth Ross is best known by academic historians: her 1972 *New Zealand Journal of History* article on the Treaty. In considering it we will again see the influence that the intersection of the cloistered, public and private lives of history exerted on her approach and argument as well as her own account of it. The intellectual, political and personal circumstances in which she came to write and revise this article, the connection between it and her earlier writings on the Treaty, the relationship between her intentions and the final product, and a careful reading of the article itself all shed light on significant aspects of her interpretation that have been lost sight of in recent decades or never understood in the first place.

But to begin this chapter the twists and turns that occurred in her life in the course of the 1960s will be described, as these suggest that she might never have come to produce what would eventually become one of the most influential pieces of work a New Zealand historian has ever written.

Returning to the texts?

Although Ross threw in her commission from School Publications to do another bulletin on the Treaty — her so-called Hobson bulletin — she continued to be passionately interested in the subject. In February 1958 she submitted a scholarly article entitled 'The Waitangi Documents' to a recently founded publication, the *Northland Magazine*, which sought to cater to lay readers in that part of New Zealand. As with nearly all her writings on the Treaty, public discussions about it prompted her to write the piece. The Labour Party had recently come to power promising it would make 6 February a public holiday to commemorate the signing of the Treaty, and the four Labour Māori MPs were determined to ensure this occurred. Ross wanted to challenge the myth of the Treaty that underpinned the commemoration.[1]

The conception of her article owed much to the textual approach she had adopted for her commission from the Government Printer. It differed, nevertheless, from the last piece of work she had written in accordance with the conventions of academic history: the paper she had given to the Victoria Historical Association. Now, she struggled to articulate her argument that there were major differences between the Māori and English texts and that the Māori text was *the* Treaty. The dismissal of her approach to the Treaty by the likes of Mary Boyd had undermined her confidence and thus her capacity to write about the Treaty in the way the cloistered milieu of the university expected.[2]

After remarking in a preliminary aside that the original documents known as the famous Treaty of Waitangi were in a very poor shape in the bowels of the Dominion Archives, Ross embarked on an analysis that again drew into question the legitimacy of the Treaty as a legal agreement as well as the commemoration of its signing on 6 February. She argued as follows. The sheets all bore the same date (6 February) irrespective of when they were written, printed or signed by the contracting parties. Hobson's signature had been forged on one sheet and replaced by that of the acting governor on another. Another sheet bore no signature. It was a matter of dispute how many of the signatures could be regarded as a sign of consent. Of the approximately 540 signatories, sixty had neither signed their own names nor placed any mark beside them. More than a hundred signatures had no dates beside them. At least fifty did not seem to have been witnessed properly. There was some duplication of signatures, with the name of one notable rangatira — Te Rauparaha — appearing twice. A small number of signatories had sought to withdraw their consent and on at least one occasion those names had not been erased from the relevant sheet. Finally, only forty or so signatures were collected at Waitangi on 6 February (one thirteenth of the total). The remaining 500 were added over a period of several months at places other than Waitangi, while many tribes were not represented at all.[3]

Ross also pursued her main point from a different angle: the grounds on which Hobson had claimed sovereignty on behalf of the British Crown. Here, she was determined to answer her critics at Victoria University College by tackling this matter through a consideration of the proclamations Hobson had issued on 21 May 1840. She noted that in declaring sovereignty over the North Island in the first of the proclamations of that date he appeared to have been satisfied that the small number of chiefs who had signed at Waitangi could and did cede all the North Island to the Queen on 6 February. But she queried the correctness of this view, arguing that by this time Hobson must have known that the tribes were not united and that consequently the agreement required the consent of all the remaining chiefs. Likewise, she contended that it was difficult to accept his claim that the principal chiefs in the North Island had accepted the Treaty by the time he made this proclamation, given that he had only received some of the sheets that were still being circulated for signatures. Ross turned next to the second proclamation to point out that Hobson had to issue this to amend the first one because he had omitted to say that he was claiming sovereignty over the South Island and Stewart Island on the grounds of the doctrine of discovery, rather than the consent of the chiefs. 'In view of all these circumstances', she concluded, 'it is not surprising that a certain amount of confusion has arisen over "The Treaty of Waitangi" (which is not in fact a treaty of either municipal or international law), and over what date or dates saw the establishment of British sovereignty in this country.'[4]

This article received a mixed reception. Michael Standish was the most sympathetic reader. He thought Ross had succeeded in demonstrating that the treaty-making was undertaken in such a slipshod way that one had to question the sincerity of those who had drawn it up. Yet he pointed out to her that she had misjudged her audience. 'You won't mind if I say that yours is learned and requires concentrated reading. Not, I imagine, the sort of thing that one would read in the bus going from Kaikohe to Rawene after an exhausting day shopping buying 3 yards of calico for the wash-house windows.'[5]

At the *Northland Magazine* its editor, the historian J. M. R. (John) Owens, had similar reservations about whether the style of her article made it suitable for the magazine, but he was keen to publish it, despite knowing that her argument was controversial or perhaps because he knew this was the case and welcomed it. The two other reviewers were of a different mind, however. Keith Sinclair declared that it was not only unsuitable for a popular journal but an academic journal as well, for it was too detailed and pedantic. The other reviewer, James Rutherford, was troubled by the main thrust of the article. He took exception to what he saw as Ross's disparaging attitude towards the Treaty. Even though he had previously brought into question the view that Britain had assumed sovereignty merely on the basis of the Treaty,[6] he felt she had gone too far in challenging the myth about it. He would have been even more dismayed if he had known what she was saying in private. In a letter she wrote to

Standish at this time she struck at the heart of the myth — that it was a benevolent act by the British Crown — by expressing the view that the Colonial Office's instructions to Hobson were 'both very well-meaning and very cynical': well-meaning in the sense that they professed concern for Māori but cynical in that they directed Hobson to treat with the chiefs for the cession of sovereignty that the British government did not really believe they had.[7]

Ross was anxious about the reception her article might receive, so much so that she hoped it would be rejected, or so she claimed. 'My Waitangi article is unsuitable in every respect', she told Standish. But when she received Sinclair and Rutherford's comments, she must have found them wounding. She held Sinclair in high regard and believed that Rutherford was the New Zealand historian most knowledgeable about the Treaty.[8]

In due course the *Northland Magazine* did reject her article, leading her to doubt whether she should persist with her work on the Treaty. In a long letter she wrote to her fellow historian Ian Wards (1920–2003) in June 1958, she remarked: 'I've gone as far as I can go. That it wasn't far enough even for the purposes of a short article on the treaty signatures you have shown pretty completely.' In part, she still believed that the task of working on the Treaty was too difficult for her because she lacked access to the historical sources. But she felt she was not up to the task and that little good would come of it if she persisted. She even went so far as to imply that she could not be regarded as a historian.[9]

Standish tried to encourage her to continue, remarking: 'You have a skilled hand at stirring up hornets' nests. Long may it remain so.' But he made a remark that she can only have found discouraging: 'no one can write the sort of thing you have written without looking into every likely and unlikely source. And these are not available to you at present. You will never satisfy the Rutherfords of this country unless you have every little thing sewn up, unless you can demonstrate that, short of a miraculous hoard of records turning up, you have seen and compared everything.'[10]

Standish was aware of Ross's enormous potential and urged her to carry on her study of the Treaty. He suggested that she write what he called a biography of each Treaty sheet. 'Start off with the drafting of the thing, or earlier if you like — who first thought of the treaty scheme and why — and then describe what happened to each sheet. Who wrote them out, who they were entrusted to (what sort of men etc), where they took them to (what sort of places were these, contact with missionaries, traders etc), what happened there, who said what, who signed (as far as possible, and what sort of people signed)?' He recommended that she discuss what happened when the sheets were returned, what copies were made for the British government, and how they compared with the copies that remained in New Zealand. He thought it would be worthwhile to tell a story about the afterlife of these sheets, too: 'What happened to the copies here would be quite interesting — fire in 1842, rats later, etc.'

(The historian Claudia Orange would undertake just this kind of exercise twenty or so years later.)[11]

Standish realised that Ross's circumstances as a married woman with two young children meant that she would be unable to embark on this project for the time being, but he was more able than her to consider things with the longer term in mind. 'You see,' he told her, 'you will have to write a book about this, even if it takes you years and years.' He had come to know Ross well enough to know that she needed such a challenge: 'I am sure you won't be happy until you do, and you will probably be even less happy if you toss off something in a carefree devilmaycare havedonewithit fashion.' He also urged her to thumb her nose at the Victoria gang, hoping that this might goad her into resuming her work on the facsimiles volume.[12]

But Ross had become so discouraged by this time that she was unable to take Standish's advice on board. Besides, she felt that she had become so immersed in the Treaty texts or documents that she had lost perspective. 'Bogged down with detail it's hard to see the broader issues', she told him. 'Right from the beginning I've been haring off after one detail after another. Differences in meaning between biblical, treaty and modern usage of rangatiratanga . . . What is a signature, and so on and so on', she continued. 'You've always had a much broader appreciation of the whole subject, a much clearer idea of how it should be tackled.' But Standish was as tenacious as Ross. He kept on trying to persuade her to pick up the threads of her work, especially her Māori angle. In congratulating her on her Waitangi bulletin for School Pubs in November 1958, he remarked: 'What Mohi Tawhai said is very apt for us — "Our sayings will sink to the bottom like a stone". We are chock-a-block with Pakeha scribble which we treasure up, and how little there is of the Maori here. Faint echoes, inarticulate protests, distant pleas.'[13]

Several months later, Pat Hattaway approached Ross, on Standish's recommendation, for advice about the reissue of the Treaty facsimiles, after the government had called on School Publications to take responsibility for this task following its decision to mark 6 February as a public holiday. Somewhat reluctantly, Ross provided a long memorandum in which she warned School Pubs about the pitfalls involved in republishing the facsimiles. In doing so she repeated most of the arguments she had made in her paper to the Victoria Historical Association. She did, however, make some of her points more forcefully, as follows. The English text was of limited significance because, except for the sheet signed at Waikato Heads, it comprised only what the British government and its agents thought or hoped the Treaty meant. What the government regarded as the official version of the Treaty was not a translation of the Māori text but merely a draft of the English text. The real authors of the Treaty were the missionaries Henry and Edward Williams because they were responsible for producing the Māori text, which she implied was the Treaty.[14]

Ross, as so often, was dissatisfied with what she had produced, but after sweating over it for a week she sent it off to Hattaway. She told her that if the facsimiles volume was to be reissued, it should include a new introduction that incorporated the research that had been done on the Treaty since it had first been published in 1877, but she was adamant that *she* would not write it. A year later, the Government Printer republished the volume but with only a short introductory note by the chief librarian at the Alexander Turnbull Library that repeated the gist of the myth about the Treaty. Ross's highly original take on the Treaty remained unknown among most New Zealanders.[15]

The research assistant

The coming years saw major changes in Ross's circumstances. At the beginning of 1960 she and her family left Motukiore after a sharp decline in enrolments at the school pointed to its imminent closure. Ian had been offered a position at Rangitāne Māori primary school in Te Kōpuru, which lay on the Poutō Peninsula on the Kaipara Harbour, in Northland. They departed with heavy hearts. 'Leaving Motukiore plain bloody awful. Didn't realise till we came to leave how deep were the roots we'd put down. Formal farewelling by a Maori community has to be lived through to be believed', Ross told her friend and fellow historian Eric McCormick. Later, she would look back on their years at Motukiore as a golden age.[16]

As there was no secondary school at Te Kōpuru, a year after they departed Motukiore their younger son Malcolm left home to join his brother Duncan at Northland College in Kaikohe. This should have meant that Ross had more time for her historical work, but it did not turn out that way. Her life was just as hectic as ever as she assumed various roles and responsibilities in the school and the community. Moreover, there was to be more upheaval. They moved again in 1963 when Ian was promoted to a position at Punaruku District High School at Hikurangi, just north of Whangārei. And that was not the end of it. Late in 1965 he was appointed to St Thomas's primary school in Kohimarama and so they returned to Auckland (where a few years earlier they had bought land at Weymouth, on an inlet of the Manukau Harbour).[17]

In the first few years in this period in her life Ross wrote hardly anything about the Treaty, though she did resume writing about her beloved far north. She tried her hand at short stories, even winning a prize in a competition judged by the former editor of the *New Zealand Listener*, Monte Holcroft. She wrote reviews of books about pre-1840 Pākehā New Zealand for the only academic history journal in Australasia, *Historical Studies: Australia and New Zealand*. She contributed an entry on the history and development of settlement to the *New Zealand Junior Encyclopedia* and entries for the *Encyclopaedia of New Zealand* on the Māori prophet and rangatira Āperahama

Taonui and the rangatira Makoare Te Taonui, the traders F. E. Maning and Thomas McDonnell, and the French émigré Baron Charles de Thierry. She periodically worked on a book about Maning and was commissioned by the Turnbull Library to write a pamphlet about early European settlement in the Hokianga.[18]

She expended a good deal of the time, which she might have spent doing her own research and writing, helping fellow historians, most of all McCormick, who was preparing scholarly editions of books by the trader Edward Markham and the artist Augustus Earle. Her unpaid work earned her acknowledgements in the prefaces of both these volumes but not the status of a co-editor, though her contribution probably warranted it. The fault probably lay as much with Ross as with McCormick, as she insisted he used the material she provided. 'My trouble is', she remarked several years later in a letter to the historian Judith Binney (1940–2011), who, like McCormick, benefited from Ross's wealth of knowledge about the far north prior to 1840, 'that once a research assistant, always a research assistant. I just can't leave well alone[;] when I see work that needs doing urgently and no one in sight to do it I leave my own pursuits and get stuck in.' She also cringed when her own work received notice and even objected to being called an author or a historian, which prompted Graham Bagnall on one occasion to accuse her of carrying her 'inverted modesty far too far'. Women of Ross's generation were accustomed to avoiding high visibility and many accepted the status of a professional writer only with great reluctance. It is possible that she was anxious about making any claim to be a professional writer or a historian because of a fear of male condescension or hostility.[19]

It was at this time that Ross began an association with the New Zealand Historic Places Trust that was to last more than twenty years. As with all the historical work she did, she threw herself into it; demanded the highest standards of scholarship from herself and others; undertook a great deal of research work that many of the men were unwilling to do; and quarrelled with some of those she worked with. Before commencing her duties for the Trust in 1959, she had reservations. She had long been ambivalent about conservation of the past, or what soon came to be commonly known as 'heritage'; she was damning of what she saw as the Trust's amateurism and antiquarianism; and she believed that it was neglecting New Zealand's pre-1800 non-Pākehā history. In agreeing to join, she might have hoped she would be able to help the Trust address these deficiencies.[20]

Nearly all the work Ross did for the Trust concerned New Zealand's far north, but she became particularly engrossed in the restoration of the Waimate mission house, which had hosted the second of the Treaty meetings, and Pompallier House, which was associated with the Catholic bishop, Pompallier, who had been a participant at the meeting at Waitangi. She also spent an enormous amount of time on a project that was provoked by an erroneous claim that the Ngāpuhi leader Hongi Hika had had a pā at Kororipo. As with so much of her historical research, this was an exercise in myth-busting, but it could also be said to be an example of Māori tribal history, thereby anticipating the research that other Pākehā historians such as Binney and Michael King only began to do a decade or more later.[21]

None of this work directly concerned the Treaty, though in 1962 Ross had returned, if only briefly, to the Treaty when the *Northland Magazine* devoted a special issue to Waitangi and asked her to contribute. In the short scholarly article she wrote on this occasion she mainly repeated some of the points she had made in her earlier writings about the Treaty, and concluded in her customary myth-breaking mode by declaring that 6 February merely marked 'the somewhat disorganised beginning of an undertaking which was never carried through to completion'. She suggested that the annual observance of Waitangi Day should be less blindly celebratory because in her opinion it could still not be said with any confidence 'He iwi tahi tātou' — 'We are one people' — as Hobson had famously declared on that day in 1840.[22]

By the end of the 1960s Ross found it increasingly difficult to carry out her historical work. While she still enjoyed the research, writing had become a real grind for her. From the middle of the decade she found it difficult to concentrate. This was partly the result of bouts of ill health, which required her to have two major operations, but it was mostly because of the poor mental health of her son Malcolm.[23] This left her sorely troubled, not least because she felt it could be attributed partly to her flaws, even her failure, as a parent.[24]

Beaglehole began to doubt whether she would realise her potential as a historian, telling one of his friends in England who reminded him of Ross: 'There's another person out here like you — she knows more about certain things than anybody else — she's capable of brilliant work, as when she writes a memorandum without thinking about it, or a letter denouncing somebody else; & yet we're all dead scared she'll slide into the grave & leave undone all the terrific work she could do, & has material to do.'[25]

Still, at this very time Ross produced one of her most brilliant pieces of work: an essay for a volume that had an intriguing title, *The Feel of Truth*, which was commissioned to mark the retirement of her two teachers at Victoria University College: Beaglehole and Wood. Her contribution was entitled 'The Autochthonous New Zealand Soil' and she gave it this introductory remark: 'You could hardly be closer to the original, autochthonous New Zealand soil, you ought to be very happy, wrote J. C. B. shortly after we went north to Hokianga. It was a dig at my reaction to his *New Zealand Scholar*. It added to my vocabulary. And it prompts me now to reminisce a little about those years on the bank of a creek at Waiwhao [i.e. Motukiore].'[26]

This essay was 'more like a short story than a piece of historical writing', the leading New Zealand educationalist W. L. (Bill) Renwick (1929–2013), a trained historian himself, was to observe nearly twenty years later. 'What she manages to convey is a sense of cultural difference in the way that the Maori of her acquaintance on the banks of the Hokianga identified with their whakapapa, tribal traditions, and the forces of wairua and tapu that are part of the fabric of their lives.' What Ross was revealing, he pointed out, was that past and present are not separable in the way academic historians assume. 'The mauri of the ancestors lives on. It is an obligation of the living to keep them alive and protect their mana. This can be baffling to a Pakeha historian, even to one who has enough Maori to be able to have a rough idea of what is being said . . . Maori and Pakeha occupy different conceptual worlds, have different forms of explanation, different forms of discourse, and they proceed under different protocols and for different purposes . . . What Ruth Ross . . . is reminding Pakeha historians trained in [Beaglehole's] school of scepticism is that, to kaumatua and kuia, tribal history is celebration.' Renwick pointed out that the New Zealand tradition that Beaglehole had spoken of in his lecture *The New Zealand Scholar* was not the issue for her. 'It was how Pakeha scholars, schooled in the [Beaglehole] tradition [of history], should perceive, try to understand, relate to, live with, and learn from the Maori with whom they associated and shared a century and a half of history, but whose heritage, traditions, and ways of experiencing the world were so different.'[27]

Renwick confessed that when he had first read Ross's essay he found it baffling and thought it eccentric, but he came to realise that he had not been ready for it because she was 'asking questions that had not occurred to [him] or to many other Pakeha'. Yet at the time it was published at least some Pākehā readers understood a good deal of what she was saying. In a review for the *New Zealand Listener* the historian John Miller, who was another one of Beaglehole and Wood's students, described Ross's narrative as the most outstanding contribution to *The Feel of Truth* and noted its distinctive nature. 'History, a report on experience or a parable?' he wrote. 'There are elements of each in this lively and sensitive narrative which ought to be read by every New Zealander.'[28]

Another seminar at Victoria

While she wrote little on the Treaty during the 1960s, Ross never lost her interest in it, as her clipping of newspaper articles testifies.[29] There was growing public discussion and debate about the Treaty at this time. This was partly the result of the ongoing campaign by the Māori MPs and others to raise the profile of Waitangi Day and to get the Treaty ratified. But it was mainly the outcome of protest by young urban Māori and their allies who began to insist towards the end of the decade that the Treaty was a 'fraud' and a 'sham'. Their voices became more audible a couple of years later in protest that was spearheaded by a new group calling themselves Nga Tamatoa (The Young Warriors), which had been formed after a Young Maori Leaders conference held at the University of Auckland. They contested the celebration of the Treaty as the symbolic expression of the myth that New Zealanders were 'one people' and the country's race relations were the finest in the world. They argued that this story glossed over what Māori had lost as a consequence of colonisation as it ignored the dispossession of land and the loss of culture and language they had suffered.[30]

This moment, the historian Miranda Johnson has pointed out, proved to be a critical historical juncture. A major paradigm shift started to occur in the discourse about the rights of Māori and the way that the relationship between Māori, Pākehā and the New Zealand state was conceived. Like indigenous peoples in Australia and Canada, Māori began to articulate distinct claims about their rights. They argued against the progressive policy of assimilation, pursued in the decades since the end of the Second World War, with its emphasis on Māori acquiring individual civil rights, having the same rights and privileges as other citizens enjoyed, and being fully integrated into the wider New Zealand society. Insisting that this was not the answer to the problems their people faced and that it was actually the cause of many of them, they called on government to recognise the collective rights of Māori and even their sovereignty on the grounds that they were the prior occupiers and first peoples of the land. In doing this, they declared that the identity of Māori people was inextricably connected to land, culture and language, and called for changes that would enable them to regain and/or revive those things.[31]

From 1971, increasingly militant Māori protest prompted Pākehā New Zealanders to pay more attention to the Treaty. Consequently, Ross's historical expertise was suddenly in demand. In other words, the public life of history, rather than its cloistered life, saw her return to a subject she had not written about for nearly ten years. In July 1971 she was asked to give a paper at a two-day seminar about the Treaty that the Department of University Extension at Victoria University of Wellington decided to mount in February the following year. This department was the part of the university responsible for public programmes. As its director remarked at the time, its brief was to stage occasional seminars in which information about and interpretation of important public issues were presented by scholars in the hope that this would deepen public understanding of them. The Department's recent makeover — it was previously called Adult Education — suggested that the university's academic staff (like those elsewhere) were no longer engaging in public debate as a matter of course, as they had in Beaglehole's day.[32]

The Extension Department's lecturer in Maori Studies, Wiremu or William (Bill) Parker (who had been encouraged to take up this position by Matiu Te Hau many years earlier), was responsible for planning the seminar, but Mary Boyd might have been a member of its organising committee. Almost certainly, she was responsible for suggesting that Ross be one of the six speakers at the seminar. Alongside Boyd, there were to be three legal scholars (K. J. Keith, Warwick McLean and R. N. Tristam) and Hēnare Kōhere Ngata, the son of Sir Apirana Ngata and a member of the New Zealand Maori Council, in which capacity he had recently been responsible for a memorandum setting out all the breaches of the Treaty's terms. In the event, it was Boyd who made the approach to Ross. She must have known her old friend would be diffident. 'Could you let me know soon if you could be persuaded to do this?' she asked. 'I think you could virtually choose your own subject! I hope you will come — particularly as you know more about the treaty on the ground so to speak than anyone else.'[33]

Ross did have mixed feelings about the invitation, but, as so often on such occasions, Ian urged her to accept. She was nonetheless anxious about talking publicly as she believed she was a poor speaker. This must have been aggravated by the fact that her one and only experience of presenting a paper about her research on the Treaty had occurred more or less under the same auspices as this one was going to be. 'My own part in proceedings fills me with considerable trepidation', she told Boyd. 'I have never done anything like this before, although in fact I am not quite sure what doing it this way is.' For the moment it seems she had forgotten what had happened on that unhappy occasion in March 1956 when Boyd had dismissed her work on the Treaty. But she soon recalled the experience, commenting to an old friend, Robert (Bob) Burnett, that she found it 'all rather ironic to be asked, on Mary's recommendation, to give a paper at this seminar'. However, she recognised that this had happened because of the political shifts that were taking place in New Zealand: whereas her approach to the Treaty had once been dismissed as historically worthless, it was now valued highly.[34]

Ross's anxiety about presenting a paper at the seminar was no doubt heightened by her fellow historian, friend and colleague at the Historic Places Trust, Ormond Wilson, who declared himself puzzled as to why she rather than Ian Wards had been invited to speak. (In the course of the next several months he would swing back and forth between helping and hindering her work on the Treaty.) She must have found Boyd's response to Wilson's query ironic. 'I'd ignore Ormond!' Boyd urged her. 'Don't you dare get cold feet as you are about the only person we all want to hear on the treaty. We all know what Ian thinks already. I'm the one who [is] really the least qualified for the job.' It seems Ross had another reason for being annoyed by Wilson's remark. 'Years and years ago now', she told Boyd, '[Ian Wards] cut me short in an exchange of ideas on the treaty, indicating that I could wait till his book was published to draw on the fruit of his researches — or so it appeared to me was his meaning'.[35]

To pick up the threads of scholarly work one has done many years earlier is never an easy task, and Ross made it harder for herself. She could have written a paper off the top of her head or revised the one she had given in Wellington in 1956, but she decided to start afresh and do more research. She hoped to find more material relating to the Treaty meetings and was keen to examine the originals of the Treaty documents, including one of the deeds that was in private hands. She was acutely aware that almost every time she returned to the texts she saw something she had never seen before. This is a common if unnerving experience for historians, but she seems to have found it especially difficult.[36]

Ross found it hard to settle on a title for her paper. She proposed 'The Treaty on the Ground', probably because Boyd had used that phrase in inviting her to speak, but Bill Parker wanted a title that would give the potential audience a better sense of what she was going to talk about. She suggested 'The Treaty documents, the Treaty meetings, the signatories'. Ross knew the university's Extension Department required the papers beforehand so they could be circulated to all the participants in the seminar, but she did not begin writing her paper until a month before the seminar and soon got into trouble trying to sort out her argument. A good part of the problem can be attributed to the fear that she might get a similar reception to the one she received fifteen or so years earlier. Recalling that occasion, she told one of her correspondents: 'I don't think I have ever found anything as difficult to write as this ruddy Waitangi thing.' She struggled to keep her paper to the length required. In the end her paper ran to more than 8000 words, and this did not include its three lengthy appendices.[37]

The MP for Southern Maori, Whetū Tirikātene-Sullivan (1932–2011), whose father had been a supporter of Tahupōtiki Wiremu Rātana and had long fought for the statutory recognition of the Treaty, and in whose footsteps she had followed, opened the seminar and chaired the first session in which Boyd and Ross gave their papers. Ross was miffed that Tirikātene-Sullivan used what she called her 'punch line', feeling it had been 'filched' from her. (Her punch line probably comprised her claim that the Māori text was *the* Treaty.) And, shortly before she was due to deliver her paper, Wilson asked her who she was going to get to read the passages in the Māori text, which did nothing for her confidence. 'I could have scragged him', she recalled after the ordeal was over. (Later, he commended her on her pronunciation.)[38]

Ross's aim was to explain what the Treaty was, how it had been drawn up, what it was thought to mean at the time, who consented to sign it, who opposed it and the reasons why. She claimed later that she had sought to approach the subject from these different angles in the hope that everyone in the audience would find something of interest in it. But the fact of the matter is that she felt torn about whether she could or should make the texts, and especially the Māori text, her focus. At the last minute she decided to add this little story after she had made her opening remarks: 'In a debate on the Treaty of Waitangi in the House of Representatives in 1865 J. E. FitzGerald said his "notion of equity between man and man . . . led him to believe that when a man signed a paper he should understand the meaning of it, and that, if this document was signed in the Maori tongue, whatever the English translation might be had nothing to do with the question".' Reverting to her script, Ross quickly tried to explain her point: 'It has always seemed to me that one must accept the Maori text as the Treaty of Waitangi. This was the text of the agreement signed by Hobson and the chiefs at Waitangi on 6 February 1840 and subsequently assented to by 460 others, over the next seven months. Therefore, any discussion of the terms of the Treaty of Waitangi must surely hinge on the meaning of this Māori text.'[39]

Her use of the word 'surely' suggests that Ross was nervous about making this argument, as does another introductory remark she made: 'To lawyers and academic historians this [i.e. her claim that the Māori text *was* the Treaty] may seem a simplistic, maybe even a wayward approach. I am neither a lawyer, nor an academic historian. Nor do I speak Maori. But I have spent a fair amount of time looking at the Treaty of Waitangi.' It seems unlikely that many of her audience would have understood the implications of the point that she was making, not least because she had not explained her rationale for telling the FitzGerald story.[40] But at least one member in the audience *did*. Tirikātene-Sullivan 'couldn't get the reference fast enough', Ross observed later.[41]

She soon plunged into a discussion about the texts and translation, determined to make a series of points that she had long been making: the English versions or texts were no more than drafts of the Treaty; the Māori text was a translation of an English draft, rather than the other way round; the text that was customarily regarded as the official version of the Treaty was an English one that had been signed only at Waikato Heads; and the text that was signed everywhere else was the Māori text. However, she did not spell out what she considered to be the implications of these points. Furthermore, she complicated matters for her audience because she was determined to share two findings from the research she had recently done but whose implications she had yet to figure out: that the several English versions differed from one another in significant ways; and that a careful comparison of them suggested that the Māori text had been translated from an earlier English version that had not survived. In regard to the former, she admitted later that she had been unable to see the wood for the trees.[42]

Next, Ross discussed the drafting of the English version. After noting that Hobson had been authorised to treat with the chiefs for the recognition of British sovereignty (an important point that historians to this day overlook, as a careful reading of the historical scholarship on the Treaty reveals), she observed that he had not been provided with a draft but was told instead that he could expect to receive a good deal of help from the missionaries — that is, she insisted, the *Protestant* missionaries. She noted that Hobson had turned to the former British Consul to New Zealand, James Busby, for help, but she was critical of his claim that he was responsible for drawing up the Treaty. She accepted that Busby had had a role in the drafting of the articles in the English text, but pointed out that his contribution to the Treaty — by which she meant the Māori text — was minimal.[43]

Ross's consideration of Busby's role led her to consider the Declaration of Independence, in which Busby did have a major hand. In 1835 he had persuaded northern rangatira to make this statement in which they both proclaimed themselves to be sovereign *and* called on the British Crown for protection. Here, she took issue with a contention Ian Wards had made in his 1968 book *The Shadow of the Land*: that the British Crown had accepted that sovereignty in New Zealand was vested in a defined Māori authority. She argued that if this had been the case, the historian would expect to find some reference to that very authority in Hobson's instructions, but there was none. (It is a point that most historians have chosen to ignore in recent years as they have repeatedly misinterpreted the Declaration and its reception by the imperial government, claiming that it amounted to an unambiguous assertion of Māori sovereignty and that the Colonial Secretary recognised Māori as sovereign when he acknowledged receipt of the Declaration on behalf of the Crown.)[44]

Ross then returned to pick up the thread of her argument about translation. Here, she repeated several points that she had advanced in her earlier writings: the English draft had been put together hurriedly; there was little time allowed for its translation into Māori; the Williamses were not the most able translators among the missionaries. She also raised the possibility that the text that chiefs had signed at Waitangi on 6 February differed to some degree from the one that had been the basis of the discussions the previous day.[45]

Ross moved next to raise her most important question about the translation, having at the beginning of her paper declared that the language of the Māori text was not 'indigenous Maori' but 'missionary-Maori'. As she had done in her earlier writings, she expressed doubt that the key concepts in the Treaty had been translated in a way that enabled the chiefs to understand what was at stake. In reference to its first article she argued that the point at issue was whether 'sovereignty' had been translated adequately by 'te Kawanatanga katoa o o ratou wenua'. In doing so she chose to rely on remarks that the former Chief Justice Sir William Martin had made about the Treaty in 1860, probably because she assumed that his words were more likely to persuade her audience of the point she wished to make. She quoted these two passages from his writings at that time: 'We called them [i.e. the rights the government was seeking] "Sovereignty"[,] the Natives called them "Kawanatanga", "Governorship"'; and 'This unknown thing [that is, unknown to Māori], the "Governorship"'. She noted that the word 'kawanatanga' had been coined by the missionaries, then moved to argue that if the Williamses 'had translated sovereignty as *te kawanatanga kapa te mana katoa me te kaha* no Maori would have been in any doubt about what was being given to the Queen', after which she hesitantly raised this question: 'But if the Maori concept of *mana* had been seen as a part of the European concept of sovereignty, would any New Zealander have signed the treaty?'[46]

Ross's next move reveals that she was more intent on explaining why the missionaries had proceeded in these ways, rather than on examining how Māori understood what was presented to them. 'Did [the Williamses], knowing that the chiefs would never sign away their *mana* to the Queen, deliberately eschew the use of this word and this concept in their translation?' she asked. But having raised that possibility she merely remarked: 'Well, your guess is as good as mine.' Moreover, she went on to observe only that she found it 'interesting' that in the Declaration of Independence the phrase 'all sovereign power and authority within the territories of the United Tribes' had been translated as 'ko te Kingitanga ko te mana i te wenua o te whakaminenga' but that in the Treaty, in which 'this same sovereign power and authority was to be ceded to the Queen, any mention of *mana* was omitted'. Ross might have pursued this point if she had been sure that Henry Williams was responsible for translating the Declaration but, having thought this to be the case fifteen years earlier, she was now uncertain who had translated it.[47]

Turning to the first part of the Treaty's second article, Ross again relied on Martin's legal authority. Noting that the British Crown had confirmed and guaranteed to all Māori 'te tino rangatiratanga' in return for the chiefs ceding 'their kawanatanga', she quoted his contention: 'To themselves they retained what they understood full well, the "*tino Rangatiratanga*," "full Chieftainship," in respect of all their lands.' She then proceeded to argue that 'te tino rangatiratanga' applied not only to their land (whenua) but to all their possessions and not just to material ones, which meant, she argued, that it included prized possessions (taonga) such as language. Yet, having made this argument, which was sympathetic to Māori aspirations, she proceeded to point out that, whereas the first clause of the second article of the English text that had been signed at Waikato included a reference to forests and fisheries, the Māori text made no reference to either. She even went so far as to raise the possibility that the 'kawanatanga' the chiefs had ceded — irrespective of whether it referred to 'a blanket authority [that was] sovereignty or merely government' — could 'cancel out any lesser guarantees given in return should this be found necessary for its due exercise'. She argued, moreover, that it was not at all clear what 'te tino rangatira' meant at the time the Treaty was signed. These remarks reveal Ross's purpose and principal argument: that because the English text had been so poorly translated, the meanings of the Treaty's provisions were ambiguous and contradictory and so could not be the basis for a proper agreement between the two parties to it.[48]

Her next move might be regarded as surprising given how often she claimed that her interpretation of the Treaty was based on its texts and how often this claim has been accepted by readers. She turned from the text of the first part of the second article to the talk about it at Waitangi. This, she held, was a better indicator of what the parties thought they were doing in making the Treaty. 'The vital question', she declared, 'is how did Henry Williams at Waitangi explain the difference between the *kawanatanga* which went to the Queen and the *tino rangatiratanga* which the chiefs and hapu and all the men of New Zealand retained.' It seemed, at this point, that she had abandoned her contention that the texts held the key to grasping the Treaty's meaning. She went on to contend (in a somewhat convoluted fashion) that in explaining the Treaty to the chiefs, Williams had probably used the same key words as he and his son had used in translating it. This led her to say, as she had said in her earlier writings: 'One wonders whether . . . the chiefs supposed they were retaining everything and had nothing left over to give to the Queen.' In support of this argument, Ross again adduced the famous words that it was believed Nōpera Panakareao had uttered at the Treaty meeting at Kaitāia: 'the shadow of the land will go to [the Governor] but the substance will remain with us'.[49]

In discussing the second part of the second article Ross turned once more to the text, albeit the English one. Here, she argued that there was little doubt that Hobson intended this to mean that the chiefs agreed to grant the British Crown the sole right of purchasing their land. But she soon returned to the way the concept of the Crown's right of pre-emption had been represented during the talk that had taken place at Waitangi and later meetings, and suggested that this raised doubts about whether it had been made clear to the chiefs that they were only going to be able to sell their land to the Crown, rather than to whomever they chose. Then, amid a long-winded discussion of this matter, she raised in an oblique manner what amounted to another question that arose out of a consideration of the talk about the Treaty rather than the texts: what did signing really signify, given that so many of those who did sign spoke vehemently against one or more of its provisions?[50]

In the next part of her paper Ross turned to what had happened after Hobson had been struck down by a stroke shortly after the Treaty meetings in the north of the North Island. She provided a long and discursive account of the proceedings, punctuating it with technical points of the kind she had made many years earlier in her article 'The Waitangi Documents'. These drew into question the legal validity of the Treaty, but she did not make an argument to that effect. Instead, in the last part of her paper, she provided a similarly flawed treatment of a matter that had long preoccupied her, arguing that in order to understand Māori opposition to the Treaty at the meetings in the Bay of Islands and the Hokianga one needed to discard Hobson's misguided attribution of it to foreign forces — French and Catholic — but few in her audience can have grasped her point. After asserting that Hobson had 'plots on the brain' she started — but only started — to make what had previously been one of her most important arguments: that Hobson's claim of sovereignty over the North Island based on Māori consent was difficult to sustain given that several chiefs and several tribes had refused to sign and no attempt had been made to obtain the adherence of those in the interior.[51]

Ross ended her paper abruptly, stating, very belatedly and very briefly, her principal argument, which she had first advanced more than fifteen years earlier: 'This, then, is how the treaty on the ground looks to me: hastily and inexpertly drawn up, ambiguous and contradictory in content, chaotic in its execution.'[52]

Ross's paper was by no means her best work on the Treaty. She had not written anything like it for many years and her skills were rusty. It must have been difficult for the audience to grasp her principal contention given that she only articulated it properly at the end. Similarly, they must have struggled to understand some of her particular lines of argument. She had shifted from one to another without any signposting; large parts of her account were discursive; and at a few stages she mounted discussions in which her point only became clear at the end. She herself recognised that her paper had several weaknesses. 'I know it wasn't a bad paper', she told her son Malcolm a few months later with her characteristic lack of confidence.[53]

Nevertheless, her paper was well received, at least by the Pākehā in the audience. It seems the Māori members were more critical. This is hardly surprising given that she had attacked the myth of the Treaty to which many still subscribed, and drawn into question whether the Treaty provided a guarantee of their rights to forests and fisheries, which had long been important to many. She reckoned that Tama (Tom) Poata, a Ngāti Porou man who was a founding member of the Maori Organisation on Human Rights that was pushing for ratification of the Treaty, spoke crossly and that 'the Ratana mob' were similarly annoyed; she told a correspondent that one of their number complimented her on providing the Māori text in one of her appendices but thought the 'rest of my paper stank'.[54]

'Te Tiriti o Waitangi: Texts and Translations'

In the wake of the seminar, Ross gave some thought to getting her paper published, but felt it needed more work and wanted to do further research. She was also discouraged by the advice that some of the historians at Victoria University had given her, that the *New Zealand Journal of History* — which had been founded in 1967 by the University of Auckland's Department of History — would not be interested in such a long piece.[55]

More likely than not, Ross would never have published this paper which many years later became famous, if two things had not happened. Shortly after the seminar, Ormond Wilson took the trouble to tell the journal's editor, Keith Sinclair, that she had delivered an interesting paper. Sinclair in turn expressed interest in it immediately, no doubt because its resolute focus on New Zealand was unusual. (At that time there was still only a few academic historians who were working exclusively on New Zealand history.)[56] As he knew Ross well, Sinclair asked to see her paper in its current form, rather than wait until she had revised it. He recognised that he had to encourage her a good deal, going so far as to tell her that when it was revised 'I think it will probably be the most important article which has been submitted to us'. He thought it wise to allow her to revise as she saw fit and to go over-length, though he begged her 'please do *not* turn it into a book!'.[57]

Ross reckoned that the article she finally published in the journal differed from her seminar paper enormously and in a particular way. According to her account, which the content of her article actually belies, it came to focus 'exclusively' on the Treaty texts, and specifically the Māori one. (There *were* major differences between her article and her paper, but they comprised its longer treatment of the *English* texts and the matter of pre-emption that derived from a focus on the English version rather than the Māori one.) Historians have tended to accept Ross's characterisation of her article (even though it is widely recognised that discrepancies sometimes appear between an author's account of their own work and the work in question). They have attributed her discussion of the Māori text to the nature of the political debate that had begun to take place at the time. There can be little doubt that contemporary discourse did influence the degree to which Ross discussed the Māori text in both her seminar paper and her article, but given that historians have made a mistake in assuming that her article was essentially a product of the early 1970s, rather than of the mid-1950s, this explanation for its focus is, at best, of limited value. There are good reasons for assuming that her lengthy consideration of the Treaty texts, and her misrepresentation of her article as one that focused exclusively on them, owed more to forces that belong to the private life rather than the public life of history.[58]

Ross's own words suggest that she was both prompted and provoked to concentrate somewhat more on the texts in her article than she had in her seminar paper — and thus return wholeheartedly to the approach she had adopted when she began work on the Treaty for her Government Printer commission in 1954 — by the response she received from the *New Zealand Journal of History*. Sinclair commissioned two readers — the linguist Bruce Biggs and the historian Judith Binney — while he and the journal's associate editor, Keith Sorrenson, who, like himself, had expertise in the history of Māori–Pākehā relations, provided comments. Biggs's report was brief and to the point. He liked the paper and just provided a series of technical points about language. His response meant a good deal to Ross. 'I have always been very conscious of how ill-equipped I am to tackle Waitangi this way. There are so many pitfalls and it has been a hard slog', she told Sinclair. 'If he thinks what I have to say on the treaty text is worth publishing, then I feel I've really passed the test.'[59]

Ross was similarly encouraged to focus on the texts of the Treaty — a move that she characterised as 'sticking to my guns' and presenting '*my* view of the Treaty' — because of the response of the historians at the journal, not least because this was in stark contrast to the reception she felt she had got when she first presented her findings to an academic audience in 1956. After telling Sinclair what had happened on that occasion — 'it was intimated to me then that my approach ... was a waste of time' — she told him that the response she had now received 'buoys me up no end. If I am no longer just a nut on the subject of the treaty, then I can change down out of this rather apologetically personal gear.'[60]

Yet while this response played a part in Ross deciding to focus somewhat more on the Treaty texts in her article and had a major role in how she represented it, it is unlikely that it alone was responsible for this change. Instead, some of the comments and suggestions Sinclair and Binney made convinced her that they had misunderstood one of her key arguments, namely that the Māori text was *the* Treaty, thereby causing a recurrence in her mind of the uncomprehending reaction she had received to her Treaty paper in 1956 and the pain that this had caused.[61]

In response to their feedback, Ross made a series of remarks to Sinclair in a firm but measured tone, telling him that it had made her aware that she had to spell some things out more clearly. In response to a query he had raised, she stated: 'There's only one Treaty of Waitangi, i.e. only one text, that signed at Waitangi and everywhere else except Waikato, and by my definition the English text signed there was the Treaty of Waikato'; and in response to references Binney had made to 'Maori texts' of the Treaty, she commented: 'Judith's several mentions of "one of the Maori texts" also show how completely I have failed to get across to her. There's only one Maori text, that is one extant one, and that's the text signed at Waitangi &c &c.' But as she went on, she became agitated, making a number of remarks that reveal that their misunderstanding of her argument about the Māori text provoked her to decide — if 'decide' is the right word given the irrational forces that were clearly at work — that she would return to her emphasis on the Treaty texts, and the Māori one in particular. She told Sinclair: 'You say: We are inclined to think it might be useful to publish the text in English and a literal English translation from the Maori. I am sorry, I don't agree. What you call "the text of the Treaty in English" is not the Treaty of Waitangi, and my article is about the Treaty of Waitangi. I strenuously object to publishing any English translation of this Maori text because, damn it, this is what about half of my paper is about, the meaning of this Maori text.'[62] But, as so often, Ross feared she had been unduly assertive (which was regarded at that time as unacceptable behaviour if you were a woman) and so backed off, saying 'I hope this doesn't sound self-opinionated'.[63]

But this was only momentary. She had strong words to say about another aspect of Binney's response to her paper. Binney had included in her reader's report a translation into English of the Māori text of the Treaty that James Rutherford had done many years earlier. Ross responded: 'It was kind and thoughtful of Judith to send the copy of Rutherford's translation', but immediately went on: 'I hope this won't sound too much like an egg-sucking grandmother, but this was my starting point 20 years ago, or very nearly so . . . Rutherford gave more thought to the treaty of Waitangi than any of his contemporaries in the academic world, or his successors . . . But his study of the treaty text was limited, and indeed perverse.' Ross then proceeded to attack the Auckland History Department on the mistaken assumption that it had been circulating Rutherford's translation, accusing it of leading both academics and students astray. She took the time to tell Sinclair she was not 'trying to roast' Binney in making these remarks. But in reality she was trying to settle a score with her (as we will soon see).[64]

As so often after such an outburst, Ross felt the need to apologise: 'I'm sorry to go on and on, but it seemed to me that although you most generously said to take all comments as suggestions and no more than that, I disagreed so fundamentally with the idea of publishing any English text/version, and any translation of the Maori text, that it was best to let you know my feeling on the subject while the paper was still relatively fresh in your mind.' She more or less concluded this letter to Sinclair by saying: 'Well, I've got that off my chest.' Another exchange of letters about this matter took place between her and Sinclair a little while later, which strengthened her resolve to stick to her guns.[65]

The emphasis she now placed on the Treaty texts, or more especially her *feeling* that this was what she was doing, almost certainly owed something to another kind of unfinished business for Ross: her failure to complete the Waitangi job Beaglehole had arranged for her in 1954 and which she had sought to execute by focusing on the Treaty texts. Very soon after the *New Zealand Journal of History* published her article, she sent a copy of it to Beaglehole's widow Elsie (Beaglehole having died a year or so earlier). In a covering letter she recalled in some detail the conflict that had occurred between her and Beaglehole fifteen years earlier, and told her she was sending her the article because it was something she 'owed John from way back'. As so often with a matter like this, she joked about what had happened, but there can be no doubting the feelings of pain, anger and aggression she had felt at the time and the repetition of them all these years later.[66]

As Ross set about revising her article, she found the going tough. In April she poured her heart out to Malcolm: 'I wish thinking came more easily to me. Or put more crudely, I wish I were not so damned dumb. When I said this not so long ago to [a Catholic priest] he asked, what made me think I was dumb. And I said, OK, maybe not exactly dumb, but I'm so bloody slow. If I slog at it, sometimes I get there in the end, but if and when I do, it's usually in a state of exhaustion.' She had some sense that the difficulty she was experiencing was a function of the originality of her treatment of the Treaty, yet for the most part she did not explain it in these terms. Referring to her seminar paper, she remarked, 'OK, so its strengths (and its weaknesses) derive from the fact that I don't follow fashions' but then continued in this vein: 'I just sit down and slog away, ploughing through the underbrush and finding my own way out in the end. But it's that finding my way out that is such slow torture. Anyone else, I always feel, given the same material, could have sorted it out in half the time and with only a tenth of the self-torture, and would have been much more readily intelligible at that.' In other words, completing the task did not put an end to the agony she felt. 'Of course, in the end, the feeling of achievement is out of all proportion to the thing achieved, until, one by one, the errors come home to roost and you want to curl up and hide in a very small hole somewhere. And then in my affliction and misery, remembering only the wormwood and the gall —

a misquotation from somewhere surely⁶⁷ — I wonder why the hell I ever try to do anything but grow cabbages.' As always, she was too hard on herself.⁶⁸

In the months that followed, Ross complained to several of her correspondents about the difficulty she was having in writing her article. She told the Hocken Librarian, Michael Hitchings: 'The article for the New Zealand Journal of History has narrowed itself down to a discussion of texts and translations and I am becoming more and more exasperated and bored and hag-ridden by it.' It was taking its toll on her physically. 'Battering the typewriter virtually non-stop for a month produced an acute case of tennis elbow', she told Wilson. 'So acute that I was alarmed, with the fair copy still to be typed.' But she was determined to meet the deadline, in large part because she had been told by the administrative assistant in the Department of History at the University of Auckland, Beverley Simmons, that Sinclair was not expecting her to do so. A few days into August she triumphantly told Malcolm: 'Took it to the history department at AU on Friday and Keith Sinclair said — I don't believe it.'⁶⁹

In submitting her article Ross provided Sinclair with a cover letter in which she made a few observations about aspects of it that she said she wanted to get off her chest. Most importantly, she felt it necessary to tell him: 'I have confined myself to a discussion of texts and translations' (though she had done no such thing). This remark makes clear that the journal's editorial team did not know she had decided to place more emphasis on this aspect of the Treaty in her article, which is to say that it reveals that they played no role in this development other than accidentally, by dint of Sinclair and Binney's misunderstanding of her argument about the Māori text in her 1972 seminar paper causing a repetition of the incomprehension that had greeted her 1956 paper and the feelings of despair and rage this had aroused in her. In this letter Ross made another remark that is important to note. She told Sinclair: 'My only theory is that the whole exercise [of making the treaty] was a hopeless shambles.' That is, as far as she was concerned, this was the principal or even the only argument she had made about the Treaty in her article.⁷⁰

The journal's editors accepted Ross's revised article even though it was much longer than the articles it published usually: some 14,000 words compared to 8000 words. Moreover, they hardly called for any changes. Ross must have been bemused, given how many changes she had had to make to her Waitangi bulletin before School Pubs deemed it ready to go to press. However, a couple of difficulties arose before it was finally published. Ross had to deal with copy-editing queries at a time when she had her hands full taking care of two toddlers (who belonged to Ian's niece). Then Binney and one of her professorial colleagues, Nicholas Tarling, marked up the galley proofs according to very different referencing conventions. Much to Ross's delight, Tarling prevailed.⁷¹

Tensions had been brewing between Ross and Binney in recent years. In 1964–65, when Binney was working on a Master's thesis at the University of Auckland on Thomas Kendall, one of the earliest Church Missionary Society missionaries in the Bay of Islands and one of the few whom Ross admitted to finding interesting, they had exchanged long letters in which they discussed in great depth and detail their mutual interest in the history of northern New Zealand prior to 1840, and particularly Māori. Ross had enjoyed the intellectual companionship this correspondence provided her, gave freely of her wealth of knowledge about Māori in that place and time, provided frank criticism of Binney's research, and even disclosed aspects of her earlier life that she normally found too painful to talk about, such as the death of first husband. If she envied the opportunities Binney had as a member of a younger generation of women who had come of age at a time when New Zealand universities were experiencing enormous growth[72] and many social, cultural and political changes were taking place,[73] this was not evident. But within a few years that had begun to change. Binney was appointed to a senior lectureship at Auckland and was thus afforded advantages Ross never had, and while she was married she had no children and so had neither the time-consuming family responsibilities Ross still had nor any inkling of what they entailed — or at least this is what Ross thought.[74]

But it was the differences between their positions in the historical profession, which both Ross and Binney characterised as those of the 'amateur' and the 'academic', that seem to have troubled Ross the most. One day in 1970 she came across a remark Binney had made about amateur historians — 'that they sometimes had quite good ideas' — that she felt was condescending and had put her in her place.[75] She resented this all the more because of the help she had freely given Binney. To make matters worse, that very same day she happened to re-read an encyclopaedia article she had written on Baron Charles de Thierry (as preparation for a forthcoming meeting with Thierry's biographer)[76] and to read in Binney's recently published book on Kendall a long appendix about de Thierry that had changed considerably since it had appeared in her MA thesis. Ross was struck by the similarities between Binney's account and her own, and was angry because Binney had not acknowledged her encyclopaedia article, even though she had clearly drawn on it, and because she believed the changes Binney had made were the result of advice and criticism she had given her. She was all the more dismayed because this episode left her feeling that she had little to show for all the help she had given Binney and others over many years, prompting her to declare that 'it is time that I used some of my own ideas instead of handing them to others'.[77]

In April 1972 Binney's comments on the seminar paper Ross had submitted to the *New Zealand Journal of History* raised Ross's hackles again, as we have seen; but several months later Ross was furious when she felt that Binney had once again used her work (her seminar paper) without any acknowledgement for an article on the Treaty Binney had published in the University of Auckland's student newspaper, which she had entitled 'Te Tiriti-O-Waitangi'. Ross complained bitterly to friends and family that Binney had been unscrupulous, had claimed expertise she did not have, and had stolen her thunder.[78]

There can be little doubt that Binney had drawn on Ross's seminar paper but she probably saw no reason to acknowledge it or to alert her readers to Ross's forthcoming article, given the nature of the publication in which her own article was to appear. In any case, she had not relied on Ross's work to the degree that Ross claimed. Curiously, in reporting this episode Ross made no reference to the fact that Binney had in effect taken issue with some of the arguments she had made in her seminar paper. Binney contended that most of the chiefs *had* grasped the issues involved in the treaty-making; she argued that the Treaty remained important because it was an attempt by British humanitarians to found a colony on the novel ground that an indigenous people possessed rights; and she concluded that it should be remembered as 'a compact of a bi-cultural society'.[79]

Ross's major and minor arguments

It is commonly believed that the principal argument of Ruth Ross's famous article in the *New Zealand Journal of History* was that there were substantive differences between the Māori text and the English texts, that the Māori text constituted *the* Treaty, and that any consideration of its meanings and implications should proceed on that basis. What has been reported of her undoubted dedication to the Māori text, and her challenge to the authority of the English one, adds force to that conviction. Yet a careful — or even a cursory — reading of her article brings this into question.

To Ross's way of thinking, the differences between the two texts constituted the best evidence for what was actually her principal argument, an argument that she expressed in the following passage as she began to draw her article to a close and for which she used many of the same words she had in writing to Beaglehole eighteen years earlier: 'The [Māori and Pākehā] signatories of 1840 were uncertain and divided in their understanding of [the Treaty's] meaning; who can say now what its intentions were? . . . However good intentions may have been, a close study of events shows that the Treaty of Waitangi was hastily and inexpertly drawn up, ambiguous and contradictory in content, chaotic in its execution. To persist in postulating that this was a "sacred compact" is sheer hypocrisy.'[80]

Furthermore, while it is undoubtedly true that a good part of her argument *was* concerned with the Treaty texts, several particular aspects of her article have been lost sight of by later commentators. Most important is the fact that her argument about the texts was inextricably bound up with her contention about the translation of the

English text into Māori, and that this underpinned her principal argument. She argued that *because* the English text had been mistranslated, the Treaty was ambiguous and contradictory, and consequently the parties to it were uncertain and divided about its meaning, and so it could not be regarded as a moral compact, let alone a legal contract.

It is also the case that in her discussion of the Māori text Ross stated that the Māori understanding of the Treaty was determined not by their *reading* it but by *listening* to what the translators of the English text told them during the Treaty meetings. 'Of even greater significance than the fact that the Treaty of Waitangi was written in . . . Maori', she declared, 'was the monopoly which the Protestant missionaries had of interpretation and explanation.'[81]

Moreover, it is noteworthy that Ross's longest discussion of any part of the Treaty concerns neither sovereignty nor rights of possession, but pre-emption. By far the largest part of her article was devoted to this matter.[82] (She had become interested in it because of the research she had done shortly before the Victoria seminar; a comment one of her fellow speakers made on that occasion; and the research she undertook after that.) Just as noteworthy is that barely any of Ross's discussion about pre-emption focuses on the Treaty texts. Most of it is concerned instead with the meanings of the term or concept of pre-emption in Britain and New Zealand at the time, and in the North American colonies earlier; the ways in which Williams and Busby reckoned they had interpreted and explained the relevant part of the Treaty at the meeting at Waitangi; the fact that Māori chiefs claimed in 1843–44 that they had misunderstood the concept when it had been explained to them in 1840; and the manner in which major political and legal figures had interpreted the pre-emption clause at that time and again in 1846–47.[83]

It is also striking that in her consideration of the first part of the Treaty's second article, her discussion of the meaning of 'te tino rangatira' is dwarfed by her discussion about several issues that arose from that article, most of all fishing rights, rather than just the matter of sovereignty as she is commonly thought to have emphasised. In the opening paragraph of her article Ross used the issue of fishing rights as her example of contemporary debate about the Treaty.[84]

One of the points I have been making applies to Ross's brief discussion of the third article: she did not so much concentrate on the texts but on the way in which various colonial players tried to mobilise this part of the Treaty in the mid to late 1840s. And it was this that led her to make one of her most memorable remarks about what she called 'the Waitangi problem':

Ever since the 1840s the New Zealander has been told that the Treaty of
Waitangi was the Maori Magna Carta. In modern times Lord Bledisloe's prayer
has been repeated each Waitangi Day 'that the sacred compact then made
in these waters may be faithfully and honourably kept for all time to come'.
Yet how many of today's New Zealanders, Maori or Pakeha, ever look at the Treaty
of Waitangi? To each one of us — the politician in Parliament, the *kaumatua* on
the marae, *Nga Tamatoa* in the city, the teacher in the classroom, the preacher
in the pulpit — the Treaty of Waitangi says whatever we want it to say.[85]

Given that Ross's argument about the Treaty texts was subsidiary to her principal argument, and her discussion of them less extensive than is commonly thought, we might ask how and why her article came to be called 'Te Tiriti o Waitangi: Texts and Translations'. This was not Ross's title. She had entitled it 'A New Look at the Treaty of Waitangi' when she submitted the final version and subsequently she took no interest in the matter. It was Binney or Sinclair, or most likely the two of them together, who were responsible for the title. They might have chosen it because of the way Ross characterised — or rather mischaracterised — her article at the point she submitted the final version (which we noted earlier). But perhaps something else was on their minds, though they were probably unconscious of it: the fierce remarks Ross had made to them when she felt they had misunderstood her argument about the Māori text. Whatever the case, it can be argued that this titling of her article proved consequential in the fullness of time (as we will see).[86]

For some time now, Ross's findings have become so familiar that it is difficult to appreciate how startlingly original they were when they finally saw the light of day in 1972, nearly twenty years after she had first formulated them. No one had previously taken the Māori text as seriously as she had or claimed that it differed from the official English text in so many important respects. No one had previously argued so strongly that the Treaty was ambiguous and contradictory and so the parties to it were uncertain and divided about its meaning. No one had published such a ferocious assault on the myth of the Treaty as a sacred covenant and the Māori Magna Carta.

Ross herself was ambivalent about her article. While she was delighted to have an article about the Treaty accepted by an academic journal, thereby fulfilling a wish she had had many years earlier, she was by no means enamoured with the focus she felt it had ended up taking. 'I'd like to do another article, for the NZJH, about who signed the treaty, why and what it signified and so on', she told Sinclair after she had submitted the final version. 'Much more fun than all this scrutinising of various texts and translations and what-have-you.'[87] In other words, a good part of her was more interested in pursuing the kind of work she had done in her primary school bulletin *Te Tiriti o Waitangi* of 1958, in which she had told of Māori perspectives of the Treaty, and her essay 'The Autochthonous New Zealand Soil' of 1969, in which she talked of Māori traditions about the past.[88]

As this account of Ross's famous article makes clear, it is a mistake to treat this text as though it amounts to a coherent or unified whole.[89] There are tensions within it, primarily because her intentions and purpose were ambiguous, contradictory, uncertain and divided. She principally argued that the Treaty was ambiguous and contradictory and that its signatories were uncertain about and divided over its meaning because she held that it existed in two texts that differed radically from one another. But she also contended that the text in Māori was *the* Treaty and that Māori perspectives of it should be recovered and understood. It is clear, then, that Ross's intentions and purpose in writing this article do not adequately account for, or exhaust, its meanings and implications.

We might have good reason to treat Ross's argument that the Treaty was ambiguous, contradictory and so forth as the text of her article; and to treat her argument that the Māori text was *the* Treaty and so forth as its subtext. But it probably also makes sense to characterise the former as her major argument (rather than its principal argument, as I have been doing up to this point) and the latter as her minor one, bearing in mind both the meaning of these terms as greater and lesser, but also the sense they have musically speaking: a piece of music can switch readily from a major to a minor key, and in so doing it immediately lends a different character and/or emotion to the same melody or idea, thereby influencing its reception.

In other words, Ross's approach to and account of the Treaty resemble the Treaty itself. This raises several different intriguing possibilities, none of which are mutually exclusive: that her ambiguous, contradictory, uncertain and divided approach to the Treaty enabled her to identify its ambiguous, contradictory, uncertain and divided meaning more than any other scholar has done to date; or that her ambiguous, contradictory, uncertain and divided intentions and purpose led her to project these characteristics onto the Treaty and consequently to exaggerate their presence in the Treaty; or that this projection led her to attribute to the Treaty characteristics that it simply did not have, though I doubt this is the case.

These possibilities reveal that Ross was engaged in an attempt to understand what the Treaty meant in its time and what it meant in her own, as have all historians of the Treaty before and since she wrote. The most engaging, if also the most perplexing, dimensions of historical interpretation tend to exist at the point where those two meanings — the meanings attributed to an event or text in the past and the meanings attributed to them in the present — are conjoined. It is at that point that the present-day dialogue with the past, which characterises all historical work, is most evidently internal and external to the historian, and so the intersections between the private and public lives of history are writ large.

A final point should be borne in mind as we proceed to the next part of this book where I seek to explain why Ross's article became famous some time after it was published. One reason why a piece of writing or a historical text becomes canonical lies in the fact that interpretation of it does not lead to any definitive conclusion, and so its history is a history of divergent or even conflicting interpretations and the different uses to which it is put by its readers. This is true of both te Tiriti o Waitangi/the Treaty of Waitangi and Ruth Ross's article.

PART 2
Te Tiriti

Chapter 4
Reading 'Te Tiriti o Waitangi'

We now turn our attention to the different contexts in which Ruth Ross's article in the *New Zealand Journal of History* was received. In doing so, our focus broadens to encompass the remarkable changes that have taken place in the fortunes of the Treaty and the way it has been interpreted since 1972.

In considering the reception of a text or a piece of work, many tend to assume that readers will read or understand it in accordance with the author's intentions.[1] When that does not occur, it is commonly believed that this amounts to a misunderstanding and thus a distortion of the work in question. Moreover, that outcome is often attributed to a kink in the process of communication that is otherwise assumed to be uncomplicated. Yet in most societies the way a piece of work is received is rarely in keeping with its author's intentions. Any text, by its very nature, is polysemic — open to being read or understood in multiple ways — though this seldom means that it is received in ways that bear no relationship whatsoever to its words.

Considering the ways that a text is received is fundamental to being able to understand its impact. This is best investigated in terms of complex series of readings that occur over time, including the process by which certain texts are canonised or become famous. Many texts reach their readers overlaid, even burdened, by earlier readings or interpretations of them, to which they are consciously or unconsciously indebted. As this suggests, canonisation involves not only a process by which certain texts are selected but the selective interpretation of those texts as well.[2]

Examining reception of an author's piece of work can shed new and unexpected light on it, revealing meanings that the author might not have conceived of, because of the nature of the public contexts in which they wrote, or because they might not have been conscious of those meanings due to personal factors. This is the case with Ross's article.

'Te Tiriti o Waitangi' and the cloistered life of history

On the publication of Ross's article in New Zealand's only academic journal of history, historians and their students in New Zealand universities were among the first to read it, not surprisingly. For the next ten years they received it by and large in a manner that was in keeping with the way she intended it to be read. This, too, is unremarkable as these readers were familiar with the conventions of the discipline of history, the cultural codes, and the political and legal contexts in which Ross had written her article. Moreover, the circumstances in which they received it did not change significantly during this period.

Before we consider in detail how Ross's article was read, it should be noted that scepticism about the myth of the Treaty had begun to emerge among historians before it was published. In the opening chapter of his 1968 book *The Shadow of the Land*, called 'The Myth of Moral Suasion', Ian Wards, like Ross, and perhaps in the light of hearing the paper she gave to the Victoria Historical Association in 1956 and having discussions with her afterwards, had already tried to cut the Treaty down to size.[3]

After its publication, Ross's article in the *New Zealand Journal of History* had a definite and traceable impact within the cloistered life of history. This can be seen in the work of Alan Ward who in 1973 published *A Show of Justice*, a study of racial amalgamation in mid-nineteenth-century New Zealand that was based on a doctoral thesis he had undertaken at the Research School of Pacific Studies at the Australian National University in the previous decade. The tenor of his brief discussion about the making of the Treaty was the same as Ross's. He remarked at one point: '[Hobson's] instructions to officers who subsequently hawked the Treaty about the country . . . suggest that he saw the task as an exercise in public relations rather than a weighty mission.'[4]

Most of Ward's discussion of the Treaty, though, was framed by his consideration of the introduction of English law in New Zealand after it had been signed. Consequently, while he had no need to re-present Ross's major argument on the ambiguous and contradictory nature of the Treaty, he had good reason to draw on her minor argument about the Māori text being the authoritative one. His focus meant he was more interested in the matter of sovereignty than she was, but his argument about the differences between the first article in the English and Māori texts, and the consequences of those differences, had much in common with hers.[5]

The impact of Ross's article on the cloistered world of academic historians is evident, albeit to a lesser degree, in Peter Adams's 1977 book *Fatal Necessity* about the British government's intervention in the islands of New Zealand in the early to mid-nineteenth century, which was based on a doctoral thesis he had undertaken at Oxford University. Unlike Ross, Adams (1944–) was primarily concerned with British policy and practice at the imperial centre rather than the colonial periphery. However, because he was similarly sceptical about the myth of the Treaty, he reproduced the principal argument she made about its first article: the English text had been translated in such a way that it was less comprehensible than it might have been if the key terms in the Declaration of Independence ('mana' and 'kingitanga') had been adopted instead, and that consequently it was a matter of guesswork as to how the Māori chiefs had understood it. Like Ross, Adams argued that the grounds upon which the British had claimed sovereignty in New Zealand rested on Hobson's proclamations of May 1840 and that the Treaty was a legal nullity. Similarly, he argued that Whitehall intended to protect Māori only so far as this was compatible with British dominance and so the Treaty could hardly be regarded as enshrining equality between the two races.[6]

Probably the best guide to the ways that Ross's article was received within the cloistered life of history, however, is a multi-authored *Oxford History of New Zealand*, which was researched and written during the 1970s and published in 1981. In the chapter he wrote, J. M. R. Owens, who, like Ross, was well versed in New Zealand's pre-1840 history, gave an account of the treaty-making at Waitangi that was clearly informed by her article.[7] First and foremost he observed that 'The Treaty of Waitangi has been described as "hastily and inexpertly drawn up, ambiguous and contradictory in content, chaotic in its execution"'. He also remarked that Hobson had acted too fast in drafting the Treaty; that he had no legal training or adviser; that it had been translated quickly by Henry and Edward Williams, and that they were, at best, inexperienced translators. Similarly, he noted that they had not so much translated the Treaty as rewritten it and had done so to make it acceptable to the Māori chiefs.[8]

Like Ross, Owens devoted much of his discussion to the Treaty texts and did so in a manner that was largely in keeping with hers. In noting the differences between the English and Māori texts and the problems translating the English text into Māori, his main point, like Ross's, was that Māori could not have understood the Treaty in the same way the British had. As Ross had done in her writings, he pointed out that Hobson had added to the confusion about the Treaty by proclaiming sovereignty over the North Island while his agents were still collecting signatures from the chiefs, and over the South Island on the basis of the legal doctrine of discovery, thereby casting doubt over when and how Britain had acquired sovereignty.[9]

Another example of the influence of Ross's article on New Zealand academic historians in the decade after it was published can be found in the doctoral thesis that James Belich (1956–) completed at Oxford University in 1982, though the Treaty was by no means central to his subject matter, the New Zealand Wars. He, too, read her article in the way she had intended. Yet he was not altogether persuaded by her textual approach and argument. 'Whether or not the different versions of the Treaty actually *created* misunderstanding [about whether the British had acquired full and real sovereignty]', he remarked, 'they certainly epitomized it.'[10]

In the ten years after Ross published her article, then, it was read by academic historians largely in keeping with her authorial intentions and so in a way that would have made sense to her. But this discussion has revealed something else important: none of the specialist studies I have discussed were the result of research undertaken in a New Zealand university. In other words, if historical consideration of the Treaty within New Zealand had been the province of the cloistered life of history alone, little would have been written about it during this period. This remained the case until well into the 1980s, one notable exception aside — the work of Claudia Orange — and when interest did grow among historians it was as a result of forces beyond the walls of the university.[11]

'Te Tiriti o Waitangi' and the public life of history

Articles in an academic journal of history are seldom read outside the cloister. Ross's was. Moreover, this occurred immediately after it was published. According to Antony Wood, the *New Zealand Journal of History*'s business manager, one of his neighbours had borrowed an offprint and become so fascinated by it that she had not done any of her household chores that day.[12]

Two months later, Ross's article struck a chord with another reader outside the university. The *Auckland Star* chose to mark Waitangi Day by publishing a review of the issue of the *New Zealand Journal of History* in which it had appeared. Nearly all this review, which was almost certainly written by one of the newspaper's former book review editors, Lawrie Moir, focused on her article even though it had not been given top billing in the journal. Ross must have been pleased. From the moment she submitted her seminar paper to the journal for consideration she hoped it would be published before the following year's commemoration of the Treaty. Of less importance to her would have been the reviewer's praise of it.[13]

As the review was framed by the ways in which the Treaty was currently being debated in public and as the recently passed Waitangi Day Act had included the English text in its schedule, Moir focused initially on Ross's argument about the differences between the two language texts. 'No doubt [the annual commemoration of the Treaty] will be accompanied by further calls for [its] ratification', he wrote, 'but which treaty is it advocated should be ratified? Or, rather, which version of the Treaty?' Yet he immediately drew attention to the connection between this question and Ross's major argument, which he rendered faithfully in these terms: 'no one can be sure today either what the treaty says or what it meant to those who signed it'. Furthermore, he continued in this fashion, relating the gist of Ross's argument about the texts and translations before quoting what would become the most famous passage in her article: 'However good intentions may have been, a close study of events shows that the Treaty of Waitangi was hastily and inexpertly drawn up, ambiguous and contradictory in content, chaotic in its execution.'[14]

It is apparent, then, that Moir understood the connection between Ross's major argument and her minor argument. Nonetheless, part of Moir's review suggests that her major and minor arguments could easily be pulled apart from one another and the relationship between them severed, and that each one could readily stand on its own and make perfect sense without the other. Yet this way of receiving her article lay in the future. The available evidence suggests that throughout the period we are presently considering — the decade immediately after its publication — Ross's article continued to be read beyond the university in the way she anticipated it would be.

The work of Tony Simpson (1945–) further suggests the way in which Ross's article was received outside the academy.[15] In 1979, having graduated with a Master's degree in politics and history from the University of Canterbury and produced radio documentaries and a book (*The Sugarbag Years*) that drew the public's attention to aspects of New Zealand's turbulent social and political history, he published *Te Riri Pakeha: The White Man's Anger*. He framed this account of the history of relations between Māori and Pākehā by telling a story about how he had once uncritically accepted the stories he had been told as a boy, which included the myth about the Treaty as a solemn covenant between Māori and Pākehā. He also alluded to encounters he had since had with the Māori world that were not unlike those Ross had in the Hokianga and which had similarly opened his eyes to their ways of seeing the past.[16]

In a chapter on the treaty-making Simpson told a story that owed a good deal to Ross's article (though he had conducted research in the Colonial Office archives while living in London). Like Ross and Ian Wards, he was intent on demolishing the myth of the Treaty as a great charter. He began by making many of the same points that she had made, but he did so more forcefully: he drew into question the ways in which the major British parties had acted; noted that several of the chiefs who had signed at Waitangi had spoken against the Treaty; observed that those who had signed had been rewarded with blankets; pointed out that some who signed later regretted having done so; claimed that important chiefs in areas untouched by European contact had not agreed to sign; and argued that the Treaty had played no meaningful legal role in the British Crown claiming sovereignty.[17]

The influence of Ross's article is most apparent in Simpson's account of what the chiefs at Waitangi signed and what they understood they were signing. Of any author who read her article in the decade after it was published, it was Simpson who most carefully reiterated her argument, even including some of the minor points she had made, such as the fact that the document signed at Waitangi on 6 February was not the same as the one that had been discussed the previous day. This is probably because his purpose was the same as hers: to demolish the myth of the Treaty. He concluded his discussion in much the same way as she had done and even used some of the same words: 'What, then, is the real meaning of the Treaty of Waitangi, if it did not mean what it said and if those who signed it did not know what they were signing? Clearly, to each actor it meant something different.' Nevertheless, Simpson was more intent than Ross had been in pronouncing that the losers in this proceeding were Māori.[18]

The academic historian Keith Sorrenson took issue with Simpson's polemical tone (and what he saw as a litany of errors) in both the book and a series of short radio programmes he had broadcast before it was published.[19] But he came off worse in the exchanges he had with Simpson in a panel discussion on national radio, the letters pages of the popular weekly magazine the *New Zealand Listener*, and in the literary quarterly *Landfall*. He was damned by a radio critic who found Simpson's talks interesting and informative and claimed that he (Sorrenson) was just a pedantic professor who took exception to history being presented in a lively fashion. This episode suggests that academic historians had lost much of the authority they had previously enjoyed in the public realm in New Zealand, at the same time as it revealed that the revisionist history of Māori–Pākehā relations, sympathetic to the plight of Māori, that Sorrenson and others had forged in the 1950s and 1960s had now become something of an orthodoxy, at least among those on the liberal wing of the political spectrum.[20]

Another example of how Ross's article was received in the public realm at this time can be found in some of the writings of Ranginui Walker (1932–2016), a Whakatōhea man from Ōpōtiki. After taking up a lectureship in the Department of Anthropology at the University of Auckland, he had welcomed the opportunity to write a weekly column, 'Korero', for the *New Zealand Listener* so that he could present a Māori view of the world to Pākehā. Several of his 'Korero' reveal that he had taken on board Ross's major argument. For example, on one occasion he cast the Treaty as 'a historical muddle' on the grounds that there were 'several English versions of the so-called treaty, none of which equate with the Maori translation signed by the chiefs'.[21]

Both Simpson's and Walker's critical remarks about the Treaty were in keeping with those made in the public demonstrations against the celebration of Waitangi Day since the early 1970s, as organisations such as Nga Tamatoa and the Waitangi Action Committee attacked it as a sham and a fraud. 'The Treaty is a fraud' was a saying seen and heard repeatedly by New Zealanders in the 1970s and into the 1980s.

The Treaty and legal scholarship

At the same time as Ross's article was being read in ways that were in keeping with her authorial intentions, it began to be received in a very different way in the legal sphere. This was something she could never have anticipated. It occurred because of the changes that were beginning to take place in legal theory, practice and history regarding the sovereignty and rights of property of indigenous peoples in Canada, Australia and New Zealand and the historic treaties that the British Crown had made in Canada and New Zealand.

In the New Zealand case, it might seem at first glance that nothing had changed. In 1971 a lawyer and part-time lecturer in the Law School at the University of Auckland, Anthony P. Molloy, published an article in the *New Zealand Law Journal* in which he attacked the claims that the Treaty of Waitangi was a valid treaty as well as the calls for it to be ratified. He argued that the courts in New Zealand gave no support for the former supposition and contended that the Treaty did not meet the requirements of international law because the Māori signatories had long been deemed to lack the characteristics that were essential for an 'international legal personality': a settled population, a defined territory, a government that the mass of the people obeyed, and independence.[22]

Molloy contended that the third of those requirements was the real hurdle for Māori, citing an 1877 judgment delivered by New Zealand Chief Justice Sir James Prendergast. In the now famous case *Wi Parata v Bishop of Wellington*, Prendergast held, among other things, that the Treaty was 'a simple nullity', having been made with a collection of tribes who did not constitute a unified, independent sovereign power recognisable in international law.[23] Molloy argued that even if the Treaty was valid in international law, no claims could be based upon it in municipal law unless it was incorporated into New Zealand law by statute. Thus, he concluded, the Treaty was 'worthless and of no effect'. What is more, he could see no point casting back 130 years into the past as a means of grappling with the present-day problems facing Māori and New Zealand.[24]

Yet only a month before Molloy's article appeared, the *New Zealand Universities Law Review* published a case note by one of Molloy's colleagues at the Auckland Law School, F. M. Auburn, entitled 'Te Tiriti O Waitangi (The Treaty of Waitangi in New Zealand Law)', in which he made a series of points contrary to Molloy's. Auburn noted that D. P. O'Connell, a New Zealand-born scholar destined to become a professor of international law at Oxford University, had recently argued that native tribes *had* been held capable of ceding territory in international law. Auburn similarly argued that a New Zealand court had on one occasion (in a 1941 case, *Hoani Te Heuheu Tukino v Aotea District Maori Land Board*) ruled that there had been a proper cession of all the rights and powers of sovereignty by the chiefs in the Treaty. He also claimed that the Treaty had recently been made part of New Zealand law (the Waitangi Day Act 1960). In a different vein, the editor of the *New Zealand Law Journal* added a note to Molloy's article suggesting that if the Treaty was regarded as valid in New Zealand law, the question of which version would be the official one could arise. But he believed the Māori version was only 'somewhat different' to the English version. He was in good company.[25]

Ross dismissed these barely nascent developments in legal scholarship. In February 1973, shortly after her article had begun to circulate in the universities beyond the circle of academic historians, Auburn sent a copy of his case note to her in the hope that she would be interested. She was not. While she realised that her article might be used to some political end — indeed she hoped it would be — she assumed that there were no grounds on which the Treaty could be recognised in New Zealand law because she held that the parties to it were uncertain and divided in their understanding of what it meant.[26]

But there was another reason why she was scathing about Auburn's work, as the brief story I will tell now reveals. In his case note Auburn had argued that the Treaty had been recognised in international law as a result of a long-running case involving the claims for land made by an American man, William Webster. But as far as Ross was concerned, what the lawyers had said on that occasion, and what this lawyer was saying to her now, amounted to historical nonsense. 'The [British American Claims] Tribunal's ignorance about the treaty was just about total, as your quotation from the pronouncement ... ["all those who had any claim to represent the aboriginal natives as politically organised, entered into a treaty ceding sovereignty to Great Britain"] so clearly demonstrates', she told Auburn. 'The tribunal knew nothing about the treaty, [Judge] Salmond made no investigation of the events surrounding the signing of the treaty, in fact there is no evidence that I recall that he was familiar even with the wording of "the English version" of the treaty, far less that he had a clue of who had signed the actual treaty documents.'[27]

Ross told Auburn that what he had said in his case note was 'beyond [her] comprehension' because she, as a historian, and he, as a legal scholar, spoke 'different languages'. At the very least, whereas typically an academic historian will conduct an inquiry into the law to understand what it meant in the past, a legal scholar will seek to interpret the law to serve contemporary ends irrespective of what it might have meant in the past.[28]

'Te Tiriti o Waitangi'

In 1974 another development in the legal sphere got under way: one that would eventually lead to the creation of the Waitangi Tribunal. This saw one of Ross's arguments taken up in a way that would have made little sense to her but which would help transform the Treaty's legal status and its place in the New Zealand polity and the country's history and culture.

What transpired amounts to a case of unintended — and thus unforeseen — consequences. This is not to suggest, though, that Ross played no role in what happened. In January 1973 she belatedly turned her mind to distributing a few offprints of her article in the *New Zealand Journal of History*. Among the recipients were the Māori MPs Matiu Rata (1934–1997) and Whetū Tirikātene-Sullivan. The Labour Party, led by Norman Kirk, had been returned to power just two months earlier for only the second time in twenty-two years; Rata had become both the Minister of Maori Affairs and the Minister of Lands; and Tirikātene-Sullivan had been appointed Minister of Tourism. 'Goodness knows who in their right senses would want to read this indigestible textual exposition', Ross remarked to Bob Burnett at the same time as she sent her article to Rata and Tirikātene-Sullivan. 'Of course, it should have been done years ago, by someone better qualified than I am to cope with the language problems, the legal problems &c &c.' She thought Tirikātene-Sullivan would read it, given she had already pinched her punch line at the seminar at Victoria University the previous year, but was less sure about Rata. But it was he and his office in Maori Affairs that first took it up.[29]

The Labour Party had been elected on the basis of a manifesto (in both English and Māori) that included a promise to examine a 'practical means' of acknowledging legally what it called 'the principles set out in the Treaty'. After introducing legislation about Waitangi Day shortly after winning office, it belatedly turned its attention to this commitment, directing its caucus committee on Māori affairs to provide a report on the matter. In undertaking this work the committee largely conceived of its task in terms of this question: whether any legislative action *could* be legally taken regarding the Treaty? Answering in the affirmative required it to demonstrate that the Treaty was a valid legal agreement and a binding one. This determined how it went about its work and how it received the material placed before it, which included the views of those scholars who had recently studied the Treaty in some depth.[30]

In this context, Ross's article was received in terms of her minor argument that the real Treaty was the one in the Māori language. The committee had no use whatsoever for her major argument about the muddled, ambiguous and contradictory nature of the Treaty, partly because it already knew that calls for the ratification of the Treaty were a source of endless confusion and so had to be set aside if any progress was to be made. The committee was struck by her minor argument that whereas the English version had long been regarded as the authoritative version, the Māori version should have primacy because it had been widely circulated and signed by most of the 540 Māori chiefs and it was the one that was first signed (at Waitangi). That this was the case was undoubtedly a source of pride for the Māori members of the committee, yet it did not claim any authority, let alone primacy, for the Māori text, unlike what was to occur just a few years later. Moreover, it held that 'the question of versions' was primarily important only in respect of the first part of the Treaty's second article, and this was because Ross had noted that the *English* version was more specific about the kinds of Māori property the Queen had guaranteed to protect than was the Māori text.[31]

Furthermore, the committee's reading of Ross's article ran contrary to her major argument that there were considerable differences between the English drafts and the Māori text and thus grossly evident ambiguity and confusion about the meaning and the implications of the Treaty. This was so because the committee was determined to demonstrate that Parliament *could* give some legal effect to the Treaty. Consequently, it asserted that the central issue was not whether the Treaty was in Māori or English but that it was a binding agreement that had been made by the Crown and the Māori chiefs. This was in keeping with its insistence that the Treaty could become 'an instrument of mutuality'. It declared: 'There is no doubt in the Committee's mind that the documents in both Maori and English were executed by both parties and therefore both of them are *equally as valid as the formal means of the Crown gaining its sovereignty*.'[32]

Shortly after it submitted its report, the committee made some changes to it, one of which was to delete the words I have just emphasised and replace them with '*equally valid as documents*'. But this should not lead us to assume that the committee wanted to tackle the question of whether sovereignty *had* been transferred from the Māori chiefs to the British Crown in 1840. It held that the Treaty's article regarding land, rather than the one about sovereignty, was the vital one. Moreover, the committee made it very clear that it did not believe that any legislative enactments regarding the first article could have any legal purpose given that British sovereignty had been in place in New Zealand for more than 130 years. Ross would have agreed.[33]

In other words, the committee did not envisage a situation in which the sovereignty of the British Crown and thus the legitimacy of the New Zealand state could be drawn into question, even though its members realised that Ross had raised the question of whether the chiefs had agreed to cede sovereignty. They were convinced that there was no point in pursuing this matter as they believed it would not help address the losses Māori had suffered. Consequently, it proceeded to recommend: 'That for the purpose of considering any proposals for the formal acknowledgement of the Treaty of Waitangi, the signed Maori and European versions are valid Treaty documents and cannot for the purpose of any study, be set aside or taken individually, but both [are] warranting recognition, and that one complements the other.' In other words, the committee believed that little was to be gained from drawing attention to the differences between the two language texts. This was a time when only a small minority of New Zealanders could see any advantage for Māori, let alone Pākehā, in speaking the political language of difference — that is, in calling for *special* rights for Māori that rested on their status as the indigenous people. Nor could they imagine calling for special rights on the grounds that Māori had rights in *land* that had a different source from those that Pākehā could claim, let alone asserting that Māori had never relinquished their sovereignty. What reigned supreme was a political language that called for Māori to be granted the same rights and privileges as those enjoyed by Pākehā New Zealanders and for the Māori people to be absorbed by the New Zealand state.[34]

Given the committee's task of working out means by which the Treaty could be given some legal effect, it is not surprising that it accepted some of the findings of the recent New Zealand legal scholarship about indigenous people, treaties and the law. It drew on the paper W. A. McKean had presented at the Victoria University seminar in February 1972, which had since been published twice. It noted his claim that the Treaty had been incorporated in New Zealand municipal law recently and that Māori were now held by legal scholars to have been competent to make the Treaty. However, it did not place great store by these legal arguments, asserting instead that, as far as Māori were concerned, 'no amount of legalistic argument' could detract from the fact that their forebears had entered into a binding agreement with the British in good faith and that the Crown had a responsibility to uphold the Treaty's principles. Clearly, the committee regarded the Treaty in the same way that Māori and some Pākehā (like Ross) had long conceived of it — as a moral agreement rather than a legal contract — and so it emphasised the *spirit* it believed the Treaty symbolised rather than any strict rights it might be said to contain.[35]

The committee might have noted an argument that McKean made about what he called the 'discrepancies' been the various English versions and the Māori version. Based on a passage about treaties in two languages that he had read in a recently published book by Lord Duncan McNair, *The Law of Treaties*, he argued that as far as international law was concerned neither language text was considered superior to the other but that each assisted the other in the interpretation unless there was a stipulation to the contrary. McKean contended that in dealing with such a treaty, legal tribunals often considered the language in which it was drafted to be more important and that this meant the English version of the Treaty, not the Māori one, was the authentic text. (In fact McNair had argued that legal tribunals might seek to ascertain the working language in which a treaty was drafted *and* negotiated.) McKean referenced Ross's article and described it as illuminating, but he dismissed her contention that the Māori text should be regarded as *the* Treaty. He could see no legal purchase in such an argument. He was far from being alone.[36]

Just as the Labour Party's manifesto had made only a vague promise about the Treaty, most of the committee's recommendations were vague. It suggested that the status of the Treaty be 'cultivated' so that it was given 'a place of honour', thereby bestowing 'a new dignity and relevance' on it. The committee realised there was a need to introduce legislation to ensure that the so-called land guarantee provided by its second article was upheld so that the many breaches that had occurred in the past could be prevented in the future, but it was reluctant to make a case based on any of the Treaty's provisions. In respect of its first and third articles, the committee doubted any legal measures were needed. As far as the second article was concerned, it realised that if the Treaty was given statutory force from the time it had been made, the government would be confronted with the issue of what to do about the lands that had been seized by the Crown. The committee assumed that it would be practically impossible to return them to Māori ownership and that the cost of doing so was beyond contemplation because almost all those lands had passed out of the Crown's hands. It considered several ways by which the Treaty might generally be given legal effect, one of which was a tribunal, but recommended instead the establishment of a permanent parliamentary standing committee, whose task it described in the most general of terms: 'uphold[ing] the Treaty of Waitangi'.[37]

Not surprisingly perhaps, on receiving the committee's report, Cabinet called on it to provide more precise recommendations for legislative enactment. The committee obliged, but only to the extent that it recommended the establishment of a tribunal 'for the purpose of maintaining, upholding, advising and hearing of any matters related to the treaty to which existing laws offer no redress'. However, once the Cabinet agreed to endorse this proposal, an unexpected question arose, and the way it was answered would, inadvertently, enable the Waitangi Tribunal to do the transformative work that it eventually undertook.[38]

How did this happen? After being instructed to perform the tasks that were required before the legislation to create the Tribunal could be drafted, the Secretary of the Department of Maori Affairs, J. McEwen, realised that an important question had to be addressed because the committee had recommended that both the English and Māori texts of the Treaty be considered in any legislative enactment. 'As the two versions differ, it will be necessary to state clearly which version is to be authoritative', McEwen pointed out to Rata. 'It can be either the English version or the Maori version, or both, but if the latter alternative is chosen, there will have to be a specific provision which empowers somebody to decide the true meaning of the words. I would suggest that the way around the difficulty would be to make both versions authoritative and expressly empower the Tribunal to decide any issues arising from the differences in wording.' Consequently, he drafted a clause that stated: 'In exercising any of its functions under this section the Tribunal shall have regard to the two texts of the Treaty set out in the First Schedule to this Act and, for the purposes of this Act, shall have exclusive authority to determine the meaning and effect of the Treaty as embodied in the two texts and to decide issues raised by the differences between them.' In time, this clause would see the matter of the two texts become central to the Tribunal's work and allow it to bestow a degree of authority on the Māori text that McEwen could never have imagined and which he had actually tried to prevent in his drafting. Nor did anyone in government anticipate that McEwen's adoption of the Labour Party manifesto's mention of 'the principles' of the Treaty would prove similarly vital to the work the Tribunal did.[39]

For the time being — for several years in fact — the potential significance of the clause about the Treaty's two texts passed largely unnoticed. In introducing the Treaty of Waitangi Bill in November 1974, Rata informed Parliament that, while the Tribunal would be required to take into consideration the differences in the two texts in exercising its functions, the government accepted that they were both valid documents. Yet Tirikātene-Sullivan was thinking along lines that would see those differences become more important. In the speech she made on this occasion she argued that the legislation was significant for several reasons. They included the fact that it embodied in statute the understanding that Māori had long had of the Treaty, and recognised their status as the tangata whenua and what she called 'their proprietorial rights as a people with a certain sovereignty'.[40]

Outside of Parliament, there were Māori who had opinions about the two texts that mirrored Tirikātene-Sullivan's and differed from those that had been articulated publicly by Rata and his advisers. This is apparent in the parliamentary Maori Affairs select committee to whom the Bill was referred, just as it is evident that most of the Māori organisations that made submissions to the committee were familiar with Ross's article. (Bob Mahuta, who was responsible for drawing up the submission on behalf of the Waikato-Tainui people, had been sent a copy of it by Ross in September 1973 after she became aware of the protest they were organising against the government's proposal to build a power station at Huntly.)[41] While each of these Māori bodies read her contentions about the texts in different ways, several took up her argument about the Treaty's first article, rather than the second article alone, and thus the matter of whether the chiefs who signed had ceded sovereignty. In the opinion of the Arahura Maori Committee, for example, the Treaty's terms had to hinge on the meaning of its Māori text. It argued that in determining the Treaty's meaning and effect the Tribunal should proceed on the grounds of that text alone, a position that it almost certainly formed by reading Ross's article given that no one else had articulated a comparable argument about the Māori text.[42]

By contrast the Ngai Tahu Maori Trust Board made clear that it believed that the differences between the two texts had been a minor causative factor in the New Zealand government's breaching of the Treaty over many years. It called on the committee to 'make it abundantly clear [to the House of Representatives] that the whole sorry story of the Treaty does not spring from the text differences alone'. Ngāi Tahu was in good company. Many Māori were pleased that the Māori text was being recognised as they saw this as a step towards winning recognition of a Māori view of the Treaty as a binding agreement between the chiefs and the British Crown that should be honoured by the New Zealand government. But they had little if any conception of how Ross's contention about the differences between the texts could aid their cause. Before this could happen, what was required was what the philosopher of science Thomas S. Kuhn famously called a paradigm shift.[43]

It would be several years — not until the early to mid-1980s — before the Waitangi Tribunal became a considerable force and a particular reading of Ross's article would enable its work. Its beginnings were unpromising. Rata had been unable to persuade the Minister of Justice Martyn Finlay and his Cabinet colleagues to grant the Tribunal the power to make inquiries into past breaches of the Treaty, even though he pointed out that the submissions to the select committee made it clear that this was what Māori wanted and that without it most of their grievances could not be addressed. Cabinet was firmly of the opinion that allowing claims to be made about breaches of the Treaty dating back to 1840 'would create an impossible situation'. As one minister put it, it would give effect 'to all the worst features of retrospective legislation, i.e. the loss of certainty in respect of completed transactions; inequity to parties who lawfully carried out contractual obligations; and confusion in respect of land presently owned or administered by the Crown'. There was also concern about the financial costs it could entail. (As well, there was a strong belief that insufficient historical records existed about the acquisition of land from Māori and that this would make it impossible to assess the merits of any claim.)[44]

In October 1975 news that Parliament had approved the creation of the Waitangi Tribunal was drowned out as a hīkoi (walk or march) from Te Hāpua in the far north, organised by Nga Tamatoa and led by an elderly Te Rarawa woman, Whina Cooper, reached the capital and presented a petition with 60,000 signatures to the Prime Minister, Bill Rowling, protesting against the continuing loss of Māori land. The following month the Labour government fell from power and the incoming National Party, which was to remain in office for three parliamentary terms, did not convene the Tribunal until 1977 and then deprived it of funding and staff. For several years it was hardly active as it received few claims. Māori felt alienated by its formal, legal practices and took their most important claims to MPs, ministers, Parliament and the Maori Land Court instead.[45]

Ross, reading and writing

Ross was aware of many, though by no means all, of the ways in which her article was being read in the ten years after it was published. She had seen the *Auckland Star* review and was probably aware that Ward, Adams and Owens had drawn on her article as she continued to read books on the history of Māori–Pākehā relations as they were published.[46]

She knew Simpson had made use of her article. She reckoned he had many simplistic, inaccurate and misleading assertions and comments, and she was very upset as a result. (She compiled a long list of them after Keith Sorrenson asked her for help prior to his appearing on the panel discussion about Simpson's radio programmes.) She was especially troubled by some of Simpson's moral strictures, particularly about Henry Williams. She probably feared they owed something to her own treatment of the missionary. By this time, she had spent several years helping the Catholic Diocese of Auckland to organise its archives, done a good deal of research on Pompallier's Auckland, and nearly completed a small book about the Anglican Church's Melanesian Mission in Auckland, all of which had softened her opinion of the Church Missionary Society missionaries. In any case, she was always more sympathetic towards religion than some of her writings might suggest. She never had anything like what commonly passes for religious conviction, but for as long as she could remember she had been intensely interested in religious belief and religious history and did not think anyone could get along in life without faith of some kind or another.[47]

Ross was perturbed by the emotionally charged nature of Simpson's work, as she was apprehensive about the impact it could have on debate about the Treaty. In her imitable fashion she told Sorrenson: 'That anyone could be so utterly irresponsible [as Simpson] makes me want to throw up. The whole subject of Waitangi and the treaty is a powder keg; that anyone so ignorant should cash in on the topic is really frightening, and he sounded so plausible. I was so steamed up about it that I very nearly wrote to you there and then.' As this reveals, academically trained historians like Ross believed that public discussion about historical matters should be conducted in a manner in which reason prevailed, even though — or because — they themselves were passionate about subjects like the Treaty.[48]

By this time Ross's interests in the Treaty had shifted somewhat, though the ambivalence and thus the tensions that had long characterised her work about it remained. In the mid-1970s she returned to the north to undertake a major conservation report for the Historic Places Trust about the so-called Treaty House at Waitangi (that is, James Busby's former residence), and wrote an essay about it and the other Treaty houses at Waitangi for a book about historic buildings in the North Island that was being compiled for the Trust.[49]

In undertaking this essay her interest in Māori historical perspectives came to the fore. She insisted that she be allowed to focus on the well-known 'Treaty House' and the other little-known one as well. 'At Waitangi more than one site is associated with the treaty and there are two treaty houses, separated one from the other by the Waitangi River and by traditional differences in Maori and Pakeha ways of looking at history', she told the book's editor, her former colleague Frances Porter. As a result, her approach and account had many similarities to her 1958 primary school bulletin *Te Tiriti o Waitangi* and her 1969 essay 'The Autochthonous New Zealand Soil'. She consulted with the relevant Māori organisation; adopted criteria for the Māori Treaty house that differed from that she would have used if she was writing about a comparable European building; asked at least two Māori men to read a draft; and, as a result of their criticisms, rewrote part of it to reveal more of the ways in which Māori had understood the Treaty as a covenant that Queen Victoria had made personally with their forefathers. Consequently, she argued that Māori had regarded the Treaty since the 1860s 'as a talisman by which Maori rights and Maori land would be restored' and 'the bastion of their rights'. She also discussed the ways in which it had been commemorated in a series of buildings and a monument that had been erected at Waitangi over many years, noting that three of those buildings had been named 'Te Tiriti o Waitangi'.[50]

Her emphasis on Māori ways of seeing similarly characterised an essay she wrote about the Māori church in Northland for the same historic buildings volume. She argued for the existence of what amounted to an indigenous Christian church. And soon after the volume was published, she remarked to her old friend Mary Boyd: 'Architecturally [Māori buildings] comprise the only truly indigenous contribution to the New Zealand scene today and it does my heart good to know that an organisation like the Historic Places Trust . . . could bring out a book at this particular juncture which is so demonstrably looking at New Zealand history with Maori and Pakeha eyes.'[51]

This was the sum of the work Ross was to do on the Treaty even though she had an opportunity to undertake a major historical study about it, which Michael Standish had urged her to do nearly twenty years earlier. Between 1976 and 1978 she held a three-year Faculty of Arts senior research fellowship in the Department of History at the University of Auckland. From today's standpoint, it is striking that when her name was put forward for this position in March 1975 neither Keith Sinclair (who was the Department's chairman at the time) nor Keith Sorrenson (who would shortly succeed him in that position) raised the prospect that she might work on the Treaty, even though both had first made a name for themselves by undertaking research in the history of Māori–Pākehā relations. Nor did Ross herself think of using the fellowship to undertake such a project. As far as Sinclair and Sorrenson are concerned, this might suggest that academic historians at this time still did not believe the Treaty was important enough to warrant further historical study. As far as Ross is concerned, she struggled to generate projects on her own, which is hardly surprising given that all the research she had done as a professional historian had been at the instigation of an employer or commissioning agent and she had always undertaken it as a part-timer, juggling this with family and other such responsibilities.[52]

Ross's term as a research fellow turned out to be an unhappy one. Having her name put forward for the position by the Department had provided an enormous boost to her morale, though she had found the prospect of holding it daunting. 'After pottering along on one's own for so long, to be recommended for something so grand is all rather unreal', she told Sorrenson. 'I hope, if it goes through, that I shan't be a disappointment to you all.' On taking up the position, she relished the fact that for the first time she not only had a room of her own that was separate from her home and family but a proper salary as well, which she had not had since she had left the War History Branch more than thirty years earlier. Nevertheless, she came to feel like a fish out of water in the Department and to believe that no member of staff except Hugh Laracy, a Pacific historian who had done a great deal of research on Catholic missionaries, was interested in what she was doing. Moreover, by the end of the fellowship she felt she had let Sinclair and Sorrenson down, complaining that it was a case of 'a lot of hard work and damn-all results', though, as always, she was too hard on herself — she had accomplished a good deal.[53]

Ruth Ross and Claudia Orange

Ross's feelings about her time as a research fellow might have been coloured by the fact that two years into her appointment she became aware that a student, Claudia Orange (1938–), had embarked on a PhD thesis in the Department on the history of the Treaty and was pursuing many of the same lines of inquiry that she once had, including an examination of Māori perspectives.

In searching for a topic, Orange had learned that at least one of her two supervisors was sceptical that there was any need for a major study of the Treaty, not least because Peter Adams's book *Fatal Necessity* had appeared recently. Partly as a result of this, she decided that she would focus largely on three other matters: the making of the Treaty 'on the ground' in New Zealand, Māori perspectives of it, and the history of its fortunes after the late 1840s. 'The Treaty on the Ground' was the title of Ross's 1972 seminar paper and the published essay that sprang from it, but it was the latter — her article in the *New Zealand Journal of History* — that exerted most influence on Orange.[54]

Not surprisingly, she sought Ross's help as she began her research. For example, in the closing months of 1978, having agreed to present a paper at a major conference to be held at the University of Auckland in January the following year, she rang Ross one weekend to pick her brains. '[There] followed a question and answer session that seemed to go on for an hour though I guess was only half that length', Ross later told Mary Boyd. 'It sounds as though she has got on to some interesting stuff . . . but she left me feeling like a large clod of earth that some very energetic bird had been digging furiously in for worms.'[55]

The paper Orange gave at the conference, which she later revised and published as an article in the *New Zealand Journal of History* in 1980, owed a great deal to Ross's article. As she remarked at the beginning of it: 'The best appreciation of Maori understanding can be found in two articles by Ruth Ross who examines in some detail the immediate circumstances surrounding the signing of the treaty.' The extent of Orange's debt is evident in her introductory paragraphs in which she briefly discussed the making of the Treaty. In fact, she reproduced Ross's argument. But the substantive part of her article, entitled 'The Covenant of Kohimarama: A Ratification of the Treaty of Waitangi', which focused on a major conference involving senior government officials and leading chiefs that was held at Kohimarama near Auckland in 1860, also makes clear how much she owed to Ross's article.[56]

Nevertheless, whereas other historians in the 1970s had received Ross's article mainly in terms of her major argument, Orange was primarily interested in her minor argument. Thus, while she noted Ross's scathing opinion of the Treaty's deficiencies — remarking that it was 'an untidy treaty' and immediately quoting the oft-quoted words that appeared near the end of her article — her main focus was on the meaning of the Treaty to Māori. In a sense, she did what Ross in good part wanted to do but found difficult to execute, partly because during the time in which she (Ross) had grown up and lived most of her life there was little interest in, if not hostility to, Māori perspectives.[57]

In adopting that focus, Orange extended the historical range of Ross's contentions about what was coming to be called by this time the Treaty's 'two texts'. That is, rather than focusing only on how the Treaty had been understood by Māori in 1840, she set about investigating how it had been understood by them in the years that followed. Moreover, she enlarged the significance of Ross's argument by insisting that there were not only two texts but what she called two treaties. Yet, however much Orange sought to establish the importance of the discussions about the Treaty at Kohimarama in Māori history, one of her main lines of argument was very Rossian. She emphasised that understanding of it among the Māori chiefs on this occasion was 'very limited' and that most 'had only a vague and confused comprehension of [it]'. She even remarked that the Treaty's clauses were 'impossibly contradictory'.[58]

In November 1981 Ross was diagnosed with bowel cancer that surgery eighteen months earlier had seemed to have taken care of. The following month she began a course of chemotherapy but soon learned that she was terminally ill. She sought out Orange and told her that she was happy to pass on to her the baton or what amounted to the mantle of being the historian of the Treaty, though she was far too humble to put it in those terms. Orange was grateful but did not realise the true meaning of this gesture as she was unaware that Ross had spent much of her life as a historian thinking and writing about the Treaty. She was in good company. Matiu Te Hau had once observed, albeit half-jokingly, that Ross's 'life-work has been and still is the interpretation of the Treaty of Waitangi', but as far as academic historians go, probably only Keith Sinclair and J. M. R. Owens were aware of how long she had been preoccupied with the Treaty.[59]

In February 1982 Ross was shown a cartoon in a weekly broadsheet that revealed that her 1972 article had become famous (see Figure 20). The cartoonist, Bob Brockie, had more or less quoted its best-known passage. Shortly afterwards, a historian at Ross's alma mater, Malcolm McKinnon, suggested to the editor of the *National Business Review* that it would be appropriate for the cartoonist to acknowledge her contribution. In doing just that, Brockie recalled that he had first heard the words he had quoted bandied around a dinner table (by someone who had read Owens's chapter in the recently published *Oxford History of New Zealand*). He remarked that the 'inspired author of this universal put-down must be gratified to see her words passing into the vernacular'. At McKinnon's suggestion, he sent Ross the original of the cartoon. By this time, she was very ill. Consequently, the cartoon and the responses it aroused, she told Boyd, 'caused quite a little flurry in the mailbox and a welcome diversion'. She had no trouble with the cartoonist's cynical take on the Treaty. 'No one could call Brockie subtle', she remarked, 'but he sure gets his point across.'[60]

When she died six months later, Ross was aware that her article had been taken up by academic historians in a way that made sense to her and that her major argument had entered public discourse. But she could not have known that a revolution in the place of the Treaty in New Zealand's legal and constitutional history was about to occur, and she would have been amazed that her article — or, rather, one of the ways in which it was received — was to play a huge role in this change.[61]

A nation in search of a new history

In the closing decades of the twentieth century a crisis emerged in the way that New Zealanders, especially Pākehā, understood themselves and their nation's history. This amounted to a problem for what had come to be called 'national identity'. Several factors were at work. New Zealanders had long regarded themselves as a people who belonged to the British Commonwealth, formerly the British Empire. But in the wake of decolonisation in Africa and Asia and Britain's decision to enter the European Economic Community and loosen many of its ties to its former settler colonies, it no longer made as much sense for New Zealanders to identify themselves in this way. At the same time, New Zealand's relationship to the Asia-Pacific region became a source of greater trade ties and a growing number of immigrants. Pākehā New Zealanders had also been taught to regard their nation as an exemplary laboratory for social democracy, but its economy was now believed by many to require radical reform that threatened to put an end to the extensive provision of social security they had enjoyed. New Zealanders had similarly been told that their nation had the best race relations in the world, but this boast was now seen to be threadbare as Māori advocates drew attention to a history of past wrongs and demanded a reconfiguration of the relationship between the indigenous people of the country and the New Zealand state. Some such as Donna Awatere began to call for the return of what they claimed their forebears had never surrendered: mana motuhake or Māori sovereignty. Most of these changes brought into question the very sovereignty of the nation and provoked a crisis of legitimacy for the New Zealand nation state.

Many Pākehā New Zealanders who played a role in governing the country began to realise that it was necessary to change the way the nation saw itself so that they could feel that they still belonged. More to the point, they came to believe that the nation's indigenous people, culture and history might best meet this need but only once the legacy of the wrongs that the New Zealand state had committed against Māori had been addressed. As a result, major changes took place in the way that the relationship between race, history and nationhood — and thus the position of Māori — was conceived. Having been marginal to New Zealand culture, society and politics for so long, taha Māori (Māori perspectives) would begin to become central to it. Moreover, whereas the New Zealand nation was conceived for many decades as one in which Māori were supposed to be treated the same as Pākehā, granted the same (that is, equal) rights and assimilated, and expected to allow their ways of doing things to recede into the past, now the nation was imagined as one in which Māori were to be treated in many respects as different from Pākehā, granted different (that is, indigenous) rights, and encouraged to retain their cultural difference and nurture their history.

The same general phenomenon occurred in two other settler states — Australia and Canada — at this time. But what happened in New Zealand was distinctive. Australia and Canada, both continental confederations that comprised an array of ethnic groups that included tiny minorities of indigenous people, chose to construe themselves predominantly as multicultural nations. New Zealand, a unitary island state whose population was less diverse ethnically than Canada and Australia and which had a much larger indigenous minority, opted to construct itself as a bicultural nation that comprised Māori, who increasingly called themselves the 'tangata whenua', or the first people of the land, and the settlers, who began more and more to call themselves 'Pākehā', or the people who had only arrived later. The new relationship between Māori, Pākehā and the New Zealand nation state would come to be interpreted largely in terms of the Treaty. New Zealanders were to be encouraged to understand much of the country's past, present and future by reference to it. For this change to take place, a new history — and particularly a new constitutional and legal history of the Treaty and its place in the nation — was required.

The story that had been told in recent decades about the Treaty and its place in the nation was no longer fit for purpose. Partly this was because it was *critical history*, as the nineteenth-century German philosopher Friedrich Nietzsche would have called it — a history that damned the Treaty, as Ross had done in her major argument, as an agreement that was hopelessly ambiguous and contradictory in its meaning, as a contract that had been repeatedly breached by the New Zealand state, and as a document that was incapable of being put to any legal or political purpose because its signatories were uncertain and divided in their understanding of its meanings. Partly this was because it was represented as a treaty that had been written in the language of the colonisers.

What was required was a history of the Treaty that had several major characteristics. It had to be a story that would emphasise the Māori text and the differences between it and the English texts. In this context it is important to note that, while there are differences between the two texts (if only because they are in two languages), in and of itself this does not dictate that those differences will be regarded as more important than the similarities. Differences and similarities abound in the world but whether one or the other is said to really count is determined by the prevailing political, social and cultural forces and thus by power, rather than empirical investigation. The history of the Treaty, at least in the decades leading up to this moment in time, testifies to this point: in a world dominated by Pākehā and assimilationist ways of seeing, it had long been represented as an agreement in which the similarities rather than the differences between the two texts were more important, so much so that the differences barely registered in most accounts. Even when those differences were acknowledged, the English text was held to be the official version and thus understood to be *the* Treaty.[62]

The new story about the Treaty had to be what Nietzsche would have called a *monumental history* — that is, one that could meet a people's need for example and inspiration in their action and struggle. Thus, the history that came to be told in the next few years held that the Treaty was a noble agreement that was, and had always been, important in the nation's history. It contended that the nation's foundations lay in the Treaty being a contract between Māori and Pākehā. It claimed that it was an agreement that both parties had made in good faith. It asserted that the Treaty had bestowed rights on the indigenous people and imposed a duty or obligation on the (British) Crown to uphold them. It argued that the Māori had ceded sovereignty to the Crown but only on the basis that it would protect rangatiratanga over their lands and other resources. It acknowledged that the Treaty had been repeatedly breached by the Crown and that this had caused enormous suffering to Māori but argued that this could be repaired by the Crown undertaking to uphold the principles of the historic agreement in an honourable manner. Finally, it maintained that, by doing this, the injustices of the past would be redressed to some degree and the New Zealand nation redeemed, as it would be re-founded on just principles, thereby going some way towards resolving the crisis of legitimacy.[63]

For a story to be able to perform the work required, it needed to provide an account of the nation's past in which the Treaty was central. It had to attribute to, and explain, the conflict that had occurred between Māori and Pākehā during the nation's history, and the consequences of that conflict, by reference to the very terms of the Treaty and the various ways in which those terms had been misinterpreted by the two parties to it. It was also assumed that the story had to provide an interpretation that could be held to reside in the Treaty document, or more specifically the norms or principles that could be said to inhere in one or other text but preferably the Māori text. Finally, it had to emphasise that the different interpretations or understandings of the Treaty lay in its two texts, but it also had to contain or limit the implications of those differences by playing down the ambiguities and contradictions and, at times, even the differences between those texts.

This new account of the Treaty would be forged by several main players or figures — the Waitangi Tribunal and the courts, Māori advocates, legal scholars and academic historians. Each of them told stories about the Treaty in distinctive ways but with the same interpretive thrust. The materials were mostly provided by Ross's article, once it was read against the grain of her major argument. All these players took up her minor argument, using a logic that seemed to lie in it and discarding her other argument so that it largely, but by no means entirely, disappeared from public view. In this process her contention about the Treaty texts and especially the text in Māori came to have a life of its own. As these various players adopted and adapted it, they influenced readers who had never read her article or were not even aware of its existence.

Both the Treaty and Ross's article about it could be readily reactivated as a result of two general factors. Language, and public language especially, is inherently ambiguous and thus contestable. Most texts, like the Treaty and Ross's article, are neither simple nor fully at the command of those who produce them, and so they will reveal more than their creators intended. They can be made to yield information or interpretations that may or may not have been the creator's intention to convey. In this case, this meant that tensions, ambivalences and contradictions that were inherent in both these texts could be used by the various key figures. More specifically, texts like the Treaty and Ross's article express historical tensions and conflicts that have been only partially resolved, which means that they often contain the history of those tensions and conflicts. People like politicians and lawyers know this and can exploit the ambiguity of past language, either to discover what its creators may have meant in their time, and/or to determine what they might find it expedient to interpret them as saying now.[64]

The New Zealand Maori Council, Eddie Durie and the Waitangi Tribunal

Before this new story about the Treaty could be forged in any thoroughgoing sense, there had to be a radical change in the way it was regarded by many New Zealanders, especially young Māori advocates and their Pākehā allies. In 1984–85, this occurred, first during a hīkoi to Waitangi and later at hui at Tūrangawaewae and Waitangi. Cynicism about the Treaty, which had been dominant since the early 1970s, was replaced by pious respect for it as a solemn contract. More and more, calls began to be made for it to be honoured. The notion of the two texts, derived from a reading of Ross's article, played a vital role in this shift.[65] By invoking the Māori text rather than the English one, these advocates were able to embrace te Tiriti o Waitangi, as they could represent it as a very different agreement from the Treaty of Waitangi they had been dismissing for many years as a sham and a fraud.[66]

This change of heart owed a good deal to the work of the New Zealand Maori Council, headed by Graham Latimer (1926–2016) of Ngāti Kahu. In a discussion paper released in February 1983, it set out kaupapa (principles that could be the basis for action) that held that the Treaty was fundamental to any attempt by Māori to regain control of their land. It began by declaring its belief that te Tiriti was the basis of British sovereignty and government in New Zealand and that in it the Crown had promised to protect Māori and guarantee them their assets. It devoted the remainder of the discussion paper to summarising the clauses of the Treaty in both their English and Māori versions, providing an interpretation of the agreement from which it drew certain principles, and arguing that it should be the foundation for all legislation on Māori matters.[67]

The Council's interpretation of te Tiriti was informed by Ross's article. She had sent a copy of it to one of its members, Hēnare Kōhere Ngata, in September 1973, after hearing him speak at the Victoria University seminar the previous year. The Council noted her major argument — 'the Treaty was drawn up by amateurs on the one side and signed by those on the other who understood little of its implications' — only to discount this contention and draw out what it deemed to be the logic of one of her other contentions about the Māori text: that Māori expected their rangatiratanga to be protected and thereby to retain it while the Crown expected to gain sovereignty over New Zealand. Drawing on Ross's argument about the texts and the translation, the Council went on to explain this contention: 'In the Treaty, the Maori people's "full"[,] "exclusive" and "undisturbed possession" (of "lands", "estates", "forests", "fisheries", and "other properties") is rendered by "te tino rangatiratanga". However, while rangatiratanga may indeed mean "possession", it also means much more than that today, as in 1840.'[68]

At the close of its discussion paper, the Council turned to consider the forums to which Māori might best present their claims about breaches of the Treaty. It was not convinced that the answer lay in allowing the courts to deal with them, recommending instead that they be considered by a body that would examine them in accordance with the 'principles' of the Treaty. It suggested that the Waitangi Tribunal could be that body but only so long as its functions were extended. Of the changes it proposed, the most important was that of empowering it to hear retrospective claims and make recommendations to the government for 'some compensatory or other remedial action'.[69]

By this time the Tribunal itself had begun to undergo major change. This has rightly been attributed to Edward (Eddie) Taihakurei Durie (1940–) of Rangitāne, Ngāti Kauwhata and Raukawa descent, who became its chair after being appointed as the Chief Judge of the Maori Land Court in 1980. As the historian Andrew Sharp has pointed out, Durie was a highly capable judge, a brilliant advocate, and a man of considerable political skill and intellectual acumen. He, more than any other figure, was primarily responsible for transforming the status of the Tribunal and revolutionising the place of the Treaty in New Zealand law, society and politics, and it was his way of reading Ross's article that was to become canonical. This said, what is often overlooked is the role that Latimer played in the changes that took place, first as the chairman of the New Zealand Maori Council, then as one of the Tribunal's three members.[70]

Soon after the Council had released its discussion paper, the Tribunal published its first major report — on the Motunui-Waitara claim — and in the next three years it would deliver findings and make recommendations on three other claims — Kaituna (November 1984), Manukau (July 1985), and Te Reo (April 1986). These reports, all of which were written by Durie, gave an enormous boost to the Tribunal's standing and set in motion a process that put the Treaty centre stage in New Zealand.[71]

Under Durie's chairmanship, the Tribunal shifted its hearings from a highly formal legal and Pākehā setting, thereby enabling the Māori claimants to present testimony in places that were very familiar to them, namely their marae (a communal and sacred meeting ground), and where their ways of relating — and relating to — the past, which differed markedly from those of academic history, came to the fore. After the first occasion this had happened, Durie pointed out that the Tribunal's governing legislation, the Treaty of Waitangi Act 1975, allowed it to receive evidence in any place and in any form it chose. He noted the implications of this change: 'The Tribunal is completely satisfied that by adopting this procedure it was able to reach the real heart of the matter.'[72]

Māori history — and by this term I mean here accounts in which Māori people, their perspectives of the past, and their ways of being in history are foregrounded — also came to be important in the stories the Tribunal heard. This had several consequences. The Tribunal came to argue that whereas Pākehā tended to consign the Treaty to the past and believe it did not have many implications for contemporary New Zealand, Māori believed it had enormous ongoing significance. It contended that the Treaty had been a regular subject of debate on marae throughout the country for more than a century. And it emphasised that Māori had long held that the Treaty amounted to a solemn pact and had given them a special place in New Zealand.[73]

Just as Māori history came to figure in the stories the Tribunal heard and told in turn, so too did another way of relating, and relating *to*, the past — that of the law. Generally speaking, the Tribunal used its governing legislation to sanction what it wanted to do. More specifically, it took that legislation's instruction to 'make recommendations on claims relating to the *practical application* of the principles of the Treaty and, for that purpose, to determine its meaning and effect and whether certain matters are inconsistent with those *principles*' as an opportunity to turn the past into a storehouse in which those principles were to be identified; to judge the actions of the Crown in the light of those principles; and, where the Crown was found to have acted inconsistently with them, to make practical recommendations to government for change that would redress the breaches of the Treaty that it had committed.[74]

The changes I have just described meant that the Tribunal would come to play a powerful role in interpreting the Treaty, and that the law and Māori history would work hand in hand in doing so. Durie had formed the view that understanding of the Treaty in New Zealand had been limited because its courts had long ruled that it had no legal status. He held that this had worked against the public exposure of a Māori view of the Treaty. If the Treaty had been regarded as irrelevant by the law, Māori opinion had been regarded as 'doubly so'. Durie reasoned that by recovering the Treaty in a legal sense, Māori perspectives would be revealed in every sense, and he proceeded accordingly.[75]

In much the same vein, he formed the opinion that to change the legal status of the Treaty it was necessary to put it in an international context. In the early 1970s indigenous people in Canada and Australia had taken to the courts claims about the land they had lost. In Canada a case, *Calder v Attorney-General of British Columbia* (1973), had resulted in a judgment that the native peoples had common law rights by virtue of their prior occupation of the land, while an Australian case, *Milirrpum v Nabalco Pty Ltd* (1971), had resulted in a ruling that aboriginal people had no such rights but nonetheless drew enormous attention to their cause.[76] These legal developments had prompted several legal scholars and a few historians in Australia, Canada and New

Zealand to embark on research about the way indigenous peoples' rights of property in land had been treated historically. Durie was aware that courts in North America had been making rulings in favour of indigenous peoples and he now became acquainted with this new legal scholarship. He sought to point out that the approach of New Zealand's courts did not compare favourably with those overseas and suggested that this should provoke New Zealanders to rethink their perception of the Treaty and reassess the making of it in a context other than just the history of New Zealand.[77]

Under Durie's chairmanship, the Tribunal chose to use the authority that the Treaty of Waitangi Act had granted it to 'determine the meaning and effect of the Treaty as embodied in the [Treaty's] *two texts* and to decide issues raised by the differences between them'. Consequently, Ross's article, or the way her minor argument about the texts was read by the members of the Tribunal as well as those who appeared before it, was to play a crucial role in the radical change that took place in the Treaty's legal status and the way the Treaty was understood.[78]

Chapter 5
The Waitangi Tribunal, the Legal Scholars and the Historians

As contexts change, so too do the ways in which texts are read. In this case, significant changes in the relevant political and legal contexts led to important changes in the way Ross's article was received and the Treaty was read. While one might expect that this would be the case for the players whose orientation to the world was political and legal, it was true of those whose orientation was historical. As Ross's text and the texts of the Treaty were read in new ways by the former, the latter tended to follow suit. Many of these changes were stark and so are easy to trace and comprehend; but many are subtle and so are harder to delineate and understand.

In this chapter I consider the ways in which Ross's work was received by the Waitangi Tribunal and the uses to which it put her minor argument; trace the changes that occurred in the work of Claudia Orange as *the* Treaty historian, which include her reading of Ross's article; discuss the emergence of legal scholarship relating to the Treaty, particularly that of P. G. (Paul) McHugh; and examine the impact of the law on the work of the historian Keith Sorrenson.

The Tribunal, the courts and 'Te Tiriti o Waitangi'

After Eddie Durie assumed the role of chair of the Waitangi Tribunal, Ross's article began to be read in particular ways that ensured it would play a crucial role in the findings that the Tribunal reached. Not only Durie and Latimer (as members of the Tribunal) but two other senior Māori figures, Hugh Kawharu and 'Sidney' Hirini Moko Haerewa Mead (as they made submissions to the Tribunal or gave evidence at its hearings) played a vital role in this respect. Kawharu (1927–2016), of Ngāti Whātua, had completed a doctorate at Oxford University in 1963, had become the foundation professor in the Department of Social Anthropology and Maori Studies at Massey University in 1970, had published a major study of Māori land tenure in 1977, he had recently been appointed as Professor of Maori Studies and Anthropology at the University of Auckland, and was the chair of the Ngati Whatua o Orakei Maori Trust Board. Mead (1927–), of Ngāti Awa, Ngāti Tūwharetoa, Ngāi Tūhoe and Tūhourangi descent, had completed a doctorate in anthropology at the University of Southern Illinois in 1968, taught in several universities in Canada, become the foundation professor of Maori Studies at Victoria University in 1977, and co-curated a major international exhibition of Māori art (*Te Maori*) and had helped to established the Ngati Awa Trust Board in the early to mid-1980s.

In the first report that the Tribunal issued after Durie became its chairman, it acknowledged that it owed its account of the Treaty's 'two texts' to Ross's article. In its subsequent reports it placed great store by interpretations of the Treaty's clauses that were advanced by Kawharu and Mead but which drew heavily on Ross's minor argument. In other words, the Tribunal came to cite Māori, professors and men — rather than a Pākehā woman who had little academic standing — as its authoritative sources of knowledge. It also referenced the work of a Pākehā legal scholar, David Williams, who had similarly taken up Ross's argument about the Treaty texts.[1]

The Tribunal's reception of Ross's article can be attributed to several factors. It is not so much that the fifth section of its governing legislation granted it, for the purposes of the Act, the sole authority to determine the meaning and effects of the Treaty as they were embodied in the Māori and English texts and to decide any issues that were raised by the differences between them. It was that the Tribunal *chose* to use this provision so it could consider those differences and treat them as of the utmost significance. Given this, it is not surprising that it invoked repeatedly the relevant section of the Treaty of Waitangi Act 1975 to legitimise what it was doing.[2]

In the decade after Ross's article was published, most historians registered her major argument that the Treaty was 'hastily and inexpertly drawn up, ambiguous and contradictory in content, chaotic in its execution' as well as the relationship between it and her minor argument that the text in te reo was the authoritative text. But the context in which her article was received by the Tribunal was very different. It was a legal commission charged with a particular legal task. This meant that the Tribunal, and those who appeared before it, read her article in terms of its minor argument. The Tribunal had no use for her major argument and never noted, let alone discussed it in its Motunui-Waitara, Kaituna, Manukau and Te Reo reports, delivered from 1983 to 1986. For Ross's article to be useful in this context, her minor argument had to be severed from her major argument, as the latter ran counter to what the Tribunal was trying to do. Any reference to it could have undermined the persuasiveness of its interpretation of the Treaty.[3]

It was relatively easy for these players — the Tribunal and those who appeared before it — to read Ross's article in a way that was contrary to her authorial intentions — to switch from its major key to its minor key. She had not spelt out the relationship between the two, let alone made it clear that her principal purpose in making the minor argument was to demonstrate and evidence her major one. This meant that readers could readily overlook the connection between them and disconnect the former from the latter, thereby lending it a different character and emotion, that of monumental rather than critical history.

The fact that Ross made so much of the Treaty texts in one way or another, rather than the contexts in which the Treaty was made, enabled the Tribunal's way of reading her article. The Tribunal and its supplicants followed suit to a large degree in that they implied that the Treaty's meaning was to be found principally in the texts instead of the contexts. For the Tribunal to be able to generate and legitimise its new interpretation of the Treaty, it was vital that it be able to remove the Treaty from the historical contexts in which it was made and insert it instead into a legal context that it created, just as Ross had done to some degree. The way it had been titled or mistitled by the *New Zealand Journal of History* — 'Te Tiriti o Waitangi: Texts and Translations' — probably aided this reception of her article. Her focus on the texts and the fact that one of her arguments about a crucial article in the Treaty owed a good deal to a legal, rather than a historical, reading of the Treaty — Justice William Martin's interpretation of it in the early 1860s, or rather the way she construed it — might have also facilitated the way in which her article was received by the Tribunal and those who appeared before it.

In the four reports being discussed here, the Tribunal believed that in considering the terms of the Treaty it was important to register Ross's main point about the texts and translations. As it stated in one of its reports, 'the Maori text is not a translation of the English text and conversely, nor is the English version a translation of the Maori' and so there were 'significant differences' between the two texts. But the implications of this argument were heightened, as far as the Tribunal was concerned, because it made a vital connection between her *historical* approach and interpretation of the Treaty and its *legal* approach to and interpretation of treaties, especially bilingual ones. It noted the points that Lord Duncan McNair had made in his classic study of treaties: that in the absence of any provision to the contrary, neither language text was to be treated as superior to the other, and that it was permissible to interpret one text by reference to the other. More importantly, it noted the legal rule of *contra proferentem*, which holds that in the event of ambiguity, provisions of a treaty should be construed against the party that drafted or proposed those provisions. It also pointed to rulings by North American courts, and legal commentary about treaties with Indian tribes, that could be treated as an extension of this rule. It is difficult to underestimate the role that this rule came to play in interpretation of the Treaty, not only among lawyers but among historians as well.[4]

The Tribunal drew on specific parts of Ross's argument about the texts to furnish itself with evidence for the various legal arguments it mounted. At the moments it argued that the Māori text should be regarded as the authoritative text, it adopted and adapted her point that this was the text most of the chiefs had signed by contending that it had played an important role in securing the consent of the chiefs. For a different reason, it invoked Ross's points about the difficulty of translating legal concepts, and the way in which Henry Williams had translated the English text, claiming that they supported an argument that it occasionally made for the need to take *both* texts into consideration if one was to understand the meaning and effects of the Treaty.[5]

But the most important argument the Tribunal derived from its reading of Ross's article undoubtedly sprang from her consideration of what had come to be regarded as its key words: 'kawanatanga', 'te tino rangatiratanga' and 'taonga'.[6] The meaning the Tribunal attributed to these words was crucial to the findings it reached about breaches of the principles of the Treaty. It either adopted Ross's argument about these words or articulated a logic that was implicit in her discussion of them (which had been elaborated by Kawharu and to a lesser extent Mead in the expert testimony they gave to the Tribunal), or else it adapted her argument to make somewhat different points, or it contested her argument to advance contrary points.

As far as 'kawanatanga' was concerned, the Tribunal mounted the following argument. In translating 'sovereignty' Williams had sought a word in Māori that did not exist because this concept was foreign to Māori culture. As 'sovereignty' had no exact equivalent in Māori, Williams had used 'kawanatanga' to translate 'all the rights and powers of sovereignty', and he had done so because the missionaries had previously used this word in translating the Bible and the *Book of Common Prayer* into Māori. 'Kawanatanga' was something less than the 'sovereignty' or the 'absolute authority' referenced in the English text. It merely meant the authority to make laws for the peace, good order and security of the realm. The word 'kawanatanga' was well chosen because, while it was one the missionaries had coined, it was a term known to Māori because of their familiarity with the Bible, and it signified what both Māori and the British Crown wanted from the agreement. Finally, in ceding kāwanatanga, the chiefs would have understood that they were only granting the Crown the right of governance and so were retaining their mana and thus their absolute power and authority.[7]

Yet, while the Tribunal clearly drew on a reading of Ross's article (whether its own or Kawharu's) in making this argument, its interpretation diverged in important respects from hers. She had begun her account of the Treaty by noting that 'kawanatanga' was used in its preamble to translate *both* 'sovereign authority' and 'government', which suggested some of the problems facing the translators and raised the question of whether they had been surmounted. She had then proceeded to argue that in the Treaty's first article the concept of sovereignty was not adequately contained in the phrase the missionaries had used to translate it, namely 'te kawanatanga katoa o o ratou wenua', adding that, however much the word 'kawana' would have been well known by Māori, the term 'kawanatanga' was an unknown thing to them. Moreover, she had gone on to imply that the translators should have used the word 'mana' instead of 'kawanatanga', as they had in translating 'sovereignty' in the Declaration of Independence in 1835, and that if they had done this in translating the Treaty the chiefs would have been in no doubt that they were being asked to cede their sovereignty to the Queen. Finally, she had suggested that the omission of 'mana' from the Māori text by Williams was no accident.[8] In essence, the difference between Ross's and the Tribunal's account of the first article amounted to this: whereas she emphasised the differences between the English and Māori texts and implied that this had resulted in ambiguity and thus confusion and misunderstanding, the Tribunal noted the ambiguity only to deny there had been any confusion and misunderstanding in order to make an argument very different from hers: that the Treaty *was* coherent and *had* been understood in the same fundamental way by both the parties to it.[9]

In its discussion of 'te tino rangatiratanga', the Tribunal mounted the following argument. 'Rangatiratanga' had no exact equivalent in English, just as 'sovereignty' had no exact equivalent in Māori. The nearest one could get to a good translation was to say that it meant 'all the powers[,] privileges and mana of a chieftain or "chieftain-ship" in the widest sense'. When 'te tino rangatiratanga' was used in the phrase 'te tino rangatiratanga o o ratou wenua kainga me a ratou taonga katoa' to translate 'lands and estates[,] forests[,] fisheries and other properties', it meant 'full authority, status and prestige with regard to their possessions and interests', or 'the fullness of control', or even 'the sovereignty of their lands'. In other words, its scope was wider than the full, exclusive and undisturbed possession guaranteed in the English text. This meant that the Treaty promised that Māori were not only to be protected in the possession of those forms of property, but in the mana to control them.[10]

The Tribunal's consideration of 'te tino rangatiratanga' clearly owed a good deal to a reading of Ross's article, just as it is apparent that there are similarities and differences in the arguments the Tribunal and Ross made. Apart from the fact that she had paid much less attention to 'te tino rangatiratanga' than the Tribunal did, she had raised questions about what it would have meant to the chiefs, rather than advancing an unequivocal argument about its meaning. She did point out that 'rangatiratanga' had been used in the Declaration of Independence, and had wondered whether its recurrence in the Māori text of the Treaty meant that 'independence' could be said to have been guaranteed to the Māori chiefs and people in it. She had proceeded to note that 'rangatiratanga' was used in two quite different ways by Pākehā: for the missionaries it meant 'kingdom', but Hobson had used it (a few months after the Treaty was signed at Waitangi) to denote 'sovereignty', prompting her to remark: 'Was it any wonder that the New Zealanders [i.e. the Maori] at first supposed the Queen had guaranteed them something more than possession of their own lands?' But in the end she had argued that the Te Rarawa chief Nōpera Panakareao had soon realised that he was mistaken in assuming that the substance of sovereignty would remain with Māori and only the shadow would go to the Queen. In other words, she made a point that was consistent with her major argument: the way in which the Treaty had been translated meant it was ambiguous and contradictory and this had resulted in confusion. *This* was the point at which the Tribunal parted company with Ross as it had no use for that contention.[11]

Regarding 'taonga', the Tribunal made the following argument. In the English text the Queen had specifically guaranteed Māori the possession 'of their lands and estates, forests, fisheries and other properties'. In the Māori text there was no specific reference to forests or fisheries 'but rather to "o rato wenua" (their lands), "o ratou kainga" (their habitations)' and, most importantly, '"me o ratou taonga katoa" (and all their treasured things)' — that is, for Māori, 'taonga' embraced all things treasured by their ancestors and so included the forests and fisheries. It argued that this was a good example of how the English and Māori languages differed in nature — the former precise, the latter metaphorical and idiomatic — and that it would be inappropriate to apply English canons in interpreting the Treaty. Nonetheless, the Tribunal concluded its first consideration of this matter in the Motunui-Waitara report by asserting that the differences between the two texts were not as substantial as might first be thought, stating: 'We consider that the Treaty envisaged protection for Maori fishing grounds because the English text specifically provided for that while the Maori text implied it.' But in the later reports it often found it useful to emphasise the differences.[12]

It is possible that Ross's consideration of 'taonga' in her article had alerted Kawharu and Mead, and in turn the Tribunal, to its potential significance in the Māori text. (She devoted more discussion to it than to 'te tino rangatiratanga'.) But if this is so, the way the Tribunal took up this matter diverged from her account of it. She noted that the definition of 'taonga' in Herbert Williams's *Dictionary of the Maori Language* was 'anything highly prized', and contended that he had used it in this way in translating the Treaty's second article; but she proceeded to point out that the Māori text mentioned only '*whenua* (land), *kainga* (homes), and *taonga katoa* (all [other?] possessions)' and to argue that it was consequently a matter of interpretation as to whether 'taonga katoa' in the Treaty *did* include natural food resources, as the Tribunal now contended. She believed that Williams did not envisage 'taonga katoa' as including fishing rights and suggested that his omission of any words signifying fisheries almost certainly stemmed from what she believed was the omission of the word 'fisheries' from the English draft that had been given to him to translate. She also contended that fishing rights were not an issue for Māori in the nineteenth century (though she later realised she was mistaken in this regard). In short, much of her argument about 'taonga' ran contrary to the contentions the Tribunal made about it.[13]

There were other moments in the four reports when the Tribunal found it advantageous to depart even further from Ross's argument by invoking what it called the wairua (spirit) of the Treaty and taking issue with her focus on its texts. In its Motunui-Waitara report, it asserted: 'A Maori approach to the Treaty would imply that its wairua or spirit is something more than a literal construction of the actual words used can provide. The spirit of the Treaty transcends the sum total of its component written words and puts narrow or literal interpretations out of place.'[14]

The Tribunal's overarching interpretation of the Treaty was at odds with Ross's. As she had argued that the Treaty was 'ambiguous and contradictory' and concluded that its signatories were 'uncertain and divided in their understanding of its meaning', she could not envisage it ever being given any legal, let alone constitutional, status. By the same token, she believed it was 'sheer hypocrisy' on the part of Pākehā New Zealanders to 'persist in postulating that this was a "sacred compact"', just as she was scathing of what she saw as the myth that the Treaty amounted to a Māori Magna Carta.[15]

By contrast, the Tribunal argued that in 1840 there had been a considerable degree of understanding between the two parties — or what it started to characterise as the 'partners' — to the Treaty about the 'principles' informing it. It asserted that the Treaty was, at least in Māori eyes, 'a solemn pact'. It also contended that the Treaty could well be described as the 'Maori Magna Carta'; indeed that it was more than an affirmation of rights granted in the past. 'It was not intended to merely fossilise a status quo, but to provide a direction for future growth and development', it declared. 'The broad and general nature of its words indicates that it was not intended as a finite contract but as the foundation for a developing social contract.' Likewise, the Tribunal held that the Treaty had established a regime for bi-culturalism rather than uni-culturalism. It opined that Pākehā need not feel threatened by this but could be proud instead, even going so far as to suggest that if Pākehā were unable to accept the rights the Treaty granted Māori they risked drawing into question their own right to be in the country. Finally, it claimed that the Treaty was not only coming to be regarded as a valid legal agreement but was well on its way to having 'the status of a constitutional instrument'. In short, whereas Ross had been intent, in her major key, on tearing down the myth about the Treaty, the Tribunal was forging a new one, in good part on the basis of its reading of her minor key. While some of its findings would have baffled Ross, just as Auburn's had, others would have troubled her if she had continued to be attached to her major argument rather than her minor one. But as the times changed she might have come to align herself more with the latter than the former.[16]

In June 1987, in the wake of the Tribunal reports I have been discussing, the Court of Appeal delivered a judgment about the Treaty in a case, *New Zealand Maori Council v Attorney-General*. This case was mounted after the Council, among others, became apprehensive that recently passed legislation would allow huge amounts of land and other assets to be transferred from the Crown to private corporations and that this would mean that the Crown's power to act on the Tribunal's recommendations to return resources to iwi (tribes) would be severely diminished. This case was to prove crucial in determining the legal and constitutional status of the Treaty, not least because the most senior judge hearing the case suggested that it might be as important to the future of the country as any that had ever come before a New Zealand court. The court agreed with the appellants that the Treaty was a document that related to what they had called 'fundamental rights'; that it should be interpreted widely as a 'living instrument' by considering developments in international rights norms since it was made in 1840; and that the law should not permit any conduct that was inconsistent with its 'principles'. In reaching its findings the court endeavoured to read and assimilate a mass of documentary material that comprised works of historical and legal scholarship, which presumably included Ross's article. It also admitted many affidavits, including ones by Latimer, Ngata, Kawharu and Orange. But the court gave most weight to the opinions the Tribunal had expressed in its recent reports.[17]

Like the Tribunal, the court took for granted that there were two language texts and that they did not convey the same meaning. This was testimony to the influence of Ross's article or at least the way it had predominantly come to be read in the last few years. Furthermore, the court accepted a contemporary translation of the Māori text that Kawharu had prepared, which owed a good deal to his reading of her article. In addition, it presented an interpretation of the key words in the Treaty that was in keeping with the ways her discussion of them had been read by the Tribunal and those who had appeared before it. Yet, the court held that what mattered in the end was not the literal words in the Treaty, or the differences between the two texts, but its principles and spirit. It noted that there were difficulties in deciding what its provisions meant but ruled that the law could decide the precise rights that the Treaty might now be taken to have implied in its use of terms such as rangatiratanga.[18]

In much the same vein, the court conceded to some degree the Rossian point that 'the basic terms' of the Treaty conflicted with one another, but argued that it had 'to be seen as an embryo rather than a fully developed and integrated set of ideas'.

The most important of these, it contended, was that the Treaty 'signified a partnership between [the] races' and, more portentously, 'a solemn compact'. It argued that the British and Māori parties to the Treaty had entered into the agreement in good faith and that it was important that the Crown now took steps in acting towards its Māori partner with the utmost good faith by ensuring that Parliament did not act in ways inconsistent with the Treaty's principles. It also argued that the Crown should accept that the Treaty had created responsibilities for it that were 'analogous to fiduciary duties' and that its 'honour' was at stake in all its 'treaty relationships'. Finally, it declared that the responsibilities the Crown had undertaken to perform were not merely passive in nature but extended to the active protection of Māori in the use of their lands and waters.[19]

In essence, what the Court of Appeal did was in line with the way the common law usually works. It brought down a judgment that *created* precise legal rights but made them appear as though they had been *discovered* in the agreement of 1840. This would have baffled Ross in one sense, given the difficulty she had comprehending the language of lawyers, but it would have struck her as familiar in another, given that she had believed that the Treaty meant to each New Zealander whatever they wanted it to mean.[20]

Claudia Orange's Treaty of Waitangi

Shortly after the Court of Appeal delivered its judgment in *New Zealand Maori Council v Attorney-General*, Claudia Orange put the finishing touches to her now famous book, *The Treaty of Waitangi*. It was a major historical study and came to be read widely.[21] She became *the* Treaty historian in the eyes of the public and has remained so ever since.

Like so many of the historians who have written about the Treaty, Orange was drawn to it, consciously or unconsciously, by forces that were deeply personal in nature. Her father, Monty Bell, had worked in Maori Affairs and Māori regularly came to the house to mull over matters with him. As a young teenager in the early 1950s she witnessed a local council trying to evict Ngāti Whātua from Auckland's Bastion Point as well as her father's helplessness in the face of it, both of which she found upsetting, perhaps even traumatic. (Many years later Ngāti Whātua would be among the first to take a case to the Waitangi Tribunal.)[22]

Orange's work on the Treaty warrants careful examination for reasons that extend beyond its influence. The first thing to note is that between the early and the mid-1980s small but significant changes took place in the way she read Ross's article and interpreted the Treaty. Of all the figures discussed in this part of the book, no one engaged with Ross's article as deeply as Orange did and her account was profoundly influenced by it. Despite or perhaps because of this, few of the major figures at this time rejected as many of Ross's arguments as she came to do. The changes in Orange's reading of Ross's article and her own interpretation of the Treaty can be charted by comparing her 1980 journal article, her doctoral thesis of 1984, and her book of 1987 that was based on that dissertation. The comparison alerts us to the degree to which the new legal and political discourses that were at work in New Zealand during this time had an impact on her work.

In both her thesis and her book Orange made little reference to Ross's major argument about ambiguity, confusion and chaos, unlike those historians who had discussed or drawn on Ross's article in the 1970s, which included herself in her 1980 'The Covenant of Kohimarama' (see pp. 110). For example, she never quoted Ross's scathing appraisal of the Treaty that the cartoonist Brockie had referenced. In large part, this change in the way she received Ross's article occurred because the changing times demanded a different kind of account from the one Ross and other historians had provided since the late 1960s. Ross, Ian Wards, Alan Ward, Peter Adams and Tony Simpson had all attacked the prevailing myth about the Treaty. They had also told a story in which the British and Pākehā New Zealanders were the principal historical actors (though Ross had done otherwise in her *Te Tiriti o Waitangi*). When Orange began her research in 1977 these historians' critical angle on the Treaty influenced her approach, so much so that she reckoned that a consideration of the myth was one of the major themes of her thesis. But she soon came to believe that a much less critical take was required and she jettisoned that theme, so much so that the word 'myth' disappeared from her account as she sought to address a larger and broader audience in her book.[23]

But even while she was working on her thesis, the political changes that were occurring prompted her to adopt a different stance from the one she held when she began work on it. As public expectations about the Treaty were heightened by an increase in official recognition and a rise in Māori protest, she became troubled by the growing divergence between Pākehā and Māori attitudes. This led her to take the long Māori struggle for a degree of autonomy in New Zealand as one of her two major themes. She hoped that by recovering that history her fellow Pākehā would acquire an appreciation of the perspective many Māori had on the Treaty and that this would minimise the increasing conflict between the two peoples. Slowly but surely, then, the fulcrum in her work shifted from *critical history* to *monumental history* (to use Nietzsche's terms again).[24]

In this context Orange became more interested in adopting and adapting Ross's minor argument on the primacy of the Māori text than previously. This was the launching pad for her consideration of Māori perspectives of the Treaty, both at the time it was signed and in the years that followed. But the degree to which her account was indebted to Ross's article faded from view with the passing of time, though those such as Keith Sorrenson, who was one of her PhD supervisors, remained cognisant of the fact. Patricide and matricide are common among scholars. Typically, as they work on a project for a long time, they tend to lose sight of how much their interpretation owes to the scholars who preceded them, even, or perhaps especially, if they come to reject their findings. Orange seemed to forget how much she owed Ross. In her thesis she did not acknowledge the help that Ross (who had died by the time Orange completed it) gave her. And as she turned it into a book, not only was there no such acknowledgement but many of the overt traces of the influence that Ross's minor argument had exerted on her interpretation disappeared because the kind of historiographical discussion that marks a thesis was removed from the text and even from the endnotes as well.[25]

What I have just described occurred in part because Orange's interpretation of the texts started to depart from Ross's at the same time as it followed a logic implicit in it. She began to argue that *the* most important difference in meaning between the two texts concerned the question of whether the transfer of sovereignty from Māori to the Crown had been made clear to the chiefs. Furthermore, she diverged from Ross by arguing that the Crown had not only undertaken to safeguard Māori land and other possessions but to uphold their authority or control over them. While Ross had suggested that the *chiefs* might have assumed that this was what they had been guaranteed, she did not argue that this was how the *British* parties to the treaty-making understood the Treaty. This subtle change in interpretation has had a profound influence on the way that the Treaty has been understood ever since.

At the same time, Orange became critical of Ross's argument about texts and translations in a way she had not been in her article 'The Covenant of Kohimarama'. This also saw her argument depart from Ross's. Whereas Ross had emphasised that the Treaty was ambiguous and contradictory, Orange now sought to play this down. In her article and thesis she had not flinched from acknowledging this aspect of the Treaty, but in her book she barely referred to it, thereby minimising the divergence of opinion and discord over the Treaty in recent times. Moreover, while she continued to accept Ross's contention that the differences between the texts caused a good deal of confusion, her explanation for those differences, and consequently the differences between Māori and the British understanding of the Treaty's terms, diverged in one important respect. Whereas Ross was inclined to draw into question whether the translators and the British agents who had sought to persuade Māori to sign had behaved in an honourable fashion, Orange came to minimise the possibility that they had not. She omitted from her book the words she had used in her thesis in this context, such as 'misleading', 'misrepresentation' and 'deception'. And she rewrote several passages. For example, in her thesis she stated: 'That no effort was made [by the missionaries to use a word that better conveyed the meaning of sovereignty than "kawanatanga"] suggests that the treaty translation was deliberately made obscure and ambiguous in order to achieve the desired end of securing British sovereignty.'

In her book, she recast this passage so it read: 'The choice of terms by Williams may not have been accidental, of course. It is possible that he chose an obscure and ambiguous wording in order to secure Maori agreement, *believing (as did most missionaries at the time) that Maori welfare would be best served under British sovereignty.*'[26]

How do we account for this divergence between Ross's and Orange's accounts? We can continue our consideration of this question by noting that Orange made the Crown's dealings in relation to the Treaty between 1840 and the present day one of the two major themes of her thesis and that she placed even more emphasis on this theme in her book, so much so that it became central to the storyline that threads its way through the book. This amounted to a new constitutional history of the New Zealand nation state that went as follows. The foundations of the New Zealand nation state are to be seen as lying in the Treaty of Waitangi that was created in both an English- and a Māori-language text. It was an agreement made in good faith by both parties, and it was a binding legal contract whereby Māori agreed to cede sovereignty to the Crown and the Crown agreed to protect te tino rangatiratanga, or the full exercise of Maori chieftainship over their lands and other property. The Crown repeatedly breached the Treaty and committed many wrongs, but Māori have repeatedly asserted their rights under it and sought to remind the New Zealand state of those rights. Now that the Crown has realised that it acted unjustly — because it is becoming familiar with the story of the Treaty that is now being told by several players — it can recognise the rights of Māori that were guaranteed to them by the Treaty and make reparation for their wrongful neglect, thereby putting an end to racial conflict and redeeming New Zealand as a nation.[27]

This argument required a historical account that had several elements that differed from Ross's. While it could allow for some degree of confusion in the making of the Treaty, it had to represent the agreement as sufficiently coherent, rather than fundamentally ambiguous and contradictory, so that both the parties could be said to have a mutual understanding of its terms and the Treaty could be thereby regarded as a binding contract. It also had to figure the Crown as a body that had generally acted in an honourable manner at the time the Treaty was made.

The growing differences between Orange's and Ross's accounts owed a good deal to the differences that had taken place in political discourses since Ross had published her article and Orange had embarked on her research. Talk about both *rights* and *sovereignty* had burgeoned in New Zealand, as in other settler societies. In Orange's thesis and her book, they became her key conceptual words and drove much of her argument.[28] Consequently, she, like political and legal advocates, turned the Treaty of Waitangi into a treaty that was said to recognise special rights and more particularly indigenous rights.[29] Furthermore, her overarching narrative, the traces of which can be glimpsed in her thesis but which became prominent in the book, came to mirror the one told by legal bodies in the early to mid-1980s. Orange had familiarised herself with all the Tribunal reports that were produced at that time, read the findings in an important High Court case of 1986 (*Te Weehi v Regional Fisheries Officer*) in which the Treaty figured, and had provided an affidavit in the Court of Appeal case. In turn, her work influenced the Tribunal.[30]

In all probability the differences between Orange's and Ross's accounts owed something to the fact that Orange's book was published by a trade publisher, rather than an academic one. At this time trade publishers were more attuned to the public life of history than were academic publishers. Moreover, the editor who oversaw the publication of Orange's book — Bridget Williams — was committed to producing scholarly research in an accessible form.[31]

As Orange turned her thesis into a book, she shed several of the most important contentions she had previously made about the history of the Treaty after its signing. She abandoned an argument that was consistent with one of the observations Ross had made in concluding her article: 'the Treaty of Waitangi says whatever we want it to say'. Orange had argued in her thesis that not only the British and Pākehā New Zealanders but Māori as well had 'tended to make use of the treaty . . . to further what they considered to be legitimate interests and to validate assumed rights'. No such observation appears in her book. In other words, while in her thesis she had acknowledged the way in which the Treaty had long been a matter of *politics* among Māori, in revising it for publication she treated this point as though it was an inconvenient truth.[32]

Orange came to find a closely related argument problematic: that the way both Pākehā and Māori had used the Treaty in political debate varied over time. At one point she had remarked in her thesis: 'This was an obvious case of Maori about-face in appealing to the treaty to legitimate a course of action. And it was by no means an isolated instance.' At another point, she had noted that there had been 'repeated re-assessment and re-interpretation [of the treaty] by both races, for Europeans *and* Maori have continued to give the treaty new meanings and to infuse into it aspirations for which originally it was never intended'. Neither of these observations ended up in the book (though there was a vague reference to 'new aspirations [giving] the treaty fresh meanings'). If they had remained, they would have undermined an argument she now wanted to make: that continuity in Māori understandings of the Treaty over time was greater than the changes that had occurred. In the same vein, Orange now played down the degree to which Māori *interest* in the Treaty had fluctuated over time.[33]

Another important way in which Orange's account diverged from Ross's and that of other contemporary historians concerned the Treaty's legal status. Her account came to be informed by the legal scholarship that began to be published in the early 1970s. Ross could make neither head nor tail of this research and concluded that historians and lawyers spoke a different language. But Orange took the work of lawyers on board and was inclined to assign enormous *historical* authority to these interpreters of the Treaty's legal meaning and implications, going so far as to describe the pertinent legal scholars as experts, even though none of them had any training in the discipline of history and two of them were undergraduate students.[34] This was a sign of things to come. Moreover, one of the ways in which Orange distinguished her work from that of Ross and other historians rested on a claim that they had neglected to give serious consideration to the role the law had played in the making of the Treaty[35] and that this had led to serious weaknesses in their understanding of the Treaty.[36]

Orange's point of departure in this regard was her contention that the Treaty was a legally valid and binding agreement. This dictated many of her arguments. She pointed out that the making of treaties was by no means unusual, whereas Ross and all other historians had treated the Treaty as though it was peculiar to New Zealand. She suggested that the British government had believed that the making of a treaty was required *legally*, whereas Adams had argued that it was an indispensable *political* preliminary. She contended that the primary purpose of the British government in making the Treaty was *legal* whereas Adams argued that its principal reason for doing so was *diplomatic*. Finally, whereas Ross and Adams had drawn into question the contention by Thomas Buick that the Treaty constituted the legal grounds upon which the British Crown had assumed sovereignty, Orange implied that the imperial government took the position that the Crown had acquired sovereignty precisely by way of the Treaty. She held to this position even though she conceded that Hobson had claimed sovereignty over the South Island on the basis of the legal doctrine of discovery, she acknowledged that there were shortcomings in what she called the Treaty negotiations, and she noted that the legal status of the Treaty in 1840 was unclear.[37]

The differences between Orange's account of the Treaty's legal status and the accounts of Ross, Adams and others sharpened as she revised her thesis for publication. In the thesis her treatment of the way in which the British government had regarded New Zealand's legal status and thus that of Māori, both before and after the making of the Treaty, was tentative. In the book this was no longer the case, and only some of the evidence that she had provided of the ambiguous way the British government had treated this matter was retained. Two examples must suffice to illustrate this point. In her book Orange omitted part of a sentence that had read 'the legal interpretation placed on the treaty itself by officials in England and in New Zealand is by no means clear' and replaced it with this passage: '[Colonial Secretary Viscount] Normanby's instructions recognised New Zealand as a "sovereign and independent state" but at the same time expressed grave doubts about Maori capacity to govern. Yet Normanby, like his predecessor Glenelg and his successor Lord John Russell, admitted that British sovereignty was to be established by cession. All three Secretaries of State for Colonies in 1840, then, appear to have regarded the treaty as a valid [legal] treaty of cession (despite later arguments to the contrary which continue to the present).' Second, Orange omitted this sentence: 'Both Hobson and Normanby were aware . . . that Maori independence or sovereignty, although recognised by Britain, was not strictly speaking cognisable in international law.'[38]

As Orange attributed more importance to the role that British law had played in the making of the Treaty, another important change occurred: the attention she had paid to Māori history diminished. This is apparent in several respects. In her thesis she had noted the moments in which Māori oral tradition had attributed significance (in the sense of both meaning and importance) to the Declaration of Independence in the years after it was signed, and she had taken care to distinguish between this and the significance Māori had given to it earlier, when it was made. But in her book the fact that Māori attributed different meanings to the Declaration at different periods of times went unremarked on. In other words, she removed from her text evidence that she had previously adduced that brought into question the historical basis upon which the Declaration was coming to be understood in contemporary New Zealand by Māori advocates and their supporters as an expression of Māori sovereignty.[39]

In her thesis Orange had been careful to distinguish between the meanings that Māori attributed to the Treaty and what the Treaty might be said to have meant to both the parties to it, but in her book she collapsed the two. Furthermore, while in her thesis she had paid considerable attention to the fact that Māori iwi had held different views of the Treaty, both at the time it was made and in the decades that followed, she did not do this in the book, with the result that Māori views tended to be represented as though they were uniform. Moreover, in discussing some of the ways that many Māori had remembered the Treaty, Orange had noted in her thesis that these had been encouraged by Europeans, but in the book she implied that there was a more or less autonomous Māori discourse about it.[40]

Finally, in discussing the way that Māori had understood the Treaty over time, in her thesis Orange had stressed that they had cast the agreement as a covenant in a religious sense; that they believed it had been forged on the basis of a special relationship between the Crown and their people; and that they regarded the Treaty primarily as a protective instrument. In other words, Orange had stressed the degree to which Māori regarded the Treaty as an agreement whose binds were religious, moral and personal in nature and so a matter of relationships. But in her book she placed less emphasis on this line of argument and even omitted parts of it in favour of presenting the Treaty as a legal agreement and a treaty of rights.[41]

In summary, a careful reading of Orange's thesis and book testifies to the degree to which political and legal discourses had come to influence the manner in which Ross's article was received and the Treaty was represented by its leading historian. Orange made changes to her argument in ways that were subtle but which nonetheless had implications for the way the Treaty was to be understood. As a result, her book became a powerful instrument for change in the public realm at the same time as a good deal of the historical richness of her thesis can be said to have been lost.

Paul McHugh, the law and the Treaty

In the same year that Claudia Orange published her book about the Treaty, the New Zealand legal scholar Paul McHugh (1958–) completed a doctoral thesis at Sidney Sussex College, the University of Cambridge, entitled 'The Aboriginal Rights of the New Zealand Maori at Common Law'. Whereas most of the legal scholars whom Orange had relied on in her account had undertaken only a modicum of research and produced short accounts of legal matters relating to the Treaty, McHugh's thesis rested on a deep excavation of the relevant historical record and provided a long exposition of his findings, some of which concerned the Treaty.[42] He can also be said to have a personal relationship to the Treaty. At least one member of his family had connections with the work of the Waitangi Tribunal, and by the time he had completed his thesis he had already published several papers about contemporary aspects of aboriginal property rights that had been drawn on by the Tribunal and the courts in New Zealand.[43]

In both his thesis and a book that he wrote a few years later, *The Māori Magna Carta*, which was not so much a work of legal history but rather a work of contemporary law, McHugh read Ross's article in the manner that had become increasingly common. Indeed, he probably attributed more importance to her contentions about the texts and translations than any of the main players at this time. On the opening page of his book he declared: 'There were, for a start, two versions of the Treaty: an English and a Māori version, with important differences between the two texts. This alone tells us that there may be outstanding issues of interpretation in relation to the Treaty of Waitangi.' Moreover, he adopted her interpretation of the Māori text — or at least the way it had been received by the Tribunal — and declared it to be authoritative. He made no reference to her major argument as it was contrary to his overall interpretation of the Treaty and ran counter to his attempt to restore it to its status as a Magna Carta. McHugh's treatment of the Treaty would have baffled Ross, not least because in his hands it assumed the guise of a legal charter rather than the moral one that had been so important in her day.[44]

The account that McHugh provided in his thesis of the making of the Treaty differed from that of earlier scholars, legal and historical alike, in several ways. He focused on the legal norms that existed at the time the British Crown tried to assume sovereignty in New Zealand and the historical process by which he believed sovereignty had been acquired, whereas historians tended to focus on the latter at the cost of understanding the former and legal scholars tended to neglect both.

He also sought to isolate the relevant legal principles at work by examining the larger and longer imperial context in which the British had formed relations with local or indigenous peoples, whereas historians and legal scholars had been inclined to neglect this past and assume that New Zealand had been annexed in a legal or constitutional vacuum.

McHugh argued that there were certain well-established principles that determined how the British Crown had established authority over non-Christian societies since the sixteenth century. He insisted that the Crown had long recognised that these societies had some juridical status and argued that the Treaty was regarded by the Crown as a legal prerequisite for assuming sovereignty in New Zealand. This meant that acquiring the consent of an indigenous people was not merely the result of some moral imperative, notwithstanding the fact that this legal requirement was unenforceable in English courts. He argued, moreover, that it was clear that the Crown *had* considered the Treaty to be a valid instrument of cession, even going so far as to contend that it was an example par excellence of a legal principle that the consent of tribal people was a prerequisite to the exercise of sovereignty over any territory, asserting that Hobson's proclamations of 21 May 1840 were no denial of that principle but simply an authoritative statement that this formal requirement had been met. Finally, he argued that the Treaty's guarantee of Māori customary law and their title to land should be regarded not so much as the source of their rights but a declaration of rules that had been recognised by the common law and, hence, that which would have applied in any event. In his book McHugh repeated these contentions; he made the same arguments about the Māori text as the Tribunal had done based on its reading of Ross's account; and he noted the same legal principles for interpreting bilingual treaties that the Tribunal had invoked. Consequently, he argued that the Treaty provided a yardstick by which the treatment of Māori could be measured.[45]

Styled as a work of legal history, McHugh's thesis had a profound impact on the way New Zealand historians approached and interpreted the Treaty in the next ten or more years, as did the law more generally. Before we consider this matter, though, it should be noted that the way in which the Treaty was being interpreted by the Tribunal, the courts and legal scholars like McHugh was by no means the only way in which lawyers were interpreting it. Shortly before the publication of McHugh's book, an Auckland legal practitioner, Guy Chapman, made a comprehensive attack on the story of the Treaty that the law had been telling, dismissing it as a myth in the common sense of that word — that is, as a falsehood. He drew on Ross's article, though, not surprisingly, he only invoked her major argument.[46]

Chapman's intervention was an expression of the depth of anxiety that many Pākehā were, not surprisingly, beginning to feel: the Treaty and the history of New Zealand more generally was being interpreted anew; the basis upon which rights and privileges were being accorded was changing; the cultural and political position of

Māori in the nation was being transformed; and relationships of power between Māori, Pākehā and the New Zealand state were shifting. All of these changes presented a challenge to Pākehā's sense of themselves and seemed in the eyes of many to threaten their place in the country. In the 1990s the place the Treaty now had in New Zealand's legal, cultural and political order was increasingly subject to attack by a handful or so of writers, most notably Stuart C. Scott in his *The Travesty of Waitangi: Towards Anarchy*. They gave voice, often in a hyperbolic fashion, to the dismay, alarm and resentment that many Pākehā were feeling about the changes taking place, and which these authors claimed were based on the abuse of history. In the following decade the leader of the conservative National Party Don Brash launched an assault on the Treaty along much the same lines and for many of the same reasons, as he sought to launch a kind of culture war that was more common across the Tasman. Scott cited Ross's major argument as the most authoritative source for his historical account of the Treaty, and part of what Brash said echoed the oft-quoted words in her article, though he does not appear to have been familiar with it.[47]

Keith Sorrenson, the Tribunal and the Treaty

The changes in the way that historians read Ross's article and the way they interpreted the Treaty in turn in the 1980s and 1990s is writ large in writings other than Claudia Orange's. I am now going to discuss just one of those historians — M. P. K. (Keith) Sorrenson (1932–) — to illustrate and explain this phenomenon.[48] I have chosen his writings for several reasons. He was one of the most senior New Zealand historians writing about the Treaty at the time and so had a good deal of authority. His writings, for the most part, were not the result of any historical research that he had conducted, and they shed an unusually large amount of light on the influence that was being exerted by the work that was being done by the other players. Finally, all but one of the essays he wrote at this time were prepared for an audience other than academic historians, which means that they do much to reveal the public life that history was having in regard to the Treaty.[49]

Sorrenson has noted that his work took a new turn in 1986 when he was appointed as one of the Waitangi Tribunal's members, first as a deputy member but subsequently as a full member. Yet one might doubt whether this did mark a fundamental departure in his life as a historian. He had long played a role in New Zealand public life: he had been a prominent member of CARE (Citizens Association for Racial Equality) and was a passionate opponent of the All Blacks touring South Africa and New Zealand hosting the Springboks; and most of the books he had written were aimed at audiences other than an academic one.[50]

Sorrenson's appointment to the Tribunal occurred after it was granted retrospective powers to investigate claims about breaches of the Treaty dating back to its signing in 1840, which was a power that Matiu Rata had sought for the body originally. In these circumstances, the Tribunal assumed that it required the expertise of an academic historian and realised that Sorrenson would be ideal, given the research he had carried out previously on the alienation of Māori land. His involvement with the Tribunal brought him into contact with two of the most powerful strands of storytelling that were at work in regard to the Treaty — those of the law and Māori history — though he was already familiar with the latter as he had grown up hearing stories about the loss of his mother's Māori land and this had played a role in his choosing to do his first substantial piece of historical research (in the mid-1950s) on the alienation of Māori land. This said, only a decade earlier, at the point Orange had expressed a wish to undertake her PhD on the history of the Treaty, he had been sceptical that there was anything much new to be said about the subject. The fact that he became a convert to Treaty history — as we can call work such as Orange's — is testimony to the changes that were occurring in New Zealand in a short period of time.[51]

In joining the Tribunal, Sorrenson sat alongside Eddie Durie and the other members on its panels, attended its hearings, and contributed to its reports. In hearing Māori claimants give testimony, he became reacquainted with stories told in the oral tradition in which the past became alive and even seemed to be relived. In listening to the stories kaumātua told about the past and its relationship to the present, he formed the opinion that there were essentially two histories in New Zealand: the Māori and the Pākehā. He also came to learn of the work of legal scholars, most importantly McHugh's doctoral thesis. But perhaps the most profound influence on him was the way in which the Tribunal itself, under Durie's leadership, was seeking to apply the 'principles' of the Treaty, which entailed telling a story in a mode that, like those of Māori oral tradition and legal scholarship, diverged from that told by the practitioners of the discipline of history. As he became more involved in the Tribunal's work, the way Sorrenson approached, interpreted and understood the Treaty gradually changed, as did the way he read Ross's article. He came to regard it as a very important piece of work, variously describing it as 'superb', 'seminal' and a 'landmark'. These shifts are evident in the essays he wrote over the next six years.[52]

Sorrenson penned the first of them in 1986, 'Maori Representation in Parliament', shortly after he became a member of the Tribunal. At this time, one of the ways he read Ross's article had much in common with the way other academic historians had received it in the period immediately after it was published: he noted her major argument and quoted her famous 'concluding' words. But he made more of her argument about the texts and translations as he became interested in the way Māori understood the Treaty and the way the Tribunal was interpreting it. This led him to claim, in much the same fashion as Ross had done, that the Māori Treaty sheets were 'the real Treaties of Waitangi'. This was in stark contrast to the way he seems to have read her article many years earlier, when he was the associate editor of the *New Zealand Journal of History*. Now, he attributed great importance to the fact that there were two versions of the Treaty, asserting that the differences between them was 'the source of a larger difference between Maori and Pakeha that has been accumulating since the Treaty was signed'.[53]

The second essay was penned by Sorrenson in 1987, entitled 'Towards a Radical Interpretation of New Zealand History: The Role of the Waitangi Tribunal'. It was the most important of any he wrote about the Treaty because it was the one most widely read; it was eventually published three times, in various versions.[54] By the time he wrote the first version he had become very familiar with the Tribunal's work. In it he sought to draw the attention of other scholars to the radical new interpretation of the Treaty that had emerged as the result of the work of historians (especially but not only Ross), legal scholars (particularly McHugh) and the Tribunal itself in its reports discussed earlier in this chapter. Most obviously, he sought to lend his personal authority to the ways the Tribunal was interpreting the Treaty.

He began by emphasising the basic points that Ross had made. But his purpose in doing so was at odds with hers. He had no interest in arguing that the differences between the Treaty's two texts were so great that they rendered it useless as a foundational document and so he made no reference to her major argument, let alone quoted the famous passage near the end of her article. Instead, he wanted to draw attention to some of the differences between the two texts because he believed they could provide the basis for what he called 'the coexistence of two peoples within one nation'.[55]

Sorrenson's purpose meant that he interpreted the Treaty's second article in a way that seemed to follow the logic of Ross's argument but drew out implications that diverged from the ones she had drawn in her article. For example, he asserted, like Orange, that because the chiefs' 'rangatiratanga o o ratou wenua o ratou kainga me o ratou taonga' had been 'expressly preserved' in the Treaty, this meant that it constituted not just 'a guarantee of their possession of land and other properties' but 'a guarantee of their autonomy and authority, above all their mana, as chiefs'. He also heightened the significance of the Treaty's two texts by asserting that 'two histories of the Treaty' stemmed from them. It was by no means clear what he meant, but in time other historians would put some flesh on the bones of this claim.[56]

After noting that Orange's soon-to-be published book asserted that the Treaty had long been important for both races in New Zealand and that she had recovered much of its 'submerged Maori history', Sorrenson observed that the work historians had done in recent times had been paralleled by that of legal scholars; he named those whose work has been referenced here (Auburn, McKean, McHugh and Williams); he noted that some of these scholars had not been content to rely on the English text but had focused on the Māori one instead; and he pointed out that their work had helped to resuscitate the Treaty as a legal entity.[57]

Sorrenson devoted most of his attention, however, to the work of the Tribunal itself. His purpose was twofold. First, he wanted to point out that it had assumed a vital role in the interpretation of the Treaty, and he wished to legitimise this development. To this end, he emphasised that Parliament had given the Tribunal the exclusive authority to interpret the Treaty, to do so in reference to both the language texts, and to decide issues raised by the differences between them. In making this point Sorrenson made no reference to the fact that the Tribunal had *chosen* to assume these powers, though he knew that Durie had had an enormous influence on its work. Most importantly, he claimed that the Tribunal was interpreting the history of the Treaty in ways that were in keeping with what he called the historical traditions of both sides: Māori oral tradition on the one hand, and academic history and legal scholarship on the other. Strikingly, he provided no evidence that this was the case as far as academic history was concerned.[58]

In a third essay Sorrenson wrote three years later, 'Giving Better Effect to the Treaty: Some Thoughts for 1990', he repeated many of the arguments he had made in his previous two essays but with a couple of subtle differences. He emphasised the importance of the argument Ross had originally made about the Treaty's two texts, even though she had never made the precise claims he now advanced, contending that the differences between the two texts — or what he again called the two treaties — were important because they were 'the source of alternative Pakeha and Maori historical traditions that lie at the heart of [New Zealand's] race relations'. Further, he asserted that there had not only been fundamental conflict between Pākehā and Māori over interpretation of the Treaty but that at the heart of this conflict were matters that sprang from the fact that there were two texts. More generally, he went further than he had done previously by adopting a contention that the law had been making, namely that the Treaty was 'not intended as a finite contract' but rather as 'the foundation for a developing social contract'.[59]

In his fourth essay, also written in 1990, 'Treaties in British Colonial Policy: Precedents for Waitangi', Sorrenson worked in a more conventional historical mode, taking the past as his focus. In doing so he revealed more sharply the degree to which his historical interpretation had diverged from the one he had previously held. This is so because he made clear that the new legal scholarship about indigenous people, especially that of McHugh,[60] had influenced his historical approach to the Treaty. He argued that it had been common practice since the fifteenth century for European nations to make treaties with non-Christian societies; that in later centuries they had few qualms about negotiating them with tribal societies; that these treaties were regarded as binding in international law; and that there was an imperial policy pertaining to this matter. All this meant, he contended, that there was nothing unusual about the Treaty, except for its Māori text. He pointed out the similarities between it and the treaties the British had made in the period immediately prior to 1840, noting that an agreement made between the British and Sherbro people of West Africa in 1825 had three articles that were virtually identical to those of the English version of the Treaty. Likewise, he pointed out the way in which North American precedents had ensured that the Treaty included a clause granting the Crown the right of pre-emption. In concluding, he took one of Ross's main points — that the Māori text was *the* Treaty — to suggest that this gave the Treaty its distinctive quality — and that New Zealanders had yet to come to terms with this fact.[61]

We have now seen how the status of the Treaty was transformed during the 1980s as several figures — the Waitangi Tribunal, the courts, Māori advocates, legal scholars and academic historians — told a new story about the Treaty, based largely on the way they had read or received Ross's article. We have noted that they did their work in several different modes: legal or quasi-legal rulings, legal scholarship, oral tradition and scholarly history. We have observed that major change occurred in the way that academic historians approached and interpreted the Treaty in the context of the shifts that took place in legal and political discourse about the rights of indigenous people.

For the most part we can do little more than guess what Ross would have made of these changes. She would have been amazed by the phenomenal rise in the Treaty's status and nonplussed that this had resulted from the fashioning of a new myth about it. She would likely have been astonished by the nature of reparative work promised by the findings and recommendations of the Tribunal and the courts, and while she would undoubtedly have welcomed this she might have been troubled as she would probably have preferred redistribution on the ground that people in need should be accorded the same rights and privileges as others in need. She would probably have been dumbstruck by the fact that her article, or rather the way it had come to be read, had played an important role in these changes. And, at the very least, she might have been ambivalent about the role that the discipline of history had played in the making of the new story about the Treaty and the change in the Treaty's fortunes.

PART 3

History

Chapter 6
Politics, Public History and Juridical History

By the end of the 1980s important questions were beginning to be raised about the story being told about the Treaty, especially by the Tribunal. Was it history? If so, what was its nature? These kinds of questions expanded during the 1990s and beyond. What might a good history of the Treaty comprise? On what grounds could or should this be determined? Even more profound questions came in their wake. How does one determine what is historically true? Is the kind of knowledge that the discipline of history creates a force for good? Was the history that was being told about the Treaty good for New Zealand, and what was the future of democracy in New Zealand, or even that of the nation itself? Clearly, the stakes involved in nearly all these questions were high, just as they remain so. Some of these questions would have been familiar to Ruth Ross; others would not have been, so much did New Zealand and the public, cloistered and private lives of history change in the decades after she died.

As with the telling of the new story about the Treaty, the discussions and debates that took place about it involved several main figures: the historians of political thought Andrew Sharp and J. G. A. Pocock; the historians Alan Ward, Michael Belgrave and W. H. Oliver; and the legal scholar turned historian Paul McHugh.[1] The positions they took were influenced by their situation or, in colloquial terms, where they were coming from, which was in turn shaped by a series of factors that included their disciplinary training, the nature of their employment, and their place of residence. Consequently, analysis of the questions that were thrown up by the new story about the Treaty, and attribution of the responsibility for it, varied between these players, though like those figures discussed earlier in this book most of them were in dialogue with one another. And as political and legal circumstances surrounding the Treaty, and the way Treaty claims were tackled, changed, so too did the positions of most of these protagonists.

In this chapter my focus is primarily on the debates that occurred about the nature of the stories that were being told about the Treaty in the context of the Tribunal's work in the 1990s — what can be called Tribunal history. In the chapter that follows, I focus on the shifts that occurred among scholars during the following two decades in the historical interpretation of the Treaty — what we can call Treaty history.

The public, politics and the present

Andrew Sharp (1940–) was among the first scholars to raise questions about the nature of the current historical discourse surrounding the Treaty. In his 1990 book *Justice and the Māori* he drew attention to a simple but profound fact: the questions being raised were pre-eminently contemporary, public and political in nature.[2] When academics with expertise about the Treaty made public pronouncements about its historical meaning, he pointed out, they were talking as much about present-day political arrangements concerning authority and rights to land as they were about the past meanings of the Treaty. In making this point he referred to the writings of Hugh Kawharu, Claudia Orange, David Williams and Ranginui Walker, but he probably had those of Paul McHugh and Keith Sorrenson in mind as well. These scholars, he argued, did not take the Māori text to be the more important and the one more worth following solely on legal grounds, but because it was more in accordance with their notions of justice. He was not passing comment on the quality of their scholarship, merely noting that when they made pronouncements about the Treaty they were making arguments that had been articulated in the world of Māori–Pākehā politics in recent times, and that they had done so either alongside or in connection with the Waitangi Tribunal.[3]

Sharp, as well as making these observations about the role that several historical figures had been playing in discussion and debate about the Treaty, sought to intervene in it. He suggested that there were fundamental difficulties in the way that the Tribunal was interpreting the Treaty. Considering the meaning of what had come to be regarded as its key words — 'kawanatanga', 'taonga' and 'te tino rangatiratanga' — he argued that no single interpretation could be given of what the Treaty meant, either in the past or the present: because it was a document in two languages, its meanings were multivalent in nature, and it was a potent symbol. In other words,

Sharp was pointing out that the Tribunal was trying to present a single understanding of a document that was simply not amenable to that kind of treatment.[4]

Sharp argued that the Tribunal faced particular difficulties in representing the Treaty in the way it had been doing. The main one arose, he argued, because it was seeking to find *strict* rights where it was unlikely they could be found. (These are the kind of rights that some people have — in this case Māori — because they correlate with duties that others have — in this case the Crown.) He argued that this brought into question the persuasiveness of the findings that the Tribunal had made about breaches of the rights of Māori by the Crown. In his view much of the Tribunal's interpretation ran counter to the rules of both legal and historical interpretation: the contents of any historical document like the Treaty are to be understood not just in terms of the linguistic usage of the time but also the meaning it had in the minds of those who created or received it. He was willing to accept that some of the ways the Tribunal was now interpreting the terms of the Treaty mirrored and extended long-standing Māori understanding of them, but he doubted whether this reflected how Pākehā had understood those terms in the past. Sharp argued that the Tribunal tended to reach findings that conflated and thereby confused present-day purposes with historical ones, and to render one-dimensional what had once been multidimensional. All this, as he observed, was in the service of rectifying injustice. 'Modern standards of what was right and wrong, just and unjust, were [being] read back into the intentions of the Treaty's signatories, and into the meaning of what they said.'[5]

There was, Sharp hastened to observe, nothing unusual in much of what the Tribunal was doing: 'European history is full of attempts to reconstruct the past to provide a guide for the present.' Nevertheless, he pointed out, there was a problem in any such reconstruction because there were undeniable differences between what had been the case in the past and what was now wanted in the future. This meant that it was evident that the Tribunal's reconstructions of the past were anachronistic; that is, it was attributing to the past, concepts or categories that could never have existed at that time. It was unlikely, moreover, that a reconstruction of the Treaty that was faithful to what *had* been the case in the past would provide a useable history. But this was the very kind of history that was required if the Treaty was to serve the moral, political and legal purposes of the Tribunal and the other players.[6]

In considering Sharp's intervention it is important to note that while he saw himself as a historian, he was a member of a department of political studies (at the University of Auckland). He had been a student and a colleague of Pocock's at the University of Canterbury when he was Professor of Political Science and had gone on to do his doctorate at the University of Cambridge where his tutor was Peter Laslett, an intellectual historian turned philosopher (and later demographer). He counted W. H. (Bill) Oliver, Keith Sinclair and Judith Binney among his friends but knew that most New Zealand historians cast him as some kind of exotic practitioner of history, as he was more interested in ideas rather than events in the past. He was not unduly troubled that many historians were telling a new kind of story about the Treaty, regarding this as normal and right. But he *was* disturbed by talk of competing sovereignties that the new Treaty story could harbour, and he sought a sounder basis for the justification of the special treatment of Māori than the one being provided by most of the main protagonists, believing that this was more likely to be found in contemporary theories of justice rather than in any interpretation of the past.[7]

By the time Sharp made his observations about the Treaty, some academic historians had become uneasy about the role that members of their profession had started to play since the Tribunal had been granted the power to hear claims about breaches of the Treaty dating back to 1840. This change in the nature of the Tribunal's jurisdiction, which took place in 1985, meant that the claims process required the telling of stories that were much more historical in nature than had previously been the case. And since a vast written archive existed due to the fact that the British Crown or the New Zealand government had mostly acquired land through some legal instrument or another (rather than by conquest or theft), and because claims to the Tribunal had to be made by reference to the law as it was in the past rather than some abstract notion of justice, the expertise of academically trained historians was now required to research and analyse that historical record, which contributed to a surge in public agencies employing historians, the first since the days of the Historical Branch for whom Ross had worked. By the same token, the role that Māori oral tradition played in the Tribunal's work declined.

Alan Ward, the Tribunal and public history

In the same year that Sharp's *Justice and the Māori* was published, the academic historian Alan Ward offered to the *New Zealand Journal of History* a paper he had presented the previous year in the Department of History at the University of Auckland. In this article he reflected on the role that professional historians like himself had been playing over the last three or so years in an inquiry that had been prompted by a claim Ngāi Tahu had presented to the Tribunal. This was the first of a long series of investigations into historical breaches of the Treaty that surpassed in scale and complexity every case the Tribunal had previously heard. Ward had become involved after Eddie Durie had asked him to advise the Tribunal in these hearings.[8]

As a professional historian, Ward's take on what was happening historically speaking was necessarily different from Sharp's. He was concerned that responsibility was being thrown onto the shoulders of historians in circumstances in which the matters at stake were of great and immediate importance — to the Māori claimants, those likely to be affected by their claims, and the nation at large. He believed that he and the team of historians he led were taking their responsibilities seriously, but he was apprehensive that they might be tackling their work with an undue degree of confidence. As well as being a senior figure in his profession, Ward was alert to the potential problems that arose when historians undertook work for a public body — what was coming to be called *public history*.[9] Like Ross, Ward had been a student of Beaglehole's, and throughout his career as an academic historian, most of which he spent in Australia, he had been involved in areas of public life in which the past was a lively presence. At the same time, he had repeatedly been troubled by the tensions between the responsibilities he believed he had assumed as a historian and those he felt as a citizen. (As with any historian, the private life of history rather than just the public life of history almost certainly played a role in both these regards.)[10]

Ward became worried about the role historians were playing in the Tribunal's work for several reasons. As they were being commissioned to work for a public body other than a university, they were required to undertake research in accordance with the agenda of some party or another in the Tribunal's claims process, rather than one of their own choosing, thereby undermining their independence. At the very least, historians were being called on to provide historical accounts that dealt with the Treaty as though it had been central to the past they were considering; at most they were being required to produce accounts that advanced the claims of the party that employed them, most obviously in cases where that party was a Māori claimant.[11]

Ward believed that the work that historians were performing in this context made it necessary for his discipline to grapple with questions about history as a particular kind of knowledge. 'The historical profession [in New Zealand] might reasonably take stock of what the concerned historians are doing', he suggested. He observed that historians were obliged from time to time to reflect on the nature of their discipline, its methods of research and theoretical standpoints, and the relationship between its modes of interpretation and those of other disciplines, but that this was especially the case in this situation. Ward was seeking the help of his fellow historians, and he must have been disappointed when it was not forthcoming.[12]

Ward had become aware that in the context of the claims process that lay at the heart of the Tribunal's task, historians and lawyers often went about their work in very different ways. Lawyers tended to claim that the facts of the past could be established quite easily, and that facts and interpretation could be readily distinguished from one another; historians were inclined to think that facts were slippery by nature and not strictly separable from interpretation. More than this, legal counsel was asking historians to accept as fact what the historians knew was not fact, and to report on the meaning of actions in the past that historians could not readily determine, even on the basis of what the lawyers were calling the balance of probability. In short, the law was demanding of history what its practitioners did not feel they could provide, thereby placing them in what Ross would have called a damned awkward position. This was especially so because all these historians were sympathetic to the claims the Māori claimants were making.[13]

At the heart of these difficulties lay the matter of historical objectivity. This was preying on Ward's mind, partly because the consensus among historians around the world about this crucial matter was collapsing in the wake of the rise of what was called post-modernism. He noted that an American historian, Peter Novick, had recently published a magisterial study about the objectivity question in which he had characterised that consensus in these terms: 'The assumptions on which [the idea of historical objectivity] rests include a commitment to the reality of the past, and to truth as correspondence to that reality; a sharp separation between knower and known, [and] between fact and value ... Historical facts are seen as prior to and independent of interpretation: the value of an interpretation is judged by how well it accounts for the facts; if contradicted by the facts, it must be abandoned. Truth is one, not perspectival.' Novick also remarked: 'The objective historian's role is that of a neutral, or disinterested, judge; it must never degenerate into that of advocate ... The historian's conclusions are expected to display the standard judicial qualities of balance and evenhandedness ... [T]hese qualities are guarded by the insulation of the historical profession from social pressure or political influence, and by the individual historian avoiding partisanship or bias ... Objectivity is held to be gravely at risk when history is written for utilitarian purposes.' (These were the conventions Ross had broken in producing her finest work on the Treaty, *Te Tiriti o Waitangi*, as we noted earlier.)[14]

As both Novick and Ward observed, the ideal of historical objectivity was now being challenged inside the academic cloister, to say nothing of outside it. There had long been historians who asserted that the writing of history was informed by the concerns of the present and who argued that historians constructed the past in the light of those concerns. But this 'relativist position', as it was called by its critics, had acquired more adherents in recent times. Furthermore, growing importance was being attached to 'relativism' in the political claims that were being made on behalf of indigenous and other such peoples on the grounds of culture, race or religion. As a historian and a democrat, Ward found this disturbing: 'If we say, from an absolutist relativist point of view, that all cultural perceptions and valuations are equally valid, that there is no one single truth, that there are as many truth claims as there are participants according to their different cultural backgrounds and perceptions, does this not mean that we are doomed to talk past each other in perpetuity?'[15]

In the context of the Tribunal's work, this was evidently a problem, argued Ward. 'Different cultural perceptions, couched in different languages, increase the possibility of different understandings of the same events.' In pointing out how this was occurring, he observed that professional historians and Māori were presenting stories that relied on different kinds of historical sources. In the case of the professional historian, it was sources that were created in writing at the time of the events that were under consideration; in the case of Māori, it was those sources that were created orally at some time distant from those events.[16] To illustrate the problem this was causing, he told a story about an incident that had occurred during the Ngāi Tahu hearings. According to an oral tradition of Ngāi Tahu, in the 1830s the British navy had enabled the Ngāti Toa chief Te Rauparaha and his men to launch a devastating attack on their ancestors. During the formal presentation of the historical evidence that Ward had been commissioned to compile for the Tribunal, one of the Tribunal's members, Bishop Manu Bennett, had tried to put this story on the historical record. Ward objected on the grounds that the written historical record revealed that this oral tradition was wrong: Te Rauparaha had been brought down on a commercial vessel, and the Crown, after learning of the murder and mayhem that had taken place, had in fact tried to prosecute the ship's captain as an accomplice to the killings. In retelling his story about this incident at the Tribunal several years later, Ward remarked: 'This is an example where the documentary evidence [invoked by himself as the professional historian] was important and outweighed the cultural memory [of Māori], sincerely held though it was.' As Ward recognised, what he was describing was a clash between two different ways of establishing historical truth. For historians, nearly all of whom were Pākehā, something they called historical facts was fundamental to this enterprise; for Māori they were not.[17]

Ward and his team of historians set about trying to tackle the questions of fact, evidence and interpretation that were being thrown up by the Tribunal's work. They did so by developing a series of principles that were in keeping with the emphasis that academic historians typically place on critical assessment of both historical sources and later accounts of the past. Ward suggested that historians working for the Tribunal or one of the parties involved in the claims process needed to keep in mind what he called basic distinctions between three different levels of reality. He argued that it was possible to determine matters of historical fact such as 'whether Te Rauparaha was taken southward in a naval or merchant ship'; 'to identify, with some precision, the various understandings that contemporary actors [i.e. those at the time] had of the events in which they participated', and here he presumably had in mind those who tried to prosecute the ship's captain; and 'to show how later generations perceived those same events and the changing meanings and values they attached to them', and here we can assume he had present-day Ngāi Tahu in mind. In doing this, Ward demonstrated that he was willing to acknowledge that Māori had different ways of understanding the past, but he disclosed that he was holding firm to a belief that history was a superior way of representing the past.[18]

At another point in the article I have been discussing, Ward posed this vitally important question: 'What can the historical profession say about the *relationship* between the lived past of, say, the 1840s, the various memories of that decade among Maori and Pakeha New Zealanders, and our current reappraisals of those events?' But he did not pursue it, presumably because he realised that it raised issues about the role that the present and the subjectivity of the historian play in the life of history that he felt were too difficult to deal with.[19]

He did, however, suggest how historians might best proceed in the situation he was describing, drawing on Novick's discussion of the recent work of a fellow American historian, Dominick LaCapra. LaCapra accepted that historians should continue to try to resolve questions about the intentions of historical actors in the past and the meanings of the statements they made, but argued that this was insufficient. A good history, he argued, should open up new avenues of inquiry and self-reflection as well as invite counter-argument. Ward suggested it would be good if both Pākehā and Māori interlocutors could follow this advice, claiming that this would enable them to consider the issues at stake from a variety of standpoints and come to terms with themselves and each other. But he realised this was asking a good deal, not least because the Tribunal's procedures were largely adversarial in nature. Besides, what he was really saying was that *Māori* needed to take heed of this advice more than Pākehā did.[20]

In 1996 Ward published an essay in which he repeated most of the arguments he had made in his 1990 article. But by this time his concern about the differences between the ways Māori on the one hand and Pākehā historians on the other were recounting stories about the past had increased. He was troubled that some Māori as well as anthropologists like Anne Salmond were claiming that Māori and Pākehā belonged to worlds that had 'wholly distinct epistemologies'. Consequently, he mounted a full-blooded defence of history against what he saw as a rising tide of relativist claims around the world, as did many historians at this time. He was particularly critical of those accounts of a people's past that were being told by one of their number — what he called 'insider history' — on the grounds that they were inevitably selective and thus partial. He had also become more critical of accounts that rested on memory — including those belonging to oral tradition — on the grounds that they were subject to change over time and so were unreliable about what had happened in the past in question. He now described these accounts as myth — that is, stories that seek to convey meanings and insights that (in his words) were 'only partly true or not true at all, in terms of detailed correspondence to the complexities of the lived past when tested against the evidence'. He called these accounts 'bad history' and claimed that they were driving out good history.[21]

In these circumstances Ward insisted that there was a need for history as it was practised by outsiders like himself. To allow the accounts of insiders to remain unscrutinised would be dangerous as it would imply that their relativistic views were being condoned. In his opinion, this was akin to bestowing 'truth-value to the racial myths of Romantic Germany and the Nazis, or those of any other bunch of butchers who peddle their one-eyed views of history to mobilise their folk and dominate others'. As far as he was concerned, not only the future of history was at stake but that of democracy as well. 'The danger of post-modernism and other relativistic theories of knowledge is that a reluctance to subject the myths and one-eyed histories of subject [i.e. insider] groups to critical scrutiny, along with the myths and one-eyed histories of imperialists, becomes nihilistic and lets in the lies of the fanatics', he warned. 'Freedom does indeed depend on intellectual vigilance and a willingness to be critical, to demand that all interpretations be subject to the test of consistency with the weight of evidence.' Ward was doing what many historians are inclined to do — treating history and memory (whether in the form of oral tradition or myth) as binary opposites, valorising history as the realm of enlightened reason and disparaging memory as the realm of mystification and irrationality.[22]

Andrew Sharp, juridical history and constitutional histories

In the mid-1990s Andrew Sharp returned to some of the questions he had raised several years earlier, aware of the unease that Alan Ward felt about the role that professional historians were being called on to play in the Tribunal's work. As a result, he formed the view that much of what he and Ward had been talking about amounted to a particular way of thinking, speaking and writing about the past that could be distinguished from that of academic history. He gave this a name: 'juridical history'.[23]

Sharp devoted two essays — one published in 1997, another in 2001 — to a consideration of this kind of history. His purpose was to describe it, account for why it had emerged in New Zealand at this time, and explain why its operations presented difficulties to professional historians. He had no interest in criticising it as a way of doing history. His point of departure comprised an important observation: that the past is not history and history is not the past. Instead, history is a story that a historian — which he used in a loose sense to include anyone who tells stories about the past — chooses to tell. He pointed out that the nature of the story a historian decides to tell is influenced by their present, and so, as the present changes, so too does the story they tell. This means that while there is only one past there can be and are many stories — histories if you like — about it over time. He went on to suggest that in the case of those who attempt to tell stories about the past by way of disciplined description, explanation and evaluation, there can be two kinds of bad history. One basically tells a story about the past so poorly that it obscures its meaning for the present. (We might call this, following Nietzsche again, 'antiquarian history', though academic history is often guilty of this weakness, too.) The other kind — which is the one Sharp was concerned with — is told mostly by those who are immersed in contemporary debates and who claim the past in question is simple and knowable when it is neither.[24]

The example of the latter kind that Sharp had in mind was 'juridical history'. He defined it as 'a mode of representing the past so as to make it available to legal or quasi-legal judgement in the present'. To his way of thinking, it tended to be a collective enterprise. 'Judges, and the historians who are subject to their judgment, have a common interest in jointly seeking to discover the rules, principles and authoritative judgments in the past that are applicable to the case at issue. And all share a common interest in seeking to focus their histories only on those doings and sufferings which can be brought under those rules, principles and authoritative judgments.' In doing juridical history, the storyteller is at the service of legal judgment and thus in the position of an inferior appealing to superior authority. This meant two things, he pointed out. The storytellers present their stories in a particular way to attain a favourable judgment; and the stories they tell must be *presentist* — that is, designed from a present-day perspective to address current problems. Not surprisingly, then, in his opinion the practice of juridical history often results in what looks like history but does not really amount to history at all.[25]

Sharp pointed out that juridical history has had a lengthy past, but he was only interested in explaining how it was working in reference to the Tribunal and the Treaty. Before doing this, though, he explained how those in the position of a judge or their equivalent (such as the chair of a legal commission like the Waitangi Tribunal) typically go about their work. Judges seek to enforce the just and proper arrangement of legal rights, responsibilities, property and authority as well as all manner of other relationships among people and between people and things. In cases in which they examine acts and omissions in the past, their purpose is to find among them the ones that have constituted present-day just and proper relationships and to discern the principles that helped to establish and authorise them. In considering those relationships, judges might realise, as plaintiffs tend to argue, that they are not currently in place, and it is their job to attend to any discrepancy between the just and proper relationships that were authorised in the past and their distortion in the present. In doing so, one ideal that judges might bear in mind is that of restoring the parties to a rightful relationship that was once established — in this case by the Treaty — but has subsequently been destroyed by unauthorised and destructive acts or omissions that have taken place since — in this case what were deemed to be breaches of the Treaty. In this situation judges generally look back in time to discover what are *commissives*: those acts or omissions that have either rightly constructed or wrongly distorted present-day law. It is these acts and omissions and their current force in the law that are of most interest to them.[26]

In the 1980s and the 1990s, Sharp pointed out, the law in New Zealand had come to regard the Treaty as the 'great commissive' of the just and proper relationship between Māori and the Crown. This was the case with the Tribunal, he contended, because it was required by its governing legislation to justify its recommendations by reference to past 'acts and omissions' and the 'principles' of the Treaty. This meant that the stories told to and by the Tribunal (as well as the courts) had to do one or more of the following to emphasise the legal significance of what had happened. They had to interpret the actions and events of the past as ones that fell under the principles of the Treaty and proceed on the assumption that it had established a just and proper relationship between Māori and the Crown, and more particularly that the Crown had entered into particular legal obligations. The Tribunal also had to describe those actions and events in such a way as to enable the answering of questions about whether rights were violated, duties (such as the one to protect) were discharged, responsibilities attended to or treated with negligence, and whether the relationship of trust between the Crown and Māori had been sustained. More generally, the stories told to the Tribunal had to establish whether the sovereign (the Crown) in certain acts or omissions had encroached on te tino rangatiratanga in breach of the contract of the Treaty which guaranteed it. It also had to portray the parties — the Crown and Māori — as agents who had legal continuity and to demonstrate that their past acts and omissions were of continuing legal relevance.[27]

Sharp argued that it was these requirements that created difficulties for historians. Three in particular caused them unease, he suggested. It is a common belief among historians that they should be free from any obligation to others, that they are obliged only to provide a historical account that is true to the past, and that they write as equals to those to whom their accounts are addressed. Consequently, they are reluctant to recognise the truth claims that other parties make on grounds that are based on some form of authority other than the discipline of history. Furthermore, historians usually want to consider the multiplicity of meanings that are inherent in historical events. As a result, they prefer to produce accounts that are complex, rather than seeking a single thread of meaning in any past event. Finally, the discipline of history privileges a form of knowledge that is rooted in a belief that what things mean to people, what things they value and what actions they are capable of conceiving, let alone undertaking, are always relative or particular to a certain moment. Consequently, historians feel impelled to pinpoint the differences that arise across time more than they are inclined to trace continuity, let alone suggest uniformity, contrary to what the law is prone to do.[28]

As well as explaining why professional historians were finding it difficult to practise their craft in the context of the Tribunal's claims process, Sharp pointed out that they had continued to produce accounts that met its requirements. He cited the example of Ward, who, having expressed his unease at the beginning of the 1990s about the demands the Tribunal was placing on him and his colleagues, had turned around and undertaken with relish a three-volume historical overview for the Tribunal that was a good example of juridical history. Sharp observed that Ward was not ashamed to say in a book in which he summarised the findings of his overview that the future of New Zealand depended on the general acceptance and resolution of Treaty claims and that the purpose of his book was to show the scale of the task and the progress that had been made towards that goal so far.[29]

In his 2001 essay Sharp suggested that in the 1990s several players, especially some Māori, were now tending to adopt another kind of approach to the past — an approach he called 'constitutional histories'. To his mind, these were histories that were more radical, both politically and intellectually, than juridical history. They did not appeal, as it were, to a judge in a settled system of rules and principles. Instead, asserting that they had never lost or ceded sovereignty, their narrators proclaimed a right to both produce their own histories and be their own judges of them. Consequently, they drew into question not only the authority of the state, but the authority of the discipline of history as well.[30]

Paul McHugh and Whig history

Among the scholars who considered the nature of the history that the main players were telling about the Treaty in the 1980s and 1990s, Sharp was not the only one whose position or orientation lay largely in departments or disciplines other than those of history. In the mid-1990s the legal scholar Paul McHugh experienced a historical turn, so much so that he came to regard himself, and to be regarded, as a legal historian rather than a lawyer. He later recalled how this had happened. 'The germ was planted by a comment after my PhD dissertation defence in January 1987. "Well, you've convinced me," the internal examiner said, "but I am not sure that it happened." The penny took a little while to drop. When it did, I realised that what was working as an argument [that I had made] for rights arising from common-law aboriginal title in the present-day New Zealand legal system was not necessarily a depiction of actual historical experience.' In other words, McHugh's interlocutor was suggesting that an account of the past that makes sense and is convincing in *legal* terms does not necessarily constitute *historical* truth. McHugh soon came to agree with this important point. But, like Sharp, he was primarily interested in describing and accounting for the way in which stories were being told in the context of the contemporary discussion and debate about indigenous rights generally and the Treaty specifically. At the same time, he came to be a practitioner of the Cambridge school of history, one of the founders of which was J. G. A. Pocock. It holds that what happened in the past is best understood in terms of the historical conditions and more especially the intellectual context of a given historical era and insists that conventional methods of interpretation often distort the meaning of past texts and ideas by reading them in the light of present-day understandings of social, cultural and political life.[31]

Here, I will consider two of the articles McHugh wrote at this time. In the first, called 'The Common-Law Status of Colonies and Aboriginal "Rights": How Lawyers and Historians Treat the Past', he argued that lawyers and historians had long recognised that their purposes differed. The lawyer, or at least the lawyer engaged in the common law, is 'concerned with problem-solving in the present' and looks to the past for 'normative guidance' into a world that *is* and in search for the authority of precedent, while historians are concerned with 'problem-solving in the past' and questions about what *was*. Yet, having made this point, he argued that what mattered most was not so much the professional calling of the lawyer and the historian but 'the *attitude* one brought towards the use of the past'.[32]

McHugh proceeded to argue, on the basis of his reading of a famous essay by an English political philosopher, Michael Oakeshott, that three such attitudes could be identified: the 'practical', the 'scientific', and the 'contemplative'.[33] Only the 'practical' and 'scientific' concerned McHugh. He pointed out that Oakeshott had argued that someone with a practical attitude to the past is 'interested in and recognises only those past events which [they] can relate to present-day activities'. This means they tend to read the past backwards, 'look[ing] to the past to explain his present world, to justify it, or to make it a more habitable and a less mysterious place'. With such an attitude, the past consists only 'of happenings recognised to be contributory or non-contributory to a subsequent condition of things, or to be friendly or hostile to a desired condition of things'. Oakeshott gave lawyers as an example of this practical attitude and in due course McHugh would cite the Tribunal as an exponent of this kind of attitude to the past. By contrast, on the basis of his reading of Oakeshott, he pointed out that a scientific attitude 'dealt "not with past events in relation to ourselves and to the habitableness of the world, but in respect of their independence of ourselves"'. This was '"history", properly speaking', or what we can call academic history.[34]

McHugh went on to argue that Oakeshott's identification of a practical attitude towards the past recalled the Cambridge historian Herbert Butterfield's renowned argument in his 1931 book *The Whig Interpretation of History*. His principal point here was that Whig or Whiggish history took a presentist attitude or approach to the past, which he defined as a form of history that 'saw the past entirely through the lenses of the present'. He then went on to note that a Danish political philosopher, Jens Bartelson, had recently described Whig history as 'the characteristic genre of presentist historiography' and argued that it usually took two forms. Bartelson had noted that one begins 'by taking an institution or an idea from the present together with the contemporary role, function or purpose presently used to justify that institution or idea, and then describes its historical development *as if* this purpose or role had governed its emergence and transformation from its origin onwards'. In the other, it 'deals with something that is absent in or remote from the present ... by accounting for that institution or practice in categories totally foreign to [the past], *as if* these understandings [or categories] ideally *should* have been available to the past ... while neglecting the categories used by the agents in that past to describe themselves and their own practices and institutions'. McHugh pointed out that in the current context of indigenous peoples making claims in British settler societies such as Australia, Canada and New Zealand for the land they had lost, *both* lawyers and historians were involved in an activity that called for the adoption of a practical attitude to the past and so were interpreting it through the lens of the present, but that they were more particularly adopting an approach in keeping with the operations of Whig history as Bartelson had described them.[35]

In his article, which began life as a paper for a conference of legal scholars in Canada and was published in a Canadian legal journal, McHugh went on to demonstrate that in settler societies a particular institution — the common law — was currently using the past in a practical manner and adopting a Whiggish approach to provide authority for a particular idea (or doctrine) — aboriginal rights, and more specifically aboriginal title to land. He pointed out that this was fulfilling an important purpose as it was enabling the law to protect or uphold indigenous peoples' rights of property in land. But he argued that the history of the common law and aboriginal rights was being neglected (which was a history that he devoted most of his article to recovering). The doctrine of aboriginal title to land was being projected back into the past and as a result it was being depicted not merely as a measure (or a concept or category as Bartelson would have it) that had been introduced only recently but also one that had been invoked in the past. In short, what McHugh was doing was providing a highly critical commentary on his own earlier writings, which had been drawn on by the Tribunal and the courts in New Zealand in the 1980s.[36]

In concluding this article McHugh made two other remarks, one in parentheses and the other in passing. He observed that the way the common lawyer was using the past might be entirely legitimate as far as the law was concerned, but he doubted that it was legitimate for a professional historian. Having said this though, he argued that the account that the common lawyer — himself really in his earlier guise — had given of aboriginal title did not purport to be a properly historical account of the past. While McHugh was correct in saying that the common lawyer had made no explicit claim to being true to the past in providing their account of aboriginal title or the Treaty, it is doubtful that those unfamiliar with the way the law works had understood that this was the case. Historians such as Keith Sorrenson had been treating the studies of legal scholars like those McHugh had written in the 1980s as though they *were* historical accounts of the past, failing to either realise or acknowledge, as Ross had done many years earlier, that the law and history often speak very different languages.

By mistaking legal scholarship for legal history, the likes of Sorrenson had either misunderstood what the common lawyers and the Tribunal were doing, or were willing to accept it because of the outcomes they promised for the future advantage of Māori specifically and New Zealand more generally. In due course McHugh would spell out that there was a fundamental difference between the legal advocate as historian and the historian as advocate, in the sense that the former was more permissible than the latter, and that this meant that historians were more likely to run into trouble in their disciplinary circles than legal scholars were in theirs.[37]

The second of McHugh's articles, 'Law, History and the Treaty of Waitangi', appeared in a special issue of the *New Zealand Journal of History* produced in 1997 in honour of Keith Sorrenson on his retirement from the Department of History at the University of Auckland. It was explicitly concerned with the way in which stories were being told about the Treaty. Like Sharp, McHugh pointed out that this was a context in which history was a politically charged exercise and so one in which 'the pressure to service the needs of the present is felt as strongly as any inclination towards preservation of the integrity of the past'. More specifically, he pointed out that the law had become 'the dominant idiom of discourse' in the historical work that was being done, despite, or rather because of, lawyers having a 'scant sense of history' in the sense that it is conceived and practised by academic historians.[38]

McHugh focused on a particular kind of history-making: one that told a story about the constitutional basis of the New Zealand state's claim to sovereignty so as to help legitimise its authority. He sought to demonstrate the ways in which several figures — historians, the Tribunal and the courts (but not himself as a legal scholar though he *had* been one of those players) — had been adopting a practical attitude to the past. He argued that in the mid to late 1980s history, loosely defined, had become the primary means for providing a new(ish) legal account of the origins of the New Zealand state in a context in which the traditional historical and legal accounts of this were no longer regarded as tenable because they marginalised Māori. He argued that this was the case because legal scholars, such as F. M. (Jock) Brookfield, had been unable to provide a 'historically-validated account' of the matter. To be more precise, he argued that historians had performed the work that was required and that they had done so by adopting a Whiggish approach to the past.[39]

McHugh pointed out that the account of the constitution of the New Zealand state that historians now provided attributed to the Treaty a foundational role. They were arguing that the state's beginnings lay in the Treaty as an act of consent or more particularly as a contract, by which the chiefs had ceded sovereignty to the Crown in return for it undertaking to protect kāwanatanga and te tino rangatiratanga and guarantee their taonga that included their rights of possession. McHugh noted that the Tribunal had adopted this 'contractarian account' but suggested that the most remarkable example of it was Claudia Orange's *The Treaty of Waitangi*. Having claimed that the foundations of the New Zealand state lay in the Treaty that she figured as a contract, Orange had set about telling a story in which she measured the performance of the Crown in reference to it, drew attention to its breaches, and called on it to make amends for those historic wrongs.[40]

In the final part of this article McHugh proceeded to make an argument about the nature of the histories that had been told about and around the Treaty since the late 1980s. This was an argument that resembled Sharp's account of constitutional histories. He observed that as the sovereignty of the New Zealand state was increasingly drawn into question, and as settling of Māori claims to land by political means had become more important than the settlement of them through legal mechanisms, the way that relations between the Crown and Māori were being conceptualised by the executive and the judiciary in New Zealand had shifted from being 'vertical' to being 'horizontal'. In other words, a few years earlier the New Zealand state was being represented as the absolute sovereign and Māori as rights-bearing subjects or citizens of that state, and sovereignty was portrayed as something that was unitary, undivided and unlimited; but now the state (or the Crown) and Māori were being figured as partners, and sovereignty was being portrayed as something that could be dual, divided and limited. In these circumstances, McHugh argued, the Whig history that Orange had told no longer sufficed. What was required was a history that was attuned to the contingent nature of national life and emphasised the importance of co-existence, dialogue and negotiation.[41]

McHugh argued that this was most likely to be met by Māori history, or more specifically Māori tribal history, rather than conventional academic history. This was the case because Māori tribal history had a robust sense of the opportunistic nature of political life and could grasp the importance of competition for and conflict over authority and power in ways that Whiggish histories could not because they were concerned with normative principles, idealistic policies and the like. McHugh discerned among some recent historical work the seeds of a newly emergent historiography of the kind that he believed was needed.[42]

W. H. Oliver and the Tribunal's use and abuse of history

In the same year that the second of McHugh's articles appeared, one of New Zealand's most eminent historians, W. H. (Bill) Oliver (1925–2015), published an article about the kind of story he believed the Tribunal had been telling. His account had some similarities to Sharp's and McHugh's critiques, but as a professional historian he was concerned to criticise this storytelling rather than merely characterise it.

He was well equipped to do this work. Since the beginning of the 1990s he had been involved in the Tribunal's work. He had been commissioned to produce a small book summarising the claims the Tribunal had received and the major reports it had produced; he had been engaged by the Crown Forestry Rental Trust (the major employer of historians doing work on Treaty claims) to report on the submissions for and against the Muriwhenua claim (which covered the large geographical expanse of the far north where Ross had lived and worked for many years); he had appeared before the Tribunal as a witness in two claims; he had been part of a research team that worked on one claim; and he had penned critical reviews for a popular magazine, one of which comprised an article reviewing the Tribunal's Muriwhenua report.[43]

Oliver began that article by noting that the Tribunal was making a sustained effort to interpret New Zealand history in a way that placed the Māori experience and memory at its centre.[44] Like nearly all the historians involved in the work of the Tribunal, he had no problem with this or the government policies and practices that ran alongside it. He welcomed the Tribunal's work as a means of redressing the injustices of the past. But, like Ward, he was concerned that the Tribunal was telling a story that was unsustainable from the point of view of the academic historian. In the Muriwhenua case the claimants had declared that all the transactions of land their ancestors had entered into with Pākehā before 1865 were understood by them merely as conditional grants of the right to use that land, or what they called 'tuku whenua', rather than irrevocable transfers of ownership. To be able to demonstrate that breaches of the Treaty had occurred, they had to deny that they had knowingly sold land, and to do this they had to claim that Māori concepts of land ownership had not changed since the beginning of British colonisation. Oliver regarded this position — that relied on the idea of 'tuku whenua' rather than 'sale' — as contentious and believed that it could be readily contested. Before the Tribunal hearings had begun, he had done just that after he had been asked by the Crown Forestry Rental Trust to read over the evidence that was to be presented by the claimants and advise whether he thought a sufficient case had been made. He had been unimpressed by the argument they wanted to mount as he believed the historical evidence did not show that their forebears had leased rather than sold their land and so he was concerned that they would be unable to convince the Tribunal. Consequently, he had advised them to abandon their tuku whenua position and adopt a very different argument — that it was massive acquisitions of land by the Crown, which had often been effected by dubious means and sometimes by fraudulent ones, that had been primarily responsible for the dispossession and subsequent impoverishment of Muriwhenua Māori — believing, quite rightly, that this argument did not suffer from the same evidentiary problems. But the claimants rejected his advice and the Tribunal ruled that there had been no genuine sales of land, even making this finding the main part of its indictment of the Crown.[45]

In discussing the Tribunal's report in his review, Oliver was reluctant to express his reservations about this outcome. Instead, he noted that while all the major arguments in favour of the tuku whenua position had been contested during the Tribunal's hearings, this had not been done exhaustively; he raised questions about those arguments in order to point out that they revealed problems that had not been discussed at any great length by historians and anthropologists; and he suggested that what had happened merely constituted a valuable starting point for discussion of the matter under investigation. Most of all, he expressed concern that the Tribunal had made a premature pronouncement in emphatic terms and that this overreaching weakened a good case for remedy.[46]

Shortly after he wrote this review, Oliver began to have more doubts about the kind of story the Tribunal required, which included the obligation to always find that the Crown was in the wrong. In particular, he started to be troubled by what he saw as the Tribunal's anachronistic treatment of the way the New Zealand state had acted in the past. He had included a brief discussion of this point in a report he had recently prepared for one of the claims submitted to the Tribunal, but he took it up at length in an essay Paul McHugh and Andrew Sharp invited him to contribute to a collection of essays they and Pocock had conceived about the uses of the past in the context of the debate about the Treaty, which was published in 2001 as *Histories, Power and Loss*. Of all the discussions of the Tribunal's historical approach, Oliver's essay was the one most widely read by New Zealand historians. Critics of Tribunal and Treaty history, such as Oliver's former colleague at Massey University, Kerry Howe, welcomed it on the grounds that Oliver was expressing publicly the doubts that many historians had been voicing in private for many years; but many of the historians closely connected to the Tribunal were dismayed by it.[47]

Unlike McHugh, Oliver believed that the Tribunal *was* making historical arguments rather than just legal ones. '[A]nyone who gives an account of the past is in the business of historiography, and never more so than when not intending to be', he argued. 'The Tribunal is too important a producer of historical writing for its own silence [about what it is doing in this respect] to be allowed to prevail.' Whereas ten years earlier he had thought the Tribunal's use of history amounted to a valid activity, he no longer thought this was the case. He contended that the Tribunal had 'a historical mentality' that was 'less concerned to recapture past reality than to embody present aspiration'. He hastened to point out that its presentism did not arise from a post-modernist approach to history — that is, one that was sceptical that there was any such thing as historical reality. Nonetheless, he suggested that its reports were 'Janus-like' because they looked to the past and the future simultaneously and exhibited 'a curious mix' of 'a commonsense respect' for the so-called historical evidence and 'an instrumental presentism' that was remarkably free of such evidence.[48]

Oliver was critical of the fact that the Tribunal was producing reports that went beyond a description of the past sufferings of Māori to the provision of what amounted to a kind of counter-factual history — that is, a history that constructs a past that did not happen but which might have done if circumstances had been different — that he believed was implausible. In this alternative account of the past, Oliver argued, the Tribunal depicted British colonisation as though it had been dependent on Māori consent and as if it could have led to a regime that was characterised by partnership, power-sharing and economic well-being for Māori rather than for Pākehā alone. In his view, the Tribunal's account of the past amounted to a 'retrospective utopia': 'This is the "future" [the Tribunal claims] that was promised in 1840 and, because the promise was subsequently broken, it is the "past" New Zealand did not have.' Unless a plausible alternative to what actually happened was provided by the Tribunal, he argued, it was merely pointing to something that it would have *preferred* to happen rather than something that might conceivably have happened, let alone one that did happen.[49]

Having made this contention, Oliver claimed that his purpose was merely to help reveal what the Tribunal was doing historically speaking: that 'it was *clearly* not writing history within the usual (if not universally observed) academic conventions'. But Oliver's position about this matter was contradictory: if it was *clear* what the Tribunal was doing, historically speaking, why was there any need for him to point this out? In fact it was by no means obvious to historians what the Tribunal was doing in this regard. It had taken Oliver himself a long time to acknowledge that the Tribunal was not representing the past in the way an academic historian would. Given his ambivalence about criticising this, it is hardly surprising that he was reluctant to pursue the contention he had made. Instead, he remarked that what the Tribunal was intending to do was 'something rather more *interesting*' than academic history. 'Interesting' is a word that we sometimes use when we do not want to be more pointed in our remarks. Nevertheless, Oliver did ask a crucial question — could the Tribunal have discharged its task by proceeding in a manner that was in keeping with the conventions of the discipline of history? — and he answered it by saying that it seemed 'reasonably safe to conclude that . . . its political effectiveness would have been severely curtailed' had it done so. This was a point Sharp had made ten years earlier.[50]

Like Ward and Sharp, Oliver had in mind two important differences between the way the Tribunal and academic history represented the past. The Tribunal's need to produce a useful history meant it was obliged to provide firm conclusions about the past whereas academic historians are more inclined to provide inconclusive, if enlightening, analyses. Further, the Tribunal's need to see the so-called historical facts in the context of the law and from a Māori perspective meant that those facts could be adjusted to its interpretive needs. Oliver noted that while the Tribunal's approach to historical context could be said to be historical in the sense that it was dealing with situations that occurred in the past, it was apparent that it did not treat them in the manner that an academic historian would, that is, seeking to understand those situations in the way the people of that past would have done. This meant, he believed, that it had an inadequate view of what constituted the reality of the past.[51]

Given his principal contention about the Tribunal's storytelling, Oliver might have concluded his essay by saying that the Tribunal was simply getting the past wrong — in other words that it was producing bad history — but he was reluctant to do so. He remarked instead that there was 'a more interesting possibility' (that word again) — that its way of putting the past to use derived from a dual intellectual ancestry: English common law and Māori tribal history. McHugh had made this point previously, but Oliver now made it more forcefully. 'Neither tradition is much concerned with the ways in which the past is unlike the present, so that in each the past and present can and do merge effortlessly into each other. Inevitably, then, each [account] lacks a sense of anachronism.' He pointed out that this way of representing the past amounted to present-minded history or Whig history. In the same vein he drew attention to the question that Sharp had raised but not pursued: whether doing 'juridical history' could really be said to be doing history at all. Once again, Oliver was reluctant to follow the logic of what he had been arguing, remarking instead: 'Clearly, neither McHugh's "common-law time" nor Sharp's "juridical history" are close to the kind of history that usually goes on in [scholarly] monographs and journals . . . [but] the concern here is not to deplore that characteristic as much as to place it.'[52]

Oliver proceeded to suggest that the Tribunal had not only been influenced by the ways that the law represented the past but the way in which history had long been done in what he called pre-industrial and pre-literate societies. This was a way of telling stories in which the differences between past, present and future time do not appear to exist, let alone matter. Māori, he argued, was an example of such a society. He argued that the Tribunal, in following suit, was 'not so much a matter of doing history as of defying it — of reasserting, to the point of reinventing, the evidences of continuity and denying the significance, if not quite the actuality, of change'.[53]

In concluding his essay Oliver made much the same observations as he made in his review of the Tribunal's Muriwhenua report: that while the Tribunal's way of doing history enabled it to arrive at emphatic conclusions that served a good purpose, this outcome was being achieved at the cost of diminishing its credibility. He would return to this point the following year in a memoir. The personal nature of this genre seems to have enabled him to express his concerns about Tribunal history more forcefully. He now made clear in no uncertain terms that he was troubled by the fact that few academic historians in New Zealand were paying any attention to the nature of the history that was being made by the Tribunal and the courts. He cited the *New Zealand Journal of History*, in which Ross's article had been published thirty years earlier, as an example, pointing out that it had given the matter scant attention. 'As a result,' he complained, 'the major context in which politics and history intersect lacks the benefit of public debate.' He proceeded to call for an analysis of what happens to history when it is pressed into service of a political process that is designed to achieve practical outcomes. He contended that this critique had to begin with an acknowledgement that it was neither surprising nor improper that history and politics should be acting together: 'It is not a matter of saying that this should not happen but of giving the results of the interaction the benefit of a stringently academic critique.'[54]

He argued that the history that was to be found in the Tribunal's reports was an extreme example of the political dimension that could be found in all historical work, and remarked that this had persuaded him that it was even more important to identify the nature of the politics behind the Tribunal's history-making and to be alive to the possibility that it was distorting the past. He cited a remark that the famous Marxist historian Eric Hobsbawm had recently made — 'It is essential for historians to defend the foundation of their discipline: the supremacy of evidence' — before reiterating that while he did not believe that politics had no place in history, 'its place must be kept under careful scrutiny'.[55]

Oliver went on to make clear that he believed that, while politics and history had previously co-existed in the Tribunal's work, a point had been reached in which politics had 'swallowed up its partner' and put an end to any dialogue between them. He was troubled by this because he was aware that some would ask: 'Why should people concerned with promoting social justice in the present be troubled by the possibility of getting a few things wrong about the past?' He thought this was a fair question and answered it like this: 'If it can be plausibly suggested that they [who enlist the past in seeking practical results in the present] have got the history wrong, and if they decline to consider the possibility that they have, they may end up looking as if they believe that any serviceable past will do. Their credibility is likely to suffer, not just as to opinions about the past but also as to aspirations for the future.'[56]

Oliver believed there were even bigger questions at stake: questions about the health of public debate and even that of the nation itself. He welcomed that there was now intense debate about what he called the dark side of the country's colonial past and noted that the Tribunal was at the heart of it; but he warned that there was a danger if it simply became a matter of 'one dogmatic assertion trying to stare down its opposite'. He believed that the historical profession had a role to perform in this debate on the basis that it could provide a more knowledgeable discussion of the matters at stake, thereby playing an adjudicating role in the disputes relating to the past that had arisen in the public domain.[57]

In closing the chapter in his memoirs in which he mainly discussed these matters, Oliver expressed another concern: that the claims process would continue to identify and exaggerate divisions in New Zealand society and thereby place the nation at risk. Consequently, he called for more attention to be given to a different kind of history. It would take as its starting point the interaction of two peoples occupying the same space and accept that the 'shared past' would 'continue to be disputed ground' but this recognition would be 'qualified by an acknowledgement that integration is also an unavoidable inheritance'. This was necessary, he argued, 'both for the well-being of the present and the integrity of the past'.[58]

J. G. A. Pocock, sovereignty and history

As Ward, Sharp, McHugh and Oliver were raising questions about the nature of the story that the Tribunal was telling about the past, J. G. A. (John) Pocock (1924–) was addressing questions about history as a form of knowledge that were arising around the Anglophone world. Its very nature — as a subject, a discourse, a form of thought, and a way of being in and acting in time — was being challenged, and he was better equipped to explore this matter than most historians. Educated at Canterbury University College and the University of Cambridge (where he was Butterfield's student), he was not only a historian of political ideas but also a historian of historical writing. He had already stimulated many of the ideas Sharp and McHugh had been pursuing and had organised a conference in which they and other scholars had discussed them. This led to *Histories, Power and Loss*, in which he had an essay that I am going to discuss shortly.[59]

Pocock is one of New Zealand's finest historians and almost certainly the one best known beyond its shores. Of all the historians — or at least the ones I have discussed so far — he was the one most able to distance himself from the issues at stake. He had been an expatriate since the mid-1960s, spending most of the time as a professor at Johns Hopkins University in the United States. That said, prior to his departure from New Zealand he had edited a small book, *The Maori and New Zealand Politics*, and had since maintained a passionate interest in New Zealand's history, culture and politics. Lately he had been struck by the fact that New Zealanders were living in interesting times and were discovering they had an interesting history. As a historian of seventeenth-century English political debates, especially during the civil war and the interregnum, he could not fail to find fascinating what was happening in New Zealand in regard to sovereignty, law and history. Like practically all the historians I am discussing, he not only sought to describe what was happening and diagnose the difficulties that had arisen; he suggested what he thought could or should be done to address them. Unlike most of those historians, though, he was interested in taking up and thinking through the big philosophical and political questions about New Zealand's future as a plural democracy that had been thrown up by the rise of the Treaty.[60]

Pocock's starting point was an assumption that if it is the mark of sovereign people such as Māori or a polity like New Zealand that it has the power to determine, or have a say in determining, what is to be its future, then this is also true in respect of its past. When two sovereigns make a treaty, each party brings to that moment, and retains afterwards, a history or a memory that recounts and justifies their sovereignty, and each of them has to continue to act in terms of the history of that sovereignty and to determine how its past is being interpreted if it is to survive as a self-affirming community.[61]

This meant that New Zealand not only found itself in a situation in which the state had chosen to acknowledge a past in which its sovereignty could be held to be conditional upon the performance of promises entailed by the Treaty; it also found itself in a situation in which there were two 'histories' at work, one Pākehā, the other Māori. This was the case not just in the sense that alternative accounts of the past were being told but also in the sense that different understandings of the very nature of 'history' were at work, and alternatives to history as a form of knowledge were being advanced by Māori. In short, this was a situation in which a struggle for power was taking place over whose way of doing 'history' would prevail.[62]

Pocock took issue with the main argument that Oliver had made in his essay in *Histories, Power and Loss*. He agreed that it was probably inexpedient to disregard the discipline of history to the point of claiming that those who had spoken in the past about the Treaty had meant something that it was historically impossible for them to have meant. Nevertheless, he contended that the attempt by historians to determine what a past statement, like the Treaty, meant is not altogether incompatible with a political or legal claim that such a statement can be interpreted in a certain way in the present — that it entails obligations to do things that were not done. He agreed with Oliver that one should not rewrite history, including that of the Treaty, exclusively as a record of how what was not done ought to have been done, and how what was done ought not to have been done, but he pointed out that by proceeding in this way it had been possible to recover knowledge about many of the injustices that had occurred.[63]

In other words, in Pocock's view it was important for New Zealand society to have the means of exploring the language that Pākehā had employed in the past to understand what the Treaty could have meant, what it was made to mean, and what it may be held to mean now. He acknowledged that there would be differences between what the historian says about past statements and actions and what the law (in the form of the Tribunal or the courts) thinks is just or expedient to say about them, but he argued that these differences may not be incompatible and that they are acceptable so long as they are recognised for what they are. He held that it was crucial to accept that the history of the Treaty — and of New Zealand more generally — was contestable and to try to live in or with that history.[64]

But how was this to be done? This question lay at the heart of Pocock's essay, just as it remains very much alive in New Zealand today. Realising that dealing with this conundrum was a very difficult task, he suggested that what was required was 'a treaty between histories', by which he meant a process of negotiation between the two sovereign powers and their different histories in the broadest sense of the word 'history'. In his essay he sought to explain why he believed such a treaty was required and what it would entail.[65]

Pocock emphasised that one needed to be cognisant of the fact that both 'sovereignty' and 'history' are European or Pākehā concepts. He realised that this point was now taken for granted in respect of 'sovereignty' (because of the attention that had been paid to the Māori text of the Treaty ever since Ross's work had been taken up in terms of her minor argument), but that there was much less awareness in regard to 'history'. Consequently, he sought to emphasise that it is a form of knowledge that is heavily imbued with Pākehā meanings, so much so that it might never be separated from them.[66]

He pointed out that Pākehā had long had several ways of doing history, which included common law history, Whig history and academic history, but that Māori had had, and continued to have, a conception of sovereignty that rested on a form of 'history' that had little in common with those Pākehā forms of historical knowledge. Most importantly perhaps, whereas the Europeans who came to New Zealand conceived of both sovereignty and history as things that were grounded in the appropriation of land, Māori affirmed, and were still affirming, that they had a relationship with land that was based on the linked concepts of mana and whenua, and told a story about their appropriation of that land by using oral tradition, whakapapa (genealogy) and myth.

Pocock noted that Pākehā do not necessarily find this Māori worldview hard to understand but that they find it difficult to enter into and relate to their own. He pointed out that many if not most Pākehā historians were inclined to say that this form of knowledge was not history in the sense that they used the word. In other words, he realised that New Zealand historians were using Pākehā conceptions and perceptions of history as the norm by which to understand and judge Māori conceptions and perceptions of the past, thereby placing their form of knowledge in a position of dominance. He accepted that it might be best to proceed in accordance with the Pākehā conception of history but he nonetheless argued that it was necessary to look for ways to resolve the problems that would arise accordingly, which included extending the meanings of history so that it allowed for Māori ways of doing and being in it.[67]

Pocock was aware that Māori were insisting on their right to adopt a particular form of knowledge. A Māori scholar, Te Maire Tau, had contended, in an essay reproduced in *Histories, Power and Loss*,[68] that what he called mātauranga Māori was an episteme designed to organise knowledge in a certain way and that it was one in which history, if this was the correct term, was at best no more than a part.[69] Tau was arguing that for Māori to reformulate this system of both knowledge and being as a series of statements about 'history' could destroy it, primarily because it ran the risk of subordinating their thinking to a Pākehā form of knowledge.[70] As Pocock noted,

Tau's argument was not dissimilar to the more radical contention that Linda Tuhiwai Smith and other Māori scholars had recently made: that history, anthropology and all disciplines that offered to examine a culture from outside were employed by those for whom knowing (or claiming to know) a culture is a means of ruling it.[71]

Pocock accepted that there was a hard core of truth in this contention. Consequently, he believed that the only remedy available was the establishment of a regime in which everyone was free to tell one another's history and enjoy the freedom to respond to that telling in ways that were critical. He was aware, though, that there was 'a sternly Pakeha view' associated with the name of a senior New Zealand historian, Peter Munz, and that Alan Ward had expressed it recently. This held that only a society in which every account of the past was exposed to interpretation, criticism and verification qualified as an open society, and that every community or culture in it had to accept that the story they told would be constantly subject to scrutiny by others and thus regarded as nothing more than provisional. Pocock was aware that the likes of Munz and Ward doubted that Māori were able or willing to meet this requirement, believing instead that the 'history' Māori told was intended only to maintain their culture and so was not history at all but myth. However, he believed that Pākehā had to consider whether or not the worldview of Māori *was* radically unlike history as a form of knowledge, and that in so doing they needed to hear and respond to what Māori were saying on the matter. In other words, they were not entitled to judge whether or not Māori were doing history. He realised that separating judgement from the authority to give judgement is no easy matter but pointed out that this was one of the reasons why a treaty between histories was required.[72]

The treaty (as a process) that Pocock was envisaging amounted to more than a mere dialogue between Pākehā and Māori histories. This was the case, he reminded his readers in concluding his essay, because in recounting one's history a people affirm their sovereignty and in doing so they recount the past in and on their own terms. A treaty between histories would mean that the histories each people tell 'mitigate and modify one another, and the debate among them may become a sharing of sovereignty'. Pocock hoped that historians, who are revisionists by vocation in the sense that they belong to a discipline that is committed to the proposition that there is always something more to be said about the past, could admit that New Zealand's sovereignty can be interpreted, recounted and configured in more ways than one, and that as a consequence they would resist looking for a solution in which one master discourse — history — absorbs the other — mātauranga Māori.[73]

Michael Belgrave, Tribunal history and Treaty history

Despite the far-reaching implications that Pocock, Sharp and McHugh raised for a consideration of the historical work that had been done on the Treaty in recent decades, very few of the historians involved in the discussions and debates about Tribunal history and Treaty history contemplated, let alone engaged with, the questions they raised.[74] Instead, nearly every historian in New Zealand who was interested in Treaty matters just ignored them, focusing instead on Oliver's essay in *Histories, Power and Loss*. That essay, as I have already noted, provoked a debate that was primarily concerned with Tribunal history — that is, histories produced in the context of the claims process — rather than Treaty history — that is, histories that are concerned with the history of the Treaty itself — and resulted in two books and several essays being published,[75] the most important of which were those written by Michael Belgrave (1954–).[76]

These historians either had had or still had a good deal of involvement in the work of the Tribunal. Most of them took exception to what Oliver had to say in both his review of the Muriwhenua report and his essay in *Histories, Power and Loss*,[77] and sought to defend the historical profession or at least the work they had been doing. Belgrave did so on several grounds. He argued that Oliver's criticism of Tribunal history had been narrowly conceived and rested on a rather selective discussion of a small number of its reports done in the mid to late 1990s. He drew attention to the multilayered nature of the historical work that had been done and argued that one had to be wary of ascribing too much coherence to it, distinguishing between the histories that the Tribunal itself told in those parts of its reports to which Oliver had drawn attention and on which he had based his analysis and argument, and the histories that historians were telling in the work they did. Belgrave claimed that Oliver had neglected to consider the lion's share of the Tribunal's historical work, which had been done by historians. He suggested that Oliver's criticism was outdated, as by the mid-2000s a staggering amount of historical work had been done, comprising more than thirty Tribunal reports; dozens of reports written by historians (and others) for the Tribunal, many of which resembled theses (partly because they were hundreds of thousands of words long); and a massive amount of research that ran to hundreds of metres of documents.[78]

Belgrave argued that the quality of the work the historians had done compared favourably with that produced in the universities, not least because it was subjected to the same kind of critical review, if not more so. He contended, moreover, that a good deal of this research was new, that some of it was of major significance, that parts of it had prompted important historiographical debates, and that historians outside the Tribunal had produced important books that had built on this work. Finally, he argued that the research that the historians did for the Tribunal rarely attempted to consider the historical events in question in accordance with the presentist principles of the Treaty, leaving that task for the Tribunal's members. In short, he contended that most of the history that historians had produced in the context of the Tribunal, including its reports, had become more like conventional history than had been the case previously (which was a change that had coincided with the departure of Eddie Durie as its chair in 2004).[79]

There is no gainsaying many of the points Belgrave made, but it is apparent that they were overdetermined and that he had not addressed adequately the substance of Oliver's criticisms, which concerned anachronism and presentism. This was the view of another historian, Grant Phillipson, who had assumed the position of manager of historical research at the Tribunal, which Belgrave once held. He pointed out that historians were still being required to accept the contention that colonisation could have been conducted more fairly than had been the case. He feared that unless they addressed Oliver's charge about counter-factual history, the whole premise upon which the history was being made in the context of the Tribunal would be undermined and the Treaty would again be seen as an agreement that could never have been upheld and which could be once more regarded as a fraud.[80]

Consequently, Phillipson and other historians still involved in the Tribunal's work set about trying to address Oliver's criticisms and thereby defend the research and writing they were doing and uphold the political, social, economic and cultural outcomes it underpinned. The way Phillipson did this typified the response of his colleagues. He essentially made two moves. He redefined 'presentism' by claiming all historical work is influenced by the present, thereby suggesting that the work he and his fellow historians were doing was unexceptional and unexceptionable. This move gutted the term of its commonly accepted meaning — that is, a form of history that sees the past entirely, or at least largely, through the lens of the present.[81] In regard to anachronism Phillipson argued that all the parties involved in the Tribunal had taken on board Oliver's criticisms of its kind of counter-factual history and had set about mending their ways accordingly, abandoning implausible counter-factual arguments and presenting more plausible counter-factual arguments on the grounds that there was considerable historical evidence that the Crown or the government often realised that it could have acted differently from the way it did, thereby honouring rather than breaching the Treaty. This meant, he claimed, that the Tribunal and its historians *could* apply the Treaty principles in ways that were not anachronistic. He argued that several of the most senior historians involved in the Tribunal's work, such as Angela Ballara, had made a strong case for the historicity of the Treaty principles. But in arguing that there was often an awareness on the part of the Crown that it could have upheld the terms of the Treaty, Phillipson and his fellow historians just assumed that the meaning of the Treaty's provisions was always at stake in the historical claims being considered, rather than providing much in the way of evidence that this was the case. Similarly, they tended to assume that the Treaty's terms were understood in the past in the way they had come to be understood in recent times. Both these assumptions were highly questionable.[82]

What is also striking is that, as far as the work of the New Zealand-based historians I have discussed in this chapter is concerned, they offered no major criticism of Claudia Orange's account of the Treaty and its history. It is difficult not to conclude that these historians did not just neglect to consider the questions that Sharp, McHugh and Pocock had raised but that, knowingly or unknowingly, they projected the weaknesses that could arguably be found in the account of the Treaty told by academic historians onto those told by the Durie-led Tribunal, and then proceeded to criticise the story it had been telling.

In doing so they made a significant error: they received the story the Tribunal told about the Treaty as though it *was* history or was meant to be read *as* history. Durie believed that many disciplines could contribute to understanding the Treaty — anthropology, history, the law, political science, sociology and a form of knowledge he called Māori knowledge — and that they all provided different perspectives on it; but while he accepted that the Treaty was a transaction that had taken place in the past, he did not concede that history had any real authority in the context of the Tribunal's work. On the contrary, he claimed that authority for the law.[83]

Durie realised that historians were puzzled by his insistence on this point, and concluded that this was so because they had an imperfect understanding of the way the law went about its work. Consequently, he sought to explain the differences between the law's approach and that of history. 'Historians, it seems to me, give meaning to an amorphous mass of facts. They see patterns and thus locate the essential principles and the developing societal norms. For lawyers operating in the lego-political world of treaty interpretation, the process is the other way round. They assess the facts against norms already prescribed, that is to say, against a given law. The alternative approaches give different conclusions.' This was so, Durie went on to point out, because the primary task of the law was 'to ensure fairness, especially where it appears that the parties may not have been equal'. And *this* meant that 'lawyers will deem [acceptable] what historians cannot countenance'. He thought it was 'unkind' of historians to call what lawyers did 'myth-making', but noted that generally lawyers were willing to 'admit to legal fictions and some to a role in nation-building'.[84]

In short, Durie never claimed the authority of history for the story the Tribunal was telling about the Treaty. This was a point that most historians have found difficult to accept, partly because the story the Tribunal told about the Treaty's past often looked like history. But it is vital that it be acknowledged so that historians, and others in turn, can grapple with the nature of the claims the Tribunal was and was not making about the Treaty and New Zealand's future.

Chapter 7
Revisionist Histories

Since the turn of the century, major changes have taken place in the historical scholarship that has a bearing on the Treaty.[1] This can be understood in part as a response to the criticism, discussed in the previous chapter, of the historical work that has been done in the context of the Tribunal's claims process. But this new or revisionist scholarship was slow to emerge and when it did it largely originated in institutions beyond New Zealand's shores.

Throughout the 1990s most academic historians continued to accept Ross's minor argument that there were significant differences between the English- and Māori-language texts and that the Māori text should be regarded as the more important. This was the case even though the merit of Ross's textual approach had been questioned as early as 1981. In the *Oxford History of New Zealand* J. M. R. Owens had argued that her emphasis on the Māori text was anachronistic given that Māori literacy was limited at the time the Treaty was made, or so he claimed. But this had no discernible impact on the work of academic historians. A few years later, a bibliographer, D. F. (David) McKenzie (1931–1999), who was Professor of English at Victoria University at the time, had more to say on the matter Owens had raised, though his work, too, had a negligible impact on historical writing about the Treaty.[2]

D. F. McKenzie, the Treaty texts, literacy and oral culture

In a small but profound book, *Oral Culture, Literacy & Print in Early New Zealand: The Treaty of Waitangi*, published in 1985 but originally presented as a public lecture in 1983, McKenzie considered the respective roles that literacy and orality had played in the making of the Treaty. He was interested in how each affected the meaning that could be attributed to it, both at the time and ever since. Like Owens, he argued that Māori literacy was limited at the time,[3] but he also suggested that this drew into question European assumptions about the chiefs' comprehension of the Treaty, the status of their signatures on the sheets, and the binding power of written statements and written consent more generally. By taking into consideration that Māori in 1840 still had an oral culture, one was more able to understand the ways in which the Treaty might now be reconstructed, interpreted and applied, he argued. His study, like the work of the Tribunal at the time he wrote, raised serious questions for the discipline of history because of the evidentiary weight it has assigned traditionally to the written word.[4]

McKenzie focused in large part on the Treaty's different texts, its range of 'signatures', and the conflicting views of its meaning and status in 1840. His consideration was informed by Ross's article, which he called 'the most perceptive analysis of the texts and their implications', though his purpose in discussing the texts was rather different from hers. Drawing on her 1972 article, he made the following points. The first English draft was cobbled together. All the English versions of the Treaty were merely drafts. Some of them had survived but the one given to Henry Williams to translate had not. This was true of the Māori version discussed at Waitangi on 5 February. It was amended that evening and copied onto a parchment that was presented to chiefs the next day to sign. As McKenzie concluded: 'It is this document in Maori, a revised version of a translation into Maori made from a composite English draft no longer extant, which is in the most literal sense the Treaty of Waitangi.'[5]

The complex nature of the Treaty texts and the problems they raised for historical interpretation did not end there, McKenzie pointed out. On the basis of his reading of the Turton compilation of the facsimiles, to which he had probably been guided by Ross, he observed that Hobson had sent five English versions of the Treaty to his political masters in Sydney and/or London; that there are minor differences in three of them; and that the other two bear a different date, differ from the others in the wording of their preamble, and diverge radically from each other in the second article. 'According to Ross,' he remarked, 'the extant Maori version, the actual treaty, as signed by the chiefs on 6 February, is not a translation of any one of these five English versions, nor is any of the English ones a translation from the Maori. They must therefore descend, with greater or lesser accuracy and no authority, from the first full English draft now lost, and made before the Maori translation in its first and revised forms.' Pointing out that an English version of the Treaty sent to the Colonial Secretary in London in 1840 was endorsed by Williams as being as literal a translation of the Māori text as was possible, McKenzie argued that this cannot have been the case.[6]

In a similar vein to Ross, he proceeded to point out that of the approximately 540 Māori signatories only seventy-two at most had placed personal signatures on the sheets as distinct from crosses, moko patterns and what seemed to be quite meaningless marks. Consequently, one was forced to conclude that the chiefs who had 'signed' the Treaty were unlikely to have read what they signed 'even in the most literal way'. The Treaty was best understood, McKenzie argued, by regarding it as an agreement that was made at Waitangi in what he called an 'oral–aural occasion'. Pointing out that it was presented to Māori by being read out to them by Williams, he argued that this meant it was received by them 'as an oral statement, not a [written] document', let alone one they had a chance to ponder over for several days or weeks, or one whose terms they had a chance to negotiate. Reverting to the texts, McKenzie argued that the Māori language was used against Māori. Following Ross's article, he contended that this was the case in several respects: Williams assumed that much of the detail of the English draft could not be expressed in Māori; the Māori he used to communicate the intentions of the British Crown was not 'indigenous Maori' but 'Protestant Pakeha missionary Maori'; and the concepts as well as many of the words in the Māori text were actually English ones notwithstanding their Māori form.[7]

McKenzie thought Māori were aware of the concepts at the heart of the Treaty, but he contended that their mode of dealing with them was oral. He implied that this — the oral–aural dimension of the treaty-making — posed a problem for the historian as it had left 'virtually no matching record to complement the [written] Pakeha one'. This was so, he argued, because while those present at Waitangi on 5 February had been free to speak, the principal written account of the chiefs' speeches that day (by the missionary printer, Colenso) did 'scant justice to the originals', and any further oral discussion about the Treaty the following day was proscribed by Hobson.[8]

Based on the historical record of the only public debate that occurred at Waitangi, McKenzie argued that Hobson and Busby had sought to mislead Māori about what was at stake and that Māori were clearly opposed to surrendering sovereignty and therefore control over their lands. Furthermore he argued, on the basis of Colenso's report of the meeting that took place the following day, that Māori had not understood the Treaty, that those who had 'signed' the Treaty had hastily put their marks to a parchment they could not read, and that this number included chiefs who had 'declaimed *against* signing'.[9]

The problem, McKenzie was quick to clarify, was not that the Māori signatories were 'pre-literate': an oral contract made in front of witnesses could be given legal standing, and marks on a written one were legally acceptable as signatures. It lay instead in the reality that the party who drafts a written document has an advantage because they 'determine and choose the linguistic terms by which to reveal or conceal [the concepts underpinning it]'. Furthermore, an oral response by a group of people is rarely unanimous about the details of a contract and is weaker in its power to bind afterwards.[10]

At this point in his book McKenzie returned to his argument about the Treaty's texts. He observed that the circumstances he had just been relating did not mean that the written documents were useless as a means of understanding the terms of the Treaty or that it was a fraud. Rather, they meant that the written documents could only be regarded as 'partial witnesses to the occasion' and that 'reconstructing a more authentic version of the understandings reached between Maori and Pakeha in 1840 is a demanding task'. He suggested that light could be cast on the Treaty by considering other written texts, most importantly the Declaration of Independence which he called 'a complementary document'. Here he followed Claudia Orange's discussion in her PhD thesis, contending that Māori understanding of the Treaty was shaped by their belief that their independence and sovereignty had been affirmed by the Declaration in 1835 and was not nullified by the Treaty. But he added force to her argument by invoking his own about the continuing primacy of oral culture: 'for the Maori one document did not supersede the other: they lived together, one complementing the other'.[11]

Following Ross's work closely, McKenzie turned to the differences between the English and Māori texts regarding what had come to be accepted as its key words: sovereignty, governorship, possessions, kāwanatanga, rangatiratanga, mana and taonga. He argued that the standards of textual and historical truth that were derived from European intellectual traditions obliged Pākehā New Zealanders today to acknowledge that the Māori version of the Treaty was 'the only authoritative document' and that on 'any reasonable reading' it surrendered less and guaranteed more in terms of sovereignty and possessions than any of the English versions.[12]

McKenzie then resumed his argument about the oral treaty. He argued that as far as Māori in 1840 were concerned, the Treaty text was the consensus they had arrived at through discussion at the meetings. He pointed out, furthermore, that an oral culture tends to assume that there will be continuing discussion and modification of such an agreement. This meant that the Treaty was 'something more comprehensive and open than the base document or any of its extant versions'. The problem for Māori had been that the documents rather than the talk had survived, and successive New Zealand governments had chosen the written English versions that best served their ends. He quoted the remark that Mohi Tāwhai had made at the Treaty meeting at Māngungu, and which he had read in Ross's article — 'the sayings of the Pakeha float light, like the wood of the *whau* tree, and always remain to be seen, but the sayings of the Maori sink to the bottom like [a] stone' — and observed: 'Manuscript and print, the tools of the Pakeha, persist, but words which are spoken fade as they fall.'[13]

Yet McKenzie pointed out that Māori oral traditions lived on in the form of Māori distrust of the written document and the refusal of some — he gave Donna Awatere as an example — to accept political decisions based on it. This meant that 'Pakeha and Maori versions of the past continue to collide'. He gave examples of this before remarking: 'At such moments literacy defines itself for many as a concordat of sword and pen, of politics and script — to the dismay and frustration of those whose modes are oral. Pakeha continue to assume "Sovereignty" where radical Maori persist in believing that nothing so sacred as *mana* has ever been ceded under the treaty, that Maori sovereignty was, and is, intact.' And, he added: 'As it happens, the Maori text supports them.' In moving to conclude his study, McKenzie argued that once written texts are placed in their contexts — and especially their oral contexts — they 'quickly deconstruct and lose their "literal" authority'. No book, he pointed out, is ever truly bound by its covers. 'The book, in all its forms, enters history only as evidence of human behaviour, and it remains active only in the service of human needs.' (He might have been talking about Ross's article.)[14]

McKenzie was not quite content, however, to let his argument about the Treaty rest there, in what he called 'a conflict of irreconcilable versions'. It was, he observed, impossible to regard either the Māori version of the Treaty as complete — though he held that it carried the highest authority — or the English ones as authoritative — though they were far more explicit about its terms. He was aware that, like many of the dramatic texts (such as Shakespeare's) with which he was familiar, 'each had been born . . . maimed and deformed, of the pressures of context'. He was also aware that in the cloistered world of scholarship, historians would deny the possibility that '"the text" of the Treaty of Waitangi [was] anything other than its distinct historical versions' and insist that any attempt to conflate them with later ones was unacceptable as this 'would be to create a text that never was'. But in his view that position was unacceptably timid. He noted that the principle of reconstructing an ideal text from all the versions of the Treaty was 'vitally operative in legal opinion on the interpretation of treaties'; he claimed that the legislation that governed the work of the Tribunal had 'recognised the social inutility of a clutter of versions as distinct from the social value of a harmonized text'; and he argued that it had affirmed an even higher principle in its Motunui-Waitara report: that 'the spirit of the Treaty transcends the sum total of its component written words and puts narrow or literal interpretations out of place'.[15]

Clearly, McKenzie's approach to and argument about the Treaty mirrored that of the Tribunal and posed a considerable challenge to the conventional ways the discipline of history interpreted written texts like the Treaty. But few historians understood the key points he was making.[16] Judith Binney and Claudia Orange acknowledged that the Treaty had been presented in an oral context, but claimed that

McKenzie had underestimated Māori literacy, the degree to which the Māori text had been discussed, and the extent to which the chiefs had understood its implications. As a result, they failed to understand his principal argument. Most of the historians who reviewed his book treated him as though he was an interloper in what they regarded as their territory, attacked his work as dangerous, and sought to diminish the chances it would be received favourably by focusing on some factual errors he had made. This helped to ensure that Ross's textual approach to the Treaty continued to hold sway among most of their fellow historians, at least for the time being.[17]

Nevertheless, McKenzie's thesis was taken up by one of New Zealand's most outstanding historians, James Belich. In an article he wrote in 1990 about recently published books on the Treaty, he pointed out that all the authors had skirted around the problems with its texts. He argued that while the tension between the cession of sovereignty in the English version and the retention of full chieftainship in the Māori version could be resolved by preferring one or the other (and obviously the latter was being preferred), this was not the case for the tension *within* the Māori version between the cession of kāwanatanga katoa and the retention of tino rangatiratanga. He contended that on the face of it, one contradicted the other. Ross would undoubtedly have agreed. Belich was similarly sceptical about the recent claim that the British Crown and its missionary advisers had given an undertaking to preserve Māori culture and autonomy, and was inclined to argue that the intent of the two parties to the Treaty was also contradictory in this regard. Again, Ross would have concurred.[18]

Like Ross, Belich was sceptical that anyone could now know what exactly the Treaty was meant to mean, though on grounds that differed from hers. He pointed out that there was a possibility that the real Treaty lay in neither the Māori nor the English texts but in the oral debates that took place, though he had his doubts about even this being the case. This meant, he suggested, that it might be reasonable to deduce its meaning from how it was subsequently implemented, but he conceded that this might beg as many questions as the provisions of the written versions or the principles of the Treaty that were being invoked by the Tribunal.[19]

Several years later, Belich added to these arguments in the first volume of his history of New Zealand. Like Ross, and for reasons that probably lay in the realm of the private life of history rather than its public life, he was determined to challenge an interpretation of the Treaty that had once again become encrusted with myth. 'Some recent writers', he complained, 'come very close to telling us that there is only one Treaty [the Māori one], and that the Tribunal is its Prophet.' He suggested that an examination of yet another version of the Treaty was required: the Treaty as it influenced what followed. He contended that in 1840 Māori had probably understood it as some kind of new deal and suggested that this was evident in their enthusiastic reception of British law and the machinery of state in the following two decades.[20]

Figure 1 Ruth Guscott (later Ruth Ross) was seated in the centre of the front row for this photograph of her class at Whanganui Girls' College in 1938 as befitting her status as head prefect. She was already known as Gus, the name that family and friends used for the rest of her life. Growing up, she counted local Māori girls among her friends, but it seems they had all left the school by this time.

Figure 2 This is one of two portraits of Ruth Guscott that were taken in the late 1930s by a leading Wellington photographer, Geoffrey Perry, who had a studio on Brandon Street, just off Lambton Quay, one of Wellington's main streets.

Figure 3 In October 1943 Ruth Guscott married George Burnard, a promising young lawyer who had been a couple of years ahead of her at Victoria University College and whom she met in the home of one of her teachers there, F. L. W. Wood. This photograph of the young couple was probably taken around this time, when he was doing military training at Fort Dorset in Wellington.

Figure 4 Ruth with one of her lifelong friends Mary Boyd, pictured in Wellington in 1944. They and other women in the Historical Branch of the Department of Internal Affairs saw themselves as modern women, and their male colleagues regarded them as formidable. Some years later, one of their colleagues, John Pascoe, referred to 'the great dynasty of the matriarchy of Ruth, Mary, Janet and Nan', and attacked Ross as 'La Belle Ross Sans Merci'.

Figure 5 This photograph of Ruth at work on her typewriter was taken in about 1944 at the Historical Branch, which was housed in the Government Building in Wellington. In what has been called 'the typewriter century' (between approximately the 1880s and the 1980s), the typewriter was a faithful companion for many writers. Ross was deeply attached to hers.

Figure 6 This photo of Ruth with some of her colleagues in the War History Branch of the Department of Internal Affairs was taken in the closing months of 1945, a year or so after her husband George died suddenly.

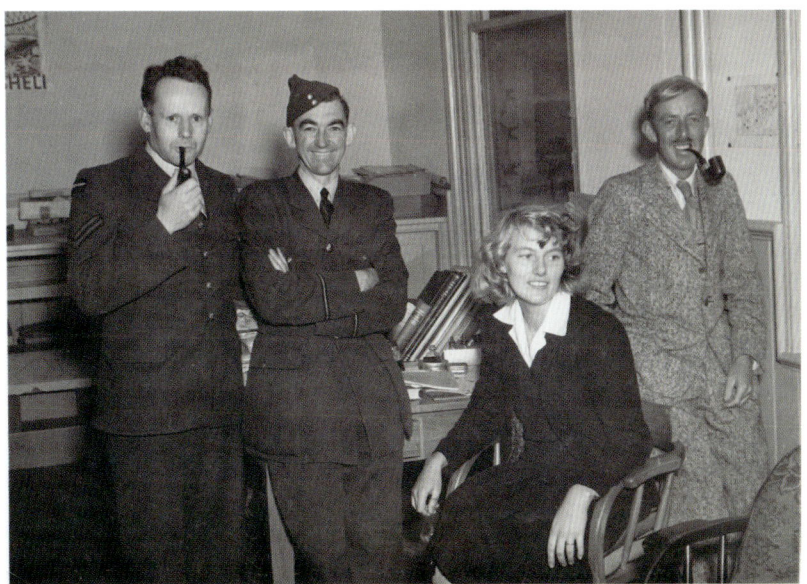

Figure 7 This photograph of Ruth and her second husband, Ian Ross, and their two boys, Duncan and Malcolm, was taken in front of their home in Arthur Crescent, Takapuna, on Auckland's North Shore, in about 1951. While the trauma Ruth suffered as the result of her first husband's sudden death had by its very nature left its mark on her, her marriage with Ian was a good one, and his skills — he had been a journalist before the war and had now become a teacher — made him an invaluable critic of her work as a historian.

Figure 8 Ross's teacher, mentor and patron, the leading New Zealand historian J. C. Beaglehole, photographed in his study in 1958. Several years earlier, he was responsible for commissioning Ross's first major work on the Treaty.

Figure 9 The historian and archivist Michael Standish, pictured here in 1961, was one of Ross's most sympathetic interlocutors. His sudden and premature death the following year must have been a blow to her at a time when the vast majority of academic historians seem to have regarded her work on the Treaty as worthless.

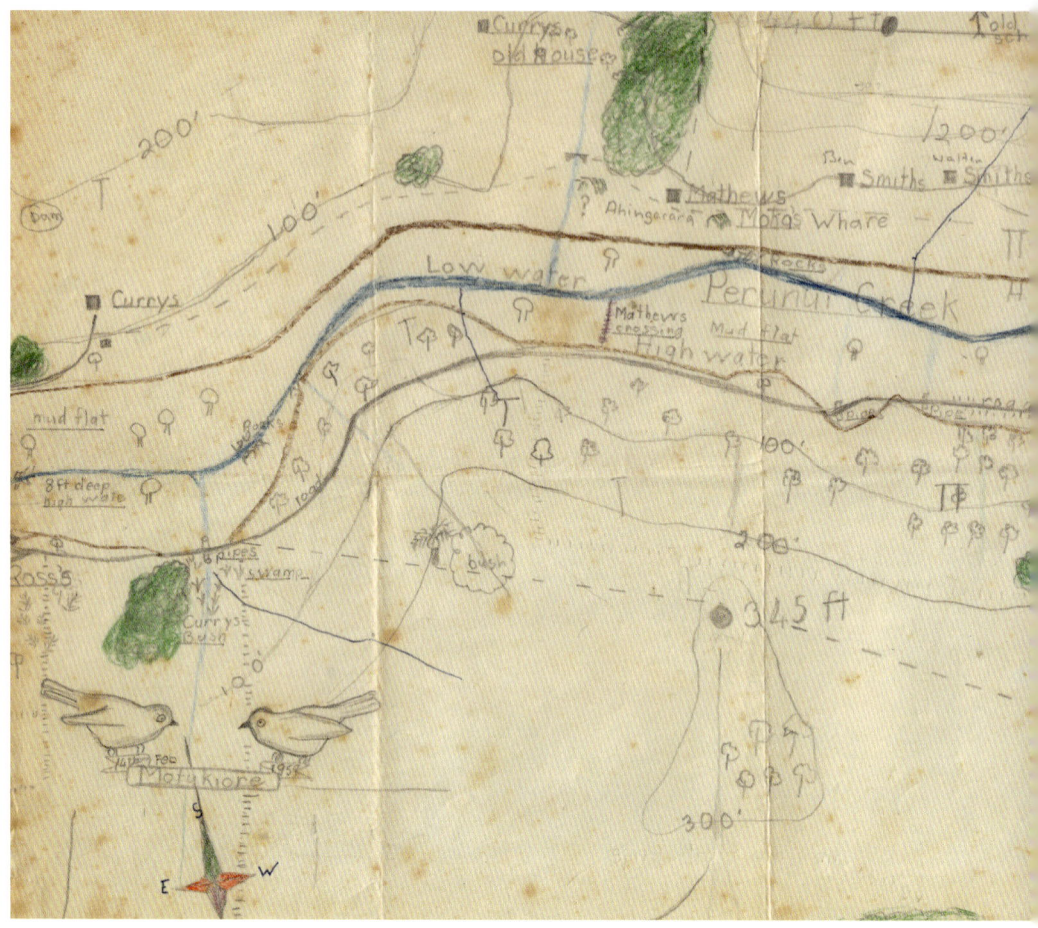

Figure 10 In 1959 Ross's son Malcolm drew this sketch map of the place where the family lived at Motukiore, on the Hokianga Harbour in New Zealand's far north, between 1955 and 1960. The Rosses' home, which lay on the Perunui Creek, is marked on the far left. The smaller annotations were made by Ruth.

Figure 12 Pictured here in about 1957 are some of the community outside the school house at Motukiore, where Ian was the principal teacher. Ross is seventh on the left, a finger resting on her cheek. For Pākehā, and especially those in the Rosses' position, they enjoyed an unusually close relationship with the local Māori people, in good part because several of the most senior men seem to have welcomed Ruth's passionate interest in the Treaty of Waitangi. Not long after they learned of this, the local tribal committee agreed, albeit after much discussion, to invite the Rosses to visit the nearby cemetery at Hairini so that she could ascertain whether any of the gravestones belonged to Ngāpuhi rangatira who had signed the Treaty at the meeting that took place at Māngungu Mission Station. Shortly afterwards, Ruth was invited to a hui at nearby Mangamuka marae.

Figure 11 Ruth walking along Perunui Creek.

Figure 13 This is a sketch of the Hokianga River from Māngungu with Maungataniwha looming in the background that the budding young Māori artist Ralph Hotere did at Ross's request, but which School Publications rejected as an illustration for a school bulletin about te Tiriti o Waitangi. However, she was delighted by the work and he gifted it to her. Many years later, Malcolm Ross, who was an artist in his own right, persuaded the historian Judith Binney to use it as an illustration for Ross's famous 1972 article about the Treaty which she included in a collection of essays compiled from the first thirty or so years of the *New Zealand Journal of History*.

Figure 14 Local rangatira were not the only Māori who lent their support to the ground-breaking work Ross did on the Treaty while she lived at Motukiore. So too did two Māori scholars, one of whom was the senior Tainui figure Pei Te Hurinui Jones, pictured here in 1957.

Figure 15 The cover of Ross's school bulletin on the Treaty, published in 1958. She preferred to be named on her publications as 'R. M. Ross' rather than 'Ruth Ross'. She once remarked that she regarded the latter as 'a particularly uneuphonious combination' but might have also thought it best to hide her gender, just as many woman writers, such as George Eliot, had done in the past by adopting a male persona.

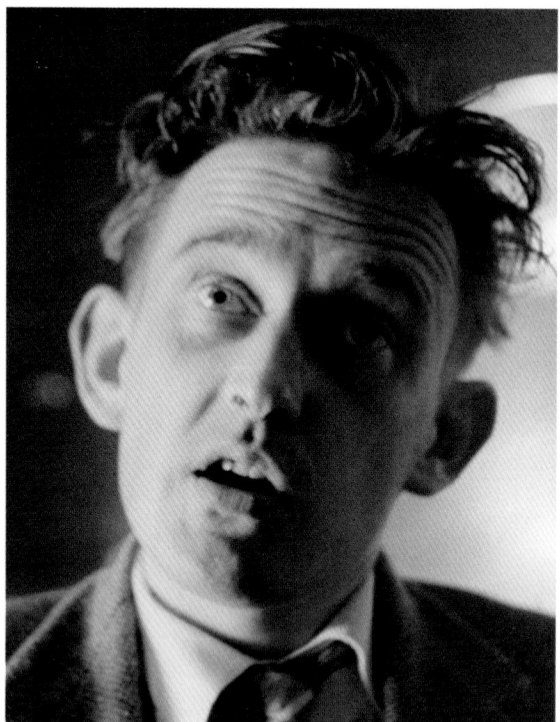

Figure 16 The poet James K. Baxter, photographed by Peter Campbell in about 1959. An editor at School Publications at the time, he played a vital role in ensuring that Ross's finest work about the Treaty — her bulletin, or small book, for school children — was published.

Figure 17 This portrait of the leading New Zealand historian Keith Sinclair was taken by the renowned New Zealand photographer Marti Friedlander in 1976. He was instrumental in shepherding Ross's 1972 journal article through to publication.

Figure 18 Members of Nga Tamatoa on the steps of Parliament in 1972, the same year in which Ross's now famous article appeared in the *New Zealand Journal of History*. The previous year they and their allies had begun to disrupt the annual celebrations of the signing of the Treaty at Waitangi in order to draw attention to their point of view.

Figure 19 The Minister of Maori Affairs Matiu Rata standing outside Parliament with a group of young Māori in October 1975, apparently ready to welcome the hīkoi from the far north that was timed to arrive as his Treaty of Waitangi Bill, which established the Waitangi Tribunal, was being debated.

Figure 20 This cartoon was produced by Bob Brockie for the *National Business Review* to mark Waitangi Day in February 1982. The oft-quoted words of Ross's article about the Treaty appear in the top-right corner. Terminally ill by this time, she must have felt that her lifetime's work on the Treaty was finally being recognised.

Figure 21 The chair of the Waitangi Tribunal, Eddie Durie (left), and one of its other members, Paul Temm, with students of the kōhanga reo at Waiwhetū in the Hutt Valley, in 1985. By this time the Tribunal had begun to transform understanding of the Treaty and revolutionise its place in New Zealand law, politics and culture, in no small part because of the way they read Ross's 1972 article.

Figure 22 The members of the Waitangi Tribunal (left to right), Rev. Manu Bennett, Sir Monita Delamere, William Wilson, Eddie Durie, Georgina Te Heuheu and Keith Sorrenson, pictured during the hearing of the Muriwhenua claim, 1988.

Lyndsay Head's revisionism

Belich aside, by the turn of the century it seemed relatively little had changed in the way academic historians in New Zealand were interpreting the Treaty. Judith Binney oversaw the publication of a book comprising twenty-two articles or essays from the nearly 400 that had appeared in the first thirty or so years of the *New Zealand Journal of History*. One section was devoted to the Treaty, reflecting the rise in academic interest since the journal was founded in 1967 (though not the number of articles the journal had published on it, as these were relatively few). As this section was entitled 'Altering the Focus', it is probably not surprising that Ross's article was the first essay. In choosing the articles or essays Binney had several criteria in mind, but they either had to have influenced the ways in which successive generations of historians had come to see the past or provided a seedbed for larger works. Binney hoped that the pieces she chose demonstrated some of the ways in which conventional ideas had been reshaped, or even overturned, by good historical research that rethought big issues. She regarded Ross's as one such essay largely because she read it in terms of its argument that the Treaty was a Māori-language document rather than her argument that there were significant differences between the Māori and the English texts. In reviewing Binney's compilation and two other collections of essays, the historian Michael King also seems to have lost sight of the latter aspect of her article. At any rate, he singled it out as the only contribution to the volume that had been superseded by subsequent research.[21]

In making this remark it is possible that King had in mind an essay by Lyndsay Head,[22] which appeared in one of the other books he was reviewing: *Histories, Power and Loss*. Head had challenged the dominant interpretation of the Treaty in a thorough-going fashion. Her essay was the most important piece of work that any historian had written about the Treaty since Claudia Orange's book first appeared in 1987 (though the focus of her essay was much broader than the Treaty). As such, it warrants a good deal of attention.

Head's research combines two fields — history and language — and at the time she wrote this essay she was a lecturer in the Department of Māori at the University of Canterbury where she was responsible for subjects about the history of Māori–Pākehā relations in the nineteenth century and the history of the Māori language. She had undertaken work for the Tribunal in which she had analysed nineteenth-century Māori-language documents and criticised the Muriwhenua claimants' 'tuku whenua' argument; she had published a series of translations of Māori historical texts; and she was undertaking a doctoral thesis about Māori political thought in the nineteenth century. Of any scholar in recent decades, Māori or Pākehā, she was probably the best equipped to analyse the Māori text of the Treaty.[23]

In her opinion, the Treaty had come to be interpreted in such a way that it had become a straitjacket. She attributed this to the influence of the legal-claims culture that had grown up as a result of the Tribunal's work, but also the broader political and legal demands that Māori were making in respect of autonomy or sovereignty. She argued that these forces made it difficult to perceive, let alone conceive of, the way in which Māori had previously understood the Treaty.[24] Consequently, she set herself the task of recovering this history.[25]

Head observed that analysis of the Treaty in recent years had come to centre on the accuracy of the translation and linguistic integrity, but argued that it had been conducted in an ahistorical fashion. This was most apparent, she suggested, in the work of scholars who were willing to ascribe authority to *present-day* Māori language and culture rather than that of the time the Treaty was made. Among the culprits she had in mind were Hugh Kawharu and David Williams. This led her to declare that it strained belief to argue that the missionary Henry Williams, knowing that the first article of the English version required Māori to transfer sovereignty to the Crown, had turned around and inserted in the second article of the Māori version a passage that meant that Māori had retained an enormous amount of that authority. Yet, she pointed out, the dominant interpretation of the Treaty was now dependent on just such a claim.[26]

To recover what she called a Māori history of the Treaty, Head set about providing an analysis that was devoted to a consideration of the relevant Māori documents of the time and their immediate contexts, though she remarked that a study with broader parameters was urgently required. (Perhaps it goes without saying that she rejected McKenzie's claim that Māori literacy was limited at the time.)[27] She complained that the study of the Treaty had come to be conducted within the limits set by textual analysis, and she suggested that this provided a fragile basis for understanding it and Māori history more generally.[28]

To understand the contexts in which Māori signed the Treaty, Head contended, one had to understand the kind of political relationship Māori were seeking to establish with the Pākehā world at that time. She argued that Māori — by which she meant those in the far north of New Zealand who had become most familiar with the world beyond its shores — were seeking to participate in a new political community and were doing so because they realised that major changes were undermining their position. She contended that this had caused important perceptual shifts among them and that consequently they were open to new political arrangements, which she characterised as those of modernity, as distinct from tradition. She argued that their pursuit of modernity in the form of those political arrangements created 'a path to the Treaty ground'. More specifically, she contended that the teachings of the missionaries provided Māori with new political ideas and what amounted to a political primer for change, and that they had persuaded them in a political sense before they had convinced them in the religious sense. In fact she insisted that it was difficult to make sense of the changes that took place among many Māori, and their openness to the political solutions that the missionaries were proposing, unless one recognised the intensity of the relationship Māori had with the Christian faith.[29]

With these points in mind, Head turned her attention to the Treaty texts and the matter of translation. Here, she was very critical of what she called loosely speculative theories, which included Ross's contention that the Williamses were inexperienced translators. Head found this argument implausible, just as she did Ross's argument that the language they used in translating the Treaty was 'missionary Maori' and so incomprehensible to Māori. Later, in her PhD thesis, Head, who has been as uncompromising in her criticism of other scholars as Ross was, described Ross's doubts about Williams and his son's ability in the Māori language as 'foolish'. She remarked that being adroit in the language was an essential ingredient in Williams's success in establishing the Church Missionary Society missionaries as an integral part of the Māori community in the far north of New Zealand, and pointed out that his son Edward had grown up speaking Māori. She observed that a comparison of Māori and Pākehā writing in Māori failed to bear out Ross's argument that the Māori these missionaries used was of a different kind to that which Māori spoke. 'For Williams, father and son, Maori was the language of communication in a cross-cultural environment', she wrote in her essay. 'Semantic improvisation would have been a common feature of everyone's speech in the world they lived in. The Europeans who translated their world into Maori were innovators by definition. However, the learning went both ways.' Williams was no longer an Englishman abroad but a local, familiar with Māori society. 'The starting point for assessing his translation of the Treaty', she insisted, 'must be the supposition that he was able to think about mana [i.e. a key Māori phenomenon] in the terms of the day.'[30]

Head discussed Williams's translation by tackling the two major debates that had arisen in recent times about the words he had chosen to convey the meaning of the Treaty's key concepts. The first debate concerned the absence or omission of any reference to 'mana' in the Treaty texts and consequently Māori misunderstanding of its terms. Head argued that the contention that Ross had been the first to make about this matter was not supported by linguistic sources dating from the time. She agreed that the speeches made at the meeting at Waitangi revealed that the chiefs were apprehensive of losing status and authority but pointed out that none of them expressed their fears in terms of a loss of mana. It would have been unlikely for them to do so, she argued. A chief exemplified mana, but the word itself was rarely uttered even though it was expressed everywhere. Paradoxically, the very power of mana was indicated by its absence in speech. 'The absence of mana from the text of the Treaty', she concluded, 'does not in itself make a case for failure of Maori understanding.'[31]

Head argued that one could pursue this matter further as it was possible to follow Williams's thinking in the words he had chosen to use in translating the Treaty. She contended that he was able to think about mana in the terms of that time. Comparing the way he had translated the concept of sovereignty in the Declaration of Independence and in the Treaty, she argued that it had been appropriate to use 'mana' to translate 'sovereignty' in the Declaration of Independence because that document had declared the existence of two sovereigns (Māori and the British in the form of the King) in 'lofty and distancing language', but that it was inappropriate to use 'mana' in the Treaty because it was a moment in which that distance was to be collapsed through a political union of Māori and the British Crown in New Zealand. As far as Williams was concerned, the localising or delegation of British authority that the Treaty portended meant that the effective functions of government were separated from the dignified ones, the former being present in New Zealand, the other being present in faraway Britain in the person of the Queen. 'In this situation,' she argued, 'neither mana nor kingitanga were plausible choices for a sovereign authority that Williams wished to convey to Maori as a local, delegated power to govern.' Delegation, Head remarked, works in terms of effective functions of government and for this reason Williams had used 'kawanatanga'. She explained that the word was derived from 'kawana (governor)' but, unlike Ross, she argued that Māori would have understood 'kawanatanga'. This was so because, first, Māori saw the governor (Hobson) in the flesh at Waitangi and realised that, while he was a man of higher status than the existing role model (Busby), he was lower than the Queen; and, second, they knew the word 'kawanatanga' from the Bible, in which it had appeared in contexts of rule. In short, she argued, 'kawanatanga' was a word or concept that the missionaries had used to refer to a specific mode of authority. 'It did not mean mana, and was not measured against it.' Hence, the absence of mana in the Māori text would *not* have prevented Māori from understanding the meaning of the Treaty in 1840.[32]

Head considered the term 'rangatiratanga' next. To begin, she turned, once again, to the Declaration of Independence to understand the use of it in the Treaty. She pointed out that Busby, who was responsible for drafting the English text, had wanted to express *independence* as an aspect of the sovereignty that was invoked in it, but that as the Māori language had no word for this, its translator had provided one by equating it with a much remarked upon aspect of the behaviour of chiefs — rangatira (their independence), hence 'rangatiratanga' in 'He Wakaputanga o te Rangatiratanga o Nu Tireni', the translation into Māori of 'A Declaration of Independence'. She pointed out that the concept of independence extended the meanings of rule and sovereignty for which the term rangatiratanga had figured in the Bible, and that the Treaty would add to that range further.[33]

She went on to argue that while recent accounts of the Treaty had concentrated on the 'literal meanings' of the Māori text on the assumption that the current meanings of its key words were the same as they had been at the time the Treaty was made, the difference between past and present usage seemed clear. 'Rangatiratanga' seldom appeared in traditional oral narratives (even though they were the appropriate venue for it) and did not appear there as an overarching concept of chiefliness, let alone an abstract authority. However, by the time the Treaty was made, she pointed out, the term had begun to appear in contexts in which it better fitted the new world than the old. Rangatiratanga was a term whose origins lay in these contexts. This was to argue that the political language of both the Declaration and the Treaty was the language of modernity rather than the language of tradition,[34] which meant that contemporary interpreters of the Treaty were making a mistake in treating rangatiratanga as though it took its meaning and force from tradition.[35]

Head turned to consider what Williams might have meant in the article that confirmed Māori in the tino rangatiratanga they possessed. The aim of the Treaty, she argued, was not to protect Māori culture, as the Tribunal had been claiming. Williams believed that it was in the best interests of Māori that their culture be transformed by modernisation (which he and his fellow missionaries offered). In any case, she contended, as the article in question concerned land, it should be interpreted in that context. The fact that the confirmation of tino rangatiratanga to Māori was paired with the arrangement by which the British Crown claimed the right to be the only buyer of their land suggested that Williams had used 'tino rangatiratanga' to refer to the guarantee of their possession of land and other such resources rather than to the protection of Māori culture.[36]

Head argued that other linguistic sources provided evidence for this argument. For example, the most common theme of the chiefs' speeches at the Treaty meeting at Waitangi was their anxiety about losing their authority over land. Therefore, she noted, '[t]here was ... good reason for the Pakeha to make a strong affirming statement not only of Maori ownership of land, but of their continuing power of decision over its alienation'. She hastened to point out that confining the meaning of rangatiratanga to land, as she had just done, did not diminish the contemporary importance of the Treaty's second article. At the time it was signed, land constituted the Māori stake in the country: it was the commodity with which they could gain access to the modernity they sought, and by owning it they controlled the most important means of limiting the power of the colonial state. 'Nothing, therefore, was of greater importance than the confirmation of ownership.' Nonetheless, she pointed out, there remained a crucial difference between the contemporary and the historical meanings attributed to rangatiratanga. 'In 1840 tino rangatiratanga did not distance Maori from the state', as was now being claimed by all the major storytellers who were discussing the Treaty, 'but fulfilled the logic of the Treaty's concern with land'.[37]

In concluding her argument about the Treaty, Head noted that Māori thinking about sovereignty and government was in a state of flux in 1840 but that their interest in new arrangements of state did not *force* them towards the British. Instead, they moved in that direction knowingly and willingly, seeing the Treaty as another way of being involved in the modern world. In doing so they believed that they were making steps towards viewing themselves as members of the same group of people, the British. This was evident in the terms of address they used: 'Queen Victoria was called to tatou Kuini, "our Queen", to tatou signifying "belonging to both Maori and Pakeha".' This familial idiom of relationships extended beyond these terms of address, she suggested. Government was seen in terms of a genealogy: it stemmed from God, as the founding ancestor of law, and devolved through the Queen to the Governor. The Treaty made Māori and Pākehā friends and united them under the authority of the Crown. It was not surprising, then, that Hobson had said to the chiefs after they signed the Treaty at Waitangi 'He iwi tahi tātou' ('We are now one people').[38]

How did academic historians respond to Head's exceptionally fine essay and the challenge it threw down to the way the main players had been interpreting the Treaty? Most of them just ignored it and many have continued to do so ever since. In 2005, however, Michael Belgrave published a major book in which he advanced several contentions that had marked similarities with her argument (though he did not acknowledge the degree to which his interpretation was indebted to her work).

Michael Belgrave's 'modern' and 'historical' treaties

Belgrave's book was the first monograph a professional historian had written about the Treaty since Orange had published her classic work in 1987.[39] In it he mostly considered the nature of the stories that had been told in the context of Māori making claims about land to the Tribunal and several earlier legal commissions of inquiry, but he also sought to advance an interpretation of the Treaty.

Here, his starting point was his criticism of the dominant interpretation of the Treaty, or at least that provided by the Tribunal. As a quick reading or misreading of the title of his book, *Historical Frictions: Maori Claims and Reinvented Histories*, might suggest, he believed that the story the Tribunal had been telling was more or less a fiction or an invented history, though for the most part he was reluctant to put it in those terms.[40] He argued that this history had emerged in the 1970s, creating what he called 'the modern treaty'. (More likely than not, it had emerged in the 1980s rather than the 1970s.) As the term 'the modern treaty' implies, Belgrave regarded this history or historical interpretation as 'presentist' (though he accepted that 'it contained echoes of the past'). He used that term to distinguish between its interpretation and an interpretation of the Treaty he called 'historical' and thus a Treaty he dubbed 'the historical treaty'. In the hands of a historian, the use of these two terms reveals the hierarchy of value that typically informs their work.[41]

Belgrave pointed out that 'the modern treaty' had dominated recent public debate and argued that the real history of the Treaty — in his terms 'the historical treaty' — had been lost from sight.[42] He set about trying to recover the past in which it had been made by providing what he regarded — and what most other historians would regard — as a properly historical interpretation. 'The extent to which the past [of the Treaty] has been reinvented on numerous occasions suggests that, in trying to understand the original events [of 1840], we have to peel back layer after layer of reinterpretation before we can understand what occurred originally', he remarked. 'Unless we strip away these layers, we cannot appreciate how far . . . variations in interpretation . . . have coloured our view of the original events.'[43]

After providing an account of what he called the origins of the 'modern' interpretation of the Treaty — which he attributed to those he called 'non-historians', thereby obscuring the role that academic historians, most of all Claudia Orange, had played in its creation — Belgrave proceeded to present his 'historical treaty'. In keeping with the times, he was mostly concerned with recovering Māori perspectives of the Treaty. He held that the worldview that informed their understanding of it in 1840 had become opaque to contemporary readers because of an undue focus on the written texts. In and of themselves, he held, the texts were extremely limited sources on which to base any historical interpretation. Moreover, he argued, the 'modern' interpretation had become so preoccupied with the texts that it had become blind to matters of *context*. The key to recovering 'the historical treaty' lay in removing the Treaty from the grip of textual analysis and recovering the 'broad contextual factors' that had shaped its meaning. More particularly, he suggested that the historian had to restore the Māori context and that this meant focusing on what he called the oral dimension of the treaty-making. Largely following McKenzie's argument at this point, he contended that Māori understanding of the Treaty was the product of the debates at the Treaty meetings and may have had little relationship to the Māori text.[44]

Still, Belgrave devoted a lot of discussion to the texts. His account of the texts bore some resemblance to the 'modern' interpretation of the Treaty in that, he, like the Tribunal and Orange, represented it as a treaty of rights. But he departed from it by paying more attention to the third article and by claiming that the rights the Crown undertook to impart in it — those of British subjects — were more important to Māori at this time than any other kind of rights.[45]

Belgrave argued that the differences between the Treaty's English and Māori texts had been overstated, thereby taking issue with one of Ross's findings. Yet in several other respects his account of the texts owed a great deal to her article and/or the way it had been received by 'modern' interpreters. He treated the Māori text as though it was *the* Treaty and his interpretation rested to a large degree on his consideration of Māori understandings of what it meant. Moreover, he cast Williams as its author, rather than merely its principal translator.[46] In these respects, for all his claim that he was challenging the 'modern' interpretation, his treaty was what we can call the Māori Treaty — that is, an interpretation that rested primarily on the Māori text. His account was Rossian, too, in that his consideration of the British players focuses on those at the colonial periphery rather than the imperial centre.[47]

The most valuable aspect of Belgrave's account of the so-called historical treaty lay in his attempt to recover the contexts in which it was made in order to explain how the Māori participants might have understood it and why some chiefs agreed to sign. He was very critical of the 'modern' interpretation of the Treaty, arguing that it distinguished between Māori and Pākehā in a simple-minded way and implied that their worlds were so different that there was no possibility that they could ever have had a common understanding of the Treaty. Belgrave did not deny there were cultural differences between Māori and Pākehā but he argued that in seeking to understand the treaty-making it was just as important to grasp the influence of culture contact as it was to understand that of culture. Otherwise, he pointed out, there was a risk of losing sight of the complex agendas of all the parties and simplifying what had happened.[48]

He held that a properly historical account revealed several important points: by the time the Treaty was made, Māori had adopted, adapted and adjusted the European ideas they had encountered; Pākehā views of the world had been influenced by Māori; there could be major differences in agendas *among* both the Māori and the Pākehā interlocutors; the lives of many Māori and Pākehā had become integrated, even intertwined, due to the relationships they had forged on the basis of trade, land, religion and marriage; consequently, the power each exercised, or the autonomy they had, was limited. All these changes meant that, even though there were major differences between the way Māori and Pākehā understood things, they were sometimes able to find common ground. As a result, Belgrave insisted, it was a mistake to claim, as 'the modern treaty' did, that in 1840 there was a distinctive Māori understanding of the Treaty that was formed independently of the cultural encounter they had had and the personal relationships they had formed with Europeans, especially the missionaries. He contended that the Treaty was best understood as the product of those relationships and thus should be regarded primarily as a 'treaty of relationships', especially one that featured protection, rather than a 'treaty of rights'. (The importance that notions of protection played in the making of the Treaty has been emphasised in more recent scholarship. In fact, it has been suggested that protection, rather than sovereignty or anything else, should be regarded as its keyword.)[49]

Belgrave maintained that a consideration of the historical contexts in which the Treaty was made reveals that the 'modern' interpretation's focus on the differences between 'sovereignty' and 'rangatiratanga' was misplaced. He advanced several arguments in this respect. He held that its legal representations of the Treaty were simplistic and obscured what was at stake in its making, at least from the point of view of the Māori participants, arguing that they did not see it primarily in terms of a transfer of sovereignty but in terms of whether they would accept a governor. In the minds of the chiefs, he maintained, the Treaty amounted to an alliance that offered them a chance to be included in a powerful British Empire and one in which they ceded some of their authority but were promised that their interests would be protected. They understood that the governor would introduce a new system of law but did not see this as a serious challenge to their own law. Finally, Belgrave argued that while the Treaty was made in a world in which Māori remained dominant, the chiefs were acutely aware that times were changing and they felt vulnerable, and that in these circumstances they believed it made sense to sign the Treaty and hoped that the British Crown would uphold the promises it had given.[50]

Belgrave argued that a study of the debates that took place at the Treaty meetings revealed that they were mostly about land and religion[51] rather than sovereignty, indeed that these matters overshadowed everything else. Most of the grievances the chiefs expressed at the Waitangi meeting concerned the transfer of land. How the government would manage this trade, and thus the issue of pre-emption, was a key theme in the debates and at the heart of the questions that were raised about Williams's translation at the time.[52] He suggested, moreover, that one of the most important messages the chiefs would have taken away from what the British or Pākehā advocates of the Treaty had declared was that Māori would be protected in their lands, and that this was a vital consideration for those who agreed to sign.[53]

Lastly, in discussing the contexts in which the Treaty was made, Belgrave implied that it should be regarded as an agreement that was made largely with the present moment in mind and that it looked backwards to the 1830s rather than forwards to some future in the 1840s that remained unknown. Hence, he claimed, it marked the end of an era rather than the beginning of a new one, not least because the world that had created, interpreted, and given the Treaty its meaning was quickly eclipsed by the new, colonial state.[54]

In concluding — if this is the right word — his discussion of this 'historical treaty', rather than reiterating the arguments he had advanced, Belgrave argued that the 'modern' interpretation had lost sight of the fact that the Treaty was 'the product of a loose and contradictory process' and the 'uncertainty' that characterised it. In other words, he more or less repeated Ross's major argument. He quoted her well-known passage that began with the words 'However good intentions may have been', before adding: 'Out of all of this confusion, she argued, it was impossible to regard the treaty as much of an agreement about anything.'[55]

Having provided his account of 'the historical treaty', Belgrave turned to his main task, that of demonstrating that the Treaty has been interpreted differently by different people at different times. As historical change has occurred, he argued, the narratives told to make sense of the Treaty have 'reinterpreted' the events of the past, even those of the recent past, thereby shaping the meanings attributed to it. His fascinating account of the life of the Treaty after the 1840s served a useful purpose in bringing into question the claim that Orange had made in her book (but not her thesis): that Māori understandings of the Treaty over time were marked by continuity more than by change.[56]

Legal history

Since the publication of Belgrave's study, there has been no major book explicitly devoted to the history of the Treaty.[57] Nevertheless, a considerable amount of research has been undertaken that has challenged the dominant historical interpretation of the Treaty in various respects. This has occurred mainly because it has departed from Ross's focus on the texts, especially the Māori one, and on what happened on the ground in New Zealand, and paid more attention to the English text and the discussion and debates about the Treaty and related matters that took place among the British in both the metropolitan centre and the colonial periphery.

Much of this scholarship has been done by practitioners of legal history, that is, by legal historians in the strict sense of that term. Earlier we encountered scholarship that appeared to be legal history and which was read by many historians as though it was (see pp. 156–57), and so some clarification is required at this point. Paul McHugh, who during this period shifted from being a legal scholar to being a legal historian, is peculiarly well qualified to provide it. 'The engagement between law and history occurs in two senses', he has pointed out. 'There is, first of all, the role and presence of the law in the past — what is normally regarded, at least in academic circles, as legal history. This involves the disinterested retrieval and recounting of the past that is specifically, or primarily legal in character. Basically, it is an inquiry into how law has operated in the past.' Second, he goes on, there is the form that 'entails the use of the law in contemporary legal fora, such as courts and statutory or extra-statutory land claims processes [such as the Court of Appeal decision in *New Zealand Maori Council v Attorney-General*, the Treaty of Waitangi Act of 1975 and the Waitangi Tribunal] in which . . . past events are presented for contemporary resolution.' McHugh further explains: 'If the main interest of the first, or what might be called "disinterested legal history", is with the past for its own sake, the second is concerned with the present-day addressing and redressing of historical processes in which the law is often implicated, if not inculpated. . . . One has to be very cautious about characterising the narratives these processes produce as disinterested legal history.'[58]

Here, I will discuss the work of two fine legal historians, Mark Hickford (1969–) and Stuart Banner (1963–).[59] Hickford is a New Zealander who did his undergraduate study in law, history and political studies at the University of Auckland (where Andrew

Sharp and Keith Sorrenson were among his teachers), but the work I am primarily discussing began as a doctoral thesis at Oxford University under the supervision of a leading English imperial historian, John Darwin, and grew into a book that was greatly influenced by Pocock, Sharp and McHugh's scholarship.[60] Stuart Banner is a legal scholar born, bred and based in the United States, who has authored several books in the field of legal history. Both he and Hickford self-consciously undertook their research at some distance from the debates that were taking place in New Zealand about the Treaty and the Tribunal.

They adopted a larger framework for their projects than any historian who did historical research about the Treaty between the 1970s and the 2000s. Banner undertook a comparative study of the ways in which Anglophone empires took possession of land in the Pacific,[61] and examined the North American and Australian continents, New Zealand and smaller islands such as Fiji. Hickford considered New Zealand in a broad Anglophone context and had considerable knowledge of what was taking place in Britain and in its settler colonies.[62]

In considering how the British treated indigenous peoples' claims to rights of property in land, Hickford's and Banner's research was informed by the same premise that informed the work of the legal scholars discussed earlier, that is, that the law had played an important role in this regard. But their account differed in fundamental ways.[63] They did not treat the law as though it was an instrument that operated in some timeless fashion but emphasised instead that it worked in ways that were highly specific to historical contexts and so varied across time and place. They were critical of the claim legal scholars and lawyers had made that the law had exerted its influence by providing a set of norms that were then applied by imperial or colonial agents. They argued instead that the law in various guises often played an important part because it was not so much the source (or cause) of how indigenous peoples' title to land was to be treated but a resource that was deployed by a large range of players, most of whom were British, to advance their political, economic and cultural agendas.

In drawing attention to the importance of practice rather than precepts, both Hickford and Banner emphasised the role that *non*-legal forces played in determining how indigenous peoples' claims to sovereignty and land were treated by Anglophone agents. Banner drew into question the claim that the law and forces such as humanitarianism located at the imperial centre played the most significant role by demonstrating that the methods by which land was acquired were remarkably diverse. In doing this, he stressed the importance of what took place on the ground at the colonial peripheries as compared to what happened in the offices of government at the metropolitan centre (London and Washington). Furthermore, he pointed to the role played by 'path dependency', arguing that the way the matter of land was treated tended to be determined by what happened at the outset of colonisation. For example, in the New Zealand case, missionaries, being among the first settlers, saw a need to negotiate with Māori so they could gain access to their land, and this practice of treating with them as though they were the owners of the land was adopted by the British entrepreneurs who followed in their wake and sought to lay claim to huge swathes of land. This practice — and the perception it helped to create about Māori as a people who had some rights of property in land — made it difficult if not impossible for the British government to contemplate the colonisation of New Zealand on any other basis than that of negotiating with Māori as a people who had a lawful right to some land.[64]

In Hickford's view, the practice of politics at the imperial centre and its interplay with political thought (which included a consideration of legal matters), rather than any abstract or normative legal principles, primarily determined how Māori interests in land were treated. Accordingly, he argued that the actual substance of Māori property rights was provided not by any legal norms but was instead the result of contestation between the major political players in Britain. This meant, he emphasised, that the nature of Māori rights in land that those players were prepared to acknowledge or accept changed over time.

Neither Banner nor Hickford devoted much attention to the Treaty, itself a mark of the degree to which this new historical scholarship was challenging the claim that the Treaty has always been central to New Zealand's history. But when they did, they made some telling observations. Banner noted that the first part of its second article in the English text — 'Her Majesty the Queen of England confirms and guarantees to the Chiefs and Tribes of New Zealand and to the respective families and individuals thereof the full exclusive and undisturbed *possession* of their Lands and Estates Forests Fisheries and other properties' (my emphasis) — was ambiguous because it was by no means clear what 'possession' meant. He pointed out that there was a considerable range of opinion inside and outside the British government as to whether Māori had rights to all the land or only the land they occupied or used in a particular way (essentially, by cultivating it).[65]

Hickford made the same point as Banner but drew out its implications for historical interpretation of the Treaty. Far from the Treaty amounting to a simple and transparent declaration of legal principles, it did not provide any answers to the question about the precise nature of the property rights that had been guaranteed to Māori. Instead, it effectively invited political dispute, thereby revealing that aboriginal title in New Zealand was malleable. 'Its second article was emblematic of a sympathetic yet formulaic, procedurally oriented vocabulary of aboriginal proprietary rights vesting in *tangata Maori*', he wrote in his inimitable fashion. 'It was formulaic and non-analysed [i.e. not defined] in that it merely recited a view of Maori as possessing "lands and estates forests and other properties" in the absence of any clarity as to what such terms signified.'[66]

Hickford argued that it was a mistake to assume that disputes about the Treaty were central to the treatment of title to land in New Zealand. Indeed, he contended that it was possible to write a history of this subject that was not preoccupied with the Treaty as it was made in 1840. At most, he suggested, the Treaty was merely one document among several that were later used by the imperial administration to attain its objective of managing both Māori and settlers in the context of overseeing the colony's territorial arrangements. He also contended that historians — his example was Peter Adams but could have been Claudia Orange — were being simplistic when they suggested that there was a correct interpretation of the Treaty's articles. There was just too much political contestation in London — and, he might have added, the colony itself — for this to have been possible. Ross, no doubt, would have agreed, but whereas Hickford accepted that this was the case, she railed against it.[67]

In 2014 a legal scholar, Ned Fletcher (1975–) — who could be said to have grown up with the Treaty, as his mother, Dame Sian Elias, was a leading Treaty lawyer — completed a 1000-page doctoral thesis about the English texts of the Treaty.[68] Several years earlier, this focus would have been welcomed, given the degree to which the Māori text had come to dominate interpretation of the Treaty. But Head and Belgrave had already pointed out that the texts were a very slender basis on which to mount major arguments about the Treaty's meaning and McKenzie had suggested that this was to be found in the oral context in which it was made; Head and Belgrave had argued that the English and the Māori understandings of the Treaty appeared to be very similar; and Fletcher accepted what has become the conventional position about the status of the different texts since the publication of Ross's article: the English texts were merely drafts and the Māori text was the authoritative text.[69]

There is another reason why Fletcher's thesis cannot be said to have broken any significant new ground, even though it rests on an extraordinary amount of historical research, is cogently argued and a pleasure to read. It amounts to a return to the past in that it repeats the contention that Banner and Hickford have drawn into question, namely that legal, moral and political norms determined the meaning and implications of the Treaty. Its principal conclusions about the historical meaning of the Treaty actually bear a striking resemblance to those that have been presented by lawyers and historians in the context of the Tribunal's work. In other words, it resembles juridical history.[70]

Perhaps the most beneficial outcome of Fletcher's colossal thesis — which is typical of the historical scholarship that has been done on the Treaty ever since Ross's famous article — is that it can help us realise that there is something very odd, historically speaking, about placing so much weight on the Treaty *as a document* and the meanings and implications it might have had in 1840. Nearly all the scholars who have worked on the Treaty in recent decades have devoted infinitely more time to thinking about the particular words chosen by its drafters (Busby and Hobson) and its translators (the Williamses) than these men were ever able to devote to the task. We would do well to remind ourselves of Ross's point that these men had to perform this job with enormous haste. In short, concentrating so much on the Treaty texts, and on their possible meanings and implications at the time they were drawn up, has led to a loss of perspective.

Post-foundational history

In 1989 J. M. R. Owens remarked that very little of the historical writing about the Treaty had ever been executed in the manner that would satisfy Herbert Butterfield, who famously argued that historians should seek to understand the past on its own terms. Instead, nearly all of it was profoundly influenced by the present and designed to meet some contemporary purpose. In other words, historians of the Treaty had failed to *historicise* the past — that is, to reveal its particularity and thus the way it differed from the present. If Owens was writing today, he would probably make the same observation. Since he wrote, there has been an enormous upsurge in historical writing about the Treaty but very little of it would meet Butterfield's requirements.[71]

Owens was not especially troubled by this phenomenon. He invoked an argument that an English medieval historian had made about scholarly accounts of the Magna Carta: there was little point trying to establish the precise historical meaning of the phrases or clauses of a historical text of this kind as there was little hope that the historian would succeed, and, besides, any attempt to do so could only lead to distortion. I am not altogether persuaded by Owens's analogy. It seems to me that it might be possible to establish something like the historical meanings of a historical document made in 1840, as compared to one created in 1215 and for which the relevant historical sources are much sparser. At any rate, I believe there is some value in trying.[72]

One of the main reasons why nearly all the historical work done on the Treaty fails to adequately represent the past in its own terms can be attributed to the fact that it takes the form of 'foundational history'. By this I mean a kind of historical work in which writers try to discern in a particular historical event or text — in this case the treaty-making or the Treaty — some norm or another that they believe created or should have created the foundations of a nation, or which they hope could re-found the nation on a more legitimate basis. Foundational history tends to configure an event or text in terms of some homogeneous *essence* or another that is deemed to be invulnerable to historical change, or even as something that exists prior to its representation in historical knowledge.[73]

In my book *Empire and the Making of Native Title*, published in 2020, I sought to provide some of the elements of what can be characterised as a *post*-foundational history of the Treaty, partly by drawing on the work of Pocock, Sharp, McHugh, Head, Belgrave, Banner and Hickford. Rather than reproducing the interpretation of the Treaty that I advanced there, I will set out the assumptions that underpinned it and the tools that I believe are required to produce a post-foundational history of the Treaty and thus what we might call a truly historical account of the Treaty.

A post-foundational history assumes that it makes no sense to treat the Treaty as though its meanings exist outside of or prior to the way it has been interpreted or represented in any historical work or text. It assumes instead that the way the Treaty has been understood has always been the result of the ways it has been interpreted by some historical actor or another, including historians, usually in the course of telling a story about it. It also assumes that the Treaty's historical significance cannot and should not be taken for granted, recognising instead that it has only been significant at particular points in time. As a result, post-foundational history does not make the mistake of claiming or implying that the Treaty has always been central in New Zealand's history.

In seeking to show *how* and *why* the Treaty has been significant at particular times, a post-foundational history takes for granted that the Treaty was the subject of contestation from the very beginning and assumes that that contestation is responsible for determining what it has meant, or is believed to have meant, at any historical moment. In other words, Ross had a point when she expostulated that the Treaty has said whatever any New Zealander has wanted it to say (though we do not need to follow her in regarding this as a problem). As a theologian remarked many centuries ago, authority has a nose like wax and so can be twisted whatever way one wants.[74]

In a post-foundational history both the Treaty *and* all the parties to its making in 1840 are treated in a way that assumes they did not have some kind of essence that has been the same over time and therefore stable, or that they have been homogeneous, undivided and autonomous subjects. Instead, it assumes there was a multiplicity of players involved in making the Treaty in 1840 and that they only came to know themselves as Māori, Pākehā, and New Zealanders over time in the context of an encounter with each other and/or as a result of the histories that have been written about that encounter, some of which have included stories about the Treaty. Likewise, it assumes that those people we now know as Māori or British or Pākehā had a range of interpretive positions about the Treaty at the time it was being made and that those positions not only influenced one another but were formed in the course of a dialogue. Similarly, it assumes that this has continued to be the case.

A post-foundational history assumes that New Zealand did not exist in any meaningful sense prior to being represented in works of history and that it has not been unitary or homogeneous over time. It recognises that at the time a British colony called New Zealand was formally established, it was not independent but part of the colony of New South Wales, the web that was the British Empire, and an indigenous world. Furthermore, it recognises that there were at least two British colonies in the islands of New Zealand in the years that immediately followed the making of the Treaty (one formed by the colonisation company known as the New Zealand Company, the other by the colonial government) and that they challenged one another's claims to sovereignty, just as the indigenous peoples challenged the claim of sovereignty made by the British Crown as well as that of their fellow indigenes.

All these assumptions mean that any history of the Treaty that seeks to be true to the past will try to capture its complexity and heterogeneity and that of the parties that have made it, thereby enabling us to see that the meanings attributed to the Treaty *were* ambiguous and contradictory, as Ross argued, though probably not to the degree that she suggested or for all the reasons she put forward. It will make clear not only that the Treaty was made in two language texts and was almost certainly understood differently by some of the parties to it, but that the interpretation of each language text should be considered as being as important as that of the other and that the meanings attributed to one should not be privileged over those attributed to the other.

Producing a post-foundational history of the Treaty requires the adoption of particular methodological approaches. One of them is comparative history. Unless we use this method we risk attributing an explanatory value to the Treaty that it does not warrant. By comparing the islands of New Zealand with other places in which British planted colonies of a similar kind, and particularly those in which the Crown did not make any treaties with indigenous peoples, we are able to see that the British government's treatment of sovereignty and rights of property in land was determined not so much by whether they had made a treaty with those peoples but by events or processes that occurred over a much longer period and which both pre-dated and post-dated the time in which a treaty was made or might have been made. In other words, adopting a comparative approach reveals that the Treaty at the time it was made was little more than a sign or a symbol of how the matters of sovereignty and title to lands were *already* being treated by the Crown and that whether a treaty was transacted or not made little difference to what happened in the early phases of colonisation. Only later did the fact that a treaty had been made in New Zealand become so important, and even then this did not remain constant. Some historians, such as Owens, have distinguished between what they call histories of the Treaty as an event and histories of the Treaty as a symbol, but this ignores that whatever significance it has had has always lain in the realm of the symbolic, and that this has been the case from the very beginning.[75]

A comparative approach sheds light on this point from another perspective. While the Treaty was one of hundreds of treaties of its kind that were made in the eighteenth and nineteenth centuries, and while its content is like some the British made elsewhere, few if any of those other treaties have acquired the importance that the Treaty of Waitangi has. This point once again reveals that the reason for its significance lies not in its making in 1840 — however much that is a necessary precondition — but in what has repeatedly been said about the Treaty ever since, which is to reiterate that its significance is the result of the telling of stories about it. The same is true of Ross's article.

Historical comparison serves a useful purpose in drawing into question an assumption that has informed most if not all histories told about the Treaty: that common or mutual understanding of its terms was — and still is — a prerequisite for peaceable relations between Māori and Pākehā. This assumption has been held not only by those who have embraced the Treaty as a foundational document and sought to reconcile its two language texts in recent times but also by those who have derided it. Yet the American historian Richard White has shown, in a celebrated study of the relationship between native, British and French players around the Great Lakes between the middle of the seventeenth century and the early nineteenth century, that these culturally diverse peoples accommodated their differences with one another by means of a process he has called 'creative misunderstanding'. As he points out, people often misinterpret the values and practices of those they encounter, but from those misunderstandings new meanings and practices can arise. Such has been the case with the Treaty over a long period of time. In other words, what troubled Ross about the Treaty — that there was so much misinterpretation of and misunderstanding about its terms — need not be an insurmountable problem, as the work of the Tribunal has shown.[76]

A post-foundational history involves working with historical sources in particular ways. Historians often make the mistake of assuming that their historical actors sought to address the questions and problems that arose in the past by using the perceptual or conceptual categories that are dominant in the present, thereby failing to pay sufficient attention to the discrepancies that exist between their use of historical sources and the uses they had for those who created them. In a post-foundational history of the Treaty, the historian pays a good deal of attention to the processes that generated any historical source, asking how and why it came into being at a particular time at a particular place, who was its author, who was their intended audience, and what was the relationship between it and other sources.[77]

In doing this vital work, the historian distinguishes between 'historical traces' and 'historical sources' — the term historians commonly use to describe the materials they work with. 'A trace is anything remaining from the past that was not made with the intention of revealing the past to us, but simply emerged as part of normal life', the American historian Allan Megill has explained. 'A source, on the other hand, is anything that was intended by its creator to stand as an account of events.' As he points out, a trace, which is created inadvertently, provides a more solid basis for historical knowledge than does evidence that people in the past intended to stand as evidence. 'The reason is that a source is inevitably mixed up with past people's conceptions and misconceptions as to what was happening, whereas a trace, at least in its pure form, is devoid of such admixture. Sources are always already interpretations of events, whereas traces are not.' Megill hastens to add: 'To be sure, "traces" do not offer us facts in a pure state — nothing does. But by virtue of being only inadvertently evidence, traces are insulated from people's conscious or unconscious wishes to remember and testify in a particular way.'[78]

In a post-foundational history of the Treaty, historians are alert to the provenance of the historical traces and sources they use in the sense of *where* they find them and *how* they came to be there. Many of the ones relevant to the history of the Treaty are to be found in the archives of government, while many of them were printed in parliamentary papers soon after they were created. This can reveal much about the factors that made the Treaty a significant text. Reflecting on the nature of those sources means that a post-foundational history of the Treaty will acknowledge the severe limitations of the historical record, especially in respect of Māori perspectives. Many historians have assumed or even asserted that the record of the Treaty meetings is much better than it is (though Ross cautioned against this) and they have projected their findings about one of the areas — the far north — in which the indigenous people had become most familiar with European newcomers onto areas where they had barely met them. They have also played down the difficulties that arise because *all* the written record of these meetings was created by British or Pākehā players rather than Māori, and the longest account (Colenso's) was only produced many years later.

Finally, a post-foundational history of the Treaty requires a particular approach to the relationship between the word and the world. Authors of foundational histories have paid little attention to the fact that human beings use words not only to refer to, or document, the world in which we live but also to shape or change it. Historians have tended to mine historical traces and sources merely to derive information about the past. This documentary mode of using traces and sources is undoubtedly a vital part of any work that claims to be historical, but it is insufficient and it cripples a historian's capacity to grasp what happened in the past. In a post-foundational history a historian seeks to interpret historical traces and sources based on the assumption that they were often deployed by people in the past who were seeking to change something in the world around them. This means that whereas the authors of foundational histories of the Treaty have been astonishingly deaf to rhetoric, the author of a post-foundational history pays a lot of attention to the ways in which many key players used language to persuade their audience to their point of view or to see things in the way they wanted them to be seen.

A post-foundational history will reveal that the Treaty, just like Ross's work on it, was the result of historical processes that were seldom linear but halting, contingent and ultimately reliant on a large degree of chance, involving as they did forces that were invariably complex, frequently incoherent, sometimes mundane, occasionally base and seldom constant — hardly, then, the stuff of foundational history. This is not to say that a post-foundational history might not provide some kind of foundations for the nation, but it will do so inadvertently rather than intentionally, and in ways that reveal that those foundations are to be found not so much in the Treaty as it was made in 1840 but in the ways it has been interpreted again and again in the years ever since.

Having said all this, it is important to note that while post-foundational histories can provide accounts of the Treaty that are truer to the past than any other histories, this does not necessarily mean that in and of themselves they are beneficial for the life of the nation. It is to this question that we will now turn.

Chapter 8
The Advantages and Disadvantages of History

All human beings need history as a form of knowledge, Friedrich Nietzsche held, just as he maintained that history belonged 'to living man' in three different respects — 'so far as he is active and striving, so far as he preserves and admires, and so far as he suffers and is in need of liberation' — and that each of these corresponded to a particular kind of history: 'a *monumental*, an *antiquarian*, and a *critical* kind of history'. He explained: 'If the man who wants to achieve something great needs the past at all he will master it through monumental history; [he] who on the other hand likes to persist in the traditional and venerable will care for the past as an antiquarian historian; and only he who is oppressed by some present misery and wants to throw off the burden at all costs has a need for critical, that is judging and condemning history.' Most historical works, even simple ones, incorporate elements of each of these kinds of history.[1]

But Nietzsche believed that history can only be a good thing when it 'serves life'. He warned that doing too much history and attributing too much value to it brought with it 'a withering and degenerating of life'. He insisted that monumental, antiquarian and critical history each had advantages for the life of an individual, people and culture, but that this was only the case if they were tempered by the other kinds. Otherwise it could grow into 'a noxious weed'. As I have suggested in earlier chapters, Nietzsche's typology is useful for understanding how the various histories

I have been describing performed their public work. But it is also useful for answering the question of how histories of the Treaty might best serve New Zealand life.[2]

Myth and history

Many of the histories that have been at work in recent decades in relation to the Treaty — Whig history, common law history, juridical history, and Māori history — have elements of *monumental history* in that they have provided what Nietzsche called 'models, teachers and comforters'. This has been advantageous for New Zealand life as it has brought to the fore aspects of the past that have long been marginalised in New Zealand society; helped to redress injustices, revive Māoritanga and restore Māori pride; and enabled the nation to recover some of its legitimacy and thereby retain the loyalty of its citizens.

Yet these histories have been disadvantageous whenever they have not been tempered by *antiquarian* and *critical history*. This has occurred when monumental history has assumed the form of myth. In everyday parlance, 'myth' refers to a statement that is considered to be false. In using this term I do not exclude that connotation but I have something more ambiguous in mind. This is so because most mythic histories have a genuine link to a genuine past. To be considered plausible, they must be able to show that they have at least a partial relationship to past reality and what is regarded as historically truthful (or at least this used to be so). In the case of the Treaty, the moral, legal and political norms that have dominated the myths that most of the main players have told about the Treaty *did* play a role in the making of the Treaty in 1840 and even more so in how it was understood later. However, those norms did *not* make up the essence or even all of the past reality. In suggesting that they did, mythic histories of the Treaty have provided simple and one-dimensional accounts that have distorted the past.[3]

In recent years some academic historians have taken issue with these mythic histories. Perhaps the best example is Michael Belgrave. His book *Historical Frictions* is informed by a conviction that a properly or truly historical account of the Treaty must be provided and that this can only be done if the historian remains true to the vocation of history. He claimed that he had recovered 'the historical treaty' and even 'the real treaty' by peeling away the myths that had grown up around the Treaty in recent times as a result of the rise of 'the modern treaty'.

The position Belgrave has adopted is by no means unusual among academic historians. For a long time they have believed that they should be myth-slayers. Certainly, this was true of Ruth Ross and her contemporaries. At much the same time as she did her work on the Treaty, W. H. Oliver asserted: 'the academic historian, dedicated to reconstructing the past as faithfully as he may, must make it his business to detect and expose the myths, legends, and fallacies which accumulate around the past of his country'. He also believed, as many historians have done since, that historians should not limit themselves to exposing myths but should use them for the valuable clues they can provide into the mentality of the people who have constructed them, thereby subordinating the accounts they give of the past to the ones produced by the discipline of history.[4]

However, if monumental history has become a noxious weed in respect of the telling of histories about the Treaty, the same can be said of history in the form that Belgrave practised it. We might call it 'historicism', while Nietzsche would have called it *antiquarian*.[5] Like Belgrave, I believe that historians who seek to construct as accurate an account of the past as is possible are more able than anyone else to provide a true understanding of the Treaty as it might have been understood in 1840, say. But I doubt there are any sound grounds for denying the status of history to mythic accounts of the Treaty, as he does by calling them 'modern' rather than 'historical'. By creating a kind of analytical opposition between 'history' and 'myth',[6] historicism runs the risk of implying that the account the historian provides of the way an event or text was understood at the time it happened or was created should be favoured over the ways it has been understood since by people who rely on other forms of knowledge than history. In other words, historicism carries the potential disadvantage of dismissing or even ruling out of order other types of history such as the mythic, which can reveal perspectives of the Treaty that were submerged and repressed at some point in time. This was one of the points that Eddie Durie was making in calling for the recovery of Māori accounts of the Treaty.

In any case, the stance that historians like Belgrave have taken towards myth is odd, given that most historians recognise that the significance of a past event tends to lie not so much in what took place but in what is later believed to have occurred. As Ross herself remarked after she had published her famous article: 'I have long maintained that it is not what happened in history which is important, but what people think happened.' This point is especially important in this context as the significance that has been attributed to the Treaty throughout New Zealand's history has undoubtedly been the result of the ways it has been understood at various moments after 1840, rather than the way it was understood at that time. In short, academic historians must be careful not to exaggerate the importance of the past in which the Treaty was made, as compared to that of the pasts in which it has since been represented.[7]

By placing too much emphasis on the particularities of the moment in which the Treaty was made in 1840, historicism runs the risk of exaggerating the changes and differences in the way the Treaty has been represented over time and thereby obscuring the continuities and the similarities in the way it has been understood. Belgrave argued that differences between the 'historical treaty' and the 'modern treaty' are so great that the two amount to 'different treaties', rather than just different interpretations of the same agreement. This contention tends to play down the repetition that occurs in the way the past can, albeit with some variation, reappear in the present. It also obscures the ways in which later interpretations are nearly always in dialogue with earlier ones. All this means that it makes little sense to talk of mythic accounts as 'inventions' or 'fictions'. One is better to describe them by using words like 'making', 'formation' and 'construction', thereby indicating that these representations are also historical in nature, albeit in a somewhat different way from that of a work that seeks to historicise the past in which a text was created or an event happened and thus capture something of its particularity.

In seeking to recover the particularities of the treaty-making in 1840, historicism carries the danger of consigning the Treaty to a long-ago past, so that it comes to be regarded as merely an object of antiquarian interest with little if any significance in the present. This was Nietzsche's concern about academic history: that in excess it can be deadly and hence no longer able to serve life. It can be argued (as Belgrave has done) that as the role of academic history has increased and that of Māori oral tradition declined after the Tribunal was granted the power to hear claims about breaches dating back to 1840, there is a risk that the purpose for which the Tribunal was created in the first place — to address contemporary Māori disadvantage — is not being fulfilled as much as it once was.[8]

Historicist accounts of the Treaty carry yet another risk in that they can lead to an insistence that the meanings the Treaty had at the time it was made should be regarded as paramount irrespective of the outcomes. A historical comparison makes this problem clear: it is generally believed that no treaties were made in Australia with the indigenous people, but the cause of justice is not served by claiming that Australia should be bound by its original denial of the indigenous people's sovereignty and rights of property in land.

As far as *critical history* is concerned, it has undoubtedly served life in New Zealand in recent decades by 'dragging' past breaches of the Treaty 'to the bar of judgment, interrogating [these] meticulously and finally condemning [them]' (as Nietzsche would say). But there are disadvantages when this kind of history becomes dominant, as it has done at some moments among both Māori and Pākehā. As J. G. A. Pocock has argued, a history that undermines the traditional mythic narratives that have long provided Pākehā with a sense of identity, may suggest that a new identity can be found merely by rejecting those myths, but those who claim to have thereby emancipated themselves will never be free and might even cripple themselves. If Pākehā are to work through difficult subjects such as the Treaty, historians must help them rethink their past by studying it in all its complexity, rather than encouraging or allowing them to believe that, somehow or other, they have no relationship to their forebears and have inherited nothing from them, such as the land their ancestors acquired and the wealth they made from it, or at the very least the culture they developed.[9] For Māori, the risk in critical history dominating the two other kinds of historical thought is that it tends to represent the past in such a way that denies the possibility that their forebears might have been implicated in some way or other in what happened. Insisting that one's ancestors had no agency is hardly a recipe for life.[10]

Another disadvantage of critical history becoming too powerful springs from the problems that occur when judgement triumphs over understanding. The remarks the French historian Marc Bloch made in this regard are worth bearing in mind. 'When all is said and done, a single word, "understanding", is the beacon light of our studies', he wrote in 1944. '"Understanding", in all honesty, is a word pregnant with difficulties, but also with hope . . . Even in action, we are far too prone to judge. It is so easy to denounce. We are never sufficiently understanding. Whoever differs from us — a foreigner or a political adversary — is almost inevitably considered evil. A little more understanding of people would be necessary merely for guidance, in the conflicts which are unavoidable; all the more to prevent them while there is yet time.'[11]

Just as problems have arisen about the proper place of the Treaty in New Zealand life as monumental, antiquarian (or academic) and critical history have become too powerful in one context or another, there is a risk that history itself as a form of knowledge has been too important in New Zealand politics, culture and society more generally. We need to ask what role history and its practitioners are best equipped to play. Many of the matters at stake in regard to the Treaty concern justice and ethics and so are legal and philosophical in nature rather than historical. Consequently, they require the kind of judgements that lawyers and philosophers are probably better trained to make (as Eddie Durie was saying). This is not to suggest that historians do not or did not have a role to play, but it does mean that they need to be clear about what role they and their discipline are best able to perform.

In praise of history?

In recent years historians have been insistent about the advantages of academic history in any public discussion and debate about the Treaty. 'It is important', Michael Belgrave declared in his *Historical Frictions*, 'that any utilitarian reconstruction of the treaty should be based on a sound interpretation of the historical treaty.' Yet he did not provide a satisfactory explanation as to *why* he believed this to be the case. He has not been alone. The same was true of Alan Ward and W. H. Oliver, to cite two notable examples that were discussed earlier.[12]

Belgrave argued that contemporary legal and political positions about the Treaty that have 'historical foundations' are 'open to criticism if those foundations prove unsustainable' as a result of their being tested by the methods of academic history. But he does not make clear why he believes that such interrogation will render 'the modern treaty' unsustainable. Moreover, having insisted on his 'historical treaty' as the correct interpretation of the Treaty, he concedes that even in 1840 the Treaty could not be pinned down to a single interpretation for the small number of British actors involved, let alone the more than 500 rangatira representing diverse communities. Furthermore, he has argued that the interpretations of the Treaty over time have been so different that 'there can never be a "true" meaning' of the Treaty. Perhaps it is no surprise, then, that there are moments when he seems to give up on his notion of 'the historical treaty' as the right interpretation and 'the modern treaty' as the wrong one, and refers instead to 'earlier treaties' and 'later interpretations'. He even seems resigned to the possibility that historically sound interpretations of the Treaty can play only a limited role in influencing what the Treaty 'can be made to mean'.[13]

Belgrave has not been alone in struggling to pinpoint the advantages of a thoroughgoing historical account of the Treaty as a force for life. Historians of his generation (which is also mine) have lost the confidence that a Beaglehole or a Ross once had in this regard, partly because of a loss of faith in historical objectivity (see p. 148). Unlike many of the historians who have worked on the Treaty in recent decades, I doubt that practising history in accordance with the conventions of the discipline makes it possible for our findings to be of much practical use, and I am sceptical that a good historical account like a post-foundational history can be empowering, let alone liberating. One way or another, it has been difficult for Treaty historians in New Zealand to reconcile the demands of their discipline with those of being a citizen, let alone those of an advocate.

This does not mean that history has nothing to offer beyond its cloistered life. To clarify what it can offer, one must consider what good history comprises and how it can be accomplished. In my view, historians should continue to strive to provide historically truthful accounts, seeking in this case to reveal what the Treaty might have meant to all the parties who made it in 1840 *and* what it has meant to various parties since. In other words, I hold that historians should commit themselves to trying to understand pasts on something like their own terms. In so doing it is crucial they do not simply *assume*, *assert* or *imply* that such and such a claim about the meaning of the Treaty is true (which increasingly characterises the work of many historians) but that they put forward arguments and evidence that justify their claims.[14]

Above all else perhaps, good history requires that historians maintain a commitment to objectivity, though not objectivity in any absolute sense, which is a notion that implies that it is possible to practise history in a way that is disinterested or neutral.[15] The pursuit of the noble dream of objectivity is inescapably conditioned by the perspectives a historian brings to their work. Commitment to objectivity does not exclude moral and political commitments but takes them for granted. Historians must be committed to being objective *and* to achieving good moral and political outcomes. Without the latter commitment, they are unlikely to be able to interpret the past in a satisfactory way, for their work will lack purpose and meaning and thus be dead or deadening. Nevertheless, historians must try to ensure that they do not cross over the razor-thin line that separates historical scholarship from political advocacy. Doing this requires self-control (though not self-immolation) so that they are both able and willing to abandon wishful thinking, accept findings that do not serve the cause they support, and discard pleasing interpretations that do not pass elementary tests of logic and evidence. This would mean, for example, that New Zealand historians would not assert, as several have done in recent years, that in 1840 some of the *British* players who were party to drawing up the Treaty understood it as an agreement in which the sovereignty of the chiefs had been guaranteed in a comprehensive sense.[16] Nor would any historian argue that Māori never knowingly engaged in transfers of land that they knew amounted to sales, as several historians have done, or that the British Crown undertook to protect Māori in the possession of all their lands, as most historians have done.

The mental acts needed to pursue the unattainable goal of objectivity requires distance, though not detachment, from one's own perceptions and convictions. By achieving something like this, historians can develop perspectives that are multifaceted. It needs to be acknowledged, though, that this is a difficult task. Historians invariably have strong personal relationships to the pasts they study, identifying emotionally (whether they are conscious of it or not) with something or other in them, and so they tend to be implicated in some way in the manner they relate to, and relate, those pasts. This identification is especially intense in the case of historians working on subjects that are highly charged emotionally, such as colonialism and thus the Treaty — all of which is to say that Ross was unexceptional and unexceptionable in this regard. But unless historians reflect on their relationships to the past and seek to counter their identification with it to some degree, they are likely to merely repeat some of the very forces that are active in it, rather than help in working them through.

The advice that the American historian Dominick LaCapra has offered about how historians might best handle their proximity to some aspect or other of the past they research and write about is useful. He has recommended that they accept or allow what amounts to an empathetic response to one or more of the subjects in their inquiry, whether those subjects be, say, a perpetrator, a collaborator, a victim, a resister or a bystander. However, he insists that historians should try to stop short of full identification with any one historical subject and recognise that there are differences between their own position and the position of that subject. At the very least this will enable historians to grasp the ways in which they probably have a relationship with subjects other than the one(s) they have been drawn to identify with. In so much of the history that has been written about the Treaty, historians have tended to identify with only one or two subject positions — most obviously with Māori as 'victims', but also Pākehā 'resisters' such as William Colenso and Sir William Martin (as Ross did) — but seldom with 'bystanders' with vested interests such as F. E. Maning (though Ross did), a 'collaborator' such as Henry Williams (unless he is made-over into a defender of Māori sovereignty or something like that), or 'perpetrators' such as the directors of the New Zealand Company who notoriously dismissed the Treaty as 'a praiseworthy device for amusing and pacifying savages for the moment'. By doing as LaCapra has suggested, historians can try to attain different degrees of proximity with the various subjects, which might enable them to understand each one of those subjects and the relations among them better (rather than merely judge them). This can help historians to acquire a more complex position in relationship to the past, a greater degree of objectivity (though not in any transcendent sense), and broader and deeper historical understanding, which might enable them to contribute to a working-through of New Zealand's difficult history.[17]

Just as historians can rightfully demand of our fellow human beings that they act fairly and honestly, readers have a right to expect that historians will strive to do the same. It makes sense for historians to declare the moral and political investments they have in their subject matter rather than pretend that they are absolutely objective or neutral, which only encourages or endorses the illusion that this is possible. Paradoxically, readers are probably more likely to conclude that a historian has been relatively objective when they know they have a moral and political commitment in spades and yet have treated the past in a way that seems fair and honest. Historians cannot expect to be trusted as storytellers unless their readers are persuaded that they have at least tried to be objective. As Allan Megill has remarked in discussing objectivity, 'truth and justice, or whatever simulacra of them remain to us, require at least the *ghost* of History if they are to have any claim on people at all. What is left otherwise is only what feels good (or satisfyingly bad) at the moment.'[18]

Striving for objectivity requires that historians adopt a critical approach to all accounts of the past, whenever they have been created. It also demands that they consider as much of the historical record as they possibly can. (Although historians cannot hope to achieve the certainty of the logically deduced kind, their accounts can still be assessed as more or less likely to be true based on how well they deal with the totality of the evidence.) In doing this, a good historian will resist adopting a single unequivocal interpretive position and be willing instead to leave their mind suspended between conflicting arguments or claims and so leave at least some matters unresolved. This has been called the principle of historical irresolution. Any claim on the part of the historian to know the past with certainty violates that principle. A good interpretation will not seek to settle once and for all the meaning of a text such as the Treaty or Ross's article about it. At best, it will seek to activate or reactivate a process of inquiry, opening up new avenues of investigation and reflection. In this regard it is vital that historians enter openly into dialogue with the past as well as other practitioners, rather than present their work as though it is the product of some kind of monologue.[19]

By continuing to practise the discipline of history in the ways I have been describing, historians can contribute to a cognitively and ethically responsible public sphere. In addition, they can perform an invaluable service by revealing how the past was different, though not altogether dissimilar, from the present, and thus something that is surprising and even astounding, which they can do only by trying to recover the past on something like its own terms. One might go so far as to say that unless a historical account has that quality of surprise it lacks any intellectual justification. By bringing to the fore a past that is no longer evident — as I trust I have done here in my account of Ross's work on the Treaty and the contexts in which she did it in the 1950s — we are able to see how the horizon of the present is not the only horizon or way of seeing. We can then engage with this alternative world and, on the basis of what we learn, act in our own.[20]

The difficulties for history

Even if historians can recover their faith in the conventions of their discipline, they will still struggle to influence the ways the history of the Treaty is understood in the public realm. As the American historian Paul A. Cohen has pointed out, myth (as well as memory) has 'an emotional power and importance — we may . . . call it a kind of subjective truth' — that academic history tends to lack. Historians ignore this at their peril. '[T]he very notion that the truth about the past . . . is necessarily and always of greater value than what people want to *believe* is true about the past may itself be little more than a myth.' Historians do well to remember that there are several different kinds of value — not only the intellectual one that they tend to favour, but moral, emotional, aesthetic and political ones as well — and that assertions about the past that are ranked highly in respect of one of those qualities may not be ranked highly at all in respect of the others.[21]

The point Cohen has raised goes to the very heart of the discipline of history. To understand why this is so, we need to know a little about its antecedents. The philosopher of history Hayden White, despite or perhaps because he has been a severe critic of the discipline, is a useful guide. All cultures, he notes, conceive of a relationship between past and present, but the West is peculiar in that it posited a disjuncture or even a break between the two and then sought to bridge it by creating the special discipline called history. Since the nineteenth century, this has driven a wedge between two notions of history that in previous times had been indistinguishable: what the philosopher Michael Oakeshott called 'the historical past', which was the preserve of academic historians who pursued a disinterested study of the past as it really was and as an end in itself, and 'the practical past', which was considered to be a storehouse of inspiring norms, ideals and examples that were deemed worthy of remembrance and repetition, which is the kind of history that ordinary people and politicians, judges, reformers, indeed most people, carry around with them as an imagined past reality, as we have seen in regard to many of the stories told about the Treaty. White points out that making this distinction between the past and the present was necessary for history to establish its status as a discipline but contends that this has robbed it of the capacity to make moral, aesthetic and political judgements. At the same time, he notes, history has set itself up as the judge and arbiter of 'practical' and other kinds of history, such as myth, even though mythic accounts have continued to address existential concerns about loss, violence, death and other such subjects. Ross was similarly critical of academic historians who stood in judgement on the works of amateur historians such as Thomas L. Buick and James Cowan.[22]

In recent decades, White points out, there has been a distinct loss of interest among ordinary citizens in the writings of most academic historians while at the same time there has been a surge of interest in the products of 'practical' history such as biography, historical films, historical novels and historic houses. In this situation, he argues, the salvation of academic history — insofar as he believes it deserves to be saved — does not lie in it vulgarising its practices by trying to do better what 'practical' history does. Rather, it involves the discipline amending its notions of history's importance as a field of study, revising its methods, and returning to the intimate relationship it once enjoyed with art, poetry, rhetoric and ethical reflection.[23]

In White's opinion, academic history cannot participate honourably in discussions of the ethical and political issues that beset a society while it has little more than its conventions to draw on, given that those conventions have rendered it unable to make cognitively legitimate judgements. In his view, academic historians are mistaken in assuming that their current practices are adequate to the task of analysing and adjudicating the most pressing public issues. He suggests that the best way for academic historians to counter any story that is supposed to have misrepresented the past — as many academic historians believe the Tribunal or the 'modern' interpretation of the Treaty have — does not lie in their providing more historical facts, but in producing better stories, by which he means stories told with greater artistic integrity and poetic force. Ross would have agreed. In cases like contemporary New Zealand, White would say, no amount of professionally established historical fact can adjudicate the contending claims of Māori and Pākehā to the land of — what should we call it so as not to prejudice the issue? Aotearoa? New Zealand? (White was referring to Palestine and Israel.)[24]

White has suggested that historians need to give more thought to the relation between ethics and the historical — ethics, as he points out, being about the difference between what was or is the case, and what ought to have been or ought to be, in some area or another of human thought, belief or action. 'The historical past is "ethical" in that its subject matter (violence, loss, absence . . . death) arouses in us the kinds of ambivalent feelings, about ourselves as well as about the "other", that appear in situations requiring choice and engagement', he has observed. 'In order to deal with these kinds of events', he has argued, 'appeal should be made to ethically rich traditions of literary expression, but it is precisely these of which, in their efforts to become "scientific" or "objective" or indeed even "neutral" historians have deprived themselves over the last century or so.' Consequently, the training of historians needs to be overhauled to re-establish the connection between the aims of historical inquiry and the traditions of artistic expression. White would probably cite Ross's bulletin *Te Tiriti o Waitangi* and her essay in *The Feel of Truth* as examples of the historical work that is required. In those two works, by setting aside the discipline's strictures about the need to distance oneself from the past to the point of detachment, its preoccupation with facts, sources, research and evidence, and its preference for analysis and making an argument, she was able to use her imagination to speculate about what might have happened and adopt literary devices to bring the past alive for her readers.[25]

The difficulties White points to have become even greater in recent times as a new chapter has begun in the history of truth. American philosopher Michael P. Lynch has pointed out that truth, upon which a good deal of public life in any democracy rests, faces an uncertain future as there is a great deal of evidence to suggest that we are no longer able to agree about how to establish what is true because many have become blind to proof. 'Without a common background of standards against which we measure what counts as a reliable source of information, or a reliable method of inquiry, and what doesn't, we won't be able *to agree on the facts*, let alone values', he has pointed out. 'When you can't agree on your principles of evidence and rationality, you can't agree on the facts. And if you can't agree on the facts, you can hardly agree on what to do in the face of the facts.'[26]

We have lived for a long time in a culture of fact, as the historian Barbara J. Shapiro has observed. Yet, as she has noted, this has only been the case since about the thirteenth century, when a new method of inquiry and a new doctrine of evidence came into being in the law. They rested on a notion that an observed act or thing — the substance of fact — was the basis of truth and the only kind of evidence that was admissible in realms where truth was being arbitrated. Prior to this, a fact, etymologically speaking, was an 'act' or a 'deed'; it did not mean something that had been established as true. Instead, trial by combat and trial by ordeal served as the means of criminal investigation and the forms of legal proof. Between the thirteenth century and the nineteenth century, though, the 'fact' spread from the law to science, history and the like. More especially, during what is known as the Enlightenment (beginning in the late seventeenth century), empiricism — the method of inquiry in the pursuit of knowledge that relies on observation, experimentation or induction, rather than on intuition, speculation and deduction — came to be regarded as the means of discovering truth as something that was impartial and verifiable. But since the 1970s this has been under assault by forces that range from fundamentalism to post-modernism, which regard empiricism as an error and either hold that the only truth is that of the divine and/or that there is no truth. As a result, the era of the fact might be coming to an end. If this is the case, the implications for history as a form of knowledge are far-reaching.[27]

History and democracy

In New Zealand, historians — and particularly those working on aspects of the past touching on Māori history — have been facing the difficulties I have been describing for some time now. As Dipesh Chakrabarty has noted, the democratisation of history-making that has taken place during the last seventy years has made it clear that history is just one way of understanding the past. In other words, in the case we are considering here the pressure on the discipline of history has arisen not so much because of the demand to include Māori perspectives of the past that it previously marginalised. (After all, the story Māori have told about the past differs little from the one Pākehā academic historians have been telling since the 1950s.) Rather, it is because other forms of knowledge than history, such as myth, oral tradition and mātauranga Māori, which the discipline was previously able to rule out as invalid ways of representing the past, have been at work in the world outside the universities and have emerged as rivals.[28]

At the same time, Māori, drawing on those other forms of knowledge to tell their stories, have been entertaining the prospect of a future New Zealand that is radically different from the way the practitioners of the discipline of history have long imagined it: one that is characterised by diversity and plurality, and that even has more than one source of sovereign power and authority. By contrast, historians have conceived of their task as one of accommodating stories that have been told from particular and conflicting perspectives and integrating them into a commonly held collective history of New Zealand that they have believed is a public good, as it transcends difference and conflict. Many historians have long assumed that it is their task to produce just such a history, a history that will be accepted as true by all New Zealand citizens. This project can be called a 'shared history'. It has undoubtedly been at work in regard to the Treaty. For example, in a book published by the New Zealand Government Printer in 1990, entitled *The Treaty Now*, W. L. Renwick spoke in terms of 'the perspective from which the treaty *must* now be seen' (as the Māori Magna Carta) and 'the way the treaty *should* now be interpreted' (as set down by the Waitangi Tribunal).[29]

Moreover, historians like W. H. Oliver have assumed that their discipline not only has a role to play in producing a history that will be shared by all New Zealanders, but that they also have a part to play in adjudicating public debates about the past by adducing reason and logic. They have believed that by practising history in terms of its fundamental categories of 'facts', 'sources', 'research', 'evidence' and 'truth', they would be able to persuade members of the public to accept their accounts of the past and settle disputes between warring parties, thereby obviating any need to resort to other means, such as emotion and rhetoric, which are deemed to lack reason.

All these assumptions have been challenged in recent decades, as we have seen. Māori, among others, have been representing the past in ways that are dominated by subjective points of view and perspectives. They have deliberately been telling stories that often rest on a blend of history, the common law, oral tradition, myth and mātauranga Māori. Many have rejected any need to seek validation from the discipline of history and have been unwilling to subject their own accounts to the historian's methods of verifying what happened in the past. Most importantly, in refusing to accept the authority that history claims for its accounts of the past and in challenging the ideal of the nation as an integrated whole, they have demanded that *their* ways of knowing the past be adopted by Pākehā and thereby become a 'shared history'.[30] Moreover, they have recently had some success in persuading New Zealand universities to conduct their work in these terms, as some emphasis has been placed on the importance of carrying out research and teaching in accordance with the principles that underpin mātauranga Māori. (This has compounded the difficulties that academics have been facing as the pursuit of neoliberal policies has devastated departments in the humanities and social sciences[31] and contributed to the decline in their capacity to be independent because of the demand that their work be useful, rather than merely relevant, and that it pay the bills.)

What I have been describing has thrown up difficulties of several kinds, not only for the discipline of history but for democracy as well. As we have seen, professional historians have long attached enormous weight to the importance of being able to assess the stories being told about the past according to whether they meet the protocols of history for determining what is true and real. But for some time now Māori have been telling stories that do not always conform to the protocols demanded by the discipline because they do not meet its definition of what constitutes a fact and evidence. In this situation many historians, among others, have been wondering how competing claims to truth will be adjudicated and worrying whether the absence of a minimum agreement about what constitutes a fact and evidence might fragment the body politic and thereby impair the capacity of the nation to function.

Other historians — most notably Pocock — have asked whether it is appropriate to insist that Māori present historical accounts that meet the rules about knowledge prescribed by Pākehā. Still others have held that the universities and the broader public realm in New Zealand continue to respect the empiricist impulses of executive government, the bureaucracy and the judiciary and so have assumed that all will be well. But given the increasing challenges that have been made to truth claims around the world, they might now feel they have less reason to be so confident. Whatever the case, many historians remain apprehensive about the differences over what constitutes historical knowledge and the conflicts that this can cause, about how these might be negotiated, or whether they can be handled at all.

In this context it has become evident, to some at least, that the project of *shared history*, irrespective of whose story or what kind of story is to be told, is flawed. This is so, it has been pointed out, because it is utopian in assuming that Māori and Pākehā can and will necessarily transcend the pull of their respective identifications so that they can agree about the truth of the injustices committed in the past. This project ignores the differences that exist between and among Māori and Pākehā, especially if we expand the meaning of Pākehā to include all non-Māori New Zealanders — tauiwi (foreign people) as they are sometimes collectively called. In any society, let alone one that contains peoples who belong to two or more cultural traditions, it is inevitable that there will be conflicting attitudes, opinions, beliefs and feelings about the past and its presence today. As Chakrabarty has remarked, 'it's damn difficult to share histories in ways that also allows us to negotiate differences. And we should not make a difficult thing seem easy.'[32]

Yet the project of shared history has done just that by ignoring the reality that, as in most countries with a difficult history, different stories about the past *are* told and upheld, in the public realm at any rate, because they are tied to what and who people identify with. Most of what is deemed to be true by ordinary citizens does not rest on proof or facts, especially when it concerns matters of race, culture and nation. As a leading Canadian academic, Michael Ignatieff (who is an academically trained historian and public intellectual and once led one of his country's major political parties), has remarked: 'shared truth about the past is possible. But truth is related to identity. What you believe to be true depends, in some measure, on who you believe yourself to be . . . People . . . do not easily or readily surrender the premises upon which their lives are based.'[33]

It should go without saying that a sense of one's collective worth is just as important for Pākehā as it is for Māori.[34] But in recent decades historians (as well as others) have not given enough thought to how the new history of the Treaty has affected those who closely identify themselves with the original European colonists. They have tended to proceed in a way that fails to recognise or least acknowledge that the way New Zealand history used to be told — and still is in some quarters — is a source of enormous meaning and value to many Pākehā. Not surprisingly, criticism of those people's allegiance to that story or history tends to fuel anger and resentment, especially when they are accused of racism, and even more so when historians and others express moral revulsion about the values, opinions and actions of their ancestors.

Every people, and especially a people who are being asked to relinquish some of their power, as Pākehā have been, need to have a view of their people's past that provides them with a modicum of self-respect and pride and a belief that they have a legitimate right to live where they do. Compared to settler Australians, Pākehā New Zealanders are fortunate in this regard. They can, if they so desire, tell a story about the Treaty along the lines that it recognised Māori as having some degree of sovereignty and rights of property, and was made by the British Crown partly with an intention of treating Māori better than they had other indigenous peoples. Moreover, they can choose to help uphold the honour of the Crown or the settler nation by doing their best to advocate or support those policies that seek to address the injustice suffered by Māori that was caused in part by their forebears or forerunners breaching the Treaty. (One of the reasons Claudia Orange's books on the Treaty have been so valuable is that they provide a story that enables this kind of identification.) What I am suggesting would see Pākehā doing more to learn about and uphold their own traditions and heritage, rather than just seeking to acquire greater knowledge of taha Māori (Māori perspectives), though that too needs to be done.

Shared history has also come to be problematic in that it tends to be told in a way that suggests that there are only two peoples and two cultural traditions in New Zealand: Māori and Pākehā. Despite current demographic profiles — in the 2018 census, nearly 30 per cent of New Zealanders stated their descent in terms other than Māori or Pākehā[35] — this bicultural framing means that there is a marked absence of other peoples in the way New Zealand's past, present and future is represented by most historians.[36] Consequently, the history that is told barely speaks to those who do not identify as either Māori or Pākehā.[37]

Given the flawed nature of shared history, what can be done? What is probably required is the abandonment of that project and its replacement by one that has been called 'sharing histories'.[38] Whereas 'shared history' largely conceives of history as a body of historical facts presented as a singular story compiled by an anonymous narrator and underpinned by one kind of knowledge about the past, 'sharing histories' assumes and accepts that historical narratives are told by people who are differently situated or positioned and who produce different kinds of knowledge about the past. That is, it acknowledges that the stories that people tell depend not only on who they are but their purpose in telling them, the circumstances in which they write or speak, the form and genre in which they do this, and their intended audience. The project of sharing histories makes plain that the conjunction between past and present is the ground upon which all such storytelling occurs. This can prompt people to reflect on the nature of the relationship they have to the history they are telling, hearing, reading or seeing, which can enable us to grasp that all historical knowledge is, to some degree, a matter of perspective and interpretation and that no one has a monopoly on historical truth. Contrary to what some might assume, the project of sharing histories does not take up a relativist position. It does not hold that all historical accounts are equal or that anything goes. It simply recognises that the most significant parts of any historical narrative are always partial and so the knowledge they produce is limited.

In sharing histories, it is assumed that all narrators will assert vigorously the value of their interpretation but acknowledge that most other interpretations have value as well. In this way, sharing histories can involve an exchange between differently situated peoples as they both tell their histories and listen, hear, read and see those of others. It can be a place of robust but (one hopes) respectful discussion, dialogue and debate. Here, the vital work of cross-cultural communication can occur so that everyone will have the opportunity to understand and respect each other's stories, even though they will continue to differ about the interpretations that they present.

The project of sharing histories assumes that New Zealand will continue to be peopled by groups with diverse histories and identities, recognises that ongoing conflict cannot be avoided but that it could nonetheless be limited, and recommends that this situation be accepted, however unsettling it might be. In other words, it assumes that national communities do not require that all conflicts be resolved, or consensus reached on all matters, and that it is better to admit the ongoing presence of different histories and seek to accommodate them through a practical and ethical commitment to democratic principles that includes respect for the civil, economic and social rights of all citizens. Sharing histories holds the possibility that a new kind of common history might be attained rather than a situation in which either Māori or Pākehā demand that the other submit to their narratives, the forms in which they tell them, and their kinds of knowledge. In Pocock's terms, this would amount to a treaty between histories. Making, let alone upholding, such a treaty will be bloody difficult, as Ross would say. Apart from anything else, the negotiation it requires means that the members of each party have to be committed to and confident enough about their own ways of doing 'history' in order to be able to engage in a thoroughgoing and critical fashion with the other's ways of doing it.

Finally, in keeping with the premises I have described here, the project of sharing histories will assume that a common understanding about the Treaty's meaning is not required for it to be a document of legal and constitutional significance; that both language texts will be taken into consideration; that debate over its interpretation can never be resolved; and that interpretations of it will change over time, though probably within certain limits.[39]

Since Ruth Ross's article was published in 1972, there have been remarkable changes in the way te Tiriti/the Treaty has been interpreted, an extraordinary rise in its status, and a great deal of change in the various lives of history. We cannot know what the future holds, but if the past is anything to go by, there will be another paradigm shift in the way that the story of the Treaty is told and the relationship between Māori, Pākehā and the New Zealand nation is figured. Te Tiriti, like history itself, is a story without an end.

Appendix: Te Tiriti o Waitangi/ The Treaty of Waitangi

The text in te reo Māori that was signed at Waitangi on 6 February 1840

Ko Wikitoria te Kuini o Ingarani i tana mahara atawai ki nga Rangatira me nga Hapu o Nu Tirani i tana hiahia hoki kia tohungia ki a ratou o ratou rangatiratanga me to ratou wenua, a kia mau tonu hoki te Rongo ki a ratou me te Atanoho hoki kua wakaaro ia he mea tika kia tukua mai tetahi Rangatira — hei kai wakarite ki nga Tangata maori o Nu Tirani — kia wakaaetia e nga Rangatira maori te Kawanatanga o te Kuini ki nga wahikatoa o te wenua nei me nga motu — na te mea hoki he tokomaha ke nga tangata o tona Iwi Kua noho ki tenei wenua, a e haere mai nei.

Na ko te Kuini e hiahia ana kia wakaritea te Kawanatanga kia kaua ai nga kino e puta mai ki te tangata maori ki te Pakeha e noho ture kore ana.

Na kua pai te Kuini kia tukua a hau a Wiremu Hopihona he Kapitana i te Roiara Nawi hei Kawana mo nga wahi katoa o Nu Tirani e tukua aianei amua atu ki te Kuini, e mea atu ana ia ki nga Rangatira o te wakaminenga o nga hapu o Nu Tirani me era Rangatira atu enei ture ka korerotia nei.

Ko te tuatahi

Ko nga Rangatira o te wakaminenga me nga Rangatira katoa hoki ki hai i uri ki taua wakaminenga ka tuku rawa atu ki te Kuini o Ingarani ake tonu atu — te Kawanatanga katoa o o ratou wenua.

Ko te tuarua

Ko te Kuini o Ingarani ka wakarite ka wakaae ki nga Rangatira ki nga hapu — ki nga tangata katoa o Nu Tirani te tino rangatiratanga o o ratou wenua o ratou kainga me o ratou taonga katoa. Otiia ko nga Rangatira o te wakaminenga me nga Rangatira katoa atu ka tuku ki te Kuini te hokonga o era wahi wenua e pai ai te tangata nona te wenua — ki te ritenga o te utu e wakaritea ai e ratou ko te kai hoko e meatia nei e te Kuini hei kai hoko mona.

Ko te tuatoru

Hei wakaritenga mai hoki tenei mo te wakaaetanga ki te Kawanatanga o te Kuini — Ka tiakina e te Kuini o Ingarani nga tangata maori katoa o Nu Tirani ka tukua ki a ratou nga tikanga katoa rite tahi ki ana mea ki nga tangata o Ingarani.

[signed] W. Hobson Consul & Lieutenant Governor

Na ko matou ko nga Rangatira o te Wakaminenga o nga hapu o Nu Tirani ka huihui nei ki Waitangi ko matou hoki ko nga Rangatira o Nu Tirani ka kite nei i te ritenga o enei kupu. Ka tangohia ka wakaaetia katoatia e matou, koia ka tohungia ai o matou ingoa o matou tohu.

 Ka meatia tenei ki Waitangi i te ono o nga ra o Pepueri i te tau kotahi mano e waru rau e wa te kau o to tatou Ariki.

Ko nga Rangatira o te Wakaminenga

The text in English that was signed at Waikato Heads in March or April 1840

Her Majesty Victoria Queen of the United Kingdom of Great Britain and Ireland regarding with Her Royal Favor the Native Chiefs and Tribes of New Zealand and anxious to protect their just Rights and Property and to secure to them the enjoyment of Peace and Good Order has deemed it necessary in consequence of the great number of Her Majesty's Subjects who have already settled in New Zealand and the rapid extension of Emigration both from Europe and Australia which is still in progress to constitute and appoint a functionary properly authorized to treat with the Aborigines of New Zealand for the recognition of Her Majesty's sovereign authority over the whole or any part of those islands — Her Majesty therefore being desirous to establish a settled form of Civil Government with a view to avert the evil consequences which must result from the absence of the necessary Laws and Institutions alike to the native population and to Her subjects has been graciously pleased to empower and to authorize me William Hobson a Captain in Her Majesty's Royal Navy Consul and Lieutenant Governor of such parts of New Zealand as may be or hereafter shall be ceded to Her Majesty to invite the confederated and independent Chiefs of New Zealand to concur in the following Articles and Conditions.

Article the first

The Chiefs of the Confederation of the United Tribes of New Zealand and the separate and independent Chiefs who have not become members of the Confederation cede to Her Majesty the Queen of England absolutely and without reservation all the rights and powers of Sovereignty which the said Confederation of Individual Chiefs respectively exercise or possess, or may be supposed to exercise or to possess over their respective Territories as the sole sovereigns thereof.

Article the second

Her Majesty the Queen of England confirms and guarantees to the Chiefs and Tribes of New Zealand and to the respective families and individuals thereof the full exclusive and undisturbed possession of their Lands and Estates Forests Fisheries and other properties which they may collectively or individually possess so long as it is their wish and desire to retain the same in their possession; but the Chiefs of the United Tribes and the individual Chiefs, yield to Her Majesty the exclusive right of Preemption over such lands as the proprietors thereof may be disposed to alienate at such prices as may be agreed upon between the respective Proprietors and persons appointed by Her Majesty to treat with them in that behalf.

Article the third

In consideration thereof Her Majesty the Queen of England extends to the Natives of New Zealand Her royal protection and imparts to them all the Rights and Privileges of British Subjects.

[signed] W. Hobson Lieutenant Governor

Now therefore We the Chiefs of the Confederation of the United Tribes of New Zealand being assembled in Congress at Victoria in Waitangi and We the Separate and Independent Chiefs of New Zealand claiming authority over the Tribes and Territories which are specified after our respective names, having been made fully to understand the Provisions of the foregoing Treaty, accept and enter into the same in the full spirit and meaning thereof in witness of which we have attached our signatures or marks at the places and the dates respectively specified.

Done at Waitangi this Sixth day of February in the year of Our Lord one thousand eight hundred and forty.

The Chiefs of the Confederation

Source: https://www.tepapa.govt.nz/discover-collections/read-watch-play/maori/treaty-waitangi/treaty-close/full-text-te-tiriti-o

Illustrations

1. Ruth Guscott's class in her final year at Whanganui Girls' College, 1938, Duncan Ross Collection.
2. Ruth Guscott, *c.* 1939, Duncan Ross Collection.
3. Ruth Guscott and George Burnard, *c.* 1943, Duncan Ross Collection.
4. Ruth Burnard and Mary Boyd, 1944, Duncan Ross Collection.
5. Ruth Burnard and her typewriter, *c.* 1944, Peter Boyd Collection.
6. Ruth Burnard, War History Branch, 1945, Duncan Ross Collection.
7. The Rosses, *c.* 1950, Duncan Ross Collection.
8. J. C. Beaglehole, 1958, Evening Post Collection, Alexander Turnbull Library.
9. Michael Standish, 1961, Archives New Zealand Te Rua Mahara o te Kāwanatanga.
10. Malcolm Ross, sketch map of Motukiore, 1959, Duncan Ross Collection.
11. Ruth Ross, Perunui Creek, *c.* 1957, Duncan Ross Collection.
12. Gathering outside Motukiore Māori school, *c.* 1957, Duncan Ross Collection.
13. Ralph Hotere, Maungataniwha, 1957, Duncan Ross Collection. Reproduced by permission of the Hotere Foundation Trust.
14. Pei Te Hurinui Jones, 1957, Pei Te Hurinui Jones Papers, University of Waikato Te Whare Wānanga o Waikato Library. Reproduced by permission of Ariana Paul.
15. The cover of R. M. Ross, *Te Tiriti o Waitangi*, 1958.
16. James K. Baxter, *c.* 1959, Alexander Turnbull Library.
17. Keith Sinclair, photo by Marti Friedlander, 1976, Marti Friedlander Archive, E. H. McCormick Research Library, Auckland Art Gallery Toi o Tāmaki, on loan from the Gerrard and Marti Friedlander Charitable Trust, 2002. Reproduction courtesy of the Gerrard and Marti Friedlander Charitable Trust.
18. Members of Nga Tamatoa, 1972, photographic negatives and prints of the Evening Post and Dominion newspapers, Alexander Turnbull Library.
19. Matiu Rata, 1975, Stuff Limited.
20. Bob Brockie cartoon, 1982, Alexander Turnbull Library.
21. Eddie Durie and Paul Temm, 1985, photographic negatives and prints of the Evening Post and Dominion newspapers, Alexander Turnbull Library.
22. Members of the Waitangi Tribunal, 1988, Dominion Post Collection, Alexander Turnbull Library.

Abbreviations

AC	Alistair Campbell	**MB**	Mary Boyd
AM	Alan Mulgan	**MGH**	M. G. Hitchings
ANZ	Archives New Zealand	**MH**	Matiu Te Hau
ATL	Alexander Turnbull Library	**MPKS**	M. P. K. Sorrenson
BP	Blackwood Paul	**MR**	Malcolm Ross
BPP	*British Parliamentary Debates*	**MS**	Michael Standish
CB	Charles Brasch	**MT**	Michael Turnbull
DB	Dora Bagnall	**NZPD**	*New Zealand Parliamentary Debates*
DR	Duncan Ross	**OW**	Ormond Wilson
EE	Enid Evans	**PE**	Pat Earle
EHM	E. H. McCormick	**PH**	Pat Hattaway
GB	Graham Bagnall	**PHJ**	Pei Te Hurinui Jones
IW	Ian Wards	**RIMB**	R. I. M. Burnett
JB	Judith Binney	**RR**	Ruth Ross
JCB	J. C. Beaglehole	**RRP**	Ruth Ross Papers
JKB	James K. Baxter	**RWK**	R. W. Kenny
JP	Janet Paul	**VUC**	Victoria University College
KS	Keith Sinclair	**WM**	Warwick McKean
LR	Lindsay Rogers		

Notes

References to Ruth Ross's Papers are to MS 1442 unless otherwise stated.

Preface

1. Throughout this book I capitalise the word 'treaty' as it has become customary to do so, but it is worth noting that this has only become a convention in recent times.
2. RR to KS, 8 May 1972, RRP, Box 84, Folder 4.
3. Chakrabarty, 'Public Life', p. 143, and *Calling of History*, pp. 6–8.
4. These papers contain innumerable letters by and to Ross relating to her work as a historian. From the early 1950s, if not earlier, she began, on the advice of a former colleague, to make carbon copies of the letters she wrote and keep those she received (RR to John Pascoe, 4 April 1956, RRP, Box 91, Folder 1). There is no reason to believe that she retained these letters for any other purpose.

Chapter 1: The Government Printer

1. See, for example, Harris with Williams, 'Rights', p. 361; Wyatt, 'Keith Sinclair', p. 14.
2. My account owes something to Rachael Bell's 'Texts' but my interpretation departs from hers in several important respects.
3. RR to KS, 8 May 1972, RRP, Box 84, Folder 4.
4. Ruth Miriam Burnard (née Guscott) Academic Record, University of New Zealand, 1938–44, ANZ, R12484935; RR to JCB, 22 September 1954, JCB Papers; RR to RWK, 28 January 1955, RRP, Box 90, Folder 2; RR to JCB, 25 February 1955, JCB Papers; RR to RWK, 8 March 1957, RRP, Box 91, Folder 1; RR to DB and GB, 17 June 1980, GB Papers, MS-Papers-1901-90-103-2/03; Bagnall, 'Ross', p. 54; DR, personal communication with the author, 11 September 2021.
5. Barrowman, *Victoria*, pp. 54–55; Hilliard, *Bookmen's*, pp. 83, 87, 91.
6. Hilliard, *Bookmen's*, pp. 83–84, 93–94, 96.
7. Burnard Academic Record; JCB, Memorandum for J. W. Heenan, 10 November 1941, ANZ, R14987658; RR to PE, 12 February 1954, ANZ, R12203920; JCB to RR, 20 December 1954, RRP, Box 90, Folder 2; RR to MT, 21 February 1955, ANZ, R12203920; RR to OW, 20 October 1971, RRP, Box 98, Folder 2; RR to MB, 27 April 1975, MB Papers; Bagnall, 'Ross', p. 54; Simmons, 'Obituary'; Boyd, 'Obituary', p. 190; Boyd, 'Ross', and 'Women', pp. 77–78.
8. University of New Zealand, Victoria University College, *Calendar*, 1939, p. 20; JCB to JP, 1 July 1953, reproduced in Beaglehole (ed.), *'I think'*, p. 299; RR to RWK, 28 January 1955; RR to JCB, 25 February 1955; JP to RR, 18 July 1955, RRP, Box 90, Folder 2; RR to MS, 18 April 1958, RRP, Box 91, Folder 2; RR to OW, 20 October 1971; Ian Ross to MB and Maurice Boyd, 7 July [1982], MB Papers; Beaglehole, *Life*, p. 295; Barrowman, *Victoria*, pp. 61, 382.
9. Ruth Fletcher to JCB, 14 November 1941, RRP, Box 24, Folder 5 (this letter was one of many Elsie Beaglehole

10 forwarded to Ross after Beaglehole's death, assuming it was written by her); JCB to JP, 29 October 1952, JP Papers, MS-Papers-5738-08; RR to OW, 20 October 1971; Bagnall, 'Ross', pp. 54–55; Beaglehole, *Life*, p. 295; Sutherland, *Paikea*, p. 230.

10 JCB, Memorandum for Heenan, 10 November 1941; Boyd, 'Women', p. 79; Beaglehole, *Life*, pp. 269, 271, 273–74, 281, 286–87.

11 In 1944 Guscott endeavoured to complete her degree by taking a couple of subjects (in political science and psychology) but had to abandon them for personal reasons: Under-Secretary, Department of Internal Affairs, to Sir Thomas Hunter, Principal, VUC, 3 April 1944, RRP, Box 90, Folder 1; Burnard to the Registrar, VUC, 27 July 1944, RRP, Box 90, Folder 1; Burnard Academic Record.

12 Ruth Guscott, Memorandum for Heenan, 16 March 1942, New Zealand Department of Internal Affairs, Centennial Publications Branch, Historical Atlas Material (henceforth Historical Atlas Material), MS-Papers-0230-007; RR to JCB, 22 September 1954; RR to BP, 5 October 1954, JP Papers, MS-Papers-5523-16; Boyd, 'Obituary', p. 188.

13 Pascoe to OW, 11 April 1960 and 13 April 1960, John Dobree Pascoe, Papers, MS-Papers-75-241-066; Boyd, 'Women', pp. 82–83; Beaglehole, *Life*, pp. 286–87.

14 Burnard, Draft of a memorandum for Heenan, undated, *c*. April 1944, RRP, Box 90, Folder 1; RR to JCB, 25 February 1955; RR to GB, 3 May 1960, GB Papers, MS-Papers-1901-90-103-2/02; Boyd, 'Women', pp. 83–84; Brookes, *History*, pp. 258–59.

15 JCB to Heenan, 5 August 1942, ANZ, R14987658.

16 Guscott, Memorandum for Heenan, 16 March 1942.

17 *Evening Post*, 20 October 1938; Foden, *Constitutional*; Guscott to Marie King, 23 August 1943, Historical Atlas Material, MS-Papers-0230-008; Burnard to Heenan, 31 March 1944, Historical Atlas Material, MS-Papers-0230-008; Burnard to Gilbert Mair, 6 April 1944, Historical Atlas Material, MS-Papers-0230-008; Burnard to King, 1 May 1944, RRP, Box 90, Folder 1; Burnard, 'Bay of Islands', 20 March 1945, Historical Atlas Material, MS-Papers-0230-009; RR to PE, 22 March 1953, ANZ, R12203920; Notes of an interview Rachael Bell conducted with Mary Boyd, June 2003.

18 Guscott to King, 23 August 1943; RR to DB and GB, 2 March 1952 and 13 March 1953, GB Papers, MS-Papers-1901-90-103-2/02; RR to JCB, 17 December 1952, RRP, Box 24, Folder 5; RR to PE, 8 February 1954 and 13 April 1954, ANZ, R12203920; RR to PHJ, 21 February 1955, RRP, Box 90, Folder 2; RR to MT, 21 February 1955 and 2 March 1955, ANZ, R12203920; RR to KS, 10 August 1956, RRP, Box 91, Folder 1; Ross, 'Review of Morrell', p. 110.

19 Beaglehole, *New Zealand*, pp. 38–39; Burnard letter, 1 October 1943, and Burnard to John Lee, 26 July 1943 [*sic*, i.e. 1944] and 7 August 1944, ANZ, R19966023; JCB to Heenan, 10 August 1944, ANZ, R19966023; Heenan to Minister of Internal Affairs, 11 September 1946, ANZ, R19966023; Ross, *New Zealand's*, pp. 5, 8–9, 16 note 13, 17, 22, 24, 26, 41, 66, 68–69.

20 Guscott, Memorandum for Heenan, 18 March 1943, Historical Atlas Material, MS-Papers-0230-008.

21 Hilliard, 'Prehistory', pp. 39–41.

22 Guscott, Memorandum for Heenan, 18 March 1943.

23 Burnard, Memorandum for Heenan, 31 March 1944.

24 Burnard to Lee, 8 June 1945, Historical Atlas Material, MS-Papers-0230-009;

25 Burnard to King, 1 May 1944; Burnard to Lee, 8 June 1945.

26 Marriage Certificate of Rex Whittington Burnard and Ruth Miriam Guscott, 15 October 1943, New Zealand Registry of Births, Deaths and Marriages, 1943/9507; Wellington Hospital, Index of Patients, entry 26 June 1944, ANZ, R2263386; Burnard to Mr N. H. Good, 10 July 1944, RRP, Box 90, Folder 1; Burnard to Lee, 26 July 1944; Burnard to the Registrar, VUC, 27 July 1944; Burnard to Lee, 1 August 1944, ANZ, R19966023; Certificate of Death for Burnard, 17 August 1944, New Zealand Registry of Births, Deaths and Marriages, 1944/25179; *Gisborne Herald*, 19 August 1944; Burnard, Affidavit, 15 September 1944, ANZ, R23137235; RR to DB and GB, 24 December 1981, GB Papers, MS-Papers-1901-90-103-2/03. I am indebted to David Dammery, a GP, for explaining the nature of both these diseases to me.

27 Burnard, Memorandum for JCB, 19 April 1944, RRP, Box 90, Folder 1; JCB, Memo for Heenan, 28 April 1944, ANZ, R14987658; Heenan, Memorandum for JCB, 10 May 1944, ANZ, R14987658; Burnard to Good, 3 May 1944, RRP, Box 90, Folder 1; RR to JCB, 25 February 1955; RR to LR, 18 April 1955, RRP, Box 90, Folder 2; RR to JB, 3 April 1969, JB Papers, MS-Papers-11115-139; RR to DB and GB, 24 December 1981; Bagnall, 'Ross', p. 56; Boyd, 'Ross'; Notes of Bell interview with Boyd.

28 A year later Ross was thrilled by the publication of *New Zealand's First Capital* in 1946, but Eric Ramsden wrote a very critical review of it that seems to have cut her deeply (Ramsden, 'Early Bay of Islands', *Evening Post*, 4 November 1946, copy held ANZ, R19966023; Bagnall, 'Ross', p. 56).

29 Burnard to Good, 3 May 1944 and 16 October 1944, RRP, Box 90, Folder 1; Burnard to Owen [Meads?], 17 October 1944, RRP, Box 90, Folder 1; Burnard to E. S. von Sturmer, 12 March 1945, Charles William Vennell Papers, MS-Papers-5922-1; Burnard to Lee, 9 April 1945 and 20 April 1945, Historical Atlas Material, MS-Papers-0230-009; Burnard to Miss Webster, 11 April 1945, Charles William Vennell Papers, MS-Papers-5922-1; RR to DB and GB, 9 December 1954, GB Papers, MS-Papers-1901-90-103-2/02; RR to CB, 4 February 1955, RRP, Box 90, Folder 2; RR to F. L. W. Wood, 8 March 1955, RRP, Box 90, Folder 2.

30 When Ian Ross's birth was belatedly registered in 1925 (Birth Certificate, New Zealand Births, Deaths and Marriages, 1925/3427), the year was listed incorrectly. The correct date — 8 July 1909 — was listed in the registry of baptisms of a Catholic church in Westport, where he was born (Certificate of Baptism, Diocese of Wellington, Parish of Westport).

31 Marriage Certificate of Ruth Miriam Burnard and Ian Munson Ross, 21 December 1945, New Zealand Registry of Births, Deaths and Marriages, 1945/64110; Brookes, *History*, pp. 258, 297; DR, email to author, 6 August 2021.

32 Salary Card for Ian Munson Ross, National Archives of New Zealand, Series 4414, Box 71; RR to JCB, 6 February 1947, ANZ, R19966023; RR to JCB, 17 December 1952; RR to LR, 18 April 1955; RR to JB, 3 April 1969; Bagnall, 'Ross', p. 56; Boyd, 'Ross'; Brookes, *History*, pp. 301, 324.

33 For copies and a discussion of each of these Treaty sheets, see Orange, *Treaty of Waitangi / Te Tiriti o Waitangi*, pp. 376–434.

34 [Turton], *Fac-Similes*; JCB to JP, 10 June 1953, JP Papers, MS-Papers-5738-09; RR to Elsie Beaglehole, 28 January 1973, RRP, Box 99, Folder 2. Beaglehole would have needed to give the Government Printer some public rationale for this commission. He might have found

35. RR to JCB, 26 May 1953 and 1 April 1954, RRP, Box 24, Folder 5.
36. RR to JCB, 26 May 1953; RR to PE, 17 June 1953, ANZ, R12203920.
37. RR to JCB, 26 May 1953; JCB to RR, 19 May 1957, RRP, Box 91, Folder 1.
38. RR to JCB, 18 July 1953 and 22 July 1953, RRP Papers, Box 24, Folder 5; JCB to JP, 22 July 1953, JP Papers, MS-Papers-5738-09; RR to PE, 27 July 1953, ANZ, R12203920; RR to JCB, 4 August 1953, RRP, Box 24, Folder 5; RR to JCB, 1 April 1954.
39. RR to JCB, 1 April 1954; RR to RWK, 19 January 1956, RRP, Box 91, Folder 1.
40. RR to JCB, 1 April 1954; Ross, 'Te Tiriti', p. 154.
41. RR to JCB, 1 April 1954.
42. *Auckland Star*, 6 June 1953, copy in Ross's Papers, Box 83, Folder 2; RR to JCB, 1 April 1954.
43. RR to JCB, 1 April 1954.
44. Ibid.
45. RR to JCB, 5 April 1954, RRP, Box 24, Folder 5, her emphases.
46. Ibid.
47. RR to KS, 24 June 1954, RRP, Box 90, Folder 2; RR to DB and GB, 16 November 1954, GB Papers, MS-Papers-1901-90-103-2/02.
48. RR to DB and GB, 16 November 1954, her emphasis.
49. Here I rely on one she gave Beaglehole in July 1957, but it is confirmed by what she told more than one of her correspondents in 1954–55.
50. RR to JCB, 2 July 1957, JCB Papers (I reference this version of this letter rather than the one in Ross's Papers [Box 91, Folder 1] as it includes handwritten amendments she made before sending it to Beaglehole); RR to MS, 6 August 1958, RRP, Box 91, Folder 2; Hilliard, *Bookmen's*, p. 51.
51. Burnard to Mair, 8 June 1944, Historical Atlas Material, MS-Papers-0230-009; Rutherford, *Hone*, p. 8; RR to JCB, 1 April 1954; RR to JCB, 5 April 1954; RR to KS, 24 June 1954; Ross, Paper, untitled and undated [1956], RRP, Box 79, Folder 4.
52. Buick, *Treaty*, pp. xvi, xvii, 89, 221–23, 297, 334; Orange, *Treaty*, pp. 234–38; Hilliard, *Bookmen's*, p. 51.
53. Ross was mistaken as this had actually occurred in the mid-1840s. See my *Empire*, p. 239 note 89.
54. Martin, *Taranaki*, pp. 13–14, 89; Martin, *Remarks*, pp. 42–43; RR to KS, 24 June 1954; RR to JCB, 2 July 1957.
55. RR to JCB, 2 July 1957.
56. RR to PH, 30 June 1954, ANZ, R12203920; RR to BP, 5 October 1954; RR to DB and GB, 16 November 1954; RR to JCB, 2 July 1957.
57. See, for example, Sorrenson, 'Towards', p. 174.
58. RR to DB and GB, 16 November 1954; RR to JCB, 2 July 1957.
59. Ross, Paper; Carr, *What*, pp. 10–14.
60. Ross, Paper; RR to DB and GB, 2 March 1952; RR to AM, 22 May 1956, RRP, Box 91, Folder 1; RR to Mr Dwyer, 14 October 1959, RRP, Box 91, Folder 3.
61. RR to RWK, 26 October 1954, RRP, Box 90, Folder 2; RR to DB and GB, 2 November 1954, GB Papers, MS-Papers-1901-90-103-2/02; RR to DB and GB, 16 November 1954; RR to PHJ, 21 February 1955; RR to JCB, 19 April 1955, RRP, Box 24, Folder 5; RR to JCB, 2 July 1957; Walker, 'Matiu', p. 185; Biggs, 'Jones'.
62. RR to EHM, 19 July 1954, RRP, Box 90, Folder 2; RR to RWK, 28 September 1954, RRP, Box 90, Folder 2; RR to RWK, 26 October 1954; RR to DB and GB, 2 November 1954, RRP, Box 90, Folder 2; RR to DB and GB, 16 November 1954;

RR to MT, 21 December 1954, ANZ, R12203920; RR to LR, 14 March 1955, RRP, Box 90, Folder 2; RR to LR, 18 April 1955; RR to JCB, 19 April 1955; RR to LR, 6 May 1955, RRP, Box 90, Folder 2; RR to MT, 9 May 1955, RRP, Box 90, Folder 2; RR to CB, 23 September 1955, RRP, Box 90, Folder 3; RR to MT, 23 September 1955, RRP, Box 90, Folder 3; RR to Mr Robertson, 25 September 1955, ANZ, R12203919; RT to RWK, 19 January 1956; RR to MT, 20 January 1956, RRP, Box 91, Folder 1; RR to DB and GB, 22 January 1956, GB Papers, MS-Papers-1901-90-103-2/02.

63 RR to JCB, 5 April 1954; RR to MS, 28 February 1956, RRP, Box 81, Folder 4.

64 Here I am principally relying on two versions of an untitled and undated paper that are held in Ross's Papers (Box 79, Folder 4). On the basis of the similarities between its content and parts of her correspondence at this time in which she discussed the Treaty and talk to this historical society, I have concluded that this is the paper she prepared for that occasion.

65 Ross, Paper.
66 *Ibid.*, my emphases.
67 *Ibid.*
68 *Ibid.*
69 *Ibid.*
70 *Ibid.*
71 *Ibid.*
72 *Ibid.*
73 *Ibid.*
74 *Ibid.*; RR to EHM, 15 June 1960, EHM Papers, MS-Papers-0166-11; RR to Henare Kohere Ngata, 9 September 1973, RRP, Box 84, Folder 4.
75 Ross, Paper. In recent years most scholars have refused to accept that the British government's position on this matter was profoundly ambiguous. For my attempt to make sense of its position, see my *Empire*, Chapter 4.
76 Ross, Paper.

77 *Ibid.*
78 *Ibid.* Ross also made these points in a letter to Ian Wards, 6 June 1958, RRP, Box 91, Folder 2.
79 Ward, 'Tribute', p. 6.
80 80 RR to RWK, 15 April 1956, RRP, Box 91, Folder 1; RR to JKB, 20 June 1957, ANZ, R12203919; RR to JCB, 2 July 1957; RR to IW, 6 June 1958; RR to MPKS, 19 March 1979, RRP, Box 73, Folder 2.
81 RR to RWK, 15 April 1956; RR to JCB, 2 July 1957.
82 About this time, Beaglehole overheard a conversation between two of Boyd's students: 'Oh how I hate that woman! The questions she asks you! And she told a boy one day he didn't know what he was talking about!' (JCB to JP, 19 March 1958, JP Papers, MS-Papers-5738-14).
83 RR to RWK, 15 April 1956; RR to EE, 9 July 1956, RRP, Box 91, Folder 1; RR to JKB, 20 June 1957; RR to JCB, 2 July 1957; RR to IW, 6 June 1958; RR to MS, 26 June 1958, RRP, Box 91, Folder 2; RR to MS, 6 August 1958; RR to PH, 9 August 1959, RRP, Box 91, Folder 3; RR to Isobel Andrews, 13 October 1959, RRP, Box 91, Folder 3; RR to GB, 3 May 1960; RR to EHM, 9 May 1960, EHM Papers, MS-Papers-0166-11; RR to R. I. M. Burnett, 11 March 1972, RRP, Box 99, Folder 1; RR to KS, 13 April 1972, RRP, Box 84, Folder 4; RR to OW, 16 August 1972, RRP, Box 99, Folder 1; RR to Beaglehole, 28 January 1973; RR to MPKS, 19 March 1979; Boyd, 'Obituary', p. 188; Munro, 'Mary', pp 124–25; McKinnon, 'Obituary', p. 32; Ovenden, *Bill & Shirley*, pp. 113, 115; Munro to the author, 26 March 2020, 29 April 2020 and 19 December 2021.
84 RR to GB, 3 May 1960; Boyd, 'Obituary', p. 188.
85 RR to JCB, 2 July 1957; RR to MS, 26 June 1958.
86 MB to RR, 2 July 1956, RRP, Box 91, Folder 1; RR to AM, 12 August 1956,

RRP, Box 91, Folder 1; RR to MS, 26 June 1958; RR to Beaglehole, 28 January 1973.

87 RR to RWK, 28 September 1954, RRP, Box 90, Folder 2; RR to DB and GB, 9 December 1954; RR to LR, 4 February 1955, RRP, Box 90, Folder 2; RR to AM, 11 April 1956, 22 May 1956 and 16 June 1956, RRP, Box 91, Folder 1.

88 Williams, 'Treaty', p. 237 note 1; RR to AM, 22 May 1956, her emphases.

89 RR to John Pascoe, 4 April 1956, RRP, Box 91, Folder 1; RR to RWK, 15 April 1956; RR to AM, 16 June 1956; RR to EE, 9 July 1956; RR to JCB, 2 July 1957; RR to BP, 1 October 1959, RRP, Box 91, Folder 3.

90 RR to MH, 31 March 1957, RRP, Box 91, Folder 1; RR to MS, 18 April 1957, RRP, Box 91, Folder 1; RR to JCB, 18 April 1957, RRP, Box 91, Folder 1; RR to JCB, 2 July 1957; RR to Burnett, 11 March 1972; RR to KS, 13 April 1972.

91 KS to RR, 17 August 1956, RRP, Box 91, Folder 1; RR to PH, 6 September 1956, RRP, Box 91, Folder 1; RR to BP, 5 October 1956, RRP, Box 91, Folder 1; RR to MS, 18 April 1957.

92 RR to MS, 23 May 1956, RRP, Box 91, Folder 1; MS to RR, 30 May 1956, RRP, Box 91, Folder 1; RR to MS, 4 July 1956, RRP, Box 91, Folder 1; RR to MS, 18 April 1957.

93 JCB to RR, 19 May 1957; Beaglehole, *Life*, p. 295.

94 *Ibid.*; RR to JCB, 2 July 1957.

95 RR to MS, 12 September 1957, RRP, Box 91, Folder 2; RR to DB and GB, 10 February 1958, GB Papers, MS-Papers-1901-90-103-2/02; RR to MS, 18 April 1958, her emphasis.

96 RR to IW, 6 June 1958; RR to PH, 2 December 1958, RRP, Box 91, Folder 2; RR to DB and GB, 28 April 1959, RRP, GB Papers, MS-Papers-1901-90-103-2/02.

Chapter 2: School Publications

1 In writing about this piece of work of Ross's I have learned a good deal from Rachael Bell's 'Window', but my interpretation diverges from hers in certain important respects.

2 RR to RWK, 26 October 1954, RRP, Box 90, Folder 2; MT to RR, 26 August 1955, ANZ, R12203919; RR to JKB, 2 November 1956 and 26 May 1957, ANZ, R12203919.

3 Southgate, 'School', p. 480; O'Brien, *Nest*, p. 18.

4 RR to PE, 22 March 1953, ANZ, R12203920.

5 RR to JCB, 26 May 1953, RRP, Box 24, Folder 5; RR to PE, 29 April 1954 and 14 June 1954, ANZ, R12203920; RR to PH, 25 June 1954, ANZ, R12203920, my emphasis.

6 For a discussion of Turnbull's career as an editor, see Munro, 'Michael'.

7 PH to RR, 13 July 1954, ANZ, R12203920; RR to PH, 15 July 1954, RRP, Box 90, Folder 2; MT to RR, 1 November 1954, ANZ, R12203920; RR to MT, 8 October [*sic*, i.e. November] 1954, ANZ, R12203920.

8 PE to RR, 22 October 1952, ANZ, R12203920; RR to PE, 6 November 1952, ANZ, R12203920; Ross, 'Material', 'Cruise', 'Rewi of the Ngatiroro', 'Rewi, the Whaler', *The Journal* and *Early Traders*.

9 Beaglehole, 'Small', p. 124; RR to AM, 12 August 1956, RRP, Box 91, Folder 1.

10 RR to PH, 6 October 1954, ANZ, R12203920; O'Brien, *Nest*, pp. 7, 18, 20, 37, 50.

11 RR to MT, 27 October 1954, ANZ, R12203920; RR to DB and GB, 22 January 1956, GB Papers,

MS-Papers-1901-90-103-2/02; Southgate, 'School', p. 480.

12 Ross was nonetheless critical of the historical errors Finlayson had made and gave him a lot of advice as to how he might address this problem. He accepted her help — or what Ross jokingly called her meddling in his affairs — and they became firm friends (RR to MT, 23 September 1955, RRP, Box 90, Folder 3, and ANZ, R12203919 [one part of this letter is held in the former, the other part in the latter]; MT to RR, 26 August 1955; RR to MT, 8 May 1959, RRP, Box 91, Folder 3).

13 RR to MT, 12 May 1955, RRP, Box 90, Folder 2; RR to Mr K. Robertson, 25 September 1955, ANZ, R12203919; RR to MT, 1 November 1955, ANZ, R12203919; RR to MS, 4 July 1956, RRP, Box 91, Folder 1; RR to BP, 5 October 1956, RRP, Box 91, Folder 1; RR to AM, 23 June 1957, RRP, Box 91, Folder 1; RR to KS, 9 July 1957, RRP, Box 91, Folder 1; Ross, 'Review of Norris'.

14 Ross, 'Cruise', p. 2; Ross, 'Rewi', p. 248; RR to PH, 15 July 1954; Ross, *Simmonds*, verso page; RR to RWK, 28 January 1955, RRP, Box 90, Folder 2; RR to PHJ, 21 February 1955, RRP, Box 90, Folder 2; RR to AC, 19 February 1956, RRP, Box 91, Folder 1.

15 See, for example, the bulletin and her stories for the *School Journal* cited in the previous endnote.

16 RR to MT, 9 May 1955, RRP, Box 90, Folder 2; RR to JKB, 14 July 1957, ANZ, R12203919; Baxter, 'Primary School', p. 312; Bell, 'Ruth', pp. 68–69. Locke could be said to have followed in Ross's footsteps at School Pubs as she wrote stories about New Zealand's history from the perspective of both Māori and Pākehā (Birchfield, *Looking*, pp. 321–22).

17 RR to RWK, 26 October 1954 and 28 January 1955; RR to MT, 19 April 1955, ANZ, R12203920.

18 Beaglehole, *New Zealand Scholar*, pp. 3–6, 17, 19, 21, 24.

19 *Ibid.*, pp. 7–9, 11, 13, 16, 19, 21, 23.

20 RR to JCB, 22 September 1954, JCB Papers; GB to RR and Ian Ross, 6 November 1954, GB Papers, MS-Papers-1901-90-103-2/02; RR to RWK, 19 January 1956, RRP, Box 91, Folder 1; Beaglehole, *Life*, p. 439.

21 RR to JCB, 22 September 1954; RR to RWK, 28 September 1954, RRP, Box 90, Folder 2; RR to DB and GB, 16 November 1954 and 9 December 1954, GB Papers, MS-Papers-1901-90-103-2/02; RR to JCB, 25 February 1955, JCB Papers; RR to AM, 16 June 1956, RRP, Box 91, Folder 1.

22 RR to JCB, 22 September 1954.

23 RR to JCB, 22 September 1954 and 25 February 1955.

24 RR to JCB, 22 September 1954.

25 *Ibid.*

26 *Ibid.*

27 *Ibid.*; RR to RWK, 28 January 1955.

28 RR to JCB, 22 September 1954.

29 *Ibid.*, her emphases; RR to DB and GB, 9 December 1954; RR to JCB, 25 February 1955.

30 RR to RWK, 28 September 1954; RR to DB and GB, 16 November 1954; GB to RR, 6 December 1954, MS-Papers-1901-90-103-2/02; RR to DB and GB, 9 December 1954; JCB to RR, 20 December 1954, RRP, Box 90, Folder 2; RR to JCB, 25 February 1955; RR to CB, 8 September 1955, RRP, Box 90, Folder 3; RR to CB, 23 September 1955, RRP, Box 90, Folder 3; RR to JCB, 18 April 1957, RRP, Box 91, Folder 1.

31 RR to JCB, 22 September 1954; RR to BP, 28 September 1954 and 5 October 1954, JP Papers, MS-Papers-5523-16; RR to DB and GB, 9 December 1954.

32 RR to BP, 5 October 1954; Finlayson, *Springing*, pp. 110, 112; Belgrave, *Dancing*, pp. 19, 31, 225; O'Malley, *New Zealand*, pp. 120, 122–23. There is some difference of opinion among

contemporary New Zealand historians about how best to characterise what happened at Rangiaowhia. See Belgrave, 'Response'.

33 RR to BP, 5 October 1954; RR to MT, 12 May 1955 and 23 September 1955; Ross, 'Review of Morrell', p. 110; RR to KS, 11 February 1959, RRP, Box 91, Folder 3; Ross, 'Correspondence', p. 106.

34 RR to MT, 12 May 1955 and 23 September 1955.

35 RR to MT, 23 September 1955.

36 Ross's essay 'The Autochthonous New Zealand Soil' provides further evidence for the argument I am making here: pp. 56–57.

37 RR to LR, 18 April 1955, RRP, Box 90, Folder 2; RR to MT, 19 April 1955; Calman, 'Māori'.

38 RR to LR, 18 April 1955 and 6 May 1955, RRP, Box 90, Folder 2; RR to GB, 15 May 1955, GB Papers, MS-Papers-1901-90-103-2/02; JCB to RR, 2 July 1955, JCB Papers.

39 RR to LR, 6 May 1955; RR to JCB, 3 June 1955, JCB Papers; RR to DB and GB, 22 January 1956; Ross, 'The School and the Community', undated paper, c. 1956, RRP, Box 48, Folder 8; RR to RWK, 8 March 1957, RRP, Box 91, Folder 1.

40 RR to JCB, 3 June 1955; Ross, 'The School'; RR to DB and GB, 22 January 1956; RR to John Pascoe, 24 May 1956, RRP, Box 91, Folder 1; RR to RWK, 13 August 1956, RRP, Box 91, Folder 1; RR to MB, 15 April 1957, MB Papers; RR to Ralph Hotere, 14 June 1957, RRP, Box 91, Folder 1; RR to AM, 23 June 1957; RR to MS, 5 July 1957, RRP, Box 91, Folder 1; Hohepa, *Maori*, pp. 23, 55.

41 RR to MT, 9 June 1955, ANZ, R12203919; RR to DB and GB, 22 January 1956; Ross, 'The School'; RR to JKB, 29 November 1956, ANZ, R12203919; Kaamira, 'Story', pp. 234–35, 244–45; Ashton, *Margin*, pp. 8–9.

42 RR to Phoebe Meikle and Millicent Hoyle, 10 October 1955, RRP, Box 90, Folder 3; RR to DB and GB, 22 January 1956; RR to EE, 9 July 1956, RRP, Box 91, Folder 1; Ross, 'The School'; RR to JKB, 12 October 1956, ANZ, R12203919; Hohepa, *Maori*, pp. 23, 124; Ross, 'Autochthonous', p. 53.

43 RR to Meikle and Hoyle, 10 October 1955.

44 *Ibid.*

45 *Ibid.*

46 *Ibid.*

47 *Ibid.*

48 MT to RR, 22 April 1955 and 2 May 1955, RRP, Box 90, Folder 2; MT to RR, 11 June 1955, quoted in RR to JKB, 26 May 1957.

49 RR to DB and GB, 9 December 1954 and 22 January 1956; RR to AM, 12 March 1956, RRP, Box 91, Folder 1; RR to RWK, 15 April 1956, RRP, Box 91, Folder 1; RR to AC, 27 April 1956, RRP, Box 91, Folder 1; RR to RWK, 13 August 1956; RR to JKB, 29 November 1956; RR to EE, 8 February 1957, RRP, Box 91, Folder 1; RR to RWK, 23 February 1957, RRP, Box 91, Folder 1; RR to MB, 15 April 1957; RR to MS, 5 July 1957; RR to JKB, 15 November 1957, ANZ, R12203919; RR to DB and GB, 10 February 1958, GB Papers, MS-Papers-1901-90-103-2/02; DR, personal communication with the author, 26 June 2021.

50 RR to MT, 9 May 1955 and 12 May 1955; RR to MT, 23 September 1955; RR to DB and GB, 22 January 1956; RR to AM, 12 March 1956; RR to KS, 10 August 1956, RRP, Box 91, Folder 1.

51 RR to RWK, 19 January 1956; RR to DB and GB, 22 January 1956; RR to AM, 12 March 1956; RR to RWK, 13 August 1956; RR to BP, 5 September 1956, RRP, Box 91, Folder 1; RR to JKB, 26 May 1957; RR to PH, 9 August 1959.

52 RR to AC, 16 August 1955, RRP, Box 90, Folder 3; RR to Meikle and Hoyle, 10 October 1955; RR to CB, 27 October 1955, RRP, Box 90, Folder 3; RR to RWK, 19 January 1956; RR to EE,

22 February 1956, RRP, Box 91, Folder 1; RR to EE, 9 July 1956, 29 November 1956 and 8 February 1957, RRP, Box 91, Folder 1; RR to MS, 5 July 1957; RR to DB, 15 July 1965, GB Papers, MS-Papers-1901-90-103-2/02; RR to MB, 21 November 1975, MB Papers.

53 RR to MT, 9 June 1955; RR to CB, 23 September 1955; RR to Meikle and Hoyle, 10 October 1955; RR to RWK, 19 January 1956; RR to MT, 20 January 1956, RRP, Box 91, Folder 1; RR to AC, 21 May 1956, RRP, Box 91, Folder 1.

54 In doing this, she was preceded by Angus Ross, who undertook fieldwork for his 1933 Master's thesis on Te Puoho's attack on Murihiku (Olssen, 'Obituary', p. 201).

55 RR to DB and GB, 22 January 1956; Ross, 'The School'; Ross, 'Treaty of Waitangi 3 Scenes', undated document, c. 1956, RRP, Box 81, Folder 4; RR to JKB, 2 November 1956; RR to JKB, 29 November 1956; RR to MS, 21 November 1958, RRP, Box 91, Folder 2.

56 MT to RR, 28 November 1955, ANZ, R12203919; RR to RWK, 19 January 1956; RR to AC, 15 June 1956, RRP, Box 91, Folder 1; RR to JKB, 20 June 1957, ANZ, R12203919; RR to Isobel Andrews, 13 October 1959, RRP, Box 91, Folder 3.

57 MT to RR, 28 November 1955; RR to Andrews, 13 October 1959.

58 RR to Robertson, 25 September 1955; RR to AM, 12 March 1956; Ross, 'The School'; Barrington, *Separate*, p. 267.

59 RR to MT, 7 March 1955, ANZ, R12203920; RR to LR, 6 May 1955; MT to RR, 26 August 1955; RR to AC, 15 June 1956; RR to JKB, 17 August 1956, RRP, Box 91, Folder 1; RR to JKB, 2 November 1956; JKB to RR, 4 February 1957, ANZ, R12203919; JKB to RR, 13 March 1957, ANZ, R12203919; RR to KS, 9 July 1957 and 22 July 1957, RRP, Box 91, Folder 1.

60 Ross, 'Treaty of Waitangi 3 Scenes'; RR to JKB, 12 October 1956.

61 RR to JKB, 20 June 1957; RR to JKB, 20 August 1957, ANZ, R12203919.

62 JKB to RR, 27 August 1956, ANZ, R12203919; RR to JKB, 29 November 1956; RR to MH, 31 March 1957, RRP, Box 91, Folder 1.

63 RR to RWK, 15 April 1956; JKB to RR, 27 August 1956; RR to BP, 5 September 1956; RR to MS, 18 April 1957, RRP, Box 91, Folder 1.

64 RR to JKB, 12 October 1956, her emphasis; JKB to RR, 18 October 1956, ANZ, R12203919.

65 JKB to RR, 18 October 1956.

66 *Ibid.*; RR to JKB, 2 November 1956.

67 RR to JKB, 2 November 1956.

68 RR to KS, 10 August 1956; RR to JKB, 2 November 1956; RR to JKB, 29 November 1956; JKB to RR, 16 January 1957 and 6 February 1957, ANZ, R12203919; RR to MH, 31 March 1957.

69 RR to MH, 6 February 1956 [sic, 1957], RRP, Box 91, Folder 1; MH to RR, undated [February or March 1957], RRP, Box 91, Folder 1; RR to MH, 31 March 1957; PHJ to JKB, undated [June 1957], ANZ, R12203919; RR to AM, 23 June 1957; KS to RR, 18 July 1957, RRP, Box 91, Folder 1.

70 *New Zealand Herald*, 21 June 1957; RR to the Editor, New Zealand Herald, undated [June 1957], RRP, Box 91, Folder 1; RR to AM, 23 June 1957.

71 JKB to RR, 19 July 1957, ANZ, R12203919; RR to KS, 22 July 1957; RR to JKB, 28 July 1957, ANZ, R12203919.

72 RR to RWK, 19 January 1956; RR to DB and GB, 22 January 1956; Ross, 'The School'; JKB to RR, 4 February 1957; RR to PH, 22 February 1957, RRP, Box 91, Folder 1; JKB to RR, 13 March 1957; RR to JKB, 24 March 1957, ANZ, R12203919.

73 RR to JKB, 28 July 1957, her emphasis.

74 *Ibid.*; JKB to RR, 15 August 1957, ANZ, R12203919; RR to JKB, 20 August 1957.

75 JKB to RR, 20 September 1957, ANZ, R12203919; RR to JKB, 27 September 1957 and 11 October 1957, ANZ, R12203919, her emphases.

76 RR to JKB, 27 September 1957, her emphasis.

77 JKB to RR, 1 October 1957.

78 RR to JKB, 11 October 1957, ANZ, R12203919.

79 RR to CB, 7 July 1954, RRP, Box 90, Folder 2; RR to MT, 9 May 1955; RR to EE, 8 February 1957; JKB to RR, 1 November 1957, ANZ, R12203919; RR to JKB, 15 November 1957.

80 RR to BP, 5 October 1954; RR to PH, 6 October 1954; MT to RR, 28 November 1955; MT to Eric Lee-Johnson, 19 December 1955, ANZ, R12203919; Lee-Johnson to RR, 2 August 1956, RRP, Box 91, Folder 1; RR to RWK, 13 August 1956; BP to RR, 28 August 1956, RRP, Box 91, Folder 1; RR to JKB, 12 October 1956; RR to AC, 20 November 1956, ANZ, R12203919; RR to JKB, 29 November 1956; MH to RR, undated [February or March 1957]; RR to MH, 31 March 1957; RR to KS, 9 July 1957; RR to JKB, 11 October 1957; RR to PH, 2 December 1958, RRP, Box 91, Folder 2; RR to MT, 8 May 1959.

81 RR to MH, 31 March 1957; RR to JKB, 1 May 1957, ANZ, R12203919; C. O'Malley to RR, 30 May 1957, RRP, Box 91, Folder 1; RR to Hotere, 14 June 1957; RR to JKB, 20 June 1957; JKB to RR, 13 March 1958, ANZ, R12203919; O'Sullivan, *Dark*, pp. 52, 57.

82 RR to JKB, 1 May 1957; RR to JKB, 20 June 1957; RR to KS, 9 July 1957; JKB to RR, 15 August 1957; RR to JKB, 20 August 1957, her emphasis; O'Brien, *Nest*, pp. 20, 105.

83 RR to JKB, 11 October 1957 and 15 November 1957; RR to JKB, 20 February 1958, ANZ, R12203919; JKB to RR, 26 February 1958, ANZ, R12203919; RR to JKB, 6 March 1958, ANZ, R12203919; JKB to RR, 13 March 1958.

84 JKB to RR, 6 December 1957, ANZ, R12203919; JKB to RR, 26 February 1958; JKB to RR, 13 March 1958; RR to JKB, 17 March 1958, ANZ, R12203919; RR to PH, 2 December 1958.

85 RR to JKB, 17 March 1958; RR to PH, 2 December 1958; RR to MT, 8 May 1959.

86 Ross, *Tiriti*, pp. 1–3.

87 *Ibid.*, pp. 4–9, 32, 35.

88 *Ibid.*, pp. 7–14.

89 *Ibid.*, pp. 15–23.

90 RR to JKB, 15 November 1957; Ross, *Tiriti*, p. 31; Ross, Memorandum for The Editor, School Publications Branch, 7 August 1959, JCB Papers.

91 Ross, *Tiriti*, pp. 31–32.

92 *Ibid.*, pp. 32–34; Pāpāhia, https://nzhistory.govt.nz/politics/treaty/signatory/1-31

93 Ross, *Tiriti*, pp. 34–35, 40, 47, her emphasis; Makoare Te Taonui, https://nzhistory.govt.nz/politics/treaty/signatory/1-123

94 Ross, *Tiriti*, pp. 38–41, 45–47.

95 *Ibid.*, pp. 42–44, her emphasis.

96 *Ibid.*, pp. 44–46, 48.

97 RR to PH, 31 October 1958, RRP, Box 91, Folder 2; KS to RR, 6 November 1958, RRP, Box 91, Folder 2; MS to RR, 12 November 1958, RRP, Box 91, Folder 2; RR to MS, 21 November 1958; RR to PH, 2 December 1958; RR to DB and GB, 28 April 1959, GB Papers, MS-Papers-1901-90-103-2/02; Boyd, 'Obituary', p. 189.

98 Novick, *Noble*, pp. 1–2.

99 RR to JKB, 20 June 1957; RR to JKB, 20 August 1957; RR to MS, 21 November 1958; RR to PH, 2 December 1958; RR to MT, 8 May 1959.

Chapter 3: The New Zealand Journal of History

1. New Zealand Labour Party, *Election Manifesto 1957*, Maori Affairs, p. 3; John Owens to RR, 26 February 1958, RRP, Box 91, Folder 2.

2. Ross, 'The Waitangi Documents', 1958, RRP, Box 91, Folder 2. Ross was more able to make her argument in her private correspondence, as more than one of the letters she wrote at this time reveals.

3. Ross, 'Waitangi Documents'.

4. *Ibid.*, her emphasis.

5. MS to RR, 11 April 1958, RRP, Box 91, Folder 2.

6. See Rutherford, *Treaty*.

7. Owens to RR, 26 February 1958; Summary of Readers' Reports for 'The Waitangi Documents', undated, RRP, Box 91, Folder 2; KS, Reader's Report for 'The Waitangi Documents', undated, RRP, Box 91, Folder 2; James Rutherford, Reader's Report for 'The Waitangi Documents', 14 April 1958, RRP, Box 91, Folder 2; RR to MS, 18 April 1958, RRP, Box 91, Folder 2.

8. RR to MS, 18 April 1958; RR to IW, 6 June 1958, RRP, Box 91, Folder 2; RR, Memorandum for the Chief Editor, School Publications Branch, Department of Education, 7 August 1959, JCB Papers.

9. Isobel Andrews to RR, 12 May 1958, RRP, Box 91, Folder 2; RR to IW, 6 June 1958. I have been unable to find the letter of Wards's that Ross references either in his papers (in the Alexander Turnbull Library) or hers.

10. MS to RR, 13 June 1958, RRP, Box 91, Folder 2.

11. *Ibid.*

12. *Ibid.*

13. RR to MS, 26 June 1958, RRP, Box 91, Folder 2; MS to RR, 12 November 1958, RRP, Box 91, Folder 2; MS to RR, 19 December 1958, RRP, Box 91, Folder 2.

14. PH to RR, 30 July 1959, RRP, Box 91, Folder 3; RR, Memorandum, 7 August 1959; RR to PH, 9 August 1959, RRP, Box 91, Folder 3.

15. RR to PH, 9 August 1959; [Taylor], *Facsimiles*, unpaginated Introductory Note.

16. RR to GB, 3 May 1960, GB Papers, MS-Papers-1901-90-103-2/02; RR to EHM, 9 May 1960, EHM Papers, MS-Papers-0166-11.

17. RR to DB and GB, 28 April 1959, GB Papers, MS-Papers-1901-90-103-2/02; RR to DB and GB, 13 February 1963, GB Papers, MS-Papers-1901-90-103-2/02; RR to DR and MR, 30 April 1963, 24 June 1963 and 18 July 1963, RRP, MS 94/23; RR to DB and GB, 19 December 1963, GB Papers, MS-Papers-1901-90-103-2/02; RR to DB, 15 July 1965, GB Papers, MS-Papers-1901-90-103-2/02; RR to JB, 3 April 1969, JB Papers, MS-Papers-11115-139; Salary Card for Ian Munson Ross, ANZ, R25043597.

18. Florence Keene to RR, 11 August 1959, RRP, Box 91, Folder 3; RR to Keene, 14 August 1959, RRP, Box 91, Folder 3; RR to T. J. Dwyer, 1 October 1959, RRP, Box 91, Folder 3; RR to Andrews, 13 October 1959, RRP, Box 91, Folder 3; RR to Dwyer, 13 October 1959, RRP, Box 91, Folder 3; Ross, 'Review of Tapp'; Ross, 'European'; Ross, 'McDonnell', 'Maning', 'Taonui', 'Thierry', and 'Review of Wright'; RR to EHM, 26 June 1961, EHM Papers, MS-Papers-0166-12; RR to JB, 26 June 1964, JB Papers, MS-Papers-1115-066; RR to JB, 3 April 1969.

19. RR to JCB, 25 February 1955, JCB Papers; RR to GB, 3 May 1960; RR to EHM, 9 May 1960, 15 June 1960, 29 September 1960 and 1 June 1961, EHM Papers, MS-Papers-0166-12;

Markham, *New*, unpaginated preface; RR to EHM, 30 June 1964, EHM Papers, MS-Papers-5292-053; RR to JB, 19 April 1965, JB Papers, MS-Papers-1115-066; Earle, *Narrative*, p. viii; RR to EHM, 23 February 1967, EHM Papers, MS-Papers-5292-053; RR to JB, 3 April 1969; RR to GB, 4 March 1971, GB Papers, MS-Papers-1901-90-103-2/03; GB to RR, 9 March 1971, GB Papers, MS-Papers-1901-90-103-2/03; Lyons, *Typewriter*, pp. 172–73.

20 Burnard to Marie King, 1 May 1944, RRP, Box 90, Folder 1; RR to AM, 12 March 1956, RRP, Box 91, Folder 1; RR to DB and GB, 30 July 1959, GB Papers, MS-Papers-1901-90-103-2/02; RR to GB, 3 May 1960; RR to EHM, 1 June 1961; RR to DB and GB, 19 December 1963, GB Papers, MS-Papers-1901-90-103-2/02; RR to EHM, 30 June 1964, EHM Papers, MS-Papers-5292-053; RR to EHM, 13 August 1964, EHM Papers, MS-Papers-5292-053; RR to GB, 16 June 1965, GB Papers, MS-Papers-1901-90-103-2/02; RR to Elsie Beaglehole, 11 October 1971, RRP, Box 98, Folder 2; RR to MB, 27 April 1975, MB Papers.

21 RR to DB and GB, 24 July 1964, GB Papers, MS-Papers-1901-90-103-2/02; RR to RIMB, 29 October 1965, enclosing a manuscript by Ross entitled 'Hongi and Kerikeri', RIMB Papers, MS-Papers-5317-6; RR to EHM, 23 February 1967; RR to JB, 3 April 1969.

22 Ross, 'Waitangi — 1840'.

23 For an account of Malcolm Ross's life and work, see Plummer, 'Legendary'.

24 RR to EHM, 13 August 1964, 23 August 1964 and 17 September 1964, EHM Papers, MS-Papers-5292-053; RR to DB and GB, 4 November 1964, GB Papers, MS-Papers-1901-90-103-2/02; RR to EHM, 24 August 1967, 12 December 1967, 10 April 1968, 23 April 1968 and 16 September 1968, EHM Papers, MS-Papers-5292-053; RR to MR, 16 March 1972 and 24 May 1972, RRP, MS 94/23.

25 JCB to Averil Lysaght, 16 October 1968, in Beaglehole (ed.), *'I think'*, p. 463; RR to JB, 3 April 1969; Beaglehole, 'List of Correspondents', in Beaglehole (ed.), *'I Think'*, p. 22.

26 Ross, 'Autochthonous', p. 47.

27 Renwick, 'Show', pp. 202–03.

28 *Ibid.*, p. 204; John Miller, 'The True Voice of Feeling', *New Zealand Listener*, 14 November 1969.

29 These are preserved in her papers, mostly Box 83.

30 Robinson, 'Making', pp. 43–44; Harris with Williams, 'Rights', pp. 358–59; Johnson, *Land*, pp. 13, 108–09, 111–12.

31 Johnson, *Land*, pp. 1, 3–4, 14.

32 Ross, Talk Delivered to the Auckland Historical Society, 19 July 1971, RRP, Box 79, Folder 4; Pauline Swain to RR, 19 January 1972, RRP, Box 84, Folder 4; Powles, 'Foreword'; Dakin, 'Preface', p. [iii]; G. Blackburn to RR, undated, c. May 1971, RRP, Box 84, Folder 4; Barrowman, *Victoria*, p. 209.

33 MB to RR, 9 July 1971, RRP, Box 98, Folder 2; Dakin, 'Preface', p. [iii]; Walker, 'Parker'.

34 RR to MB, 14 July 1971, RRP, Box 98, Folder 2; RR to RIMB, 11 March 1972, RRP, Box 99, Folder 1; RR to KS, 13 April 1972, RRP, Box 84, Folder 4; RR to MR, 6 June 1972, RRP, MS 94/23.

35 MB to RR, 20 August 1971, RRP, Box 84, Folder 4; RR to OW, 1 November 1971, RRP, Box 98, Folder 2; OW to RR, 19 January 1972, RRP, Box 99, Folder 1; RR to RIMB, 11 March 1972; RR to Beaglehole, 28 January 1973, RRP, Box 99, Folder 2.

36 RR to Mr T. Lovell-Smith, 28 October 1971, RRP, Box 84, Folder 4; RR to OW, 1 November 1971; RR to Warren Winstone, 29 January 1972, RRP, Box 84, Folder 4.

37 RR to Bill Parker, 8 November 1971, RRP, Box 84, Folder 4; Victoria University of Wellington, Department of University Extension, Programme

for Weekend Seminar on Te Tiriti o Waitangi / The Treaty of Waitangi, 19–20 February 1972, copy in RRP, Box 84, Folder 4; OW to RR, 19 January 1972; RR to OW, 2 February 1972, RRP, Box 99, Folder 1; RR to J. C. Couling, 8 February 1972, RRP, Box 84, Folder 4; RR to RIMB, 11 March 1972.

38 Programme for Weekend Seminar; RR to RIMB, 11 March 1972; RR to RIMB, 28 January 1973, RIMB Papers, MS-Papers-5137-8.

39 Ross, 'The Treaty on the Ground', typescript, RRP, Box 79, Folder 1; RR to GB, 21 June 1972, RRP, Box 84, Folder 4; RR to MGH, 17 July 1972, RRP, Box 84, Folder 4; Ross, 'Treaty', p. 16.

40 Ever diligent, Ross recognised this and addressed the problem in her two subsequent publications about the Treaty. She omitted the story from the published version of her paper ('Treaty', p. 16) and made clear her point in telling it in her *New Zealand Journal of History* article, as follows: 'James Edward FitzGerald remarked in a debate on the Treaty of Waitangi in the House of Representatives in 1865: "if this document was signed in the Maori tongue, whatever the English translation might be had nothing to do with the question." He went on to point out: "Governor Hobson might have wished the Maoris to sign one thing, and they might have signed something totally different. *Were they bound by what they signed or by what Captain Hobson meant them to sign?*" To which one would now add the question: Was the Crown bound by what Hobson signed, or by what he assumed its meaning to be? Any attempt to interpret the provisions of the Treaty of Waitangi, or to understand what the signatories, both Hobson and the New Zealanders, thought it meant, must review the circumstances in which the agreement was drawn up, taking into account all the relevant texts' ('Te Tiriti', pp. 129–30, my emphasis). As a matter of interest, FitzGerald answered the question he had posed in this manner: 'The real fact was, that the Maoris were bound by what they signed, and the English by what they signed' (11 August 1865, *New Zealand Parliamentary Debates 1864 to 1866*, p. 292).

41 Ross, 'Treaty', p. 16; RR to GB, 21 June 1972.

42 Ross, 'Treaty', pp. 16–17, 19, 21, 23, 25; RR to Henare Kohere Ngata, 9 September 1973, RRP, Box 84, Folder 4.

43 Ross, 'Treaty', pp. 17–18.

44 *Ibid*., p. 18; Ross, 'Te Tiriti', p. 130 note 10. See my discussion of the Declaration in *Empire*, pp. 115–17.

45 Ross, 'Treaty', p. 19.

46 Martin, *Taranaki*, pp. 13–14; Ross, 'Treaty', pp. 16, 19–20.

47 Ross, Paper, untitled and undated [March 1956], RRP, Box 79, Folder 4; Ross, 'Treaty', p. 20; RR to GB, 3 July 1972, RRP, Box 84, Folder 4.

48 Ross, 'Treaty', pp. 20–22.

49 *Ibid*., pp. 22–23.

50 *Ibid*., pp. 23–25.

51 *Ibid*., pp. 25–30.

52 *Ibid*., p. 30.

53 'The Treaty on the Ground' was published with very few changes under the same title in *The Treaty of Waitangi*; unless stated otherwise, I have cited the published version; RR to MR, 7 April 1972, RRP, MS 94/23; RR to OW, 23 July 1972, RRP, Box 99, Folder 1; RR to KS, 3 August 1972, RRP, Box 84, Folder 4.

54 RR to RIMB, 11 March 1972; RR to KS, 13 April 1972.

55 RR to KS, 5 March 1972, RRP, Box 84, Folder 4; RR to MR, 16 March 1972.

56 The content of all the issues of the journal published up to this time evidences this point.

57 KS to RR, 1 March 1972, RRP, Box 84, Folder 4; RR to KS, 5 March 1972; Beverley Simmons to RR, 7 March 1972, RRP, Box 84, Folder 4; RR to RIMB, 11 March 1972; KS to RR, 7 April 1972, RRP, Box 84, Folder 4, his emphasis; KS to RR, 19 April 1972, RRP, Box 84, Folder 4; RR to OW, 16 August 1972, RRP, Box 99, Folder 1.

58 RR to KS, 5 March 1972; RR to WM, 22 March 1972, RRP, Box 84, Folder 4; RR to MGH, 17 July 1972, RRP, Box 84, Folder 4; RR to OW, 17 July 1972, RRP, Box 99, Folder 1.

59 Bruce Biggs, Reader's Report on Ross's Paper, 16 March 1972, RRP, Box 84, Folder 4; RR to KS, 13 April 1972.

60 RR to KS, 13 April 1972, her emphasis.

61 Binney, Some Textual Points on Ross's Paper, undated, RRP, Box 84, Folder 4; KS to RR, 7 April 1972.

62 It seems clear that Sinclair had suggested the inclusion of both the English text and an English translation of the Māori text so that readers could readily grasp Ross's argument, but she does not seem to have realised this was the case.

63 RR to KS, 13 April 1972; Brookes, *History*, p. 320.

64 RR to KS, 13 April 1972.

65 *Ibid.*; KS to RR, 19 April 1972; RR to KS, 8 May 1972, RRP, Box 84, Folder 4; KS to Ruth Ross, 16 May 1972, RRP, Box 84, Folder 4.

66 RR to Beaglehole, 28 January 1973.

67 The passage Ross referenced comes from the Bible, the Book of Lamentations, 3:19–22.

68 RR to WM, 22 March 1972; RR to MR, 23 March 1972 and 7 April 1972, RRP, MS 94/23; RR to WM, 9 April 1972, RRP, Box 84, Folder 4; RR to GB, 21 May 1972, RRP, Box 84, Folder 4; RR to Judith S. Hornabrook, 18 June 1972, RRP, Box 84, Folder 4; RR to MGH, 20 June 1972, RRP, Box 84, Folder 4.

69 RR to KS, 8 May 1972; RR to MR, 20 June 1972, RRP, MS 94/23; RR to OW, 21 June 1972, OW Papers, MS-Papers-90-094-3; RR to Hornabrook, 5 July 1972, RRP, Box 84, Folder 4; RR to MGH, 17 July 1972; RR to OW, 23 July 1972; RR, Diary, 1972, entry 4 August, RRP, Box 88, Folder 1; RR to MR, 6 August 1972, RRP, MS 94/23.

70 RR to KS, 3 August 1972.

71 Simmons to RR, 25 August 1972, RRP, Box 84, Folder 4; RR to OW, 5 October 1972, OW Papers.

72 For example, the University of Auckland had 9300 students in 1970, almost ten times as many as Victoria University College had had approximately thirty years earlier (Sinclair, *History of the University*, pp. 245–46; Barrowman, *Victoria*, p. 61).

73 For example, by 1972 the Department of History at the University of Auckland had twenty members of staff of whom five were women (University of Auckland, *Calendar*, 1972, pp. 27–28).

74 RR to DB and GB, 2 March 1952, GB Papers, MS-Papers-1901-90-103-2/02; JB to RR, 20 June 1964, JB Papers, MS-Papers-1115-066; RR to JB, 26 June 1964; RR to JB, 19 April 1965, JB Papers, MS-Papers-1115-066; JB to RR, 12 May 1965, JB Papers, MS-Papers-1115-066; RR to JB, 3 June 1965, JB Papers, MS-Papers-1115-066; RR to JB, 3 April 1969.

75 This is how Ross characterised Binney's remark, but what she actually said (in an interview with a journalist) was more condescending: 'the amateur historians who come forward sometimes with quite helpful facts' (*Zealandia*, 8 January 1970).

76 Ross had also focused on de Thierry in an interesting article she wrote about how historians go about their research: 'Writing'.

77 Ross, 'Thierry'; Binney, *Legacy*, Appendix 3; RR to MR,

27 January 1970, RRP, MS 94/23; RR to GB, 4 February 1970, GB Papers, MS-Papers-1901-90-103-2/03; RR to MPKS, 1 March 1979, RRP, Box 73, Folder 2.

78 RR to OW, 16 August 1972; Binney, 'Tiriti'; RR to MR, 21 September 1972, RRP, MS 94/23; RR to OW, 5 October 1972; RR to MR, 6 October 1972 and 12 October 1972, RRP, MS 94/23; RR to OW, 17 October 1972, RRP, Box 99, Folder 1. Ross took the opportunity to wreak revenge a couple of years later when Sinclair asked her to referee a short article that Binney had submitted to the journal about a 'treaty' akin to the Treaty of Waitangi that the Governor of New South Wales, Sir George Gipps, had tried to persuade Ngāi Tahu (who were visiting Sydney) to sign. Ross took great delight in pointing out that this had been the subject of a book published many years earlier — Edward Sweetman's 1939 *The Unsigned New Zealand Treaty* — upon which Sinclair rejected the paper and sent her a note thanking her for saving the journal from embarrassment: Binney, 'Shorter Communications: The Other "Treaty"', copy in RRP, Box 84, Folder 4; Simmons to RR, 22 November 1974, RRP, Box 84, Folder 4; RR to KS, 28 November 1974, RRP, Box 84, Folder 4; KS to RR, 3 December 1974, RRP, Box 84, Folder 4.

79 Binney, 'Tiriti'.

80 Ross, 'Te Tiriti', p. 154.

81 *Ibid.*, pp. 138, 151.

82 This was one of the least satisfactory parts of Ross's article, though she alone cannot be held to be responsible for it. Feeling she was out of depth in considering this legal matter, she had consulted a legal scholar, Warwick McKean, after hearing him speak at the Victoria seminar. But he gave her poor advice, telling her that at the time the Treaty was made the right of pre-emption, legally speaking, meant the right of first refusal, that is, it merely required vendors, in this case Māori, to offer their land for sale to the Crown first and that in the event that it refused to buy they could then sell to whomever they pleased (WM to RR, 24 March 1972, RRP, Box 81, Folder 5; Ross, 'Te Tiriti', p. 144). In fact, legally, pre-emption meant that the Crown had an exclusive right of purchase and so Māori could sell to no one else but the Crown.

83 Ross, 'Te Tiriti', pp. 143–52.

84 *Ibid.*, pp. 129, 141–43.

85 *Ibid.*, pp. 153–54.

86 RR to KS, 3 August 1972; RR to Simmons, 29 August 1972, RRP, Box 84, Folder 4; RR to J. C. Dakin, 13 October 1972, RRP, Box 84, Folder 4; RR to KS, 8 November 1971 [*sic*, 1972], RRP, Box 84, Folder 4.

87 She made much the same remark to Hitchings and Wilson the previous month: RR to MGH, 17 July 1972; RR to OW, 23 July 1972.

88 RR to DB and GB, 16 November 1954, GB Papers, MS-Papers-1901-90-103-2/02; RR to KS, 3 August 1972.

89 If anyone one wants more evidence of this point, it can be found in the closing paragraph of the final version of the article Ross submitted to the journal, or rather her commentary about it. The article read: 'McLean, translating Gore Browne's opening speech at the Kohimarama Conference, called the treaty *te kawenata o Waitangi*. If Waitangi 1840 held any real promise for the future, it was perhaps in Hobson's few words to each man as he signed: *He iwi tahi tatou*. Can we ever be one people till the Maori language is taught in schools to all our children?' Ross confessed to Wilson that she did not know how to finish the article and had 'grasped at this straw', which she called 'the straw of *te kawenata o Waitangi*'. 'What I'm after', she tried to explain, 'is a change in attitude, so that some instruction in Maori language,

history &c is part of the common core, so that just as kids are taught to speak and write English . . . they should be taught how to pronounce Maori, to learn something of the Maori history of their region as they learn something of its European history' (Ross, 'A New Look at the Treaty of Waitangi', typescript, RRP, Box 79, Folder 4; RR to OW, 16 August 1972).

Chapter 4: Reading 'Te Tiriti o Waitangi'

1. A good deal has been written about the reception of texts. My approach here owes something to the work of the cultural theorist Stuart Hall. See his 'Encoding'.
2. LaCapra, *Rethinking*, p. 45.
3. Wards, *Shadow*, Chapter 1.
4. Ward, *Show*, pp. ix, 42–45.
5. Ibid., p. 44.
6. Adams, *Fatal*, pp. 9–10, 15, 158, 161–64, 245.
7. This was also true of another general history published three years later: King, *Maori*, p. 48.
8. Owens, 'New Zealand', pp. 51–52.
9. Ibid., p. 52.
10. Belich, *New Zealand Wars*, p. 19, my emphasis.
11. Owens, 'Historians', p. 11.
12. Antony Wood to RR, 8 December 1972, RRP, Box 84, Folder 4; RR to RIMB, 28 January 1973, RIMB Papers, MS-Papers-5137-8.
13. RR to KS, 13 April 1972, RRP, Box 84, Folder 4; L. M., 'Waitangi Legacy', *Auckland Star*, 5 February 1973.
14. Ross, 'Te Tiriti', p. 129; L. M., 'Waitangi'.
15. Another example is a historical novel published in 1982: Grover, *Cork*, pp. 129–30.
16. Simpson, Te Riri, pp. 1–3, 30; 'Self-portrait: Tony Simpson', February 2022, https://www.newsroom.co.nz/self-portrait-tony-simpson
17. Simpson, Te Riri, pp. 1, 30, 47–48; 'Self-portrait'.
18. Simpson, Te Riri, pp. 49–52.
19. Academic historians were not the only ones to criticise the book on these grounds. See Ray Knox, 'Fools or Villains or . . .?', *New Zealand Listener*, 3 May 1980.
20. MPKS to RR, 14 June 1979, RRP, Box 82, Folder 1; Sue McCauley, 'Jumbled Drums', *New Zealand Listener*, 21 July 1979; Keith Sorrenson, Letter to the Editor, *New Zealand Listener*, 18 August 1979; Tony Simpson, Letter to the Editor, *New Zealand Listener*, 8 September 1979; RR to MB and Maurice Boyd, 2 October 1979, MB Papers; Sorrenson, 'Sorrenson Reviews'; Simpson, 'Simpson Replies'; Sharp, *Justice*, pp. 3–4; Belgrave, *Historical*, p. 49.
21. Walker, *Nga Tau*, pp. 10, 67–68, 74.
22. Molloy, 'Non-Treaty', pp. 193–95.
23. For a recent historical consideration of this case, see Williams, *Simple*.
24. Molloy, 'Non-Treaty', pp. 195–96.
25. Pope, '[Note]'; Auburn, 'Tiriti', pp. 309–11.
26. F. M. Auburn to RR, 6 February 1973, RRP, Box 84, Folder 4; RR to Auburn, 23 February 1973, RRP, Box 84, Folder 4; John O. Ross to RR, 8 November 1973, RRP, Box 90, Folder 2.
27. Auburn, 'Tiriti', p. 309; Auburn to RR, 6 February 1973; RR to Auburn, 23 February 1973.
28. RR to Auburn, 23 February 1973.
29. RR to Matiu Rata, 25 January 1973, RRP, Box 84, Folder 4; RR to Whetū Tirikātene-Sullivan, 27 January 1973, RRP, Box 84, Folder 4; RR to RIMB, 28 January 1973.

30 New Zealand Labour Party, *1972 Election*, pp. 34, 36; Report of the Government Caucus Committee of Maori Affairs on the Treaty of Waitangi, 5 February 1974, ANZ, R20825944.
31 Committee Report.
32 *Ibid.*, my emphasis.
33 *Ibid.*; Revised Report of the Government Caucus Committee of Maori Affairs on the Treaty of Waitangi, 29 February 1974, ANZ, R20825944.
34 Committee Report.
35 *Ibid.*
36 McNair, *Law*, pp. 432–34; McKean, 'Treaty', pp. 237, 239–40, 247, 301 note 6.
37 Committee Report.
38 Rata, Memorandum for Cabinet, 7 March 1974, ANZ, R20827494; Committee Revised Report.
39 J. McEwen, Secretary, Maori and Island Affairs Department, to Rata, 19 June 1974, ANZ, R20972377.
40 NZPD, 8 November 1974, pp. 5726, 5728.
41 See McCan, *Whatiwhatihoe*, pp. 228–33.
42 RR to Robert Mahuta, 9 September 1973, RRP, Box 84, Folder 4; Hoana Rapatini, Submission to the Select Committee, 3 February 1973, Arahura Maori Committee, Submission to Select Committee, undated, and Nga Tamatoa, Submission to Select Committee, 7 May 1975, ANZ, R20972377.
43 Ngai Tahu Trust Board, Submission to Select Committee, 1 March 1975, ANZ, R20972377; Arahura Committee Submission.
44 J. H. Dark, for Secretary, Department of Maori and Island Affairs, Memorandum, Treaty of Waitangi Bill, 12 June 1975, and Rata to the Minister of Justice, Martyn Finlay, 18 June 1975, ANZ, R21530636; E. W. Williams, Deputy Secretary, Department of Maori and Island Affairs, to Rata, 20 June 1975, and Draft Letter of Minister of Lands by the Director-General of the Department of Lands, to Rata, undated, [June 1975], ANZ, R3949183; Office of the Minister of Maori Affairs, Memorandum for Cabinet, 16 July 1975, ANZ, R20825493.
45 Sharp, *Justice*, pp. 75–76.
46 Copy of L. M., 'Waitangi', in RRP, Box 83, Folder 1; RR to MB and Maurice Boyd, 12 January 1980, MB Papers.
47 RR to MR, 7 April 1972, RRP, MS 94/23; MPKS to RR, 14 June 1979 and RR to MPKS, 19 June 1979, RRP, Box 82, Folder 1; RR to MB and Maurice Boyd, 2 October 1979; RR to MB, 20 October 1979, MB Papers.
48 RR to MPKS, 19 June 1979.
49 Ross, Report on Old British Residency, 1975, RRP, Box 80, Folder 2.
50 RR to Frances Porter, 5 September 1977, RRP, Box 38, Folder 1; RR to Rev. R. D. Rakena, 1 June 1978, RRP, Box 38, Folder 1; RR to Porter, 4 October 1978, RRP, Box 38, Folder 1; RR to MH, 4 October [1978], RRP, Box 38, Folder 1; Ross, 'Waitangi Treaty Houses'.
51 Ross, 'Maori Church'; RR to MB and Maurice Boyd, 12 January 1980.
52 RR to KS, 2 April 1975, RRP, Box 73, Folder 2; KS to RR, 4 April 1975, RRP, Box 73, Folder 2; RR to MB, 21 November 1975, MB Papers; RR to MB, 2 December 1978, MB Papers; RR to MPKS, 1 March 1979, RRP, Box 73, Folder 2; MPKS to RR, 6 March 1979, RRP, Box 73, Folder 2; RR to MPKS, 19 March 1979, RRP, Box 73, Folder 2.
53 RR to KS, 2 April 1975; RR to EHM, 5 October 1975, EHM Papers, MS-Papers-5292-053; RR to MPKS, 6 October 1975, RRP, Box 73, Folder 2; RR to DR and Heather Ross, 14 October 1975, RRP, Box 38, Folder 1; RR to MB, 2 December 1978; Salesa, 'Obituary', pp. 44–45.
54 Orange, 'Treaty', p. 10, and *Treaty*, p. ix; Orange, 'A Treaty Conversation', Auckland Writers' Festival, 14 May

55 RR to MB, 2 December 1978.
56 Orange, 'Covenant', pp. 61–62.
57 Ibid., p. 61.
58 Ibid., pp. 62, 68, 77–78.
59 MH to RR, undated [February or March 1957], RRP, Box 91, Folder 1; Orange to RR, 28 April 1980, RRP, Box 38, Folder 1; RR to MB and Maurice Boyd, 22 April [1980] and 7 May [1980], MB Papers; RR to DB and GB, 7 May [1980], GB Papers, MS-Papers-1901-90-103-2/03; RR to MB, 18 May [1980], MB Papers; RR to MB and Maurice Boyd, 20 November 1981, MB Papers; RR to Orange, 25 November 1981, RRP, Box 84, Folder 4; RR to DB and GB, 24 December 1981, GB Papers, MS-Papers-1901-90-103-2/03; RR to EHM, 15 March 1982, EHM Papers, MS-Papers-5292-053; Orange, personal communication with the author, 19 March 2021.
60 *National Business Review*, 8 February 1982; Malcolm McKinnon, Letter to the Editor, *National Business Review*, 15 February 1982; Bob Brockie to RR, 23 February 1982, RRP, Box 82, Folder 1; Brockie, Letter to the Editor, *National Business Review*, 1 March 1982; RR to MB and Maurice Boyd, 3 March 1982, MB Papers.
61 For a superb account of the changes that took place regarding the Treaty in the 1980s and 1990s, see Sharp, *Justice*.
62 In this paragraph I am drawing both on Thomas Kuhn's famous argument in his 1962 book *The Structure of Scientific Revolutions* and a more specific argument an American historian, Thomas Laqueur, has made in discussing a different but not dissimilar subject matter to mine (*Making*, p. 10).
63 For a consideration of several of these points, see Johnson, *Land*.
64 Here I have adapted an argument that J. G. A. Pocock makes about the Treaty alone: 'Treaty', pp. 76–77.
65 See, for example, Williams, 'Tiriti', pp. 161, 164.
66 Waitangi Action Committee, *Te Hikoi*; Blank et al. (eds), *He Korero*; Orange, *Treaty*, p. 249; Yensen et al. (eds), *Honouring*; Sharp, *Justice*, pp. 87–90.
67 New Zealand Maori Council, *Kaupapa*, pp. 3–4; Sharp, *Justice*, pp. 77, 87–88.
68 RR to Hēnare Kōhere Ngata, 9 September 1973, RRP, Box 84, Folder 4; Maori Council, *Kaupapa*, pp. 4–5.
69 Maori Council, *Kaupapa*, pp. 35–38.
70 Sharp, *Justice*, p. 77.
71 Ibid., pp. 77–78; Sorrenson, 'Epilogue', p. 301.
72 Treaty of Waitangi Act 1975, Second Schedule, Section 5, Clauses 2 and 6, Section 6, Clause 1; Waitangi Tribunal, *Report on Motunui-Waitara*, p. 5.
73 Waitangi Tribunal, *Report on Motunui-Waitara*, pp. 45, 51; Waitangi Tribunal, *Report on Kaituna River*, p. 14; Waitangi Tribunal, *Report on Manukau*, pp. 65, 67–68; Johnson, 'Making', p. 117.
74 Treaty of Waitangi Act 1975, Preamble, my emphases.
75 Durie, 'Treaty', p. 158.
76 For an excellent book that considers these developments in all three jurisdictions, see Johnson, *Land*.
77 Waitangi Tribunal, *Report on Motunui-Waitara*, pp. 45–49; Waitangi Tribunal, *Report on Kaituna River*, pp. 16–18.
78 Treaty of Waitangi Act 1975, Section 5, Clause 2, my emphasis.

Chapter 5: The Waitangi Tribunal, the Legal Scholars and the Historians

1. Waitangi Tribunal, *Report on Motunui-Waitara*, p. 46; Waitangi Tribunal, *Report on Kaituna River*, pp. 12–14; Waitangi Tribunal, *Report on Manukau*, p. 65; Waitangi Tribunal, *Report on Te Reo*, p. 20. See also Waitangi Tribunal, *Report on Orakei*, p. 185.

2. Waitangi Tribunal, *Report on Motunui-Waitara*, p. 47; Waitangi Tribunal, *Report on Kaituna River*, p. 12; Waitangi Tribunal, *Report on Manukau*, p. 65; Waitangi Tribunal, *Report on Te Reo*, p. 20. See also Waitangi Tribunal, *Report on Motunui-Waitara*, p. 46.

3. As far as I know, the Tribunal did not note Ross's major argument until 1988, by which time Keith Sorrenson had become a member. In its report on the Muriwhenua fishing claim the Tribunal asserted that it regarded her statement 'However good intentions may have been, a close study of events shows that the Treaty of Waitangi was hastily and inexpertly drawn up, ambiguous and contradictory in content, chaotic in its execution' as 'substantially correct', only to turn around and state that in its view 'the terms [of the Treaty] were not so much contradictory as complementary' (Waitangi Tribunal, *Report on Muriwhenua*, p. 213).

4. Waitangi Tribunal, *Report on Motunui-Waitara*, pp. 46–47; Waitangi Tribunal, *Report on Kaituna River*, pp. 16–17; Waitangi Tribunal, *Report on Manukau*, pp. 64–65. See also Waitangi Tribunal, *Report on Orakei*, pp. 180–82.

5. Ross, 'Te Tiriti', pp. 136, 138, 140–41; Waitangi Tribunal, *Report on Motunui-Waitara*, p. 49; Waitangi Tribunal, *Report on Kaituna River*, p. 13; Waitangi Tribunal, *Report on Manukau*, p. 65.

6. Google Ngram Viewer, which charts the frequency with which words appear each year in the books that have been digitised by Google, suggests that there was a marked rise in the use of these three words after the early to mid-1980s — that is, the time when the Tribunal reports, drawing on Ross's article and/or those who had read it, began to take them up.

7. Waitangi Tribunal, *Report on Kaituna River*, pp. 13–14; Waitangi Tribunal, *Report on Manukau*, pp. 67–68. See also Waitangi Tribunal, *Report on Orakei*, pp. 189, 207.

8. In its *Manukau* report, the Tribunal sought to counter Ross's arguments regarding both the Declaration of Independence and Williams's translation of it (p. 68).

9. Ross, 'Te Tiriti', pp. 139–41; Waitangi Tribunal, *Report on Kaituna River*, pp. 13–14; Waitangi Tribunal, *Report on Manukau*, pp. 67–68. See also Waitangi Tribunal, *Report on Orakei*, pp. 189, 207.

10. Waitangi Tribunal, *Report on Kaituna*, p. 13; Waitangi Tribunal, *Report on Motunui-Waitara*, pp. 50, 52; Waitangi Tribunal, *Report on Manukau*, p. 67; Waitangi Tribunal, *Report on Orakei*, p. 185.

11. Ross, 'Te Tiriti', pp. 142–43.

12. Waitangi Tribunal, *Report on Motunui-Waitara*, p. 50; Waitangi Tribunal, *Report on Kaituna*, p. 13; Waitangi Tribunal, *Report on Manukau*, pp. 68–69; Waitangi Tribunal, *Report on Te Reo*, pp. 20, 22–23.

13. Ross, 'Te Tiriti', pp. 141–42; RR to DB and GB, 28 July 1978, RRP, Box 38, Folder 1.

14. Waitangi Tribunal, *Report on Motunui-Waitara*, p. 47; Waitangi Tribunal, *Report on Kaituna River*, p. 19. See also Waitangi Tribunal, *Report on Muriwhenua*, p. 189.

15. Ross, 'Te Tiriti', p. 154.

16 Waitangi Tribunal, *Report on Motunui-Waitara*, p. 52; Waitangi Tribunal, *Report on Kaituna River*, pp. 14, 19–20; Waitangi Tribunal, *Report on Manukau*, pp. v, 69–70; Waitangi Tribunal, *Report on Te Reo*, p. 22.

17 *New Zealand Maori Council v Attorney-General*, *New Zealand Law Reports*, vol. 1, 1987, pp. 651, 655–56, 661–62; Sharp, *Justice*, p. 58.

18 *New Zealand Maori Council v Attorney-General*, pp. 663, 672–73, 690–91, 702, 712–15.

19 *Ibid.*, pp. 663–64, 673–74, 682–84, 702–04.

20 Sharp, *Justice*, pp. 167, 177.

21 Orange, *The Treaty of Waitangi* has sold more than 40,000 copies: https://www.bwb.co.nz/books/the-treaty-of-waitangi/

22 Diana Dekker, 'A Work in Progress', *New Zealand Listener*, 6 February 2021.

23 Orange, 'Treaty', unpaginated abstract, pp. 7–8, 24, 265, and *Treaty*, p. 5.

24 Orange, 'Treaty', pp. 11–12, and *Treaty*, p. 2.

25 Orange, 'Treaty', pp. ii, 8, 12, 137, 142, 145–48, and *Treaty*, pp. ix, 1, 41–43, 46; Sorrenson, 'Epilogue', p. 298.

26 Orange, 'Treaty', pp. i, 1, 125–27, 148, 177, 186, 239, 252–53, 330, and *Treaty*, pp. 4, 33, 41, 57, 91, my emphasis. Orange attributes the change I note in the two passages I quote here to further research she conducted for her book, but I doubt this is a sufficient explanation for it (Orange, personal communication with the author, 6 December 2021).

27 Orange, 'Treaty', unpaginated abstract, and *Treaty*, p. 1.

28 In the book, by my count, *rights* appears 290 times, *sovereignty* 230 times. In a comparable book — Buick's — these words in respect of Māori appear far fewer times.

29 Orange, 'Treaty', unpaginated abstract, p. 379, and *Treaty*, pp. 41, 58, 105–06, 144, 164.

30 Orange, *Treaty*, pp. 249–54; Durie, 'Treaty', pp. 160–61.

31 Bridget Williams, personal communication with the author, 13 April 2022.

32 Ross, 'Te Tiriti', p. 154; Orange, 'Treaty', pp. 12–13, and Orange, *Treaty*, p. 2.

33 Orange, 'Treaty', pp. 12, 18–19, 387–88, 573–74, my emphasis, and *Treaty*, pp. 4, 145–46, 218, 226.

34 In noting the former scholarship in her thesis, Orange referenced the work of Auburn, Molloy and McKean (noted earlier in this book) but also Betty Carter and J. D. Sutton (p. 9), but it is apparent that she also read the work of an earlier scholar of international law, M. F. Lindley, and a historian with a legal bent, John M. Ward (p. 125 note 1).

35 Orange overstated her case in this regard. Adams had taken one aspect of this seriously — the degree to which the British government considered Māori to be the owners or even the sovereigns of New Zealand — and her account of this did not differ substantially from his (cf. Orange, *Treaty*, p. 23 and Adams, *Fatal*, pp. 56–57), however much the significance they assigned to the role of the law differed. One of the main differences in their accounts arose from the fact that Orange neglected to pay sufficient attention to a matter that Adams regarded as important, namely the role that legal concepts and practices about protection played in the imperial government's consideration of whether it might intervene in New Zealand's affairs (see *Fatal*, pp. 52–55, 59–60, 62–63, 68).

36 Orange, 'Treaty', pp. 2, 10, 14.

37 Adams, *Fatal*, p. 11; Orange, 'Treaty', pp. 14, 20, 94, 125–26, 142, and *Treaty*, pp. 1–3, 8, 21–23, 28, 30–33, 35–36, 41, 55, 60, 65–66, 69, 85–86, 222, 235.

38 Orange, 'Treaty', pp. 95–96, 121, 241–42, 244, 260, and *Treaty*, pp. 23, 30, 87.

39 Orange, 'Treaty', pp. 85, 95, 176, and *Treaty*, pp. 21, 23.

40 Orange, 'Treaty', pp. 18, 248, and *Treaty*, p. 88.

41 Orange, 'Treaty', unpaginated abstract, 13–14, 18, 24, 89, 92–95, and *Treaty*, pp. 56–57, 226–27.

42 McHugh was by no means the only legal scholar who did work relating to the Treaty. Apart from those I have already named, there was Fredericka Hackshaw, F. M. Brookfield and Benedict Kingsbury. But McHugh's scholarship exerted the most influence historically speaking.

43 McHugh, *Māori*, p. xv. For this work, see, for example, 'Legal Status', 'Aboriginal Rights and Sovereignty', 'Aboriginal Servitudes', and 'Aboriginal Rights at Common Law', p. 10.

44 McHugh, 'Aboriginal Rights at Common Law', pp. i, 2–5, 5 note 10, 9, 93, 113–14, and *Māori*, pp. xiii, 1, 3 note 1, 4.

45 McHugh, 'Aboriginal Rights at Common Law', pp. i, 6–9, 11, 62–63, 71, 75, 78, 85, 94, 97–98, 102, 106, 111, 265, 303–04, and *Māori*, pp. 1–7.

46 Chapman, 'Treaty'. For McHugh's response to this attack, see 'Constitutional'.

47 Scott, Travesty, pp. 24, 26, 79, 148; Brash, Speech to the Orewa Rotary Club, 27 January 2004, https://www.scoop.co.nz/stories/PA0401/S00220/nationhood-don-brash-speech-orewa-rotary-club.htm. For a discussion of these writers, see Hill, Anti-Treatyism.

48 Another way to chart these changes would be to examine the shifts that occurred over time in Alan Ward's take on the Treaty. At the very least one could compare the accounts he gave of the Treaty in his 1973 book *A Show of Justice* and in his 1999 book *An Unsettled History*, but this could be extended to consider his other writings, most of which are listed in the bibliography of this book. I could also have taken some of the writings of Judith Binney as an example. See her 'Maori', 'Two Communities' and 'Kawanatanga'.

49 In his *Ko te Whenua* Sorrenson provides information, at the foot of the opening page of each of these essays, about their original provenance.

50 Ward, 'Tribute', p. 7; Innes, 'Bibliography', p. 189.

51 Sorrenson, 'Purchase', 'Land Purchase', 'Politics of Land', 'Introduction', pp. 4, 7, and 'Epilogue', p. 298; Orange, 'A Treaty Conversation', Auckland Writers' Festival, 14 May 2021, https://www.writersfestival.co.nz/look-and-listen/videos/Page1/a-treaty-conversation-claudia-orange-2021

52 Sorrenson, 'Introduction', pp. 2, 7, 'Towards' in his *Ko te Whenua*, p. 218, 'Waitangi', p. 284, and 'Epilogue', p. 298.

53 Sorrenson, Note on Judith Binney's Reader Report, undated [*c.* March 1972], RRP, Box 84, Folder 4; Sorrenson, 'Maori Representation', pp. 160–61.

54 It first appeared in the *New Zealand Journal of History*, vol. 21, no. 1, 1987, pp. 173–88 (which is the one that will now be cited here) and was then updated twice, in Kawharu (ed.), *Waitangi: Maori and Pakeha Perspectives of the Treaty of Waitangi*, Oxford University Press, Auckland, 1989, pp. 158–79, and in his *Ko te Whenua*, pp. 217–37.

55 Sorrenson, 'Radical Interpretation', pp. 173–74.

56 *Ibid.*

57 *Ibid.*, pp. 174–75.

58 *Ibid.*, pp. 175–88.

59 Sorrenson, 'Giving', pp. 238, 245, 249.

60 He also referenced a 1987 Master's thesis by Tom Bennion (which was later distilled into an article, 'Treaty-Making', a 1990 article by Sir Kenneth Keith, and a 1987 book by the Australian historian Henry Reynolds, *The Law of the Land*, in which he had worked in the mode of a legal advocate ('Treaties', p. 307 notes 5, 11, 26, 33).

61 Sorrenson, 'Treaties', pp. 40–54.

Chapter 6: Politics, Public History and Juridical History

1. My purpose here is not to provide a comprehensive account of this debate in the sense of discussing every figure. I am aware that historians and legal scholars other than the ones I consider were involved — such as J. M. R. Owens, Michael Bassett and Richard Boast — but the positions they adopted did not differ in any fundamental sense from those of the players I discuss. Nor do I attempt to discuss every argument that these protagonists made, not least because this would lead to unnecessary repetition.
2. Sharp's senior colleague Richard Mulgan also took up these matters in his 1989 book, *Māori, Pākehā and Democracy*, but the Treaty only formed part of his focus. I will discuss parts of his account in the closing chapter.
3. Sharp, *Justice*, pp. 9, 19–20, 82.
4. Ibid., pp. 132–33.
5. Ibid., pp. 132, 134–35, 139.
6. Ibid., pp. 139–40.
7. Andrew Sharp, personal communication to the author, 1 January 2022.
8. Ward, 'History', p. 150 note 1; Boast, 'Lawyers', p. 91; Belgrave, 'Obituary', p. 210.
9. See Dalley and Phillips (eds), *Going*.
10. Ward, 'History', p. 150; Ward, 'Tribute', p. 7; Hempenstall, 'Tasman'; Belgrave, 'Obituary', p. 209.
11. Dalley, 'Finding', p. 25; Byrnes, 'Jackals', pp. 113, 115.
12. Ward, 'History', p. 151.
13. Ibid., pp. 150, 152, 155. The questions Ward was raising mirrored those that historians were raising elsewhere in the world as the law played an increasing role in representing the past and the work of professional historians was pressed into service in court cases and the like. See, for example, Evans, 'History'.
14. Novick, *Noble*, pp. 1–2.
15. Ward, 'History', p. 157.
16. Ibid., pp. 157–60.
17. Ibid., pp. 151–52; Ward, 'Historical Method', pp. 152–53.
18. Ward, 'History', p. 152.
19. Ibid., p. 151, my emphasis.
20. Ibid., pp. 160, 162, 164.
21. Ward, 'Historical Method', pp. 141, 146–47, 149, 151–52.
22. Ibid., pp. 146–48, 150–51.
23. Sharp, 'History', pp. 159–61.
24. Ibid., pp. 159–60.
25. Ibid., pp. 160, 166; Sharp, 'Recent', pp. 31–32.
26. Sharp, 'Recent', p. 34.
27. Sharp, 'History', pp. 163–64; Sharp and McHugh, 'Introduction', p. 4; Sharp, 'Recent', pp. 37, 44.
28. Sharp, 'History', pp. 162, 166–67, 171–72, 178, and 'Recent', pp. 44–45, 56.
29. Sharp, 'Recent', pp. 41–42.
30. Ibid., pp. 56–60.
31. McHugh, 'History of the Modern Jurisprudence', p. 221. He wrote several essays that are relevant to the discussion I conduct here: 'Historiography', 'Law', 'Common-Law', 'History of Crown Sovereignty' and 'Tales'.
32. McHugh, 'Common-Law', pp. 393–94, his emphasis.
33. Oakeshott also identified another attitude that he called 'historical', arguing that it had a general affinity to the scientific one but diverged from it in important respects: 'Activity', pp. 153–59.
34. Oakeshott, 'Activity', p. 148; McHugh, 'Common-Law', pp. 394–95.
35. Bartelson, *Genealogy*, p. 57, his emphases, cited by McHugh,

36 McHugh, 'Common-Law', pp. 396–97, 428–29.
37 Ibid., pp. 427–28; McHugh, 'History', pp. 209, 224.
38 McHugh, 'Law', pp. 38, 49.
39 Ibid., pp. 38–39, 43–46.
40 Ibid., pp. 45–48.
41 Ibid., pp. 49–51, 57.
42 Ibid., pp. 55–57.
43 Oliver, Claims, p. 1, 'Pandora', 'Getting', 'Is Bias', Looking, pp. 155–63; Tennant, 'Obituary', p. 154, and 'Oliver'.
44 Several months later, Oliver contributed an opinion piece to a newspaper in which he made the same fundamental argument: 'Waitangi Tribunal Relied on an Insecure Argument', New Zealand Herald, 16 October 1997.
45 Oliver, 'Is Bias', pp. 17–18; Oliver, Looking, pp. 157–58.
46 Oliver, 'Is Bias', pp. 18–19.
47 Oliver, Social, pp. 12–13, Looking, pp. 164–65, and 'Future'; Howe, 'Review', p. 203; Phillipson, '2001', p. 21. Howe was not altogether correct in saying that historians had not said these things before publicly. For example, his colleague J. M. R. Owens had done so several years earlier: 'A Nation with a Distinctive Experience and Identity', New Zealand Herald, 7 February 1990.
48 Oliver, Claims, pp. 2–3, and 'Future', pp. 9, 20.
49 Oliver, 'Future', pp. 10, 13–20.
50 Ibid., pp. 20–21, my emphases.
51 Ibid., pp. 21, 215 note 26.
52 Ibid., pp. 21–23.
53 Ibid., pp. 23–25.
54 Ibid., p. 27; Oliver, Looking, pp. 167–68.
55 Oliver, Looking, p. 168.
56 Ibid., pp. 166, 169.
57 Ibid., pp. 169–70.
58 Ibid., p. 170.
59 Sharp, 'Representing', p. 29; Pocock, 'Historian', p. 112; Sharp and McHugh, 'Introduction', p. 7.
60 Pocock, Ancient, pp. vii, xi, 'Historian', p. 89, 'Uniqueness', p. 482, and 'Treaty', p. 76.
61 Pocock, 'Historian', pp. 91, 99, 'Uniqueness', pp. 483, 485, and 'Treaty', p. 80.
62 Pocock, 'Law', p. 495, 'Politics', pp. 224, 231, 233 note 12, 'Historian', pp. 90, 94, 96–97, and 'Treaty', p. 76.
63 Pocock, 'Treaty', pp. 77–78. Several years later Jim McAloon was to make a similar kind of argument: see his 'By Which'.
64 Pocock, 'Treaty', p. 78.
65 Ibid., p. 80.
66 Ibid., pp. 80–81.
67 Ibid., pp. 81, 84, 87–88.
68 Tau, 'Matauranga'.
69 Michael Belgrave has suggested that the Tribunal's history-making came under attack from Māori on the grounds that it failed to recognise properly Māori ways of dealing with the past that were consistent with their historical knowledge, but the evidence he has cited for this — Tau's essay and a book by H. C. Evison — does not support his claim as Tau made no such argument in regard to the Tribunal, and Evison is a Pākehā scholar (though closely connected to Ngāi Tahu): Belgrave, 'Tribunal', pp. 36, 52 note 8.
70 Pocock knew that Tau had begun by thinking he might be able to reconcile the two ways of conceiving the past — mātauranga Māori and history — both of which he admired. But in the end he abandoned the project as too daunting, at least for the time being (Sharp, personal communication to the author, 1 January 2022).
71 Pocock, 'Treaty', pp. 89, 93.

72 Ibid., pp. 89–92, 226 note 23.

73 Pocock, 'Historian', p. 111, and 'Treaty', pp. 94–95.

74 This point is evidenced by the bibliographical references in the work listed in the next endnote.

75 The books were the memoir by Oliver and Byrnes's *Waitangi Tribunal*; the main articles or essays were Belgrave, 'Tribunal', McAloon, 'By Which', Byrnes, 'By Which', and Belgrave, 'Looking'.

76 Sharp to John Pocock, 13 December 2001, Andrew Sharp, Personal Papers; Howe, 'Review', pp. 203–04; Belgrave, 'Looking', pp. 230, 247 note 2. The earlier articles and essays included Belgrave, 'Something', Byrnes, 'Jackals', Howe 'Two', Byrnes, *Waitangi*.

77 See, for example, McAloon, 'By Which'. For Oliver's response, see his 'Reply'.

78 Belgrave, 'Something', p. 102, and 'Looking', pp. 230–31, 236–37; Sharp to Pocock, 13 December 2001, Andrew Sharp Papers (held by Sharp).

79 Belgrave, 'Something', p. 100, 'Tribunal', pp. 45, 51, and 'Looking', pp. 232, 235, 243, 245–46.

80 Phillipson, '2001', pp. 25, 27–29, 44.

81 The legal scholar David Williams did the same in an article he published in 2014: 'Historians', p. 148.

82 Phillipson, '2001', pp. 23–24, 29, 33, 35, 45.

83 Durie, 'Treaty', pp. 158, 160–61.

84 Ibid., pp. 161–63.

Chapter 7: Revisionist Histories

1 In this chapter I do not seek to provide a comprehensive account of all the new scholarship that was available at the time I wrote the book. Rather I discuss work that I consider to be representative of it.

2 Owens, 'New Zealand', pp. 39, 51–52; McKitterick, 'McKenzie'.

3 This contention, which comprised the largest part of his thesis, was controversial and remains so (Ballantyne, 'Christianity', pp. 153–55, and 'Paper', pp. 209–10).

4 McKenzie, *Oral*, pp. 9, 19; McKenzie, *Bibliography*, p. 129.

5 McKenzie, *Oral*, pp. 32–33, 33 note 76.

6 Ibid., p. 33.

7 Ibid., pp. 34–35.

8 Ibid., pp. 35, 36 note 80.

9 Ibid., pp. 35–37, his emphasis.

10 Ibid., pp. 37, 40.

11 Ibid., pp. 40–41.

12 Ibid., pp. 41–44, 43 note 82.

13 Ross, 'Te Tiriti', p. 152; McKenzie, *Oral*, pp. 44–45, 44 note 85.

14 McKenzie, *Oral*, pp. 45, 45 note 86.

15 Ibid., pp. 45–47.

16 To be fair, McKenzie's argument was not as cogent as I trust I have rendered it here.

17 Binney, 'Review'; Claudia Orange, 'Knowing What they Signed', *New Zealand Listener*, 1 August 1987. Cf. Sorrenson, 'Context', Brooking, 'Review', and Belich, 'Hobson's', p. 203; McKitterick, 'McKenzie', p. 310.

18 Belich, 'Hobson's', pp. 202–03.

19 Ibid., pp. 203–04.

20 Belich, *Making*, pp. 193–97. In a footnote Belich describes Ross's article as an important work on the Treaty (p. 465 note 45).

21 Binney, 'Introduction', pp. 2, 4–5, 8; Interview with Judith Binney, *Whenua*, Radio New Zealand, 18 September 2001; King, 'Argument', p. 9.

22 This said, King chose not to make any reference to Head's chapter in this review. By contrast, another historian, Kerry Howe, devoted the largest part of his review of this book to discussing it, partly because he recognised that it was a very important essay and drew attention to the fact that historical paradigms in regard to the Treaty had changed so much in the previous twenty years, and partly because he saw it as supporting the attack he had made in 2001 on both the way the Treaty had come to dominate historical research on Māori–Pākehā relations and the nature of this scholarship ('Review', and 'Two Worlds?', pp. 51, 56–58).

23 Head, 'Analysis', p. 2.

24 Head also argued that, much earlier, the wars of the 1860s had made this difficult: 'Pursuit', p. 98.

25 Head, 'Pursuit', pp. 97, 99–100, 103, 109.

26 Ibid., pp. 104, 107, 228–29 note 27.

27 See Head and Mikaere, 'Was 19th'.

28 Head, 'Pursuit', pp. 99, 104.

29 Ibid., pp. 99, 101–03.

30 Ibid., p. 105; Head, 'Land', p. 16 note 7.

31 Head, 'Pursuit', pp 104–05.

32 Ibid., p. 106.

33 Ibid.

34 Head might have acknowledged that Ross had been on to something when she distinguished between missionary Māori and traditional Māori, and thereby recognised that Ross's argument had probably played some part in enabling her to make hers.

35 Head, 'Pursuit', pp. 106–07.

36 Ibid., p. 107.

37 Ibid., pp. 107–08.

38 Ibid., pp. 108–11.

39 Historians such as Donald Loveridge had produced major reports for the Tribunal but none of them saw the light of day. See, for example, his 'Knot' and 'Object'.

40 Occasionally, he did use the words 'invented' or 'invention': *Historical*, pp. 78, 85.

41 Belgrave, *Historical*, pp. 15, 43, 45, 56–57.

42 Belgrave derived the term 'the historical treaty' from his Massey University colleague J. M. R. Owens, who had also referred to 'the original treaty': Owens, 'Treaty', p. 13; Belgrave, *Historical*, p. 342 note 22. Owens himself might have derived both these terms from reading Richard Mulgan's *Māori, Pākehā and Democracy* (see pp. 90, 112 and 117).

43 Belgrave, *Historical*, pp. 38–39, 43, 45.

44 Ibid., pp. 45–55, 60, 65, 71.

45 Ibid., pp. 57, 59–62.

46 His account differed from hers, though, in two important respects. He argued that Williams believed that he had provided a proper translation of the English text and so had not radically changed the Treaty; and he contended that seeing Williams as someone who had engaged in deliberate deception was to view him in a way that was inconsistent with his character (*ibid.*, pp. 59, 61).

47 Belgrave, *Historical*, pp. 58, 65, 69.

48 Ibid., pp. 37, 63.

49 Ibid., pp. 29, 37–39, 58–59, 64. Tony Ballantyne, Andrew Sharp and I have discussed in various ways the role that discourses about protection played in the making of the Treaty: Ballantyne, *Entanglements*, especially pp. 231–34, 244–49; Sharp, *World*, Chapters 24 and 25; Attwood, *Empire*, Chapter 4. On 'keywords', see Raymond Williams's famous book of this name.

50 Belgrave, *Historical*, pp. 29, 52, 61–63, 65–66.

51 I do not discuss Belgrave's argument in respect of religion here because I do not believe he evidences it adequately.

52 Several years earlier, Belgrave had challenged the dominant interpretation of the Treaty in a journal article

53 Belgrave, *Historical*, pp. 63, 65, 67, 89, 112.

54 *Ibid.*, pp. 29, 61, 66.

55 *Ibid.*, p. 64.

56 *Ibid.*, pp. 7, 25–26, 28, 45. An argument made by Vincent O'Malley might be read in a similar way. He suggested that the Treaty was less important to Māori after its signing than were the undertakings that the Crown gave to them when it purchased land — what he called hundreds of little treaties: 'Treaty-Making', especially pp. 140, 146, 151.

57 This said, my book *Empire* has a good deal to say about the Treaty. Furthermore, the legal scholar Ned Fletcher has been revising his PhD thesis on the English text of the Treaty for publication, and it appeared just as this book was going to press. (I briefly discuss his thesis later in this chapter.) Orange has also recently published a new book that she has rightly described as a study 'independent' of her earlier ones, but her interpretation of the Treaty remains unchanged (*Treaty of Waitangi / Te Tiriti o Waitangi*, p. 7).

58 McHugh, *Aboriginal Title*, p. 274.

59 Their work was by no means the only important research done by legal historians that has a bearing on the Treaty. See also the work of McHugh — for example, *Aboriginal Societies*, 'Pretty', and 'Most Decorous'. The work of an American legal historian Lauren Benton has also been very influential. See, for example, her *Law*, *Search*, 'Possessing', and 'Beyond'. Other legal scholars have similarly shed historical light on the Treaty by focusing on the decade or so immediately after it was made. For example, Shaunnagh Dorsett demonstrates that despite the Treaty's third article the government did not intend to subject Māori to British law in all instances, especially in respect of intra-Māori matters, and suggests that it understood sovereignty and jurisdiction as quite different matters: *Juridical Encounters*.

60 Hickford to author, 6 and 11 October 2021. See his 'Making' and *Lords*, but also 'Decidedly' and 'Vague'.

61 For Banner's own discussion of this focus, see *Possessing*, p. 4.

62 See Hickford's opening chapter in his *Lords*. This has also been true of the work of Ballantyne, though from the perspective of cultural history. See several of his essays in his *Webs* and *Entanglements*, especially Chapter 6. From a different perspective, a Canadian historian, John C. Weaver, also did this in his remarkable book *The Great Land Rush*.

63 For a discussion of other aspects in which it was different, see my 'History'.

64 This at least was an account that Banner's overall argument implied for the islands of New Zealand. I spelt this argument out in *Empire*, pp. 38, 104, 199, 403–04.

65 Banner, *Possessing*, p. 61. Banner's other discussion of the Treaty — which was devoted to the other part of its second article and thus to the right of pre-emption that the British Crown acquired (*ibid.*, p. 67) — was less significant because other historians (such as Belgrave) had already emphasised its importance.

66 Hickford, 'Making', pp. vi–viii, 106, 162, 208–10, 232.

67 *Ibid.*, pp. 163–64, 275, 308.

68 This is available online: https://researchspace.auckland.ac.nz/handle/2292/24098

69 Fletcher, 'Praiseworthy', pp. iii, xi, 75–83.

70 *Ibid.*, pp. iii–iv, xiii, xv.

71 Butterfield, *Whig*, p. 16; Owens, 'Historians', p. 18.

72 Owens, 'Historians', p. 4.
73 Here I follow Prakash, 'Writing', *passim*.
74 See Porter, 'Nose', pp. 155–56. I am indebted to Andrew Sharp for drawing my attention to this saying.
75 Owens, 'Treaty', p. 6.
76 White, *Middle*, p. x.
77 Ashplant and Wilson, 'Whig', pp. 11, 13, 15, and 'Present', pp. 255, 265–70.
78 Megill, *Historical*, pp. 25–26. I provide an example of a historical source, as Megill and I define it, in *Empire*, pp. 163–64.

Chapter 8: The Advantages and Disadvantages of History

1 Nietzsche, *On the Advantage*, pp. 14, 18–19, his emphases; Davison, *Use*, p. 11.
2 Nietzsche, *On the Advantage*, pp. 7, 18, 23.
3 In much of this discussion of myth I have drawn on Cohen, *History*, especially pp. 17, 211–14.
4 Oliver, 'History'.
5 The approach I adopt in *Empire* might also be called historicist.
6 It might be said that I have done the same in some of my earlier work. See, for example, 'Law'.
7 RR to Henare Kohere Ngata, 9 September 1973, RRP, Box 84, Folder 4.
8 Belgrave, 'Colonialism', p. 228.
9 My formulation here owes a good deal to the New Zealand-born and raised Australian anthropologist Gillian Cowlishaw: 'Studying', p. 27.
10 Nietzsche, *On the Advantage*, p. 21; Pocock, 'Antipodean', p. 9.
11 Bloch, *Historian's*, pp. 118–19.
12 Belgrave, *Historical*, pp. 46, 55.
13 *Ibid.*, pp. 39, 46, 55–56.
14 See Megill's introduction to *Historical* on this matter.
15 My take on objectivity is informed by Mommsen, 'Moral', Haskell, 'Objectivity', and Megill, *Historical*.
16 For an example further to the ones I have already provided, see Binney, 'Maori', p. 27, and 'Kawanatanga', p. 78.
17 LaCapra, *Writing*, pp. 78–79.
18 Megill, *Historical*, p. 59, his emphasis.
19 *Ibid.*, pp. 2, 4, 128; LaCapra, *Writing*, p. 38.
20 Megill, *Historical*, pp. 2, 40, 215.
21 Cohen, *History*, pp. xi, xv, 7, 295, his emphasis.
22 White, 'Public', pp. 334–35.
23 *Ibid.*, p. 335.
24 *Ibid.*, p. 336.
25 *Ibid.*, p. 338.
26 Lynch, *Praise*, p. 9, his emphasis.
27 See Shapiro, *Culture*, Chapter 2.
28 In this and the following paragraphs I draw heavily on some of Chakrabarty's work. See his *Provincializing*, Chapter 4, and 'Public'.
29 Renwick, *Treaty*, pp. 9–10, my emphases.
30 See, for example, Mahuika, 'Closing'.
31 For example, whereas the Department of History at the University of Auckland had about twenty tenured members of staff in 1977, it barely has half that number now, yet the number of students it teaches has increased (University of Auckland, *Calendar*, 1977, pp. 30–31; https://www.arts.auckland.ac.nz/people/history).
32 Chakrabarty, 'Reconciliation', p. 14.
33 Ignatieff, *Warrior's*, pp. 173–74, 185.
34 In the following paragraphs I draw on Richard Mulgan's *Māori, Pākehā and Democracy*.

35 See https://www.stats.govt.nz/news/new-zealands-population-reflects-growing-diversity

36 There are notable exceptions — for example, the work of Tony Ballantyne and some of his colleagues.

37 This point has been repeatedly made by Ballantyne. See, for example, his *Webs*, pp. 16, 55–56, 60–61, 80.

38 See, for example, Goodall, 'Too'.

39 For example, a notion that the Treaty did *not* guarantee to Māori the rights and privileges of British subjects would be ruled out, though there would still be debate about what this provision meant in the past and what it means today.

Bibliography

Archives

37th Parliament — Maori Affairs Committee — Bills — Public Bills — Treaty of Waitangi [Session 3], Agency ABGX, Series 16127, Box 13, R315765, Archives New Zealand Te Rua Mahara o te Kāwanatanga, Wellington.

Application for consent to sale — Robert Hugh Standish to Ian Munson Ross and Ruth Miriam Ross, Agency BBAE, Series 5632, Box 1099/d, R24114617, Archives New Zealand Te Rua Mahara o te Kāwanatanga, Auckland.

Auckland Education Salary Cards, Agency ABEP, Series 4414, Box 71, R25043597, Archives New Zealand Te Rua Mahara o te Kāwanatanga, Auckland.

Burnard, Rex Whittington, Agency AAOM, Series 6030, Box 154, R23137235, Archives New Zealand Te Rua Mahara o te Kāwanatanga, Wellington.

Burnard, Ruth Miriam (née Guscott), Academic Record, University of New Zealand, 1938–44, W3119, Box 19, R12484935, Archives New Zealand Te Rua Mahara o te Kāwanatanga, Wellington.

Cabinet Meeting 1.4.74, Agency AAFD, Series 807, Box 294, R20823034, Archives New Zealand Te Rua Mahara o te Kāwanatanga, Wellington.

Centennial Records — Centennial National Historical Committee — Staff etc., Agency AGCO, Series 833, Box 2048, R14987658, Archives New Zealand Te Rua Mahara o te Kāwanatanga, Wellington.

Land — Maori Land — General, Agency AAFD, Series 811, Box 1241, R20825493, Archives New Zealand Te Rua Mahara o te Kāwanatanga, Wellington.

Maori Affairs — General, Agency AAFD, Series 811, Box 1334, R20825944, Archives New Zealand Te Rua Mahara o te Kāwanatanga, Wellington.

Maori Affairs — General, Agency AAFD, Series 811, Box 1334, R20827494, Archives New Zealand Te Rua Mahara o te Kāwanatanga, Wellington.

Probate Records for Rex Whittington Burnard, Agency AAOM 6030, Box 154, R23137235, Archives New Zealand Te Rua Mahara o te Kāwanatanga, Wellington.

Public School Syllabus and Instruction — Primary School Bulletins — Correspondence with Authors — 25 October 1950–23 May 1955, Agency ACIG, Series 17274, Box 5, Part 2, R12203920, Archives New Zealand Te Rua Mahara o te Kāwanatanga, Wellington.

Publications — Special New Zealand — Booklet entitled 'New Zealand's First Capital' by Mrs R. M. Ross, Agency ACGO, Series 8333, Box 2928, R19966023, Archives New Zealand Te Rua Mahara o te Kāwanatanga, Wellington.

Ross, Ruth Miriam, Will, Agency BBAE, Series 1570, Box 3443, R20242876, Archives New Zealand Te Rua Mahara o te Kāwanatanga, Auckland.

Salary Card for Ross, Ian Munson, Agency ABEP, Series 4414, Box 71, R25043597, Archives New Zealand Te Rua Mahara o te Kāwanatanga, Auckland.

Salary Card for Ross, Ruth Miriam, Agency ABEP, Series 4414, Box 71, R25043632, Archives New Zealand Te Rua Mahara o te Kāwanatanga, Auckland.

School Publications — Bulletins — Correspondence with Writers and Artists — Primary (also Correspondence on Parts 3 and 4 School Journals) — 28 April 1955–20 April 1960, Agency ACIG, Series 17274, Box 6, Part 3, R12203919, Archives New Zealand Te Rua Mahara o te Kāwanatanga, Wellington.

Treaty of Waitangi — General and Policy and Submissions by New Zealand Maori Council (including Race Relations Bill Submissions 1971), Agency ACIH, Series 16036, Box 164, R21530636, Archives New Zealand Te Rua Mahara o te Kāwanatanga, Wellington.

Treaty of Waitangi Act & Decisions of the Tribunal, Agency ABWN, Series 6095, Box 382, R3949183, Archives New Zealand Te Rua Mahara o te Kāwanatanga, Wellington.

Treaty of Waitangi Act 1975, Agency ABRC, Series 6860, Box 321, Part 1, R20972377, Archives New Zealand Te Rua Mahara o te Kāwanatanga, Wellington.

Treaty of Waitangi Act 1975, Agency ABRC, Series 6860, Box 321, Part 2, R20972378, Archives New Zealand Te Rua Mahara o te Kāwanatanga, Wellington.

Wellington Hospital, Death Register, August 1936 to September 1944, Agency ADHM, Series 23149, Box 237, R22847841, Archives New Zealand Te Rua Mahara o te Kāwanatanga, Wellington.

Wellington Hospital, Index of Patients, Agency ABRR, Series 6911, Box 6, R2263386, Archives New Zealand Te Rua Mahara o te Kāwanatanga, Wellington.

Manuscripts

Bagnall, Austin Graham, Papers, Alexander Turnbull Library, MS-Papers-1901-90-103-2/02, 1901-90-103-2/03 and 1901-90-103-2/04.

Beaglehole, John Cawte and his family, Papers, Alexander Turnbull Library, MS-Papers-11535-186.

Binney, Judith, Papers, Alexander Turnbull Library, MS-Papers-1115-066 and 11115-139.

Boyd, Mary, Papers, Personal Letters from Family, 1940–2011, J. C. Beaglehole Room, Victoria University of Wellington.

Burnett, Robert Ian McKenzie, Papers, Alexander Turnbull Library, MS-Papers-5317-6 and 5137-8.

McCormick, Eric, Papers, Alexander Turnbull Library, MS-Papers-5292-053, 0166-11 and 0166-12.

New Zealand Department of Internal Affairs, Centennial Publications Branch, Historical Atlas Material, Alexander Turnbull Library, MS-Papers-0230-007, 0230-008 and 0230-009.

Pascoe, John Dobree, Papers, Alexander Turnbull Library, MS-Papers-75-241-066.

Paul, Janet Elaine, Papers, Alexander Turnbull Library, MS-Papers-5738-08, 5738-09, 5738-14 and 5523-16.

Ross, Ruth, Papers, Auckland War Memorial Museum Library, MS 94/23 and 1442.

Vennell, Charles William, Papers, Alexander Turnbull Library, MS-Papers-5922-1.

Wilson, George Hamish Ormond, Papers, Alexander Turnbull Library, MS-Papers-90-094-3.

Parliamentary Papers

British Parliamentary Papers, Report from the Select Committee on New Zealand, Together with Minutes of Evidence, Appendix, and Index, 1844, Paper no. 556.

New Zealand Parliamentary Debates 1864 to 1866.

Newspapers and Magazines

Auckland Star

The Dominion

Evening Post

Gisborne Herald

National Business Review

New Zealand Herald

New Zealand Listener

Otago Daily Times

Zealandia

Other Material

Adams, Patricia and R. M. Ross, 'Hokianga Homes of Missionary, Magistrate, and Pakeha Maori', in Frances Porter (ed.), *Historic Buildings of New Zealand: North Island*, Cassell New Zealand, Auckland, 1979, pp. 22–29.

Adams, Peter, *Fatal Necessity: British Intervention in New Zealand 1830–1847*, Auckland University Press/Oxford University Press, Auckland, 1977.

Appleby, Joyce et al., *Telling the Truth About History*, Norton, New York, 1994.

Ashplant, T. G. and Adrian Wilson, 'Whig History and Present-Centred History', *Historical Journal*, vol. 31, no. 1, 1988, pp. 1–16.

——, 'Present-Centred History and the Problem of Historical Knowledge', *Historical Journal*, vol. 31, no. 2, 1988, pp. 253–74.

Ashton, Jennifer, *At the Margin of Empire: John Webster and Hokianga, 1841–1900*, Auckland University Press, Auckland, 2015.

Attwood, Bain, 'Difficult Histories: The Museum of New Zealand Te Papa Tongarewa and the Treaty of Waitangi Exhibit', *The Public Historian*, vol. 35, no. 3, 2013, pp. 46–71.

——, *Empire and the Making of Native Title: Sovereignty, Property and Indigenous People*, Cambridge University Press, Cambridge, 2020.

——, 'History, Law and Aboriginal Title', *History Workshop Journal*, no. 77, 2014, pp. 283–90.

——, 'The Law of the Land or the Law of the Land? History, Law and Narrative in a Settler Society', *History Compass*, vol. 2, no. 1, 2004, pp. 1–30.

——, 'Towards a Post-Foundational History of the Treaty', in Mark Hickford and Carwyn Jones (eds), *Indigenous Peoples and the State: International Perspectives on the Treaty of Waitangi*, Routledge, London, 2019, pp. 94–110.

Auburn, F. M., 'Te Tiriti O Waitangi (The Treaty of Waitangi in New Zealand Law)', *New Zealand Universities Law Review*, vol. 4, no. 3, 1971, pp. 309–11.

Aves, Dora, *The Maori and the Crown: An Indigenous People's Struggle for Self-Determination*, Greenwood Press, Conn., 1999.

Awatere, Donna, *Maori Sovereignty*, Broadsheet, Auckland, 1984.

Bagnall, A. G., 'Ruth Miriam Ross, 1920–1982', *Turnbull Library Record*, vol. XVI, no. 1, 1983, pp. 54–61.

Ballantyne, Tony, 'Christianity, Colonialism and Cross-Cultural Communication' (2005), in his *Webs of Empire: Locating New Zealand's Colonial Past*, Bridget Williams Books, Wellington, 2012, pp. 137–58.

——, *Entanglements of the Body: Missionaries, Māori, and the Question of the Body*, Duke University Press, Durham, NC, 2014.

——, 'Paper, Pen and Print' (2011), in his *Webs of Empire: Locating New Zealand's Colonial Past*, Bridget Williams Books, Wellington, 2012, pp. 205–27.

——, 'Writing the Colonial Past', in his *Webs of Empire: Locating New Zealand's Colonial Past*, Bridget Williams Books, Wellington, 2012, pp. 283–95.

Ballantyne, Tony and Brian Moloughney, 'Introduction: Angles of Vision', in Tony Ballantyne and Brian Moloughney (eds), *Disputed Histories: Imagining New Zealand's Pasts*, Otago University Press, Dunedin, 2006, pp. 9–24.

Ballara, Angela, 'Nene, Tāmati Wāka', *Dictionary of New Zealand Biography*, first published in 1990, updated November 2001, Te Ara: The Encyclopedia of New Zealand, https://teara.govt.nz/en/biographies/1n2/nene-tamati-waka

——, 'Patuone, Eruera Maihi', *Dictionary of New Zealand Biography*, first published in 1990, updated November 2010, Te Ara: The Encyclopedia of New Zealand, https://teara.govt.nz/en/biographies/1p12/patuone-eruera-maihi

Banner, Stuart, *Possessing the Pacific: Land, Settlers and Indigenous People from Australia to Alaska*, Harvard University Press, Cambridge, MA, 2007.

Barrington, John, *Separate but Equal? Māori Schools and the Crown 1967–1969*, Victoria University Press, Wellington, 2008.

Barrowman, Rachel, *Victoria University of Wellington 1899–1999: A History*, Victoria University Press, Wellington, 1999.

Bartelson, Jens, *Genealogy of Sovereignty*, Cambridge University Press, Cambridge, 1995.

Baxter, James K., 'The Primary School Bulletin' (1957), in John Edward Weir (ed.), *James K. Baxter Complete Prose*, vol. 1, Victoria University Press, Wellington, 2015, pp. 312–15.

Beaglehole, Diana, 'The Maori in the *School Journal*: 1907–1981', *Education*, vol. 31, no. 1, 1982, pp. 38–41.

Beaglehole, J. C., 'History and the New Zealander', in *The University and the Community: Essays in Honour of Thomas Alexander Hunter*, Victoria University College, Wellington, 1946, pp. 98–124.

——, 'Introduction', in Ruth M. Allan, *Nelson: A History of Early Settlement*, A. H. & A. W. Reed, Wellington, 1965, pp. vi–xi.

——, *New Zealand: A Short History*, George Allen & Unwin, London, 1936.

——, 'The New Zealand Mind', *Australian Quarterly*, vol. 12, no. 4, 1940, pp. 40–50.

——, *The New Zealand Scholar: Margaret Condliffe Memorial Lecture, Canterbury University College, 21 April 1954*, Canterbury University College, Christchurch, 1954.

——, 'A Small Bouquet for the Education Department', *Arts Year Book*, no. 7, 1951, pp. 123–29.

Beaglehole, Tim, *A Life of J. C. Beaglehole: New Zealand Scholar*, Victoria University Press, Wellington, 2006.

Beaglehole, Tim (ed.), *'I think I am becoming a New Zealander': Letters of J. C. Beaglehole*, Victoria University Press, Wellington, 2013.

Belgrave, Michael, 'Colonialism Revisited: Public History and New Zealand's Waitangi Tribunal', in David Dean (ed.), *A Companion to Public History*, Wiley Blackwell, Hoboken, NJ, 2018, pp. 217–30.

——, *Dancing with the King: The Rise and Fall of the King Country, 1864–1885*, Auckland University Press, Auckland, 2017.

——, *Historical Frictions: Maori Claims and Reinvented Histories*, Auckland University Press, Auckland, 2005.

——, 'Looking Forward: Historians and the Waitangi Tribunal', *New Zealand Journal of History*, vol. 40, no. 2, 2006, pp. 230–50.

——, 'Obituary: Professor Alan Dudley Ward ONZM, 1935–2014', *New Zealand Journal of History*, vol. 49, no. 2, 2015, pp. 209–13.

——, 'Pre-emption, the Treaty of Waitangi and the Politics of Crown Purchase', *New Zealand Journal of History*, vol. 31, no. 1, 1997, pp. 23–37.

——, 'Response to Martin Fisher, 'Review of *Dancing with the King*', *Reviews in History*, https://reviews.history.ac.uk/review/2267

——, 'Something Borrowed, Something New: History and the Waitangi Tribunal', in Bronwyn Dalley and Jock Phillips (eds), *Going Public: The Changing Face of New Zealand History*, Auckland University Press, Auckland, 2001, pp. 92–109.

——, 'The Storm Before the Calm: The Treaty of Waitangi Since the 1960s', in Rachael Bell et al. (eds), *The Treaty on the Ground: Where We are Headed, and Why it Matters*, Massey University Press, Auckland, 2017, pp. 55–70.

——, 'The Tribunal and the Past: Taking a Roundabout Path to a New History', in Michael Belgrave et al. (eds), *Waitangi Revisited: Perspectives on the Treaty of Waitangi*, Oxford University Press, Auckland, 2005, pp. 35–55.

Belich, James, 'Hobson's Choice', *New Zealand Journal of History*, vol. 24, no. 2, 1990, pp. 200–07.

——, *Making Peoples: A History of the New Zealanders From Polynesian Settlement to the End of the Nineteenth Century*, Allen Lane, Auckland, 1996.

——, *The New Zealand Wars and the Victorian Interpretation of Racial Conflict*, Auckland University Press, Auckland, 1986.

——, 'The New Zealand Wars, 1845–1870: An Analysis of their History and Interpretation', DPhil thesis, University of Oxford, 1982.

Bell, Rachael, 'Ruth Ross: New Zealand Scholar/Treaty Scholar', MA thesis, Massey University, 2005.

——, '"Texts and Translations": Ruth Ross and the Treaty of Waitangi', *New Zealand Journal of History*, vol. 43, no. 1, 2009, pp. 39–58.

——, 'A Window for Revisionism: Presenting Te Tiriti in the Primary School Bulletins, 1957', *New Zealand Journal of History*, vol. 48, no. 2, 2014, pp. 119–35.

Bennion, Tom, 'Treaty-Making in the Pacific in the Nineteenth Century and the Treaty of Waitangi', *Victoria University of Wellington Law Review*, vol. 35, no. 1, 2004, pp. 165–205.

Benton, Lauren, 'Beyond Anachronism: Global Legal Politics and the History of International Law', *Journal of the History of International Law*, vol. 21, no. 1, 2019, pp. 1–34.

——, *Law and Colonial Cultures: Legal Regimes in World History, 1400–1900*, Cambridge University Press, Cambridge, 2002.

——, 'Possessing Empire: Iberian Claims and Interpolity Law', in Saliha Belmessous (ed.), *Native Claims: Indigenous Law against Empire, 1500–1920*, Oxford University Press, New York, 2012, pp. 19–40.

——, *A Search for Sovereignty: Law and Geography in European Empires, 1400–1900*, Cambridge University Press, New York, 2009.

Benton, Lauren and Benjamin Straumann, 'Acquiring Empire by Law: From Roman Doctrine to Early Modern European Practice', *Law and History Review*, vol. 28, no. 1, 2010, pp. 1–38.

Berkhofer, Robert F. Jnr, *Beyond the Great Story: History as Text and Discourse*, Belknap Press of Harvard University Press, Cambridge, MA, 1995.

Biggs, Bruce, 'Jones, Pei Te Hurinui', *Dictionary of New Zealand Biography*, first published in 1998, Te Ara: The Encyclopedia of New Zealand, https://teara.govt.nz/en/biographies/4j11/jones-pei-te-hurinui

Binney, Judith, 'History and Memory: The Wood of the Whau Tree, 1766–2005' (2009), in her *Stories Without End: Essays 1975–2010*, Bridget Williams Books, Wellington, 2010, pp. 323–51.

——, 'Introduction', in Judith Binney (ed.), *The Shaping of History: Essays from The New Zealand Journal of History* (2001), ebook, Bridget Williams Books, Wellington, 2018, pp. 1–10.

——, 'Kawanatanga and Rangatiratanga, 1840–1860', in Judith Binney et al., *The People and the Land/Te Tangata me Te Whenua: An Illustrated History of New Zealand 1820–1920*, Allen & Unwin New Zealand in association with Port Nicholson Press, Wellington, 1990, pp. 77–97.

——, *The Legacy of Guilt: A Life of Thomas Kendall*, Auckland University Press, Auckland, 1968.

——, 'The Maori and the Signing of the Treaty of Waitangi', in David Green (ed.), *Towards 1990: Seven Leading Historians Examine Significant Aspects of New Zealand History*, GP Books, Wellington, 1989, pp. 20–31.

——, 'Māori Oral Narratives, Pākehā Written Texts: Two Forms of Telling History' (1987), in her *Stories Without End: Essays 1975–2010*, Bridget Williams Books, Wellington, 2010, pp. 71–85.

——, 'Review of D. F. McKenzie, *Oral Culture, Literacy and Print in Early New Zealand: The Treaty of Waitangi*', *Political Science*, vol. 38, no. 2, 1986, pp. 185–86.

——, 'Te Tiriti-O-Waitangi', *Craccum*, vol. 46, no. 22, 1972, p. 6.

——, 'Two Communities, 1820–1839', in Judith Binney et al., *The People and the Land/Te Tangata me Te Whenua: An Illustrated History of New Zealand 1820–1920*, Allen & Unwin New Zealand in association with Port Nicholson Press, Wellington, 1990, pp. 11–33.

Birchfield, Maureen, *Looking for Answers: A Life of Elsie Locke*, Canterbury University Press, Christchurch, 2009.

Blank, Arapera et al. (eds), *He Korero Mo Waitangi, 1984*, Te Runanga o Waitangi, Ngaruawahia, 1985.

Bloch, Marc, *The Historian's Craft* (1944), translated by Peter Putnam, Manchester University Press, Manchester, 1992.

Boast, R. P., 'Lawyers, Historians, Ethics and Judicial Process', *Victoria University of Wellington Law Review*, vol. 28, no. 1, 1998, pp. 87–112.

Bodenheimer, Rosemarie, *The Real Life of Mary Ann Evans: George Eliot, her Letters and Fiction*, Cornell University Press, Ithaca, NY, 1994.

Boyd, Mary, 'Obituary: Ruth Ross 1920–82', *New Zealand Journal of History*, vol. 16, no. 2, 1982, pp. 188–90.

——, 'Race Relations in New Zealand 1815–1845', MA thesis, University of New Zealand, 1944.

——, 'Ross, Ruth Miriam', *Dictionary of New Zealand Biography*, first published in 2000, Te Ara: The Encyclopedia of New Zealand, https://teara.govt.nz/en/biographies/5r26/ross-ruth-miriam

——, 'Women in the Historical Profession: Women Historians in the 1940s', *Women's Studies Journal*, vol. 4, no. 1, 1988, pp. 76–87.

Brookes, Barbara, *A History of New Zealand Women*, Bridget Williams Books, Wellington, 2016.

Brooking, Tom, 'Review of D. F. McKenzie, Oral Culture, Literacy and Print in Early New Zealand: The Treaty of Waitangi', *Archifacts*, no. 3, 1986, pp. 36–37.

Buick, Thomas Lindsay, *The Treaty of Waitangi, or How New Zealand Became a British Colony* (1914), 3rd edn, Thomas Avery and Sons, New Plymouth, 1936.

Butterfield, Herbert, *The Whig Interpretation of History*, G. Bell and Sons, London, 1931.

Byrnes, Giselle, 'By Which Standards? History and the Waitangi Tribunal: A Reply', *New Zealand Journal of History*, vol. 40, no. 2, 2006, pp. 214–29.

——, 'Jackals of the Crown? Historians and the Treaty Claims Process', in Bronwyn Dalley and Jock Phillips (eds), *Going Public: The Changing Face of New Zealand History*, Auckland University Press, Auckland, 2001, pp. 110–22.

——, *The Waitangi Tribunal and New Zealand History*, Oxford University Press, Auckland, 2004.

——, 'What if the Treaty of Waitangi had not been signed on 6 February 1840?', in Stephen Levine (ed.), *New Zealand as it Might Have Been*, Victoria University Press, Wellington, 2006, pp. 27–39.

Byrnes, Giselle (ed.), *The New Oxford History of New Zealand*, Oxford University Press, Auckland, 2009.

Cain, Susan, *Quiet: The Power of Introverts in a World that Can't Stop Talking*, Penguin Books, London, 2013.

Calman, Ross, 'Māori Education — Mātauranga — The Native Schools System, 1867 to 1969', Te Ara: The Encyclopedia of New Zealand, http://www.TeAra.govt.nz/en/maori-education-matauranga/page-3

Cammell, Kathryn Anne, 'Ruth Ross and Te Tiriti o Waitangi', BA Honours thesis, University of Auckland, 2018.

Carr, E. H., *What is History?* (1961), Penguin Books, Harmondsworth, 1964.

Carter, Betty, 'The Incorporation of the Treaty of Waitangi into Municipal Law', *Auckland University Law Review*, vol. 4, no. 1, 1980, pp. 1–18.

Chakrabarty, Dipesh, *The Calling of History: Sir Jadunath Sarkar and his Empire of Truth*, University of Chicago Press, Chicago, 2015.

——, *Provincializing Europe: Postcolonial Thought and Historical Difference*, Princeton University Press, Princeton, NJ, 2000.

——, 'The Public Life of History: An Argument Out of India', *Public Culture*, vol. 20, no. 1, 2008, pp. 143–68.

——, 'Reconciliation and its Historiography: Some Preliminary Thoughts', *UTS Review*, vol. 7, no. 1, 2001, pp. 6–16.

Chapman, Guy, 'The Treaty of Waitangi: Fertile Ground for Judicial (and Academic) Myth-Making', *New Zealand Law Journal*, no. 7, 1991, pp. 228–36.

Cohen, Paul A., *History in Three Keys: The Boxers as Event, Experience and Myth*, Columbia University Press, New York, 1997.

Cowlishaw, Gillian, 'Studying Aborigines: Changing Canons in Anthropology and History', in Bain Attwood and John Arnold (eds), *Power, Knowledge and Aborigines*, La Trobe University Press in association with the National Centre for Australian Studies, Monash University, Melbourne, 1992, pp. 20–31.

Cross, Máire and Caroline Bland, 'Gender Politics: Breathing New Life into Old Letters', in Caroline Bland and Máire Cross (eds), *Gender and Politics in the Age of Letter-Writing, 1750–2000*, Ashgate, Aldershot, 2004, pp. 3–14.

Dakin, J. C., 'Preface', in *The Treaty of Waitangi: Its Origins and Significance: A Series of Papers Presented at a Seminar Held at Victoria University of Wellington, 19–20 February 1972 Under the Auspices of the Department of University Extension of the University*, Victoria University of Wellington, Wellington, [1972], p. ii.

Dalley, Bronwyn, 'Finding the Common Ground: New Zealand's Public History', in Bronwyn Dalley and Jock Phillips (eds), *Going Public: The Changing Face of New Zealand History*, Auckland University Press, Auckland, 2001, pp. 16–29.

Dalley, Bronwyn and Jock Phillips (eds), *Going Public: The Changing Face of New Zealand History*, Auckland University Press, Auckland, 2001.

Davison, Graeme, *The Use and Abuse of Australian History*, Allen & Unwin, Sydney, 2000.

de Certeau, Michel, *Heterologies: Discourse on the Other*, translated by Brian Massumi, Manchester University Press, Manchester, 1986.

Dorsett, Shaunnagh, *Juridical Encounters: Māori and the Colonial Courts 1840–1852*, Auckland University Press, Auckland, 2017.

Durie, E. T. J., 'Part II and Clause 26 of the Draft New Zealand Bill of Rights', in Andrew Sharp (comp.), *A Bill of Rights for New Zealand*, Legal Research Foundation, Auckland, 1985, pp. 173–93.

——, 'The Treaty in Maori History', in William Renwick (ed.), *Sovereignty & Indigenous Rights: The Treaty of Waitangi in International Contexts*, Victoria University Press, Wellington, 1991, pp. 156–69.

Earle, Augustus, *Narrative of a Residence in New Zealand. Journal of a Residence in Tristan da Cunha*, edited by E. H. McCormick, Clarendon Press, Oxford, 1966.

Evans, Richard J., 'History, Memory and the Law: The Historian as Expert Witness', *History and Theory*, vol. 41, no. 3, 2002, pp. 326–45.

Finlayson, Roderick, *The Springing Fern*, Whitcombe and Tombs, Christchurch, 1965.

Firth, Raymond, *Primitive Economics of the New Zealand Maori* (1929), Routledge, New York, 2011.

Fletcher, Ned, 'Foundation', in Simon Mount and Max Harris (eds), *The Promise of Law: Essays Marking the Retirement of Dame Sian Elias as Chief Justice of New Zealand*, LexisNexis New Zealand, Wellington, 2020, pp. 67–89.

——, 'A Praiseworthy Device for Amusing and Pacifying Savages? What the Framers Meant by the English Text of the Treaty of Waitangi', PhD thesis, University of Auckland, 2014.

Foden, N. A., *The Constitutional Development of New Zealand in the First Decade (1839–1849)*, L. T. Watkins, Wellington, 1938.

Foucault, Michel, 'Nietzsche, Genealogy, History', in his *Language, Counter-Memory, Practice: Selected Essays and Interviews*, edited by Donald F. Bouchard, Cornell University Press, Ithaca, 1977, pp. 139–64.

Gardner, James B. and Paula Hamilton, 'The Past and Future of Public History: Developments and Challenges', in James B. Gardner and Paula Hamilton (eds), *The Oxford Handbook of Public History*, Oxford University Press, Oxford, 2017, DOI: 10.1093/oxfordhb/9780199766024.013.29.

Gay, Peter, *Freud for Historians*, Oxford University Press, New York, 1985.

Gibbons, Peter, 'Cultural Colonization and National Identity', *New Zealand Journal of History*, vol. 36, no. 1, 2002, pp. 5–17.

——, 'Non-Fiction', in Terry Sturm (ed.), *The Oxford History of New Zealand Literature in English* (1991), 2nd edn, Oxford University Press, Auckland, 1998, pp. 25–104.

Ginzburg, Carlo, *History, Rhetoric, and Proof*, University Press of New England, Hanover, NH, 1999.

Glover, Gary A. M., *Collision, Compromise and Conversion during the Wesleyan Hokianga Mission 1827–1855*, Gary Allan Malcolm Glover, Nelson, 2018.

Goodall, Heather, 'Too Early or Not Soon Enough? Reflections on Sharing Histories as Process', *Australian Historical Studies*, vol. 33, no. 118, 2002, pp. 7–24.

Grover, Ray, *Cork of War: Ngati Toa and the British Mission, an Historical Narrative*, John McIndoe, Dunedin, 1982.

Hall, Stuart, 'Encoding and Decoding in the Television Discourse' (1974), in David Morley (ed.), *Stuart Hall: Essential Essays, Vol. 1*, Duke University Press, Duke, NC, 2015, pp. 257–76.

Harris, Aroha, *Hīkoi: Forty Years of Māori Protest*, Huia Publishers, Wellington, 2014.

Harris, Aroha with Melissa Matutina Williams, 'Rights and Revitalisation: 1970–1990', in Atholl Anderson et al., *Tangata Whenua: A History*, Bridget Williams Books, Wellington, 2015, pp. 358–86.

Haskell, Thomas L., 'Objectivity: Perspective as Problem and Solution', *History and Theory*, vol. 43, no. 3, 2004, pp. 341–59.

Hayward, Janine, '"Flowing from the Treaty's Words": The Principles of the Treaty of Waitangi', in Janine Hayward and Nicola R. Wheen (eds), *The Waitangi Tribunal: Te Roopu Whakamana i te Tiriti o Waitangi*, Bridget Williams Books, Wellington, 2004, pp. 29–40.

Head, Lyndsay, 'An Analysis of Linguistic Issues Raised by Margaret Mutu (1992) "Tuku Whenua or Land Sale?" and Joan Metge (1992) "Cross Cultural Communication and Land Transfer in Western Muriwhenua 1832–1840"', Waitangi Tribunal, Wai 45, G005, 1992.

——, 'Land, Authority and the Forgetting of Being in Early Colonial Maori History', PhD thesis, University of Canterbury, 2006.

——, 'The Pursuit of Modernity in Maori Society: The Conceptual Bases of Citizenship in the Early Modern Period', in Andrew Sharp and Paul McHugh (eds), *Histories, Power and Loss: Uses of the Past — A New Zealand Commentary*, Bridget Williams Books, Wellington, 2001, pp. 97–121.

Head, Lyndsay and Buddy Mikaere, 'Was 19th Century Maori Society Literate?', *Archifacts*, no. 2, 1988, pp. 17–20.

Hempenstall, Peter, 'Tasman Epiphanies: The "Participant History" of Alan Ward', *Journal of New Zealand Studies*, nos 4/5, 2006, pp. 65–80.

Hickford, Mark, '"Decidedly the Most Interesting Savages on the Globe": An Approach to the Intellectual History of Maori Property Rights, 1837–53', *History of Political Thought*, vol. 27, no. 1, 2006, pp. 122–67.

——, 'Interpreting the Treaty: Questions of Native Title, Territorial Government and Searching for Constitutional Histories', in Brad Patterson et al. (eds), *After the Treaty: The Settler State, Race Relations and the Exercise of Power in Colonial New Zealand: Essays in Honour of Ian McLean Wards*, Steele Roberts, Wellington, [2016], pp. 92–131.

——, *Lords of the Land: Indigenous Property Rights and the Jurisprudence of Empire*, Oxford University Press, Oxford, 2011.

——, 'Making "Territorial Rights of the Natives": Britain and New Zealand, 1830–1847', DPhil thesis, University of Oxford, 1999.

——, '"Vague Native Rights to Land": British Imperial Policy on Native Title and Custom in New Zealand, 1837–53', *Journal of Imperial and Commonwealth History*, vol. 38, no. 2, 2010, pp. 175–206.

Hill, Richard S., *Anti-Treatyism and Anti-Scholarship: An Analysis of Anti-Treatyist Writings*, Treaty of Waitangi Research Unit, Stout Research Centre for New Zealand Studies, Victoria University of Wellington, Wellington, 2002.

Hilliard, Chris, *The Bookmen's Dominion: Cultural Life in New Zealand 1920–1950*, Auckland University Press, Auckland, 2006.

——, 'A Prehistory of Public History: Monuments, Explanations and Promotions, 1900–1970', in Bronwyn Dalley and Jock Phillips (eds), *Going Public: The Changing Face of New Zealand History*, Auckland University Press, Auckland, 2001, pp. 30–54.

Hobsbawm, Eric, *On History*, Abacus, London, 1998.

Hohepa, P. W., *A Maori Community in Northland* (1964), A. H. & A. W. Reed, Wellington, 1970.

Howe, Kerry, 'Review of Andrew Sharp and Paul McHugh (eds), *Histories, Power and Loss*', *New Zealand Journal of History*, vol. 36, no. 2, 2002, pp. 203–04.

——, 'Two Worlds?', *New Zealand Journal of History*, vol. 37, no. 1, 2003, pp. 50–61.

Hunter, Ian, 'Natural Law, Historiography, and Aboriginal Sovereignty', *Legal History*, vol. 11, no. 2, 2007, pp. 137–67.

Ignatieff, Michael, *The Warrior's Honor: Ethnic War and the Modern Conscience*, Vintage, London, 1999.

Innes, Stephen, 'A Bibliography of Writings by M. P. K. Sorrenson', *New Zealand Journal of History*, vol. 31, no. 1, 1997, pp. 189–94.

Johnson, Miranda, *The Land is Our History: Indigeneity, Law and the Settler State*, Oxford University Press, New York, 2016.

——, 'Making History Public: Indigenous Claims to Settler States', *Public Culture*, vol. 16, no. 1, 2008, pp. 97–117.

Jordanova, Ludmilla, *History in Practice*, 3rd edn, Bloomsbury Academic, London, 2019.

Kaamira, Himiona, 'The Story of Kupe' (translated by Bruce Biggs), *Journal of the Polynesian Society*, vol. 66, no. 3, 1957, pp. 232–48.

Kenny, Robert W., *The New Zealand Journal 1842–1844 of John B. Williams of Salem, Massachusetts*, Peabody Museum of Salem and Brown University Press, 1956.

King, Michael, 'Argument without End', *New Zealand Review of Books*, vol. 12, no. 2, 2002, pp. 9–10.

——, *Being Pakeha: An Encounter with New Zealand and the Maori Renaissance*, Hodder and Stoughton, Auckland, 1985.

——, *Being Pakeha Now: Reflections and Recollections of a White Native*, Penguin, Auckland, 1999.

——, *Maori: A Photographic and Social History*, Heinemann, Auckland, 1983.

——, *The Penguin History of New Zealand*, Penguin, Auckland, 2003.

Kuhn, Thomas S., *The Structure of Scientific Revolutions* (1962), 4th edn, University of Chicago Press, Chicago, 2012.

LaCapra, Dominick, *History and Criticism*, Cornell University Press, Ithaca, NY, 1985.

——, *Rethinking Intellectual History: Texts, Contexts, Language*, Cornell University Press, Ithaca, NY, 1983.

——, *Soundings in Critical Theory*, Cornell University Press, Ithaca, NY, 1989.

——, *Writing History, Writing Trauma*, Johns Hopkins University Press, Baltimore, MD, 2001.

Laqueur, Thomas, *Making Sex: Body and Gender from the Greeks to Freud*, Harvard University Press, Cambridge, MA, 1990.

Lindley, M. F., *The Acquisition and Government of Backward Territory in International Law*, Longmans, Green and Co., London, 1926.

Loveridge, Donald M., '"The Knot of a Thousand Difficulties": Britain and New Zealand, 1769–1840', Brief of Evidence in the Matter of the Treaty of Waitangi Act 1975 and in the Matter of Te Paparahi o te Taki (Northland Inquiry), Wai 1040 #A18, 2009.

——, '"An Object of the First Importance": Land Rights, Land Claims and Colonisation in New Zealand, 1839–1852', Report for the Crown Law Office for Wai 863, 2004.

——, 'Professor Alan Dudley Ward: He Poroporoaki: A Farewell', *Maori Law Review*, no. 2, 2015, https://maorilawreview.co.nz/2015/02/profesor-alan-dudley-ward-he-poroporoaki-a-farewell/

Lynch, Michael P., *In Praise of Reason: Why Rationality Matters for Democracy*, Norton, New York, 2016.

Lyons, Martyn, *The Typewriter Century: A Cultural History of Writing Practices*, University of Toronto Press, Toronto, 2021.

McAloon, Jim, 'By Which Standards? History and the Waitangi Tribunal', *New Zealand Journal of History*, vol. 40, no. 2, 2006, pp. 194–213.

——, 'Revisiting *The Shadow of the Land*', in Brad Patterson et al. (eds), *After the Treaty: The Settler State, Race Relations and the Exercise of Power in Colonial New Zealand: Essays in Honour of Ian McLean Wards*, Steele Roberts, Wellington, [2016], pp. 20–39.

McCan, David, *Whatiwhatihoe: The Waikato Raupata Claim*, Huia Publishers, Wellington, 2001.

McCormick, E. H., *An Absurd Ambition: Autobiographical Writings*, Auckland University Press, Auckland, 1996.

McHugh, P. G., 'Aboriginal Rights and Sovereignty: Commonwealth Developments', *New Zealand Law Journal*, no. 2, 1986, pp. 57–63.

——, 'The Aboriginal Rights of the New Zealand Maori at Common Law', DPhil thesis, University of Cambridge, 1987.

——, 'Aboriginal Servitudes and the Land Transfer Act 1952', *Victoria University of Wellington Law Review*, vol. 16, no. 4, 1986, pp. 313–35.

——, *Aboriginal Societies and the Common Law: A History of Sovereignty, Status, and Self-Determination*, Oxford University Press, Oxford, 2004.

——, *Aboriginal Title: The Modern Jurisprudence of Tribal Land Rights*, Oxford University Press, Oxford, 2011.

——, 'Aboriginal Title in New Zealand Courts', *Canterbury Law Review*, no. 2, 1984, pp. 235–65.

——, 'The Common-Law Status of Colonies and Aboriginal "Rights": How Lawyers and Historians Treat the Past', *Saskatchewan Law Review*, vol. 61, no. 2, 1998, pp. 393–429.

——, 'Constitutional Myths and the Treaty of Waitangi', *New Zealand Law Journal*, no. 9, 1991, pp. 316–19.

——, 'The Historiography of New Zealand's Constitutional History', in P. A. Joseph (ed.), *Essays on the Constitution*, Brooker's, Wellington, 1995, pp. 344–67.

——, 'A History of Crown Sovereignty in New Zealand', in Andrew Sharp and Paul McHugh (eds), *Histories, Power and Loss: Uses of the Past — A New Zealand Commentary*, Bridget Williams Books, Wellington, 2001, pp. 189–211.

——, 'A History of the Modern Jurisprudence of Aboriginal Rights: Some Observations on the Journey So Far', in David Dyzenhaus et al. (eds), *A Simple Common Lawyer: Essays in Honour of Michael Taggart*, Hart Publishing, Oxford, 2009, pp. 209–32.

——, 'Law, History and the Treaty of Waitangi', *New Zealand Journal of History*, vol. 31, no. 1, 1997, pp. 38–57.

——, 'The Legal Status of Maori Fishing Rights in Tidal Waters', *Victoria University of Wellington Law Review*, vol. 14, no. 3, 1984, pp. 247–73.

——, *The Māori Magna Carta: New Zealand Law and the Treaty of Waitangi*, Oxford University Press, Auckland, 1991.

——, '"The Most Decorous Veil which Legal Ingenuity Can Weave": The British Annexation of New Zealand (1840)', in Kelly L. Grotke and Markus J. Prutsch (eds), *Constitutionalism, Legitimacy, and Power: Nineteenth-Century Experiences*, Oxford University Press, Oxford, 2014, pp. 300–20.

——, '"A Pretty Gov[ernment]": The "Confederation of United Tribes" and Britain's Quest for Imperial Order in the New Zealand Islands during the 1830s', in Lauren Benton and Richard J. Ross (eds), *Legal Pluralism and Empires, 1500–1850*, New York University Press, New York, 2013, pp. 233–58.

——, 'Tales of Constitutional Origin and Crown Sovereignty in New Zealand', *University of Toronto Law Journal*, vol. 52, no. 1, 2002, pp. 69–99.

McKay, Frank, *The Life of James K. Baxter*, Oxford University Press, Auckland, 1992.

McKean, W. A., 'The Treaty of Waitangi Revisited', in G. A. Wood and P. S. O'Connor (eds), *W. P. Morrell: A Tribute*, University of Otago Press, Dunedin, 1973, pp. 237–49.

McKenzie, D. F., *Bibliography and the Sociology of Texts*, Cambridge University Press, Cambridge, 1999.

——, *Oral Culture, Literacy & Print in Early New Zealand: The Treaty of Waitangi*, Victoria University Press with the Alexander Turnbull Library Endowment Trust, Wellington, 1985.

McKinnon, Malcolm, 'Obituary: Mary Beatrice Boyd, 8 October 1921–8 March 2011', *New Zealand International Review*, vol. 36, no. 3, 2011, p. 32.

McKitterick, David, 'Donald Francis McKenzie 1931–1999', *Proceedings of the British Academy*, vol. 115, 2002, pp. 297–315.

MacLean, Chris, *John Pascoe*, Craig Potton Publishing in association with the Whitcombe Press, Nelson, 2003.

McLintock, A. H., *Crown Colony Government in New Zealand*, Government Printer, Wellington, 1958.

McNair, Arnold Duncan, *The Law of Treaties*, Clarendon Press, Oxford, 1961.

Mahuika, Nēpia, '"Closing the Gaps": From Postcolonialism to Kaupapa Māori and Beyond', *New Zealand Journal of History*, vol. 45, no. 1, 2011, pp. 15–32.

Markham, Edward, *New Zealand or Recollections of it*, edited by E. H. McCormick, Government Printer, Wellington, 1963.

Martin, William, *Remarks on Notes Published for the New Zealand Government, January 1861, and in Mr Richmond's Memorandum on the Taranaki Question, December 1860*, Melanesian Press, Auckland, 1861.

——, *The Taranaki Question*, 3rd edn, W. H. Dalton, London, 1861.

Megill, Allan, *Historical Knowledge, Historical Error: A Contemporary Guide to Practice*, University of Chicago Press, Chicago, 2007.

Molloy, Anthony P., 'The Non-Treaty of Waitangi', *New Zealand Law Journal*, no. 9, 1971, pp. 193–97.

Mommsen, Wolfgang, 'Moral Commitment and Scholarly Detachment: The Social Function of the Historian', in Joep Leerssen and Ann Rigney (eds), *Historians and Social Values*, Amsterdam University Press, Amsterdam, 2000, pp. 45–55.

Mulgan, Richard, *Māori, Pākehā and Democracy*, Oxford University Press, Auckland, 1989.

Munro, Doug, 'Mary Boyd, 1921–2010', *Journal of Pacific History*, vol. 47, no. 1, 2012, pp. 123–26.

——, 'Michael Turnbull, G. R. Elton and the Making of *The Practice of History*', *The Historical Journal*, vol. 58, no. 3, 2015, pp. 805–25.

Munz, Peter, 'A Personal Memoir', in Peter Munz (ed.), *The Feel of Truth: Essays in New Zealand and Pacific History, Presented to F. L. W. Wood and J. C. Beaglehole*, A. H. & A. W. Reed for Victoria University of Wellington, Wellington, 1969, pp. 9–24.

New Zealand Maori Council, *Kaupapa: Te Wahanga Tuahihi*, New Zealand Maori Council, [Wellington], 1983.

Neumann, Klaus et al. (eds), *Quicksands: Foundational Histories in Australia and Aotearoa New Zealand*, UNSW Press, Sydney, 1999.

New Zealand Labour Party, *Election Manifesto 1957*, New Zealand Labour Party, Wellington, 1957.

——, *1972 Election Manifesto*, New Zealand Labour Party, Wellington, 1972.

Ngata, H. K., 'The Treaty of Waitangi and Land: Parts of the Current Law in Contravention of the Treaty', in *The Treaty of Waitangi: Its Origins and Significance*, University Extension Publications, Wellington, [1972], pp. 49–57.

Nietzsche, Friedrich, *On the Advantage and Disadvantage of History for Life* (1874), translated by Peter Preuss, Hackett Publishing Company, Indianapolis, 1980.

Novick, Peter, *That Noble Dream: The 'Objectivity Question' and the American Historical Profession*, Cambridge University Press, New York, 1988.

Oakeshott, Michael, 'The Activity of Being an Historian' (1955), in his *Rationalism in Politics and Other Essays*, Methuen, London, 1962, pp. 137–67.

O'Brien, Gregory, *A Nest of Singing Birds: 100 Years of the New Zealand School Journal*, Learning Media, Wellington, 2007.

Oliver, W. H., *Claims to the Waitangi Tribunal*, Waitangi Tribunal Division, Department of Justice, Wellington, 1991.

——, 'The Future Behind Us: The Waitangi Tribunal's Retrospective Utopia', in Andrew Sharp and Paul McHugh (eds), *Histories, Power and Loss: Uses of the Past — A New Zealand Commentary*, Bridget Williams Books, Wellington, 2001, pp. 9–29.

——, 'Getting Facts on Your Side', *New Zealand Review of Books*, vol. 5, no. 2, 1995, p. 15.

——, 'History, Myths in New Zealand', in A. H. McClintock (ed.), *An Encyclopaedia of New Zealand*, originally published in 1966, https://teara.govt.nz/en/1966/history-myths-in-new-zealand

——, 'Is Bias One-Sided?', *New Zealand Review of Books*, vol. 7, no. 2, 1997, pp. 17–19.

——, *Looking for the Phoenix: A Memoir*, Bridget Williams Books, Wellington, 2002.

——, 'Pandora's Envelope: It's All about Power', *New Zealand Review of Books*, vol. 5, no. 1, 1995, pp. 18–20.

——, 'Reply to Jim McAloon', *New Zealand Journal of History*, vol. 41, no. 1, 2007, pp. 83–87.

——, *The Social and Economic Situation of Hauraki Maori after Colonisation*, Hauraki Maori Trust Board, Paeroa, 1997.

Olssen, Erik, 'Obituary: Angus Ross, 1911–2000', *New Zealand Journal of History*, vol. 36, no. 2, 2002, pp. 201–02.

——, 'Where to From Here? Reflections on the Twentieth-Century Historiography of Nineteenth-Century New Zealand', *New Zealand Journal of History*, vol. 26, no. 1, 1992, pp. 65–77.

O'Malley, Vincent, *The New Zealand Wars/Ngā Pakanga o Aotearoa*, Bridget Williams Books, Wellington, 2019.

——, 'Treaty-Making in Early Colonial New Zealand', *New Zealand Journal of History*, vol. 33, no. 2, 1999, pp. 137–54.

O'Malley, Vincent et al. (eds), *The Treaty of Waitangi Companion: Māori and Pākehā from Tasman to Today*, Auckland University Press, Auckland, 2010.

Orange, Claudia, 'The Covenant of Kohimarama: A Ratification of the Treaty of Waitangi', *New Zealand Journal of History*, vol. 14, no. 1, 1980, pp. 61–82.

——, *An Illustrated History of the Treaty of Waitangi*, Allen & Unwin New Zealand in association with Port Nicholson Press, Wellington, 1990.

——, *An Illustrated History of the Treaty of Waitangi*, 2nd edn, Bridget Williams Books, Wellington, 2004

——, 'Knowing What they Signed', *New Zealand Listener*, 1 August 1987, pp. 60–62.

——, *The Treaty of Waitangi*, Allen & Unwin New Zealand in association with Port Nicholson Press, Sydney/Wellington, 1987.

——, *The Treaty of Waitangi*, revised edn, Bridget Williams Books, Wellington, 2011.

——, 'The Treaty of Waitangi: A Study of its Making, Role and Interpretation in New Zealand History', PhD thesis, University of Auckland, 1984.

——, *The Treaty of Waitangi / Te Tiriti o Waitangi: An Illustrated History of the Treaty of Waitangi*, Bridget Williams Books, Wellington, 2020.

O'Regan, Tipene, 'Old Myths and New Politics: Some Contemporary Uses of Traditional History', *New Zealand Journal of History*, vol. 26, no. 1, 1992, pp. 5–27.

O'Sullivan, Vincent, *The Dark is Light Enough: Ralph Hotere: A Biographical Portrait*, Penguin Books, Auckland, 2020.

Ovenden, Keith, *Bill & Shirley: A Memoir*, Massey University Press, Auckland, 2020.

Owens, J. M. R., 'Historians and the Treaty of Waitangi', *Archifacts*, no. 1, 1990, pp. 4–21.

——, 'Missionaries and the Treaty of Waitangi', *Wesleyan Historical Society (New Zealand) Journal*, no. 49, 1986, pp. 1–25.

——, 'New Zealand before Annexation', in W. H. Oliver and B. R. Williams (eds), *The Oxford History of New Zealand*, Oxford University Press, Wellington, 1981, pp. 28–53.

——, 'The Treaty of Waitangi: Event and Symbol', *British Review of New Zealand Studies*, vol. 3, 1990, pp. 6–14.

Palmer, Matthew S. R., *The Treaty of Waitangi in New Zealand's Law and Constitution*, Victoria University Press, Wellington, 2008.

Paul, Janet (ed.), *Eric Lee-Johnson*, with a biographical introduction by E. H. McCormick, Paul's Book Arcade, Hamilton, 1956.

Phillips, Jock, 'Our History, Our Selves: The Historian and National Identity', *New Zealand Journal of History*, vol. 30, no. 2, 1996, pp. 107–23.

Phillips, Jock and Bronwyn Dalley, 'Introduction', in Bronwyn Dalley and Jock Phillips (eds), *Going Public: The Changing Face of New Zealand History*, Auckland University Press, Auckland, 2001, pp. 7–13.

Phillips, Mark Salber, 'Distance and Historical Representation', *History Workshop Journal*, no. 57, 2004, pp. 123–41.

——, *On Historical Distance*, Yale University Press, New Haven, 2013.

Phillipson, Grant, 'Bay of Islands Maori and the Crown 1793–1853', An Exploratory Overview for the CFRT, Wai 1040 #A1, 2005.

——, 'Talking and Writing History: Evidence to the Waitangi Tribunal', in Janine Hayward and Nicola R. Wheen (eds), *The Waitangi Tribunal: Te Roopu Whakamana i te Tiriti o Waitangi*, Bridget Williams Books, Wellington, 2004, pp. 41–52.

——, '2001, a Waitangi Tribunal Odyssey: The Tribunal's Response to the "Presentism" Critique', *Melbourne Historical Journal*, vol. 40, no. 1, 2012, pp. 21–48.

Plummer, Matt, 'Legendary Obscurity: The Working Life of Malcolm Ross', MA thesis, Victoria University of Wellington, 2010.

Pocock, J. G. A., *The Ancient Constitution and the Feudal Law: A Study of Historical Thought in the Seventeenth Century* (1957), Cambridge University Press, Cambridge, 1987.

——, 'The Antipodean Perception', in his *The Discovery of Islands: Essays in British History*, Cambridge University Press, Cambridge, 2005, pp. 3–23.

——, 'The Historian as Political Actor in Polity, Society and Academy', *Journal of Pacific Studies*, vol. 20, 1996, pp. 89–112.

——, 'Law, Sovereignty and History in a Divided Culture: The Case of New Zealand and the Treaty of Waitangi', *McGill Law Journal*, vol. 43, no. 3, 1998, pp. 483–506.

——, 'The Politics of History: The Subaltern and the Subversive', *Journal of Political Philosophy*, vol. 6, no. 3, 1998, pp. 219–34.

——, 'The Treaty Between Histories', in Andrew Sharp and Paul McHugh (eds), *Histories, Power and Loss: Uses of the Past — A New Zealand Commentary*, Bridget Williams Books, Wellington, 2001, pp. 75–95.

——, 'The Uniqueness of Aotearoa', *Proceedings of the American Philosophical Society*, vol. 145, no. 4, 2001, pp. 482–87.

Pope, Jeremy, '[Note]', *New Zealand Law Journal*, no. 9, 1971, p. 197.

Porter, H. C., 'The Nose of Wax: Scripture and the Spirit from Erasmus to Milton', *Transactions of the Royal Historical Society*, series 5, vol. 14, 1964, pp. 155–74.

Powles, Guy, 'Foreword', in *The Treaty of Waitangi: Its Origins and Significance: A Series of Papers Presented at a Seminar Held at Victoria University of Wellington, 19–20 February 1972 Under the Auspices of the Department of University Extension of the University*, Victoria University of Wellington, Wellington, [1972], p. i.

Prakash, Gyan, 'Writing Post-Orientalist Histories of the Third World: Perspectives from Indian Historiography', *Comparative Studies in Society and History*, vol. 32, no. 2, 1992, pp. 383–408.

Renwick, W. L., '"Show Us These Islands and Ourselves . . . Give Us a Home in Thought": Beaglehole Memorial Lecture, 1987', *New Zealand Journal of History*, vol. 21, no. 2, 1987, pp. 197–214.

——, *The Treaty Now*, GP Books, Wellington, 1990.

Robinson, Helen, 'Making a New Zealand Day: The Creation and Context of a National Day', *New Zealand Journal of History*, vol. 46, no. 1, 2012, pp. 37–51.

——, 'Simple Nullity or Birth of Law and Order? The Treaty of Waitangi in Legal and Historiographical Discourse from 1877 to 1970', *New Zealand Universities Law Review*, vol. 24, no. 2, 2010, pp. 259–76.

Rogers, Lindsay, *Guerilla Surgeon*, Collins, London, 1957.

Ross, R. M., 'The Autochthonous New Zealand Soil', in Peter Munz (ed.), *The Feel of Truth: Essays in New Zealand and Pacific History, Presented to F. L. W. Wood and J. C. Beaglehole*, A. H. & A. W. Reed for Victoria University of Wellington, Wellington, 1969, pp. 47–59.

——, 'Bishop's Auckland', in Frances Porter (ed.), *Historic Buildings of New Zealand: North Island*, Cassell New Zealand, Auckland, 1979, pp. 80–89.

——, 'Correspondence', *New Zealand Journal of History*, vol. 13, no. 1, 1979, pp. 105–06.

——, *Early Traders*, School Publications Branch, Department of Education, Wellington, 1957.

——, 'European Settlement: The Early Years', in T. J. Dwyer (ed.), *The New Zealand Junior Encylopaedia*, vol. 1, New Zealand Educational Foundation (Northern), Wellington, 1960, pp. 128–37.

——, 'Evolution of the Melanesian Bishopric', *New Zealand Journal of History*, vol. 16, no. 2, 1982, pp. 122–45.

——, *A Guide to Pompallier House*, New Zealand Historic Places Trust, Wellington, 1970.

——, *The Inland Mission of Te Waimate*, New Zealand Historic Places Trust, Wellington, 1968.

——, 'McDonnell, Thomas', in A. H. McClintock (ed.), *An Encyclopaedia of New Zealand*, originally published in 1966, http://www.TeAra.govt.nz/en/1966/mcdonnell-thomas

——, 'Mangungu Cemetery', *Northland: A Regional Magazine*, vol. 5, no. 4, 1962, pp. 21–27, and vol. 6, no. 2, 1963, pp. 27–37.

——, 'Maning, Frederick Edward', in A. H. McClintock (ed.), *An Encyclopaedia of New Zealand*, originally published in 1966, Te Ara: The Encyclopedia of New Zealand, http://www.TeAra.govt.nz/en/1966/maning-frederick-edward

——, 'The Maori Church in Northland', in Frances Porter (ed.), *Historic Buildings of New Zealand: North Island*, Cassell New Zealand, Auckland, 1979, pp. 54–67.

——, 'The Material of History: European Trade and Settlement: New Zealand Before 1840', *Post-Primary School Bulletin*, vol. 6, no. 7, 1952, pp. 113–43.

——, *Melanesians at Mission Bay*, New Zealand Historic Places Trust, [Wellington], 1983.

——, 'Old Kororareka: New Russell', in Frances Porter (ed.), *Historic Buildings of New Zealand: North Island*, Cassell New Zealand, Auckland, 1979, pp. 30–37.

——, 'Review of E. J. Tapp, *Early New Zealand: A Dependency of New South Wales 1788–1841*', *Historical Studies: Australia and New Zealand*, vol. 9, no. 33, 1959, pp. 102–04.

——, 'Review of H. C. M. Norris, *Armed Settlers*', *Education: A Magazine for Teachers*, vol. 6, no. 2, 1957, p. 67.

——, 'Review of Harrison M. Wright, *New Zealand, 1769–1840: Early Years of Western Contact*', *Historical Studies: Australia and New Zealand*, vol. 9, no. 35, 1960, pp. 331–32.

——, 'Review of W. P. Morrell and D. O. W. Hall, *A History of New Zealand Life*', *Historical Studies: Australia and New Zealand*, vol. 8, no. 29, 1957, pp. 109–10.

——, 'Rewi of the Ngatiroro', *School Journal: Part 4*, vol. 47, no. 8, 1953, pp. 248–54.

——, 'Rewi, the Whaler', *School Journal: Part 4*, vol. 47, no. 9, 1953, pp. 258–63.

——, 'Taonui, Aperahama', in A. H. McClintock (ed.), *An Encyclopaedia of New Zealand*, originally published in 1966, http://www.TeAra.govt.nz/en/1966/taonui-aperahama

——, 'Taonui, Makoare', in A. H. McClintock (ed.), *An Encyclopaedia of New Zealand*, originally published in 1966, http://www.TeAra.govt.nz/en/1966/taonui-makoare

——, 'Thierry, Charles Philip Hippolytus, Baron de', in A. H. McClintock (ed.), *An Encyclopaedia of New Zealand*, originally published in 1966, http://www.TeAra.govt.nz/en/1966/thierry-charles-philip-hippolytus-baron-de

——, *Te Tiriti o Waitangi*, School Publications Branch, Department of Education, Wellington, 1958.

——, 'Te Tiriti o Waitangi: Texts and Translations', *New Zealand Journal of History*, vol. 6, no. 2, 1972, pp. 129–57.

——, 'Te Tiriti o Waitangi: Texts and Translations', in Judith Binney (ed.), *The Shaping of History: Essays from The New Zealand Journal of History*, Bridget Williams Books, Wellington, 2001, pp. 90–113.

——, 'Two Great Battles in the Far North', *Journal of the Auckland Historical Society*, no. 7, 1965, pp. 21–23.

——, 'Waitangi Treaty Houses', in Frances Porter (ed.), *Historic Buildings of New Zealand: North Island*, Cassell New Zealand, Auckland, 1979, pp. 46–53.

——, 'Waitangi — 1840', *Northland: A Regional Magazine*, no. 21, 1963, pp. 7–14, 68.

——, 'The Writing of History', *Northland: A Regional Magazine*, vol. 5, no. 2, 1962, pp. 5–11.

Ross, Ruth, 'Crossing the Bar', *School Journal: Part 4*, vol. 50, no. 3, 1956, pp. 10–16.

——, 'The Cruise of the Magnet', *School Journal: Part 4*, vol. 46, no. 1, 1952, pp. 2–13.

——, 'The Family Tree', *School Journal: Part 4*, vol. 50, no. 2, 1956, pp. 53–59.

——, *The Journal of George Simmonds*, School Publications Branch, Department of Education, Wellington, 1954.

——, 'The Jubilee Mug', *School Journal: Part 4*, vol. 50, no. 1, 1956, pp. 2–8.

——, 'Muka', *School Journal: Part 4*, vol. 50, no. 4, 1956, pp. 10–16.

——, *New Zealand's First Capital*, Department of Internal Affairs, Wellington, 1946.

——, 'The Treaty on the Ground', in *The Treaty of Waitangi: Its Origins and Significance*, University Extension Publications, Wellington, [1972], pp. 16–34.

Royal Society of New Zealand / Te Apārangi, 'Aotearoa New Zealand's Histories: A response to draft curriculum', 2021, https://www.royalsociety.org.nz/assets/Aotearoa-New-Zealand-histories-response-to-draft-curriculum-May-2021-digital.pdf

Rutherford, James, *Hone Heke's Rebellion 1844–1846: An Episode in the Establishment of British Rule in New Zealand*, Auckland University College Bulletin no. 34, Auckland, 1947.

——, *The Treaty of Waitangi and the Acquisition of British Sovereignty in New Zealand, 1840*, Auckland University College Bulletin no. 36, Auckland, 1949.

Rutherford, James (ed.), *The Founding of New Zealand: The Journals of Felton Mathew*, A. H. & A. W. Reed, Dunedin, 1940.

Salesa, Damon, 'Obituary: Hugh Laracy', *Journal of Pacific History*, vol. 51, no. 1, 2016, pp. 43–47.

Salmond, Anne, *Tears of Rangi: Experiments Across Worlds*, Auckland University Press, Auckland, 2017.

Scott, Stuart C., *The Travesty of Waitangi: Towards Anarchy*, The Caxton Press, Christchurch, 1995.

Shapiro, Barbara J., *A Culture of Fact: England, 1550–1720*, Cornell University Press, Ithaca, NY, 2000.

Sharp, Andrew, 'History and Sovereignty: A Case of Juridical History in New Zealand/Aotearoa', in Michael Peters (ed.), *Cultural Politics and the University in Aotearoa/New Zealand*, Dunmore Press, Palmerston North, 1997, pp. 159–81.

——, *Justice and the Māori: The Philosophy and Practice of Māori Claims in New Zealand since the 1970s* (1990), 2nd edn, Oxford University Press, Auckland, 1997.

——, 'Recent Juridical and Constitutional Histories of Maori', in Andrew Sharp and Paul McHugh (eds), *Histories, Power and Loss: Uses of the Past — A New Zealand Commentary*, Bridget Williams Books, Wellington, 2001, pp. 31–60.

——, 'Representing *Justice and the Maori*', *Political Theory Newsletter*, no. 4, 1992, pp. 27–38.

——, 'Treaty of Waitangi: Reasoning and Social Justice in New Zealand?', in Paul Spoonley et al. (eds), *Nga Take: Ethnic Relations and Racism in Aotearoa/New Zealand*, Dunmore Press, Palmerston North, 1991, pp. 131–47.

——, *The World, the Flesh and the Devil: The Life and Opinions of Samuel Marsden in England and the Antipodes, 1765–1838*, Auckland University Press, Auckland, 2016.

Sharp, Andrew and P. G. McHugh, 'Introduction', in Andrew Sharp and Paul McHugh (eds), *Histories, Power and Loss: Uses of the Past — A New Zealand Commentary*, Bridget Williams Books, Wellington, 2001, pp. 1–7.

Simmons, E. R., 'Obituary: Ruth Miriam Ross', *Archifacts*, no. 23, 1982, Supplement, p. i.

Simpson, Tony, *Te Riri Pakeha: The White Man's Anger*, Alister Taylor, Martinborough, 1979.

——, 'Tony Simpson Replies to M. P. K. Sorrenson', *Landfall*, no. 137, 1981, pp. 120–22.

Sinclair, Douglas, 'Land: Maori View and European Response', in Michael King (ed.), *Te Ao Hurihuri: The World Moves On — Aspects of Maoritanga*, revised edn, Longman Paul, Auckland, 1977, pp. 86–106.

Sinclair, Keith, *A History of New Zealand*, Penguin Books, Harmondsworth, 1959.

——, *A History of New Zealand*, revised edn, Penguin Books, Melbourne, 1969.

——, *A History of the University of Auckland, 1883–1983*, University of Auckland Press, Auckland, 1983.

——, *The Maori Land League: An Examination into the Source of a New Zealand Myth*, Auckland University College Bulletin no. 37, Auckland, 1950.

——, 'New Zealand', in Robin W. Winks (ed.), *The Historiography of the British Empire-Commonwealth: Trends, Interpretations, and Resources*, Duke University Press, Durham, NC, 1966, pp. 174–96.

——, *The Origins of the Maori Wars* (1957), 2nd edn, New Zealand University Press, Wellington, 1961.

——, 'Why are Race Relations in New Zealand Better than in South Africa, South Australia or South Dakota?', *New Zealand Journal of History*, vol. 5, no. 2, 1971, pp. 121–27.

Smith, Linda Tuhiwai, *Decolonizing Methodologies: Research and Indigenous Peoples*, University of Otago Press, Dunedin, 1999.

Sorrenson, M. P. K., 'Context as Well as Text', *PSA Journal*, vol. 78, no. 8, 1986, p. 16.

——, 'Epilogue', in his *Ko te Whenua te Utu / Land is the Price: Essays on Maori History, Land and Politics*, Auckland University Press, Auckland, 2014, pp. 292–303.

——, 'Giving Better Effect to the Treaty: Some Thoughts for 1990' (1990), in his *Ko te Whenua te Utu / Land is the Price: Essays on Maori History, Land and Politics*, Auckland University Press, Auckland, 2014, pp. 238–55.

——, 'Introduction', in his *Ko te Whenua te Utu / Land is the Price: Essays on Maori History, Land and Politics*, Auckland University Press, Auckland, 2014, pp. 1–8.

——, 'Land Purchase Methods and their Effect on Maori Population', 1865–1901' (1956), in his *Ko te Whenua te Utu / Land is the Price: Essays on Maori History, Land and Politics*, Auckland University Press, Auckland, 2014, pp. 90–105.

——, 'Maori Representation in Parliament' (1986), in his *Ko te Whenua te Utu / Land is the Price: Essays on Maori History, Land and Politics*, Auckland University Press, Auckland, 2014, pp. 157–216.

——, 'M. P. K. Sorrenson Reviews Tony Simpson', *Landfall*, no. 136, 1980, pp. 382–84.

——, 'The Politics of Land', in J. G. A. Pocock (ed.), *The Maori and New Zealand Politics*, Blackwood and Janet Paul, Hamilton, 1965, pp. 21–45.

——, 'The Purchase of Maori Lands, 1865–1892', MA thesis, Auckland University College, 1955.

——, 'Review of Tony Simpson, *Te Riri Pakeha*', *Landfall*, no. 136, 1980, pp. 382–84.

——, 'Towards a Radical Interpretation of New Zealand History: The Role of the Waitangi Tribunal', *New Zealand Journal of History*, vol. 21, no. 1, 1987, pp. 173–88.

——, 'Towards a Radical Interpretation of New Zealand History: The Role of the Waitangi Tribunal' (1989), in his *Ko te Whenua te Utu / Land is the Price: Essays on Maori History, Land and Politics*, Auckland University Press, Auckland, 2014, pp. 217–37.

——, 'Treaties in British Colonial Policy: Precedents for Waitangi' (1991), in his *Ko te Whenua te Utu / Land is the Price: Essays on Maori History, Land and Politics*, Auckland University Press, Auckland, 2014, pp. 40–54.

——, 'Waitangi: Ka Whawhai Tonu Matou' (1998), in his *Ko te Whenua te Utu / Land is the Price: Essays on Maori History, Land and Politics*, Auckland University Press, Auckland, 2014, pp. 273–91.

——, 'The Waitangi Tribunal and the Resolution of Maori Grievances' (1995), in his *Ko te Whenua te Utu / Land is the Price: Essays on Maori History, Land and Politics*, Auckland University Press, Auckland, 2014, pp. 256–72.

Southgate, Brent, 'School Publications', in Roger Robinson and Nelson Wattie (eds), *The Oxford Companion to New Zealand Literature*, Oxford University Press, Auckland, 1998, pp. 480–81.

Stead, C. K., *South-West of Eden: A Memoir, 1932–1956*, Auckland University Press, Auckland, 2010.

——, *You Have a Lot to Lose: A Memoir, 1956–1986*, Auckland University Press, Auckland, 2020.

Stenhouse, John, 'God's Own Silence: Secular Nationalism, Christianity and the Writing of New Zealand History', *New Zealand Journal of History*, vol. 38, no. 1, 2004, pp. 52–71.

——, 'Introduction', in John Stenhouse (ed.), *Christianity, Modernity and Culture*, ATF Press, Adelaide, 2005, pp. 1–20.

Sutherland, Oliver, *Paikea: The Life of I. L. G. Sutherland*, Canterbury University Press, Christchurch, 2013.

Sutton, J. D., 'The Treaty of Waitangi Today', *Victoria University of Wellington Law Review*, vol. 11, no. 2, 1981, pp. 17–42.

Tau, Te Maire, 'Matauranga Maori as an Epistemology', in Andrew Sharp and Paul McHugh (eds), *Histories, Power and Loss: Uses of the Past — A New Zealand Commentary*, Bridget Williams Books, Wellington, 2001, pp. 61–73.

[Taylor, C. R. H.], *Facsimiles of the Declaration of Independence and the Treaty of Waitangi*, Government Printer, Wellington, 1960.

Tennant, Margaret, 'Obituary: W. H. Oliver, 14 May 1925–16 September 2015', *New Zealand Journal of History*, vol. 50, no. 1, 2016, pp. 153–54.

——, 'Oliver, William Hosking', *Dictionary of New Zealand Biography*, first published in 2021, Te Ara: The Encyclopedia of New Zealand, https://teara.govt.nz/en/biographies/603/oliver-william-hosking

Thwaites, Ian, *Auckland Museum People 1929–89*, The author, Auckland, 2015.

Trapeznik, Alex, 'Public History in New Zealand: From Treaty to Te Papa', in Paul Ashton and Alex Trapeznik (eds), *What is Public History Globally? Working with the Past in the Present*, Bloomsbury Academic, London, 2019, pp. 107–20.

[Turton, H. Hanson], *Fac-Similes of the Declaration of Independence and the Treaty of Waitangi*, Government Printer, Wellington, 1877, reprinted 1892.

University of Auckland, *University of Auckland Calendar*, University of Auckland, Auckland, 1972 and 1977.

University of New Zealand, Victoria University College, *Calendar*, University of New Zealand, Wellington, 1939.

Waitangi Action Committee, *Te Hikoi ki Waitangi, 1984*, Waitangi Action Committee, Auckland, 1984.

Waitangi Tribunal, *He Whakaputanga me te Tiriti / The Declaration and the Treaty: The Report on Stage 1 of the Te Paparahi o Te Raki Inquiry*, Legislation Direct, Wellington, 2014.

——, *Report of the Waitangi Tribunal on the Kaituna River Claim (WAI 4)* (1984), 2nd edn, Waitangi Tribunal, Department of Justice, Wellington, 1989.

——, *Report of the Waitangi Tribunal on the Manukau Claim (WAI 8)* (1985), 2nd edn, Waitangi Tribunal, Department of Justice, Wellington, 1989.

——, *Report of the Waitangi Tribunal on the Motunui-Waitara Claim (WAI 6)* (1983), 2nd edn, Waitangi Tribunal, Department of Justice, Wellington, 1989.

——, *Report of the Waitangi Tribunal on the Muriwhenua Fishing Claim (WAI 22)* (1988), 2nd edn, Waitangi Tribunal, Department of Justice, Wellington, 1989.

——, *Report of the Waitangi Tribunal on the Orakei Claim (WAI 9)* (1987), 2nd edn, Waitangi Tribunal, Department of Justice, Wellington, 1991.

——, *Report of the Waitangi Tribunal on the Te Reo Claim (WAI 11)* (1986), 2nd edn, Waitangi Tribunal, Department of Justice, Wellington, 1989.

——, *Te Whanganui a Tara me ona Takiwa / Report on the Wellington District*, Legislation Direct, Wellington, 2003.

Walker, Piripi, 'Parker, William Leonard', *Dictionary of New Zealand Biography*, first published in 2000, updated January 2002, Te Ara: The Encyclopedia of New Zealand, https://teara.govt.nz/en/biographies/5p11/parker-william-leonard

Walker, Ranginui, 'Matiu Te Auripo Te Hau', in Nicholas Tarling (ed.), *Auckland Mind & Matters*, University of Auckland, Auckland, 2003, pp. 180–87.

——, *Nga Tau Tohetohe / Years of Anger: A Selection of 'Korero' Columns from the* New Zealand Listener, edited by Jacqueline Amoamo, Penguin Books, Auckland, 1987.

——, 'The Treaty of Waitangi: As the Focus of Māori Protest', in I. H. Kawharu (ed.), *Waitangi: Maori and Pakeha Perspectives of the Treaty of Waitangi*, Oxford University Press, Auckland, 1989, pp. 263–79.

Walters, Mark D., 'Brightening the Covenant Chain: Aboriginal Treaty Meanings in Law and History after Marshall', *Dalhousie Law Journal*, vol. 24, no. 2, 2001, pp. 75–138.

Ward, Alan, 'Historical Claims under the Treaty of Waitangi: Avenue of Reconciliation or Source of New Divisions?', *Journal of Pacific History*, vol. 28, no. 2, 1993, pp. 181–203.

——, 'Historical Method and Waitangi Tribunal Claims', in Miles Fairburn and W. H. Oliver (eds), *The Certainty of Doubt: Tributes to Peter Munz*, Victoria University Press, Wellington, 1996, pp. 140–56.

——, 'History and Historians Before the Waitangi Tribunal: Some Reflections on the Ngai Tahu Claim', *New Zealand Journal of History*, vol. 24, no. 2, 1990, pp. 150–67.

——, 'Interpreting the Treaty of Waitangi: The Maori Resurgence and Race Relations in New Zealand', *The Contemporary Pacific*, vol. 3, no. 1, 1991, pp. 85–113.

——, 'Land and Law in the Making of National Community', in William Renwick (ed.), *Sovereignty & Indigenous Rights: The Treaty of Waitangi in International Contexts*, Victoria University Press, Wellington, 1991, pp. 115–29.

——, 'Land is the Price', *Journal of Pacific History*, vol. 50, no. 2, 2015, pp. 241–45.

——, *A Show of Justice: Racial 'Amalgamation' in Nineteenth Century New Zealand*, Auckland University Press/Oxford University Press, Auckland, 1973.

——, 'The Treaty and the Purchase of Maori Land', *New Zealand Journal of History*, vol. 22, no. 2, 1988, pp. 169–74.

——, 'A Tribute to Keith Sorrenson', *New Zealand Journal of History*, vol. 31, no. 1, 1997, pp. 6–8.

——, *An Unsettled History: Treaty Claims in New Zealand Today*, Bridget Williams Books, Wellington, 1999.

Ward, Damen, 'A Means and Measure of Civilisation: Colonial Authorities and Indigenous Law in Australasia', *History Compass*, vol. 1, no. 1, 2003, pp. 1–24.

Ward, Judith, 'The Invention of Papahurihia', PhD thesis, Massey University, 2016.

Wards, Ian, *The Shadow of the Land: A Study of British Policy and Racial Conflict in New Zealand 1832–1852*, Historical Publications Branch, Department of Internal Affairs, Wellington, 1968.

Weaver, John C., *The Great Land Rush and the Making of the Modern World, 1650–1900*, McGill-Queen's University Press, Montreal and Kingston, 2003.

Webber, Jeremy and Colin M. Macleod (eds), *Between Consenting Peoples: Political Community and the Meaning of Consent*, UBC Press, Vancouver, 2010.

White, Hayden, 'The Public Relevance of Historical Studies', *History and Theory*, vol. 44, no. 3, 2005, pp. 333–38.

White, Richard, *The Middle Ground: Indians, Empires, and Republics in the Great Lakes Region, 1650–1815*, Cambridge University Press, New York, 1991.

——, 'Using the Past: History and Native American Studies', in Russell Thornton (ed.), *Studying Native Americans: Problems and Prospects*, University of Wisconsin Press, Madison, 1998, pp. 217–43.

Williams, David V., 'Historians' Context and Lawyers' Presentism: Debating Historiography or Agreeing to Differ', *New Zealand Journal of History*, vol. 48, no. 2, 2014, pp. 136–60.

——, 'Originalism and the Constitutional Canon of Aotearoa New Zealand', in Mark Hickford and Carwyn Jones (eds), *Indigenous Peoples and the State: International Perspectives on the Treaty of Waitangi*, Routledge, London, 2019, pp. 57–74.

——, *A Simple Nullity? The Wi Parata Case in New Zealand Law & History*, Auckland University Press, Auckland, 2011.

——, 'Te Tiriti o Waitangi', in Arapera Blank et al. (eds), *He Kerero Mo Waitangi, 1984*, Te Runanga o Waitangi, Ngaruawahia, 1985, pp. 159–70.

——, 'Te Tiriti o Waitangi: Unique Relationship Between Crown and Tangata Whenua', in I. H. Kawharu (ed.), *Waitangi: Maori and Pakeha Perspectives of the Treaty of Waitangi*, Oxford University Press, Auckland, 1989, pp. 64–91.

Williams, Raymond, *Keywords: A Vocabulary of Culture and Society*, Fontana, London, 1976.

Williams, Trevor, 'The Treaty of Waitangi', *History*, n.s., vol. 25, no. 99, 1940, pp. 237–51.

Wright, Douglas, *Ghost Dance*, Penguin Books, Auckland, 2004.

Wyatt, Philippa, 'Keith Sinclair and the History of Humanitarianism', *New Zealand Journal of History*, vol. 54, no. 2, 2020, pp. 1–19.

Yensen, Helen et al. (eds), *Honouring the Treaty: An Introduction for Pakeha to the Treaty of Waitangi*, Penguin, Auckland, 1989.

Acknowledgements

In researching and writing this book I have incurred many debts. I am grateful to the many fine archivists and librarians who enabled the research, most of all at the Auckland War Memorial Museum Library (where Ruth Ross's papers are held) and the National Library of New Zealand, but also the Alexander Turnbull Library; Archives New Zealand / Te Rua Mahara o te Kāwanatanga; the Hocken Library; the Bodleian Library, University of Oxford; the J. C. Beaglehole Room, Victoria University of Wellington; and the University of Auckland Archives.

I owe special thanks to Rachael Bell whose work alerted me to Ruth Ross's papers and who generously lent me the notes of an interview she conducted with Mary Boyd. Most of all, I am indebted to my brother Ian who tirelessly undertook most of the research. Without his help, it would have been impossible to write this book as the lockdowns necessitated by the COVID-19 pandemic prevented me from travelling to New Zealand more than once.

Many people shared with me their memories of Ruth Ross, patiently and kindly answered my questions, and provided me with other kinds of help: Craig Ayrey, Michael Belgrave, James Belich, Peter Boyd, Raewyn Dalziel, Sir Edward (Eddie) Taihakurei Durie, Paul Hamer, Mark Hickford, Charlotte Macdonald, Malcolm McKinnon, Doug Munro, Claudia Orange, Brad Patterson, Tony Potter, Frances Porter, Philip Rainer, Tom Rennie, Andrew Sharp, Iain Sharp, Peter Simpson, Keith Sorrenson, Ian Thwaites and Bridget Williams. Ruth's surviving son, Duncan, took a keen interest from the outset. He and his wife Heather welcomed me into their home and talked to me about Ruth, and he lent me photographs and showed me around the Hokianga. As always, my father took a keen interest in what I was doing and provided help with genealogical matters.

All monographs, despite their name, are collaborative intellectual efforts. This one owes much to the work of many scholars who have written about the Treaty, some of whom were once my teachers: Ross herself, Peter Adams, Stuart Banner, Michael Belgrave, Rachael Bell, James Belich, Judith Binney, Thomas L. Buick, Lyndsay Head, Mark Hickford, Miranda Johnson, Donald Loveridge, A. H. McClintock, P. G. McHugh, D. F. McKenzie, W. P. Morrell, Claudia Orange, Matthew Palmer, J. G. A. Pocock, Andrew Sharp, Keith Sinclair, Keith Sorrenson, Alan Ward, Damen Ward, Ian Wards, John C. Weaver and Trevor Williams. I have also benefited enormously from the rich conversations I have had with several historians over many years on subjects that have ranged across sovereignty, native title, protection, the Treaty, the public life of history and the nature of history more generally: Michael Belgrave, Lauren Benton, Dipesh Chakrabarty, Adam Clulow, Graeme Davison, Claudia Haake, Mark Hickford, Paul McHugh, Miranda Johnson, Andrew Sharp and Damen Ward.

Acknowledgements

Tony Ballantyne, Dipesh Chakrabarty and Miranda Johnson read the proposal for Auckland University Press and provided me with wonderful advice. Sam Elworthy has been an exemplary publisher from start to finish.

Several people read the manuscript, or parts of it, and provided invaluable advice, criticism and instruction: Craig Ayrey, Tony Ballantyne, Barbara Brookes, Stephen Foster, Miranda Johnson, Duncan Ross, Robert Ross, Andrew Sharp and John Stenhouse. My brother read several drafts, more than he probably cares to remember. I am grateful for his careful reading and stringent criticism. Duncan Munro's design work was superb, Mike Wagg's copy-editing, Gillian Tewsley's proof-reading and Glenys Daley's indexing were exemplary, and Katharina Bauer and her production team were a joy to work with. All this input has made for an incomparably better book. I alone am responsible for any deficiencies.

I am grateful for the subvention my programme at Monash University provided to assist with the cost of the book's publication.

Finally, I wish to thank my partner Claudia Haake and our daughter Katarina Attwood for putting up, yet again, with my absent-mindedness as I worked on this book.

Index

An endnote is indicated by a page number followed by n and then the note number.
A plate is indicated by *Fig.* followed by the number of the figure.

aboriginal title, 135, 154, 156, 187–88
academic history
    discipline of, 62, 107, 153, 155, 161, 203–5
    evidence and, 28, 149, 163, 193–94, 202–3, 207, 209
    historical irresolution, 89, 150, 161, 204–5
    historical objectivity, 107, 148, 202–4, 249n16
    historicism, 161, 190, 199–200, 249n5, 249n6
    myths contested, 8, 94, 198–99, 249n6
    past/present disjuncture, 62, 71, 190, 205–6
    role in public life of history, 201–2, 205–6, 209
    tensions with other forms of knowledge on, 166, 205–9
    written sources, 4–5, 9, 36, 149, 193–94
    see also cloistered world of history
Adams, Peter, 95, 128, 132, 189, 242n35
Allan, Ruth (née Fletcher), 6, 31
amateur historians, 5, 84, 206
anachronisms, 145, 160, 169, 171
Angus, Rita, 35
antiquarianism, 5, 9, 69, 151, 197, 199
Arahura Māori Committee, 105
assimilation, 72, 103, 112–13
Auburn, F. M., 99–100
Auckland Star, 14, 96
'Autochthonous New Zealand Soil, The' (essay by Ross), 70–71, 88
Awatere, Donna, 112, 175

Bagnall, Graham, 69
Ballantyne, Tony, 248n62, 250n36
Ballara, Angela, 169
Banner, Stuart, 186–88, 248n65
Bartelson, Jens, 155–56
Baxter, James K., 35, 50, 52–56, 57, *Fig. 16*

Beaglehole, J. C., *Fig. 8*
    New Zealand Scholar, The, 37–38, 70–71
    relationship with Ruth Ross, 5–6, 12–14, 16, 31, 70, 82
    research and, 4–5, 7
    students of, 5–6, 147
    and the Treaty, 8
Beeby, C. E., 33
Belgrave, Michael, 182–86
    and the diversity of Treaty interpretations, 185–86, 202
    and historical context of the Treaty, 183–86, 198–200, 201, 247n42, 247n46, 247n51, 247n52
    and 'the modern Treaty', 198–99, 247n40
    and Tribunal history, 168–69, 182–83, 245n69
Belich, James, 96, 176
Bennett, Manu, 149, *Fig. 22*
Benton, Lauren, 248n59
biculturalism, 112, 125, 211
Biggs, Bruce, 80
bilingual treaties, 121–22, 135
Binney, Judith
    essays from *New Zealand Journal of History*, 177, *Fig. 13*
    and Māori understanding of the Treaty, 175–76
    relationship with Ruth Ross, 69, 80–81, 84–85, 236n75, 237n78
    'Te Tiriti-O-Waitangi' article, 85
Bledisloe, Lord, 17
Bloch, Marc, 201
Boyd, Mary (née Mackersey), 6–7, 27–28, 62, 72–73, 227n82, *Fig. 4*
Brash, Don, 136
breaches of the Treaty
    acknowledgement of, 25, 73, 104, 106, 112–13, 158
    investigation of, 116, 137, 146, 159, 200
    reparation for, 117, 130, 152, 158

Index

British acquisition of sovereignty
    on grounds of discovery, 21, 65, 132
    by means of proclamations, 14, 21, 52, 65, 95
    by means of the Treaty, 99, 102, 113, 115, 130, 135, 157, 185
    see also Hobson, William
Brockie, Bob, 111, *Fig. 20*
Brookfield, F. M. (Jock), 157
Buick, Thomas Lindsay, 16–17, 29, 132, 206
Burnard, R. W. (George), 7–8, 10–11, *Fig. 3*
Burnard, Ruth *see* Ross, Ruth
Busby, James, 75, 107, 173, 180
Butterfield, Herbert, 155, 190

Calder v Attorney-General of British Columbia, 117
Cambridge school of history, 154–55
Campbell, Alistair, 35
Carr, E. H., 18
Chakrabarty, Dipesh, xii, 208, 210
Chapman, Guy, 135
Church Missionary Society missionaries, 18, 84, 107, 179, 187–88
cloistered world of history, xii, 94–96, 175, 177
    see also academic history
Cohen, Paul A., 205
Colenso, William, 173, 204
comparative history, 187, 192–93
constitutional history, 130, 154, 157–58
contra proferentem, 122
Cooper, Whina, 106
Court of Appeal, 126–27
Cowan, James, 28–29, 206
critical history, 113, 128, 197, 200–201
cross-cultural negotiations, 165–67, 193, 200, 212
Crown Forestry Rental Trust, 159
Crown/Māori partnership, 125, 127, 158, 161

Darwin, John, 187
Declaration of Independence
    document, 12
    significance, 133, 174
    sovereignty concept in, 22, 75–76, 77, 95, 123, 180
Delamere, Monita, *Fig. 22*
discovery, doctrine of, 21, 65, 95, 132
Dorsett, Shaunnagh, 248n59
Durie, Edward Taihakurei (Eddie), 116–18, 120, 137, 168, 170, 199, *Fig. 21*, *Fig. 22*

Earle, Pat, 34
Elias, Sian, 189
Emerson, Ralph Waldo, 37
empiricism, 208, 210
Evans, Enid, 48

Facsimiles volume
    Ross's commission, 12, 29–30, 225n34
    Ross's letter regarding reissue of, 67–68
    Ross's research for, 13, 14–17, 19–20
    Ross's unique approach to, 18
    Turton's compilation, 12, 172
Finlayson, Roderick, 35–36, 42, 229n12
Firth, Raymond, 18
FitzGerald, J. E., 74, 235n40
Fletcher, Ned, 189, 248n57
Fletcher, Ruth *see* Allan, Ruth (née Fletcher)
Foden, N. A., 8
foundational history, xi, 17, 113, 130, 157–58, 190, 194
Fyfe, Frances *see* Porter Frances (née Fyfe)

Glenelg, Lord, 132
good history, 150, 202–5
Government Printer, 12, 19, 29, 68
Guscott, Ruth *see* Ross, Ruth

Hairini cemetery, Motukiore, 44–45
Hattaway, Pat, 34, 67
He Wakaputanga o te Rangatiratanga o Nu Tireni *see* Declaration of Independence
Head, Lyndsay, 177–82, 247n22, 247n24, 247n34
Heenan, Joe, 6, 8
Hickford, Mark, 186–89
Hikurangi, *ix*, 68

historians' changing perspectives
    lack of interest in New Zealand history prior to 1970s, 26, 79, 235n56
    Ross and the debunking of Treaty myths, 94–96, 128
    disputing the Tribunal's use of history, 146, 153–54, 156, 158–63, 168–70, 244n1, 246n75
    transforming interpretation of the Treaty, 128, 136, 138–40, 243n48
    understanding historical contexts, 178, 182–85, 187–89
Historic Places Trust, New Zealand, 69, 107–8
Historical Branch, Internal Affairs, 6–11, *Fig. 5*
historical fiction, 33, 36–37, 62
historical irresolution, 89, 150, 161, 204–5
historical objectivity, 107, 148, 202–4, 249n16
'historical past' *see* academic history
historical sources, 4–5, 17, 193–94
historical traces, 9, 193–94
'historical treaty', 182–85, 198–99, 201–2, 247n42
historical truth, 62, 148–49, 205, 207–8, 209–10, 212
historical v. legal approaches, 100, 134, 147, 155–57, 165, 170, 244n13
historicism, 161, 190, 199–200, 249n5, 249n6
histories of New Zealand
    Māori and Pākehā histories, 137–39, 149, 165
    a shared history, 208–11
    sharing histories, 211–12
    Treaty significance in, 26, 112–14, 117, 135, 140, 191–93
historiography
    antiquarian history, 5, 9, 69, 151, 197, 199
    comparative history, 187, 192–93
    constitutional history, 130, 154, 157–58
    critical history, 113, 128, 197, 200–201
    foundational history, xi, 17, 113, 130, 157–58, 190, 194
    juridical history, 151–54, 162, 189, 198
    monumental history, 113–14, 121, 128, 197–98, 240n63
    post-foundational history, 190–95, 202
    post-modernist history, 160
    presentist history, 145, 152, 155–57, 160–62, 168–69, 182, 246n81
    Whig history, 155–58, 162, 198
Hitchings, Michael, 83
Hoani Te Heuheu Tukino v Aotea District Maori Land Board, 99
Hobbs, John, 51, 60, 61
Hobsbawm, Eric, 163
Hobson, William
    attitude to treaty-making, 20–21, 24, 61, 65, 94, 95, 173
    Colonial Office's instructions, 7, 24, 66, 75, 132–33
    health, 59, 78
    proclamations, 14, 21, 28, 52, 65, 95, 132, 135
    role in treaty-making, 20–21, 60, 70, 172
    see also British acquisition of sovereignty
Hokianga, *ix*, 10, 43–44, 53, 69, *Fig. 13*
Hongi Hika, 69
Hōreke, *ix*, 43, 62
Hotere, Hone Papita Raukura (Ralph), 56–57, *Fig. 13*
Howe, Kerry, 160, 245n47, 247n22
Huirama, 50

Ignatieff, Michael, 210
indigenous property rights
    common law rights, 135, 154, 156, 187–88
    land claims, 117–18, 156, 240n76
    path dependency and, 187–88
    political discourse and, 99, 130, 140, 187, 192
    see also Māori property rights
insider histories, 150
Internal Affairs Department, 6–11, *Fig. 5*, *Fig. 6*

Johnson, Miranda, 72
Jones, Pei Te Hurinui, 19, 51–52, *Fig. 14*
juridical history, 151–54, 162, 189, 198

Index

kāwanatanga
    meaning compared to sovereignty, 22, 76–77, 122–23, 180
    meaning in relation to tino rangatiratanga, 17, 23, 60, 77, 176
Kawharu, Hugh, 120, 126, 178
Kendall, Thomas, 84
King, Michael, 177, 238n7, 247n22
King Country, *ix*, 41
kīngitanga, as used in the Declaration of Independence, 22, 77, 95
Kohimarama Conference, 110
Koroi, Tutere, 44–46
Kuhn, Thomas S., 106, 240n62
Kupe, 44

Labour Party, 64, 101–5
LaCapra, Dominick, 150, 203–4
Lands and Survey archives *see* Old Land Claim files
language, contestable nature of, 89, 93–94, 114–15, 119
Laqueur, Thomas, 240n62
Laracy, Hugh, 109
Laslett, Peter, 145
Latimer, Graham, 115–16, 120
Lee-Johnson, Eric, 47, 56
legal historians, 154, 186, 248n59
legal scholarship, 99–100, 103, 132, 134–35, 138, 242n34, 243n42
legal v. historical approaches, 100, 134, 147, 155–57, 165, 170, 244n13
Locke, Elsie, 36–37, 229n16
Loveridge, Donald, 247n39
Lynch, Michael P., 207

Mackersey, Mary *see* Boyd, Mary (née Mackersey)
Mahuta, Bob, 105
mana
    omission from te Tiriti, 22–23, 61, 76–77, 95, 123, 179–80
    as used in the Declaration of Independence, 22, 77, 123, 180
mana motuhake *see* Māori sovereignty

Māngungu, *ix*, 44, 48, 57, 58, *Fig. 13*
    see also Wesleyan Mission, Māngungu
Maning, F. E., 10, 21, 60–61, 69, 204
Māori history
    as different from Pākehā concept, 35–36, 71, 117, 137, 149–50, 165–67, 208–10
    oral traditions, 41–42, 137, 149, 200, 209
    tribal history, 41, 70, 158, 162
Māori identity, 72, 166
Māori literacy in 1840, 171–72, 176, 178, 246n3
Maori Organisation on Human Rights, 79
Māori property rights
    common law aboriginal title and, 135, 154, 156, 187–88
    indigenous rights v. same rights as Pākehā, 26, 72, 103, 105, 112
    path dependency and, 187–88
    political discourse and, 130, 140, 187, 188–89, 192
    Treaty guarantees of, 79, 113, 115, 130, 138, 188–89, 203
Māori sovereignty
    British view of, pre-Treaty, 24, 66, 76, 132–33, 187, 192, 227n75, 242n35
    as ceded in the Treaty, 99, 102, 113, 115, 130, 135, 157, 185
    as an indigenous right, 72, 105, 112
    as referenced in the Declaration, 133, 174, 180
    as referenced in the Treaty, 138, 203
Māori worldview
    as different from Pākehā, 49, 70–71, 150, 166, 174–75
    impacts of cross-cultural contact on, 159, 178–79, 181–82, 184–85
    see also Māori history; mātauranga Māori
Māori/Crown partnership, 125, 127, 158, 161
Martin, Sir William, 17, 76, 121, 204
mātauranga Māori, 166, 209, 245n70
Matiu, 44
Maungataniwha, 48, 57, 60, *Fig. 13*
Maunsell, Robert, 21
McAloon, Jim, 245n63
McCormick, Eric, 38, 69
McDonnell, Thomas, 69
McEwen, J. M. (Jock), 104–5
McHugh, Paul, 134–35, 154–58, 248n59

McKean, W. A. (Warwick), 103, 237n82
McKenzie, D. F. (David), 171–76
    historians' reactions to, 175–76, 178, 246n3, 246n16
    and Māori literacy in 1840, 172, 246n3
    and Treaty as an oral contract, 173–74, 189
    and Treaty texts, 172–73, 174
    and the Tribunal's approach, 175
McKinnon, Malcolm, 27, 111
McNair, Lord Duncan, 103, 121–22
Mead, Hirini Moko Haerewa (Sidney), 120
Megill, Allan, 193–94, 204
Milirrpum v Nabalco Pty Ltd, 117
Miller, Harold, 8
Miller, John, 71
missionaries, 8, 10, 60, 86, 107, 178–81, 187
    see also Church Missionary Society missionaries
'modern treaty', 182–84, 198, 202
Moir, Lawrie, 96
Molloy, Anthony P., 99–100
monumental history, 113–14, 121, 128, 197–98, 240n63
Motukiore
    community, 44–45, 48, 53, 68, Fig. 12
    Hairini cemetery, 44–45
    location of, *ix*, xi, 43, Fig. 10
    Perunui Creek, Fig. 11
    school, 43, 48, 49, 68, Fig. 12
Mulgan, Alan, 28, 49
Mulgan, Richard, 244n2, 247n42
Munro, Doug, 27
Munz, Peter, 167
Muriwhenua, land claims of, 159–60, 177
Muriwhenua fishing claim, 242n3, Fig. 22
mythic histories, 198–200, 205–6
myths, definition of, 135, 198
myths challenged
    benevolence of the British Crown, 66
    missionaries' impact on Māori communities, 8, 10
    the 'modern treaty', 198–99
    race relations in New Zealand, 72, 95, 112
    Treaty as the Māori Magna Carta, 14, 17, 25, 87, 125
    veneration of the Treaty, 8, 17, 87, 97

national identity, 111–12, 240n61
    see also Māori identity; Pākehā identity
National Party, 106
Native Land Court records, 9, 10
Nene, Tāmati Wāka, 44, 50, 59
New Zealand Company, 192, 204
New Zealand Herald, 52
New Zealand Historic Places Trust, 69, 107–8
New Zealand history *see* histories of New Zealand
New Zealand Journal of History
    article by McHugh, 157–58
    article by Orange, 110
    article by Ross *see* 'Tiriti o Waitangi: Texts and Translations, Te'
    article by Ward, 146–50
    articles from first 30 years, 177, Fig. 13
    editors, 79–80, 83, 236n62, 237n78
New Zealand Listener 'Korero' column, 98
New Zealand Māori Council, 73, 115–16
New Zealand Maori Council v Attorney-General, 126
Nga Tamatoa, 71–72, 98, 106, Fig. 18
Ngai Tahu Maori Trust Board, 105–6
Ngāi Tahu Tribunal hearings, 146, 149
Ngata, Apirana, 18
Ngata, Hēnare Kōhere, 72, 115
Ngāti Whātua, 127
Nietzsche, Friedrich, 113, 151, 197–200
Normanby, Lord, 24, 132–33
Norris, H. C. M., 35
North Island, British acquisition of sovereignty, 21, 65, 78, 95
Northland Magazine, 64–66, 70
Novick, Peter, 148, 150

Oakeshott, Michael, 155, 206, 244n33
O'Connell, D. P., 99
Old Land Claim files, 7, 9
Oliver, W. H. (Bill), 158–63
    and role of academic historians in public history, 162–63, 198–99, 201, 209
    and the Waitangi Tribunal, 159–63, 165, 168–69, 245n44
O'Malley, Cliff, 56

Index

O'Malley, Vincent, 41, 248n56
oral traditions, 9, 137, 149, 150–51, 175
Orange, Claudia, 109–11, 127–34
    changing Treaty stance of, 128–33, 242n26, 248n57
    as leading Treaty historian, 127, 211
    and the legal status of the Treaty, 131–33, 157–58, 242n34, 242n35
    and Māori perspectives, 128–29, 131, 133, 175–76
    personal background of, 109, 127
    Ross's influence on, 109–11, 127–29
Owen, R. E., 12, 19, 29
Owens, J. M. R. (John), 7, 65, 95, 111, 171, 190, 245n47, 247n42
Oxford History of New Zealand, 95

Pākehā identity, 112, 125, 135–36, 200, 210–11
Panakareao, Nōpera, 23, 78, 124
Pāpāhia, 57, 60
Parker, Wiremu (Bill), 72, 74
partnership of Māori and Crown, 125, 127, 158, 161
Patuone, Eruera Maihi, 44, 59
Paul, Janet (née Wilkinson), 5, 56
Phillipson, Grant, 169
Poata, Tama (Tom), 79
Pocock, J. G. A. (John), 154, 164, 165–67, 200, 212, 245n70
Pompallier, Bishop Jean-Baptiste, 10, 60, 69
Porter, Frances (née Fyfe), 6, 108
post-foundational history, 190–95, 202
post-modernism, 148, 151, 160, 208
'practical past', 155–57, 163, 202, 206
pre-emption, 23, 61, 78, 86, 185, 238n82, 247n52, 248n65
Prendergast, Sir James, 99
presentism, 145, 152, 155–57, 160–62, 168–69, 182, 246n81
principles of the Treaty, 101, 103, 105, 113–14, 117, 125–27
private life of history, xiii, 203
    and Belich, 176
    and Orange, 127
    and Ross, 18–19, 62, 82, 88
    and Ward, 147

proclamations of sovereignty, 14, 21, 28, 52, 65, 95, 132, 135
protection discourse, 184, 242n35, 247n49
protests, 71, 98, 106
public history, 147, 161
public life of history, xii
    impacts of political discourse on the, 71–72, 112–14, 128, 130–31, 133
    role of academic history in the, 201–2
    Ross and the, xi, 14, 64, 73, 96–97

race relations in New Zealand, 8, 42, 72, 98, 112, 136, 139
rangatiratanga
    meanings of, 60, 124, 126, 138, 180–81
    as used in the Declaration of Independence, 124, 180
    see also tino rangatiratanga
Rangiaowhia, *ix*, 41–42, 229n32
Rata, Matiu, 101, 105, 137, *Fig. 19*
ratification of the Treaty, 79, 97
relativism, 148, 150–51
Renwick, W. L. (Bill), 70–71, 209
Ross, Angus, 231n54
Ross, Duncan, 40, *Fig. 7*
Ross, Ian, 11, 43, 68, 225n30, *Fig. 7*
Ross, Malcolm, 70, 234n23, *Fig. 7*, *Fig. 10*
Ross, Ruth
    characteristics
        angry outbursts, 53–55, 81
        determination, 5, 19, 82–83
        helping other historians, 47, 69, 109–10
        identifying as a New Zealander, 38–40, 42
        integrity, 5, 19
        perfectionism, 5, 13, 30, 67, 69
        prejudice regarding missionaries, 8, 10, 19, 34, 107
        rebellious spirit, 4, 8, 19
        self-doubt, 5, 19, 31–32, 51, 64, 67, 82
        talents, 5, 7, 70
    early life, 4–6, 39–40, 224n11, *Fig. 1*, *Fig. 2*
    employment
        commissions, 12, 29–30, 34–35, 37, 47, 49, 58, 225n34

at Internal Affairs Historical Branch, 6–11, *Fig. 5*
at Internal Affairs War History Branch, 11, *Fig. 6*
at University of Auckland Department of History, xiii, 108–9
family life
    family responsibilities, xi, 11–12, 13, 47, 83
    marriage to George Burnard, 7–8, 10–11, *Fig. 3*
    marriage to Ian Ross, 11–12, 41–43, 68, *Fig. 7*
    sons, xiv, 12, 68, 70, *Fig. 7*
health, 48, 70, 110–11
as a historian
    and the discipline of academic history, 9, 13, 34, 36, 62, 66, 148
    and inseparability of past and present, 42, 48, 50, 71, 88
    letter-writing, 14, 48, 84, 233n2
    myth-busting, 8, 17, 70, 87, 125
    originality, 18, 82, 87
    research practices, 9, 13, 48
    views shaped by political context, 26, 110, 126
passionate interests
    Māori history, 9, 36, 41–43, 49, 108, 237n89
    Māori language, 48–49, 237n89
    the Treaty, 7–8, 19, 34, 62, 87
professional relationships
    with academic historians, 28–29
    with Claudia Orange, 109–10
    with Fred Wood, 5, 30, *Fig. 3*
    with J. C. Beaglehole, 5–6, 12–14, 16, 30–31, 40, 70, *Fig. 8*
    with James K. Baxter, 52–56
    with Judith Binney, 81, 84–85, 236n75, 237n78
    with Keith Sinclair, 66, 79, 81, 111, 236n62
    with Mary Boyd, 27–28, 72–73, *Fig. 4*
    with Michael Standish, 65–67, *Fig. 9*
Ross, Ruth: published work
    Encyclopaedia of New Zealand entries, 68–69
    Feel of Truth, The see 'Autochthonous New Zealand Soil, The' (essay by Ross)
    Historic Places Trust reports and essays, 69, 107–8
    Historical Studies reviews, 68
    New Zealand Journal of History see 'Tiriti o Waitangi: Texts and Translations, Te' (article by Ross)
    New Zealand Junior Encyclopedia entry, 68
    New Zealand's First Capital, 8–9, 11, 225n28
    Northland Magazine article, 70
    see also 'Waitangi Documents, The'
    School Publications stories and bulletins, 34–35, 48
    see also Tiriti o Waitangi, Te (bulletin by Ross)
    'Treaty on the Ground, The' (paper by Ross), 74–79, 235n53
Ross, Ruth: seminars
    for University Extension, Victoria University, 72–73, 74–79, 80–81, 235n53
    for Victoria Historical Association, 20–26, 27–28
Ross, Ruth: transformative influence
    on cloistered life of history, 94–96, 110, 127–29, 171, 176–77
    on public life of history, xi, 111, 120–25, 176–77, 238n15, 241n3
    that the Māori text is the Treaty, 101–2, 110, 114, 120, 128–29, 171
    that the Treaty is flawed, 94–96, 97, 111, 128
Ross, Ruth: Treaty arguments
    ambiguity and contradictions in the Treaty, xii, 14, 25, 59–60, 77, 78, 86, 88, *Fig. 20*
    authoritative version: the Māori text, 15, 18–19, 20, 50, 67, 74, 81, 85, 88, 235n40
    biased records of Treaty meetings, 21, 58
    differences between Māori and English texts, 15–16, 22–23, 77, 87, 123–25, 226n53

Ross, Ruth: Treaty arguments (*cont.*)
   English texts analysis
      as drafts of the Treaty, 15, 20, 50, 67, 75
      inexpert and hasty formulation, xii, 14, 30, 75
      the Waikato sheet and, 15, 20, 75, 81
   Hobson's attitude to treaty-making, 20–21, 24, 60, 61, 65
   legal significance of the Treaty, 14, 21, 24, 64, 86, 100, 125, 235n40
   Māori text analysis
      as 'missionary-Māori', 18, 76, 179, 247n34
      translation issues, xii, 20–21, 22, 60, 76–77, 123–25, 241n8
   Māori understanding of Treaty terms, 21, 60–61, 86, 108
   Protestant missionaries' role, 10, 18, 51, 75, 86, 123
   ratification implications, 25–26, 46
Ruru, Henare, 9
Russell, Lord John, 132
Russell, *ix*, 8, 10, 11
Rutherford, James, 17, 18, 65–66, 81

Salmond, Anne, 150
School Publications, 33–36, 67
   see also *Tiriti o Waitangi, Te* (bulletin by Ross)
'scientific' history *see* academic history
Scott, Stuart C., 136
Selwyn, George Augustus, 41–42
Shapiro, Barbara J., 207
Sharp, Andrew, 116, 144–45, 151–54, 240n61
Sherbro treaty, 140
Simmons, Beverley, 83
Simpson, Tony, 97–98, 107, 238n19
Sinclair, Keith
   as editor of *New Zealand Journal of History*, 79, 83, 236n62, *Fig. 17*
   responses to Ross's work, 53, 62, 65, 81
   at University of Auckland, 16, 108
Smith, Linda Tuhiwai, 166
Sorrenson, Keith 136–140
   as assistant editor of *New Zealand Journal of History*, 80, 138

   essays showing shifts in understanding, 137–40
   issues with Simpson's book, 98, 107
   at University of Auckland, 108, 157
   as Waitangi Tribunal member, 136–37, 138, 156–57, 241n3, *Fig. 22*
South Island, British acquisition of sovereignty, 21, 65, 95, 132
sovereignty, forms of, 22, 158, 164, 167, 208
   see also British acquisition of sovereignty; Crown/Māori partnership; Māori sovereignty
sovereignty, translation of
   compared to rangatiratanga, 115, 123–24, 176, 178, 184
   in the Declaration, 22, 77, 95, 123, 180
   as kāwanatanga in te Tiriti, 17, 22, 61, 76–77, 122–23, 180
Standish, Michael, 30, 65–67, *Fig. 9*
Stephen, James, 26
Sweetman, Edward, 237n78

tangata whenua status, 42, 105, 112
   see also Māori property rights
taonga, as used in te Tiriti, 23, 46, 77, 124–25, 157
Taonui, Āperahama, 68
Tarling, Nicholas, 83
Tau, Te Maire, 166, 245n70
Tāwhai, Mohi, 44, 58, 67, 174
Taylor, E. Mervyn, 57
Taylor, Jack, 44, 62
Taylor, Nan (née Wheeler), 6
Taylor, Richard, 59
Te Hau, Matt (Matiu), 19, 41, 52, 111
Te Heuheu, Georgina, *Fig. 22*
Te Kōpuru, *ix*, 68
Te Rauparaha, 64, 149
Te Taonui, Makoare, 60, 69
Te Weehi v Regional Fisheries Officer, 131
Te Whaiti, 50
Te Whata, Eru, 44–46
Temm, Paul, *Fig. 21*
Thierry, Charles de, 69, 84, 236n76

tino rangatiratanga
   meaning compared to possession, 116, 123, 138, 181, 185
   meaning in relation to kāwanatanga, 17, 23, 60, 77, 176
   as used in te Tiriti, 22–23, 60, 77, 123, 130, 175, 178, 181
   see also rangatiratanga

Tirikātene-Sullivan, Whetū, 74, 75, 101, 105

Tiriti o Waitangi, xi, 15, 102, 115, 122, 140, 174, 183, 213
   see also Treaty of Waitangi

Tiriti o Waitangi, Te (bulletin by Ross)
   final drafts, 52–56, 62
   first draft, 49–51
   the four parts of, 49–50, 58–61
   as historical fiction, 37, 62, 148
   illustrations for, 47, 56–58, Fig. 15
   reactions to, 62

'Tiriti o Waitangi: Texts and Translations, Te' (article by Ross)
   arguments
      major argument, 85–86, 88
      minor argument, 81, 85, 87
   discussions
      diverse interpretations of the Treaty, 87
      fishing rights issue, 86
      myths about the Treaty, 87
      pre-emption, 80, 86, 237n82
      Protestant missionaries' role, 86
   as revision of seminar paper, 79–81
   textual focus, 80, 82–83, 87, 237n87
   see also Ross, Ruth: transformative influence

Treaty of Waitangi
   articles
      first, 22, 122, 180
      second, 15–16, 22–23, 77, 116, 124–25, 188
      third, 23, 183, 248n59, 250n39
   authoritative versions
      both texts, 104, 121–22
      English text, 18, 75, 103, 113
      Māori text, xii, 15, 102, 122, 140, 174, 183
   contexts
      imperial policies, 135, 139–40
      Māori world in 1840, 178–79, 181–82, 183–85
   differences between Māori and English texts, 22–23, 76–77, 113–14, 120, 124–25, 171–72, 183
   Māori understanding of, 60–61, 110, 173, 176, 178–82, 184
   perceptions of
      as an alliance, 184–85
      as a contract, 106, 115, 117, 125, 127, 157
      as the founding document, xi, 17, 113, 115, 130, 157–58
      as fraud, 71, 98, 115
      as having multiple interpretations, 185–86, 191–92, 202, 212–13, 248n56
      as involving rights and duties, 126–27, 130, 145, 153, 183, 242n28
      as legally valid, 95, 97, 99, 100, 113, 117, 125, 130, 133, 235n40
      as a living instrument, 126, 139
      as a nullity, 95, 99
      as an oral contract, 173–74, 176
      as a solemn covenant, 97, 103, 133
   principles of, 101, 103, 105, 113–14, 117, 125–27
   signatories, 45, 60–61, 64, 78, 173, 235n40
   Treaty documents, 12, 20, 45, 64, 172
   Treaty meetings, 57, 60, 76, 77, 78, 173, 179, 185, 194
   see also breaches of the Treaty

Treaty of Waitangi Act 1975, 105–6, 116–17, 118, 120, 175

'Treaty on the Ground' (paper by Ross)
   and English drafts of the Treaty, 75, 80
   and Māori text, 74, 76–77
   and oral explanations of the Treaty, 77–78
   reactions to, 78–79, 80–81, 235n53
   research for, 73

tuku whenua, 159, 177, 203

Turnbull, Michael, 34, 46

Turton, H. Hanson, 12

University Extension, Victoria University, 72, 74
University of Auckland, 236n72
    History Department, 79, 81, 236n73, 249n31
    University College Adult Education, 18, 19

Victoria Historical Association, 20, 74
Victoria University College, 4–6, 236n72
Victoria University Extension, 72, 74

Waikato, *ix*, 41
Waimate, *ix*, 59, 69
Waitangi, *ix*, 17
Waitangi Action Committee, 98
Waitangi Day
    legislation, 96, 100
    observance, 52, 64, 67, 70, 71, 98
'Waitangi Documents, The' (Ross), 64–66
Waitangi Tribunal
    applying Treaty principles, 117, 137, 153, 169
    Durie's influence, 116, 120, 137, 170, 199
    establishment of, 104–6
    first decade, 106
    governing legislation, 106, 116–17, 118, 120, 175
    historians' role in claims process, 146–47, 149, 153, 160, 168–69, 200
    key Treaty words, 122–23, 241n6
    legal approach, 116–17, 121, 157, 162, 170
    Māori history approach, 116–17, 139, 159, 162, 200, 245n44
    members, 116, 120, 136–37, *Fig. 21*, *Fig. 22*
    reports, 116, 124, 125, 175, 241n3, 241n8
    Treaty interpretation, 117, 125, 139, 144–45, 161
    use of Ross's arguments, 120–25, 241n3
    and useable history, 145, 161
Walker, Ranginui, 98
Ward, Alan, 146–51
    changing Treaty stance of, 153–54, 243n48
    and historical objectivity, 148–49
    and inviting counter-arguments, 150, 167

    and Māori history, 26, 94
    and relativism, 150–51
    and the role of historians in the claims process, 147–49, 151, 201
Wards, Ian, 28, 73, 76, 94
Weaver, John C., 248n62
Webster, William, 100
Wesleyan Mission, Māngungu, 44, 51, 58, 59–61
Whanganui, *ix*, 4
Wheeler, Nan *see* Taylor, Nan (née Wheeler)
Whig history, 155–58, 162, 198
White, Hayden, 205–7
White, Richard, 193
Wi Parata v Bishop of Wellington, 99, 238n23
Wilkinson, Janet *see* Paul, Janet (née Wilkinson)
Williams, Bridget, 131
Williams, David, 120, 178, 238n23, 246n81
Williams, Edward, 18, 67, 95, 179
Williams, Henry
    as collaborator, 107, 130, 204, 247n46
    competency as translators of Edward and, 21, 76, 95, 178, 179–80
    role in Treaty discussions, 76, 77–78, 172
    translation of te Tiriti, 8, 18, 67, 76–77, 122–23, 125, 130, 183
Williams, Trevor, 29
Williams, William, 21
Wilson, Ormond, 73, 74, 79
Wilson, William, *Fig. 22*
women's role, 5, 6–7, 12, 27, 69, 81, 236n73
Wood, Antony, 96
Wood, F. L. W. (Fred), 4–5, 30, 70
Woon, William, 61